PSYCHEDELICS

*The Uses and Implications
of Hallucinogenic Drugs*

BERNARD AARONSON is head of the Section of Experimental Psychology, Bureau of Research in Neurology and Psychiatry, Princeton, New Jersey. He is a well-known investigator in the field of consciousness expansion. His article on "Hypnosis, Depth Perception, and the Psychedelic Experience" appears in Charles Tart's *Altered States of Consciousness*.

HUMPHRY OSMOND is the Bureau's Director of Research in Neurology and Psychiatry. The man who first coined the term "psychedelics," he is the co-author (with Abram Hoffer) of *How to Live with Schizophrenia*, *Chemical Basis of Clinical Psychiatry*, and *New Hope for Alcoholics*.

Psychedelics

*The Uses and Implications
of Hallucinogenic Drugs*

EDITED BY

BERNARD AARONSON AND
HUMPHRY OSMOND

ANCHOR BOOKS
DOUBLEDAY & COMPANY, INC.
GARDEN CITY, NEW YORK

Grateful acknowledgment is made to the following for permission to reprint their copyrighted material.

THE BOBBS-MERRILL COMPANY, INC., AND INTERNATIONAL JOURNAL OF PARAPSYCHOLOGY
For "Drugs and Mysticism," by Walter N. Pahnke. Reprinted from *International Journal of Parapsychology*, Vol. 8 (1966), No. 2. Also appeared in *The Use of LSD in Psychotherapy and Alcoholism*, edited by Harold A. Abramson. Copyright © 1967 by Harold A. Abramson. Reprinted by permission of the publishers.

INTERNATIONAL JOURNAL OF PARAPSYCHOLOGY
For "Peyote Night," by Humphry Osmond, from *Tomorrow*, Vol. 9 (1961), No. 2.

LOTHAR G. KNAUTH
For "The *Teonanacatl* in Pre-Conquest Accounts and Today," by Lothar G. Knauth, in *Estudios de Cultura Nahuatl*, 1962, Vol. 3.

FRED B. ROTHMAN & CO., AND CALIFORNIA LAW REVIEW
For "Psychedelics and Religious Experience," by Alan Watts, California Law Review, Vol. 56 No 1, January, 1968. Copyright © 1968, California Law Review, Inc.

THE WILLIAMS & WILKINS COMPANY, BALTIMORE, AND ARTHUR DEIKMAN
For "Implications of Experimentally Induced Contemplative Meditation," by Arthur Deikman, in *The Journal of Nervous and Mental Disease*, 142: 101–116, 1966.

CONTENTS

PART I
INTRODUCTION

INTRODUCTION: PSYCHEDELICS, TECHNOLOGY, PSYCHEDELICS

BERNARD S. AARONSON AND HUMPHRY OSMOND

Any culture may be regarded as a ramification of a particular technology applied to the particular set of local conditions within which that culture is situated. The term "technology," as used here, refers to the entire set of devices, whether mechanical, chemical, or linguistic, by which adaptations of individuals to their environments are enhanced. Plows, clubs, radios, airplanes, fertilizers, drugs, breakfast cereals, grammars, and concepts are each implements and instances of technology, which influence and are influenced by one another. Some implements operate by directly altering the environment in response to the demands of the individual, as when we turn on an air conditioner on a hot day. Others operate by altering the individual to meet the demands of the environment, as when we "make the last one for the road coffee." Still others may attempt to integrate the two, as when we read a book to gain knowledge that will help us in particular situations.

All systems of technology have certain common characteristics in terms of how they affect those who use them. They set up ways of looking at the world in terms of which new experiences can be encoded. One of the best illustrations of this is given in an old Jewish folk song in which the singing of a new cantor on the Sabbath is heard by a tailor in terms of how one sews a suit of clothes, by a cobbler in terms of making shoes, and by a carpenter in terms of cutting wood. Systems of technology focus attention on certain kinds of relationships and particular ways of conceptualizing those relationships. It is probably no accident that the great Chinese book on time, the *I Ching*, with its emphasis on seasons and changes and on ways of adapting to these and on the right time for initiating and carrying through action should have arisen as a vegetable oracle, the product of a farming people.

Conceptualizations, once arrived at, interact to produce new conceptualizations, new technology, from which, once more, new concepts and new needs may emerge. Television, for instance, derives as a concept from motion pictures and radio and, even though it was introduced only a comparatively short time ago, has rapidly become a central part of homes at all levels of society in our culture. Watching television has tended to produce a more uniform culture through greater exposure to common stimuli, has reduced the amount of time available for free interaction by members of any particular household, and has resulted in the creation of such implements as "TV trays" and "TV dinners" to accommodate the need for more time around the television set. Automobiles have made possible the movement to the suburbs, the virtual end of public transportation in many parts of our country, and a resultant increased dependency on private means of transportation. In its turn, this has produced a more mobile population, a proliferation of roads, a tendency to think of distance in terms of units of time, the destruction of the countryside, and an increased need to deal with air pollution.

Any technological innovation in any area expands to fill all the analogous gaps to which it can be applied. The technology of clubs developed into the technology of axes and hoes, and, in modern America, into the technology of baseball. Any technological system has a degree of play that makes possible the development of new technologies, which may not be immediately useful, but can become functional or can be combined to be functional when the need arises. The technique for producing light shows has long been available but remained essentially unused until the advent of psychedelic drugs produced its impact on a generation accustomed to TV diffraction patterns.

The technology of drugs is one of the oldest technologies and probably began when our ancestors browsed their way through the forests and found that, among the foods they sampled, some produced interesting changes in how they felt, how they perceived, and how they could accommodate themselves to the world. Substances that alter consciousness are found in use among probably all the peoples of the world

(Taylor, 1963).[1] In particular, substances containing alcohol and caffeine seem to be used nearly everywhere, and hemp and its derivatives also seem widely used.

Substances whose main effect is to stop hunger are classed as foods. Even though it is now customary to present an analysis of the chemical composition of many of the foods we eat on the sides of the containers in which they are packaged, their action tends to be studied in laboratories of nutrition rather than in those of pharmacology. The kinds of detailed study of effects on particular structures and organ systems that have historically characterized pharmacological study are rarely undertaken with foods.

Substances that increase conviviality or stimulate the individual are often treated as foods if they can be eaten, or as more like drugs (without usually naming them such) if they must be smoked. Alcohol, coffee, tea, and chocolate represent the edible class of these substances, as does cannabis and its derivatives in many Moslem and Eastern countries. Cannabis and tobacco probably represent the principal common substances smoked. The continuing agitation against the use of alcohol and cannabis by various groups in our culture suggests the anomalous position of these kinds of substances on the food–drug continuum. The fear and anxiety over the moral and physical degradation that might result from enslavement to coffee, tea, and chocolate when these were introduced into Europe are another case in point. It should also be noted that many tobacco smokers often have trouble conceptualizing tobacco as a drug, for the term "drug" has developed very specialized meanings.

Among the foods sampled by our ancestors, some sustained life, others destroyed it. Still others seemed to remove illness. Sometimes those foods that destroyed life could also sustain it and remove illness if administered in proper ways and in proper amounts. It is hard to say when the division of edibles into foods and poisons and into foods and drugs arose, for the divisions already existed at the beginning of recorded history. Legends of the witch woman and the wizard

[1] For information on all references cited in this book, see the Bibliography following the last article.

and their herbs, or of the apple whose scent drives away disease are very old. A technology of drug use is found in all cultures along with a technology of poisons, and the control of that technology is vested in individuals with priestly or semipriestly functions, or in others with claims to special relationships with the supernatural. As the amount of knowledge around the use of the healing arts grew, the priesthood, which dealt in healing, gradually gave way to a more secularized group, with specialized training, called physicians. Another group claimed jurisdiction over the preparation of these substances and were called apothecaries or, more recently, pharmacists. These experts knew which drugs to prescribe and when. It was also apparent that these substances could sometimes be dangerous when improperly compounded or improperly used, so it was important to listen when they told you how to use the possibly dangerous substances in which they dealt. In addition, since they dealt in alleviating suffering, a "good guy" image was easy to come by. As a result, a drug in this context became something that was used on the advice of a physician, and that it was foolhardy to use otherwise.

While a tradition of using minor remedies for things like colds or warts existed, reasonable people left the control of drugs in the hands of the experts. Even patent medicines derived their fundamental cultural status from the implied approval of these groups, or had to go back to their precursors, the medicine men and shamans of primitive days. To this day, television advertisements for patent medicines that will cure headaches, sinus congestion, or "tired blood" are delivered by friendly, fatherly looking men in white coats. On the other hand, the development of modern research technology made possible an expansion of the number of substances recognized as specifics against particular ailments and increased the range of illnesses and conditions for which drugs could be used. In particular, the realization that food-deficiency diseases exist, and the development of vitamin pills to be used as a food supplement, created a dynamic tension between the restricted use of drugs and the use of pills as food. Subsequently, the modern development of mood-changing drugs such as tranquilizers, and their promiscuous prescription by physicians to such a point that some minor tranquilizers can now be purchased without a prescription, completed the breach. We became a pill-using culture, although the earlier caution about the use of drugs remained as a nagging sense of guilt.

Alongside the medically controlled and related concept of drugs, a second conception exists of drugs as substances that produce depressing but exotic sleep states to which the user becomes easily addicted, to the exclusion of the claims and pleasures of ordinary life. In Homer's *Odyssey*, Ulysses and his crew visit the Land of the Lotus Eaters, whose inhabitants are addicted to a fruit that, when tasted, puts the user into a sleep in whose dreams all thoughts of home and country are forgotten. In our country, in our time, when somebody says he feels "drugged," he is generally referring to a state of depressed apathy. In contrast to this, we may often refer to a situation in which we have been gratified as one in which we have been "fed." A product that does not sell is referred to in business as "a drug on the market," but a new concept or a new perception may be "food for thought." It is a commonplace to hear how opium, the prototype for this conception, destroyed the initiative and capacity for constructive activity of the people in many Eastern countries and kept them from the progress and well-being of the Protestant ethic. It is a fact, moreover, that China did fight a losing war to keep British enterprise from bringing in opium, because the rulers of China felt that the effects of opium addiction would enervate their population.

For us, drugs are often seen as substances used in strange and alien cultures whose customs are the material from which travelogues are made and to which the intrepid traveler may venture only at the risk of being debauched. The early writings on opium by Thomas De Quincy, and the accounts of hashish experiences by Théophile Gautier and Fitzhugh Ludlow stress the exotic nature of the experience. Even Coleridge's famous poem *Kubla Khan*, written from an opium dream, in which the legendary ruler builds a pleasure dome in Xanadu over a hidden sacred river where women mourn for demon lovers and Abyssinian maids play dulcimers, bears out this aura of the strange. Drugs are substances that not only render us unable or unwilling to function in ordinary life, but make available exotic and forbidden landscapes. In these landscapes, the images of nightmare from which we have fled since childhood, move and take shape.

This view of the dangerous nature of drugs is further buttressed by the modern concept of "the drug addict"—an individual so enslaved by his need to escape "reality," a euphemism for the disappointments attendant on the need to survive, that he seeks these dangerous substances to the exclusion of the more conventional activities that keep society functioning. This immediately arouses the fear that if one person finds "illegitimate" states so attractive, others will follow because of their inherent superior pleasure-giving quality. The strictures by Louria (1966) on the hedonism of drug use emphasize this fear. Similar attitudes are expressed in the fear and condemnation of homosexuals by many perfectly adequate and well-adjusted heterosexuals, and in the horror felt by some parents when they find their children masturbating.

The drug addict is seen as becoming less controlled and more apt to express impulses that our society frowns upon, as his drug use continues. He is finally so taken over by his need, and so debauched, and so unable to make his own way, that he is forced to turn to crime to prolong a life that is now a threat to the survival of others. These negative images play an important role with respect to any substance labeled "drug" and not medically prescribed or available in a pharmacy. It is interesting to note that cough medicines containing codeine, an addicting drug, are available without prescription in many of our states, and that, at least until recently, paregoric, which contains a small quantity of opium, was freely available without prescription for use with infants. That these concepts represent an important aspect of the affective reaction to drug use is shown by the fact that campaigns against drug abuse in general, and the use of psychedelics in particular, have centered around appeals to these images.

Psychedelics are the newest addition to drug technology in our culture. While the use of many of these substances in their plant form is very old, their use in our culture is very recent, apart from minor experimentation by early scientists concerned with consciousness, such as William James, Weir Mitchell, and Havelock Ellis (DeRopp, 1957). Written descriptions of the use of hemp date from about 1250 B.C. Datura preparations are used in magic and witchcraft in many areas of the world. Amanita muscaria, the fly agaric mushroom, was not only probably used by the ancient Vikings when they went into battle, but, according to recent evidence, may have been the legendary soma of the founders of Hinduism (Schultes, 1969; Wasson, 1969). It is not possible to say how far back the use of peyote, ololiuqui, or of psilocybe mexicana goes, for the records were destroyed by the Roman Catholic missionaries to the conquered people of Mexico in their zeal for the welfare of the souls of their charges.

The central property of any of the substances labeled psychedelic is the enhancement of experience. In the anti-drug writings in the popular and semipopular press, psychedelics have even been condemned as offering "instant experience." They seem to step up the capacity of the organism to respond to fine gradations of stimulus input, to enhance response to stimulation at the upper and lower levels of perceptual responding, and to break down the barriers imposed by the different sensory avenues through which stimulation is received, in order to produce new perceptions, a greater frequency of illusions, and, more rarely, hallucinations. Before Osmond (1957b) coined the word "psychedelic," they were more commonly referred to as psychotomimetics or hallucinogens to stress their capacity to mimic psychoses or induce hallucinations. In contrast, depressants, such as alcohol and the barbiturates, and narcotics, such as opium and morphine, reduce attention to stimulus input, although hypnagogic and dreamlike states are possible with all of these. Stimulants, such as the amphetamines and caffeine, may enhance endurance, improve mood, and increase alertness and work capacity, but they do not promote attention to the fine nuances of sensory experience as do the psychedelics.

The ability of the psychedelics to produce enhanced capacity for experiencing, and for interrelating the data of experience, is central in understanding both their significance

and their popularity. Very few books that deal with psychedelics fail to include individual protocols of such experiences. Metzner (1968), Ebin (1961), and Watts (1962) have
published entire books containing nothing but protocols of
psychedelic experience. Huxley's great book *The Doors of
Perception* (1954), which probably marks the beginning of
the modern psychedelic movement, is also such a protocol
from his famous initial encounter with the Belle of Portugal
rose to his final return to "that reassuring but profoundly
unsatisfactory state known as 'being in one's right mind.'"
Timothy Leary's recent autobiographical account of psychedelia, *High Priest* (1968a), is also presented in terms of
psychedelic "trips." In discussing the use of psychedelics in
therapy for various emotional disorders, Hoffer and Osmond
(1967) stress that LSD, psilocybin, and mescaline may all
be equally effective. "It is the experience, not the compound
which induces it, which is responsible."

The stress on enhanced experiencing as the fundamental
characteristic of these substances leads, in the literature, to
a stress on the importance of the setting in which the drug
is taken. In order for the enhanced capacity for experience
created by these substances to show itself, an adequate range
of stimuli must first be available to be experienced. Administration of psychedelics under conditions of sensory deprivation seems to abolish most of the usual effects attributed
to them (Pollard, Uhr, and Stern, 1965). Hoffer and Osmond
(1967) stress the importance of providing adequate environmental support to produce the kinds of experience required to produce change in personality. Alpert and Cohen
(1966) also stress the need for adequate settings to provide
psychedelic experiences.

On the other hand, as the stimulus situations presented
to the drug taker increase in complexity, the variability of
possible responses to those stimuli increases, especially when
there is perceptual heightening. For this reason, along with
the emphasis on setting, a companion emphasis on set—the
attitudes, motivations, preconceptions, and intentions that individuals bring to their experiences—has arisen. Mogar (1965a,
1965c) has suggested that contradictory results in different
experiments on the effects of psychedelics on different func-

tions can be accounted for by considering the differences in set and setting. Leary, Litwin, and Metzner (1963) have suggested that the total effect of an exposure to psilocybin could be accounted for entirely in terms of set and setting. Krippner (1965) has pointed out that the psychotomimetic reactions of the early studies with LSD occurred within the context of a laboratory in which the individual taking the drug was surrounded by white-coated physicians who were looking for evidence that an analogous situation to schizophrenia was being produced. Hyde (1960) showed that when psychedelics were administered to a variety of normal subject groups under conditions in which they were confronted with impersonal, hostile, and investigative attitudes on the part of others, the subjects responded with devaluative distortions and hostility. Flexibility, familiarity, and the presence of others with a common culture ameliorated the psychotomimetic aspects of the reaction, while rigidity, unfamiliarity, non-acceptance, and absence of others with a common culture exacerbated them.

While few would seek enhanced experience if that experience were negative, the ability to enhance the capacity for experience is an important reason for the increased popularity of psychedelics. People tend to do what they are good at. Well-co-ordinated, well-muscled individuals are apt to be involved in athletics; those with good number ability are apt to enjoy working with numbers. One of the best predictive devices for vocational success is the Strong Vocational Interest Inventory, which provides scores based on the similarity of an individual's interest patterns to those of individuals who are successful in their chosen fields. Virtually everyone has the capacity to react, judge, and seek out experience. People will often go on long and arduous journeys just to see things, or will buy recording equipment, radios, or television just to provide themselves with stimulation. They will register for difficult courses of instruction with no demonstrable practical consequences for themselves, in order to enhance their experience. This is not unique to man, for animals show a similar pattern of experience seeking (Welker, 1961). In human societies, the theater, the church, sports spectaculars, the pomp and ceremony of parades, the rides, color, and glitter of carnivals, all are institutions created to meet the need for enhanced experience. We are built to process stimuli, and an important part of living is seeking out stimuli to be processed. The popularity of psychedelics is not only a function of this general characteristic of stimulus seeking, but it also suggests the relative infrequency of bad experiences resulting from their use, unless we wish to posit masochism as an equally fundamental characteristic of biological adjustment.

Because psychedelics focus attention on individual experience, some important social consequences arise from their use. Individual experience is on the one hand unique to the experiencer, and on the other characterized by great transpersonal commonality as one goes deeper into the self (Aaronson, 1968d). In spite of the scientific validity of the behaviorist critique that private experience is not available for scientific observation, for each of us, as individuals, our own experiences have a veridicality shared by few other things in this world. We not only seek experience, we respond in terms of our experiences, and accord a special hearing to those who can "speak from experience." Immediate experience is of greater consequence to the individual experiencing it than any promise of future good or ill made by a personal or impersonal authority figure. Any parent who has had to take a child to face a shot administered to him by his kindly pediatrician can testify to this. Any smoker who lights up contentedly as he reads the warning on his cigarette pack also shows its validity.

When individual experience is emphasized, the generalized verbal formulas for societal control based on hoary and long-unquestioned precepts become open to question as they are filtered through the individual consciousness. Various institutions maintain their authority by means of symbols and concepts that evoke traditional emotional reactions, and the more-rational verbal responses function as unconscious rationalizations of these reactions. That is, many logical arguments turn out to be simply elaborations of illogical emotional biases. These traditional emotional biases are inculcated from the earliest age at home, in the schools, and in the propaganda organizations for children, such as the Boy

Scouts, the Girl Scouts, the YMCA, and other groups. Similar institutions exist in Communist and Fascist societies, except that there the conditioning tends to be more frenetic and compulsive than in our own. The attention to the ways in which these symbols can affect us makes plain the inherent illogic of conventional wisdom. Once the question of "Why, indeed, should I respond in this way?" has been posed, many of the structures of society will tumble if answers cannot be found rooted in the existential being of the questioner.

Many of the consequences of this kind of questioning can be seen not only among the hippies and in Leary's concept of society as a collection of television stage props (1968b), but in the kinds of questions posed by those of our young people who have not obviously taken on the extreme styles of life represented either by the hippies or by Leary. The use of marijuana is sufficiently widespread among our young adult groups that attitudes developing from attention to one's own consciousness have pervaded their style of approach to the world. Before the question of "What career shall I choose?" can be answered, the question of "Why should I choose a career?" must be settled. Before one can agree to fight for flag and country, the existential meaning of flag, country, death, killing, freedom, and a host of other concepts must be considered. The source of power is not seen as being conferred from on high, but as arising from the behavior toward the power wielder of those over whom power is exercised. This attitude has tremendous implications with regard to the kinds of behavior that will be displayed toward the traditional holders of power and the traditional methods of displaying power.

The development of similar emphases on personal revelation and personal consciousness at various points in the history of Christendom led to the formation of many of our existing Protestant denominations and the replacement of the old Catholic concept of an ordained priesthood with a new concept of the priesthood of all believers. The so-called "generation gap" is a mirage that results not from the traditional need of the young to make their way in a world of already established people nor from any traditional traits of impatience or idealism, although all these may be factors, but from differing amounts of attention to the importance of individual experience. Because of the greater willingness of young people to try new things, the consciousness-changing chemicals had their greatest effect along peer-group lines.

Because of the fact that each individual consciousness is located in a body, increased awareness of the body and of our functions as biological organisms seems to occur in the psychedelic-user population. This is not the kind of stress on the body traditionally associated with weight lifting or the overdevelopment of body parts that give a good male or female image, but desire for a well-functioning body that is pleasant to experience. This has led to an interest in hatha yoga and in tai chi, the Indian and Chinese systems of exercise whose aim is not muscular development, but peace, coordination, and good bodily functioning. All bodily functions and bodily needs are more apt to be accepted and, even more important, respected. The ancient verbal taboos limiting sexual behavior have been weakened by the non-verbal nature of psychedelic experience. Excretory functions are accepted without embarrassment. Preferences develop for simple foods with more concern about how these may affect the body, although there is some tendency for this concern to turn to cultishness. Clothes are no longer used to hide the body, but to emphasize the body as the source of experience. The greater openness with regard to the physical self has been accompanied by relaxation of the taboo against touching other people and being touched by them, an event of overriding social consequence in changing the character, intensity, scope, and available possibilities in any interpersonal relationship.

Beyond the perception of the body itself, the enhanced sensory experience has called attention to the pleasures and insights that can be obtained directly from sensory experience. Light shows and modern rock music reflect some of the visual and auditory experiences produced by psychedelics. Aldous Huxley (1956) has pointed out the luminous intensity of colors found in "the antipodes of the mind," and this is mimicked by Day-Glo paints and the eerie glow of colors under black light. The greater sensitivity to color reflections, color shadows, and afterimages, especially as they appear reflected on glossy surfaces like skin, has led to the modern fashion of body painting. Along with the perception of oneself as a biological organism, with its consequent emphasis on the simple and natural, there has been an increased awareness of the complexity and beauty of natural phenomena. This has been further elaborated by the fact that, with many of the psychedelics, the retinal structure of the eye itself enters into the perception, as Klüver (1966) has pointed out. This has complicated the drive for simplicity with a preference for the baroque. The resulting dynamic tension appears in all forms of psychedelic decoration, music, literature, and art. Masters and Houston (1968) have shown this well in their recently published book on psychedelic art, which runs the gamut from simple meditative expressions to welters of clashing stimulation designed to make the viewer leave his senses through overstimulation of his senses.

Going deeply into one's own experience leads to insights beyond those experienced when the focus of attention is on what is experienced rather than the mode of experience itself. The appearance of reality is no longer taken at face value, but is seen as an interaction with the perceptual apparatus of the perceiver. This means that the usual existential primacy given the world around us, probably because we are built to process information coming to us from the outside, gives way to an equality of perceiver and perceived, so that the perception itself becomes the primary datum in a conscious sense, as it has always been without our realization. This is, indeed, one of the goals of many meditative systems, and meditation as such has become a popular activity among the psychedelic subgroup and those influenced by them. Indeed, movement within the self away from its more-surface manifestations inevitably invokes religious imagery (Masters and Houston, 1966; Aaronson, 1968a), although images invoking religious feelings may be possible at all levels of consciousness. The sense that depth is expanded, common in psychedelic experiences, is like the environmental conditions most commonly associated with mystical experience, and mystical experiences can be produced by experimentally providing experiences of enhanced depth (Aaronson, 1967d). Movement within reaches the level of archetype and myth and may transcend these to a point of ultimate mystical union. The archetypes may be an elaboration of current material featured in the concerns of the popular press, as Barron (1967) has pointed out. They may derive from early impressions and concerns fed by other technologies in our culture. Tom Wolfe (1968), for instance, has pointed out the prevalence of imagery from the comic books dear to children in the late thirties and early forties in the group centering around Ken Kesey. They may derive from fundamental perceptions of our own structures and modes of functioning. Barron (1967) has noted, "an experience of Christ, i.e. of Christ free from the institutional embodiment known as Christianity, is common to many psychedelic "trips." Christ on the cross may then be understood simply as "consciousness impaled on the human form, mind hung to die on body to expiate our voluntary participation in the world's heavy materialism." This manner of thinking and perceiving, the concentration on archetype, the sense of an indwelling, immanent God, and the interest in meditation have correspondingly created an interest in those forms of religion that stress these notions: Hinduism, and Tibetan and Zen Buddhism. Psychedelic experience is fundamentally religious, as any experience of life taken as an experience of life must be. Braden (1967) has pointed out that the fundamental thrust of psychedelic experience is religious and its fundamental challenge is to the forms of organized religion. It is one of the forces contributing to the ferment in contemporary Christianity that is presently leading one of the oldest and most tradition-bound of Christian churches to re-evaluate its forms, its structure, and many of the engrafted beliefs of its development.

The development of any new major innovation in technology affects profoundly the life and structure of the society in which it occurs. The development of psychedelics is such a major innovation, which promises revolutionary changes and is, in fact, already producing them. Psychedelics may have a potential impact on society equivalent to that of the machine, which in setting off the Industrial Revolution, created much of what we now consider our "natural" and "traditional" styles of life and forms of organizing society. At the time of the beginning of the Industrial Revolution, those dispossessed by the new forms blamed the machines and tried to wreck them in the Luddite rebellion. Our modern Luddites are not the dispossessed, but those who exist at the very center of the power structure. The alteration of values, the questioning of rules by those who have had psychedelic experiences, create much consternation, often by their very own children, among individuals who have made their way by those rules and under the value system of the existing society. In addition, the negative implications of the concept "drug," noted earlier in this discussion, are not without their effects.

Confronted by danger, each carries out his social function. The mass media simultaneously point at the wonders of psychedelic experience and view them with alarm. Psychologists, psychiatrists, and sociologists, whose business it is to find abnormality in deviance, find abnormality in deviance. Government agencies introduce regulations, lawmakers make laws, and policemen police. The upshot of all this activity is that it is now almost impossible to carry out legitimate research with psychedelics. A large user population has developed that uses bootleg drugs, sometimes containing dangerous impurities, and almost certainly producing revenue for organized crime. Drugs are now used by individuals who, under a system of controlled access to them, would probably not have been exposed to them and run the risk of injuring themselves. It is difficult to set up safeguards for the proper use of the major psychedelics when this use is illegal. One segment of our population exists under conditions reminiscent of prohibition, while the other looks on with alarm. A crisis in confidence has been created that cuts across generational lines. A great many people who normally would be law-abiding are placed in the position of outlaws, with marked implications for their further relationships to society and its institutions.

It is beyond the scope of this paper to do any more than outline briefly some of the implications of psychedelic technology and some of its associated problems. The rest of this book is devoted to filling in the picture in more detail. At the present time, the repressive attitudes toward this new technology are so strong that its effects can only show themselves in strange and aborted forms. Perhaps the situation will be eased to permit more-open and controlled development of what is now clandestine and uncontrolled. Hopefully.

PART II

THE NATURE OF THE EXPERIENCE

The fundamental reason for taking psychedelics is the experiences they produce. These experiences may be of many kinds. Walter Pahnke (1967) has recently classified them into five types: *psychotic*, characterized by fear, paranoid symptoms, confusion, impairment of abstract reasoning, remorse, depression, isolation, and/or somatic discomfort; *psychodynamic*, in which unconscious or preconscious material becomes vividly conscious; *cognitive*, characterized by "astonishingly lucid thought"; *aesthetic*, with increased perceptual ability in all sense modalities; and *psychedelic mystical*, marked by all the characteristics of spontaneous mystical experience observed in the literature. These experiences may be the cause for the effects of psychedelics on behavior. They are also the fundamental thing that must be explained if psychedelics and their effects are to be understood.

In the papers that follow, samples of experience with the major psychedelic drugs are presented. No claims are made with respect to their representativeness. The experiences are grouped by drug, so that states produced by different drugs may be compared. Examination of these accounts suggests that the differences among the experiences are less than their similarities. The entire range of phenomena listed by Masters and Houston (1966) as occurring in the course of psychedelic experiences appears among them. It is also apparent that the set of the subject toward the experience, and the setting in which the drug is taken, are of overriding significance in determining the kind of experience achieved.

The mescaline papers deal with what may be regarded as psychotomimetic experiences. The paper by Humphry Osmond is a reprint of one not generally available, which gives a sense of the impact of these chemicals in the early days of their use and provides a sense of the excitement aroused among psychiatrists and psychologists who felt that here at last was a way to understand schizophrenia. The paper by Sinnett discusses these issues in more detail.

The psilocybin papers both come from Harvard Psilocybin Project, whose results catapulted psychedelia into the mass media, and its originators out of Harvard. These studies had two aspects: those using ordinary volunteers, and a special project utilizing prisoners. The general development of the project is discussed by Leary (1968) in *High Priest*. The controversy that has surrounded this situation has obscured the fact that interesting and seminal observations have been made here and that nobody has pursued them further. The paper by Jonathan Clark deals with a drug experience he had in the course of the prisoner-rehabilitation project. The paper by Stanley Krippner focuses on the experience of a volunteer in the experiments that were carried out with non-prisoners.

Both the LSD experiences reproduced here are examples of experiences produced under controlled conditions during the time when LSD was legal and obtainable. Should the hysteria over LSD ever abate, experiences like these, under professional supervision, might be available to individuals screened against the likelihood of psychiatric abnormality and with set and setting controlled to provide maximum safeguards against any deleterious effects. The purpose of Aaronson's experience was to see what psychedelics were like; Richardson's experience was to help him solve a problem. Both, however, have therapeutic overtones.

The paper by Stafford shows the ways in which psychedelics tend to be used at present in the community of users. The substance spoken of as "yage" was probably not yage, but harmine or harmaline. Of special interest are the use of one psychochemical to ameliorate any difficulty arising from the use of another, and the use of marijuana in conjunction with the experience without any thought that the marijuana might influence the experience. Elements of this experience lead Mr. Stafford to speculate on psychedelics in general and their possible future impact on society.

ON BEING MAD

HUMPHRY OSMOND

Perhaps you are shocked at this unhygienic title and feel that some comfortable synonym should have been substituted for that harsh three-letter word; but surely there are occasions when a spade should be called a spade and semantic niceties left to those who don't have to dig for a living. During the past fifty years we have had a welter of theories explaining the great insanities, and each fresh batch spawns a new terminology, usually in bastard Greek, which cuts less sharply than the edged words of the plain tongue. We cushion ourselves, with catatonia and complexes, with schizophrenia and the Oedipus story, with the id and the sphaira, from the hard facts that we don't know what is wrong with our patients and we don't care to guess what they are enduring.

These new formidable words, *schizophrenia, dementia praecox,* and *paranoia,* are weightier but less penetrating than the old short ones, *daft, crazy,* and *mad,* and by their very size they fend us from our patients and stop them from coming too close to us. They insulate "us" from "them." Schizophrenia, the greatest and most incomprehensible of our adversaries, is schizophrenia, and that handy label allows us to pigeonhole the patient and think no more about him. The thinking has already been done for us by the masters of our mystery, who have each, according to his lights, described the illness, outlined its course, laid down methods of treatment, and usually indicated how it is caused. It sometimes looks as if there is nothing more to be said.

And yet, one can read whole books of psychiatry and never know what it feels like to be mad, which is a pity, because our ignorance makes it harder to help patients; and we become more inclined to rely on stale authority rather than on fresh observation and experiment. A useful but neglected source of information might be patients who have recovered, but, for various reasons, they are commonly reticent about their experiences. A hospital patient who frequently discusses his delusions and hallucinations with doctors and nurses does not enchance the likelihood of discharge; indeed, patients must often feel that the less they talk about such matters the more chance they have of leaving. Afterward, the patient may not wish to recall visions of an anarchic world in which primitive instinctual drives manifest themselves, untrammeled by the usual internal prohibitions. In addition, doctors, nurses, and friends often combine to make the patient so ashamed of his illness that he dare not talk of it. We do not understand and we cannot forgive the madman's defiance of our well-ordered, safe, but precarious little world.

Nevertheless, heroic souls have given us some remarkable accounts of their illnesses. One of the most vivid that I know is *The Witnesses* (1938), by Thomas Hennell. He wrote, about a prolonged schizophrenic illness, with the penetrating eye of a skilled artist. Unfortunately, his book is hard to get. Another famous book was by Clifford Beers, *A Mind That Found Itself* (1908). Beers referred to his illness as being a manic-depressive one, but this may have been a piece of necessary self-deception, brought about by the extremely gloomy prognosis that it was customary to give to dementia praecox in those days. J. H. Ogdon's *Kingdom of the Lost* (1946), published in 1947, is a good book marred by too much polemic and too little description. *Wisdom, Madness and Folly* (1952), by John Custance, is a fine piece of work dealing courageously with very severe episodes of mania and depression. It is interesting to compare this with some of the more frankly schizophrenic illnesses. These four books, and there are doubtless many others, will help the alert and sympathetic reader to picture that other world which our patients inhabit, and from which we must try to rescue them.

However, even the best-written book must fail to transmit an experience that many claim is incommunicable, and the doctor often wishes that he could enter the illness and see with a madman's eyes, hear with his ears, and feel with his skin. This might seem an unlikely privilege, but it is available to anyone who is prepared to take a small quantity of the alkaloid mescaline or a minute amount of the ergotlike substance lysergic acid diethylamide, which transmits the taker into another world for a few hours. In a recently published paper, the similarity between the mescaline and schizophrenic experiences was noted, and it was observed that mescaline reproduced every single major symptom of acute schizophrenia, though not always to the same degree, and a detailed table showed that the two states have much in common.

Mescaline, which is now usually produced synthetically, occurs naturally as the active principle of the peyotl, a cactus found in New Mexico and called, after Lewin, a great connoisseur of strange drugs, anhalonium lewinii. It has been known for many years, and its chemical formula, which is quite simple, resembles that of adrenalin. This important fact has only recently been recorded. The mescal buttons have been used by Indian tribes in divinatory and religious ceremonies for many hundreds of years. It is of interest that the U. S. Narcotics Control Bureau has some evidence that mescal taking is slowly spreading northward among the Indians in Saskatchewan. It would not surprise the writer if these unlucky people, whose culture has been overwhelmed by our own, should turn to experiences that even we, with our astonishing ingenuity, cannot match.

It is not, however, by tables or statements that we are made aware of the nature of unusual experiences, so the writer will take some rough notes, transcribed by a mescaline taker, as a basis for describing the effect of this drug, and then will discuss the application, of any information we may derive from observations of this sort, to people suffering from schizophrenia and other severe illnesses.

The subject was a psychiatrist, aged thirty-four, married, and in good health. The experiment took place in his colleague's (John) flat in London. Present in the flat during the experiment was a friend (Edward) who had a tape recorder, and John's wife (Vanna). The flat was in a back street that leads to Wimpole Street, in the center of the fashionable doctors' area in London. The experiment began shortly after midday on an August afternoon, when the subject took four hundred milligrams of mescal on an empty stomach. A condensed version of the notes taken at the time, and his recollections, will be used in this account of his experience.

About half an hour after taking the mescaline, I noticed an uneasy sense of rising tension and a need to move around the room. Chancing to look across the street at the window opposite, I saw that it was curiously sharp. It seemed to be made of old yellowing ivory which had, perhaps, been long buried and then cleaned. John was inclined to discount this observation, because he thought that it would be about an hour before I noticed anything, but I knew that there was something wrong with the window opposite. Shortly after this, a sense of special significance began to invest everything in the room; objects which I would normally accept as just being there began to assume some strange importance. A plain wooden chair was invested with a "chairliness" which no chair ever had for me before. In the many thousand stitches of a well-worn carpet, I saw the footprints of mankind plodding wearily down the ages. Barbed wire on a fence outside was sharp and bitter, a crown of thorns, man's eternal cruelty to man. It hurt me.

I noticed, about this time, that when I shut my eyes, I saw sparkling lights flashing across the darkness. I was restless and walked into another room, where I was alone. I remember how brilliantly sharp the little objects on a dressing table were. I ran my fingers over my old corduroy slacks and, as I did so, the most vivid memories began to well up in my mind of dangerous times in the past when I had worn them. Memories of the London blitz, of seagoing during the war, these had a curious quality which is hard to put into words. I was at first aware that I was simply recalling something that had once happened to me, but gradually I began to feel that I was not merely recalling, but re-experiencing the past. The room had peeling white wallpaper, and behind this was a patch of green, a milky jade green. I was much interested in this patch of green until I realized that I was looking at the winter sea, and that if I stayed there any longer, I would see a ship sinking in a storm, and that once again our ship would plow through those unhappy survivors in pursuit of a submarine. I did not wish to see all that again. I returned to the other room and asked John to come in and join me. To live comfortably, the past should remain in its place.

By now, everything was brilliantly sharp and significant: if I fixed my attention on a flower, I felt that I could spend all day in contemplating it. A faded carnation was worth a lifetime study. Although the world was sharper and brighter, it was also infinitely more fluid and changeable. A bird in the street, a sparrow small and far away, might suddenly become the focus of one's attention, the most important thing one had ever seen, the most important thing in the world, the bird of the world, a key to the universe. Beauty, a terrible beauty, was being born every moment. Phrases such as "I have seen with the eye of the world, the eye of the newborn and the new dead" sprang to my tongue apparently without construction.

Gradually, all sense perception became increasingly vivid—sight, sound, taste, touch, and smell all grew in intensity, and with this I noticed that things seemed distorted, especially if I became worried.

I can only give glimpses of the strange, often frightening, and sometimes very beautiful world which began to replace the familiar one. For instance, John, sitting in his chair opposite, became the focus of my attention, and as I gazed at him he began to change. I might have been looking at an impressionist portrait of him and, as I thought of this, he leered at me in an unpleasant way. The lighting changed, the whole room was darker and more threatening and seemed to become larger, the perspectives changing. However, as soon as John spoke again, I realized that it was only my strange condition. Then I looked out of the window at the building opposite, which towered up like a cliff, immensely tall; yet, about an hour before, it had seemed quite ordinary.

Shortly after this, Edward came with the recording machine, and by the time they had set it up I was in the full flood of the psychosis. I hadn't met Edward before, and when he brought the machine to me, the unfamiliarity made me afraid. He urged me not to be afraid of it, but as he brought it closer it began to glow, a dull purple which turned to a deep cherry red, and the heat of it overwhelmed me as when a furnace door is opened in your face. I knew that it could not be; yet it was so. However, as I got accustomed to the microphone, it assumed a normal appearance and I was able to speak into it.

I also noticed that my hands tingled and had a curious dirty feeling which seemed to be inside the skin. I scrutinized one hand and it appeared shrunken and clawlike: I realized that beneath the dried leathery skin was bone and dust alone—no flesh. My hand had withered away, yet I could remind myself that this unusual happening had been induced simply by taking mescal.

John had no radio or phonograph, so that we could not discover how I responded to music. From time to time I would close my eyes and become absorbed in the brilliant visions which I then saw. These had become very complicated and of singular beauty; showers of jewels flashed across this inner vision, great landscapes of color spread out before me, and almost any thought would be accompanied by a vision which was often supernaturally beautiful. These are, I believe, indescribable, using the word in an exact sense. Language is a means of communicating experiences held in common and is, therefore, unsuitable for matters which are out of common. Glittering fountains of liquid jewels, pearly depths of the infinite, the apricot clouds of eternity's sunrise, seen through a shimmering filigree of the finest silver mesh, do not begin to describe these enchanting mindscapes.

From time to time I recorded snatches of sentences which gave some idea of what I saw, but to give true account of them would require a tongue, a brush, a pen, an art which I do not possess, and a language which does not exist.

My companions roused me from my absorption with these things and suggested a walk. I would not have gone out alone, for I felt that this inner reality might break out, as it were, from its place, and invade the everyday world. Every so often the walls of the room would shiver, and I knew that behind those perilously unsolid walls something was waiting to burst through. I believed that would be disastrous; these two worlds must remain discrete. Not all the visions were pleasant, but I found that as long as I remained calm and observed them as a series of never-to-be-forgotten experiences, all would be well. If I became frightened, their quality might change and they would become more and more threatening. It was essential to remain calm and to refuse to be overwhelmed. If it became unbearable, I discovered that I could reduce the tension by concentrating on pleasant, reassuring themes, such as my wife and little daughter, but of course my companions had to discourage this, since we were engaged in an experiment.

Before the walk, I asked for some water. I drank the glass which John brought, and found that it tasted strange. I wondered if there might be something wrong with it: poison crossed my mind and almost at the same time the story of Socrates and the hemlock cup; and with that a calculation made by a physicist who claimed that every glass of water contains an atom of Socrates, due to diffusion in the twenty-five or so centuries since his death. I looked into the glass of water. In its swirling depths was a vortex which went down into the center of the world and the heart of time. My companions dragged me away from the water for a walk.

In the alleyway, just before we went out, a dog barked and its piercing reverberant howl might have been all the wolves in Tartary. Once on the street, the distortion of perspective became evident. The distances were immense, the colors vivid; the August sun burned on a purple patch of willow herbs on a bomb site with such intensity that I had to shade my eyes. Everything was sharp as a painting by Vermeer.

One house took my attention. It had a sinister quality, since from behind its drawn shades, people seemed to be looking out, and their gaze was unfriendly. We met no people for the first few hundred yards, then we came to a window in which a child was standing, and as we drew nearer, its face became piglike. I noticed two passers-by who, as they drew nearer, seemed humpbacked and twisted, and their faces were covered with wens. The wide spaces of the streets were dangerous, the houses threatening, and the sun burned me.

I was glad to be back in the flat; there at least my world was partly under control; outside, the hoot of a passing taxi, the brilliant color of a dress, or the sudden move of a stranger taking me off my guard would burst torrentially into my whole sensory experience.

Once indoors, I could sup deep in horror with Macbeth, or exult like a mystic in the oneness of eternity, or wallow in jewels like Shylock, but at least I only had to open my eyes to be comparatively safe. Not as safe as I would like to have been, as it was particularly difficult to get accustomed to the changes in body image. At one moment I would be a giant in a tiny cupboard, and the next, a dwarf in a huge hall. It is difficult enough to explain what it feels like to have been Gulliver, or Alice in Wonderland, in the space of a few minutes, but it is nearly impossible to communicate an experience which amounts to having been uncertain whether one was in Brobdingnag or Lilliput.

In spite of everything, I could, with an effort, behave almost normally. My wife telephoned, and I was able to talk to her quite sensibly. She was unable to understand why I didn't wish to return home that night, and I was unable to explain that I could not be sure from one minute to the next how I would experience my surroundings. A twisted string might suddenly become a snake, and if I became panicky, would writhe toward me.

An unexpected happening was an extreme sensitivity to other people's feelings toward me or toward each other. I have not seen this recorded elsewhere and, since it exerts a considerable influence on one, it seems worth noting. I experienced my friends' criticism of me as physical discomfort. If they urged me to do something I didn't want to do, I was jarred, and this jarring was sometimes accompanied by a burning taste and smell.

Most unexpected was my response to a slight difference of opinion between John and his wife. This was a minor affair, due to her wanting me to eat, and John wishing me to discuss my experiences and satisfy his scientific curiosity. The room, which had been brilliantly lighted, became dark, the colors lost some of their vitality, and I felt her criticism of him as a bitter taste, an acrid smell, and an ill-localized pain somewhere between my shoulder blades and down my spine. All the time, my three companions were changing, sometimes with reference to my inner experiences.

After seven hours the effects began to wear off and, in addition, I had learned to prevent myself from panicking by concentrating on pleasant themes when I seemed to be growing too afraid, and by observing with as much detachment as possible. I did not in this experiment attempt free association; the huge volume of associations due to the psychosis was as much as I could cope with, but I believe that this could be done and might be useful in exploring the roots of personality. I doubt whether this should be tried at a first venture, for there seems to be a real danger that more anxiety may be generated than one can deal with. It is best to become accustomed to the mescal world before exploring it.

By midnight, twelve hours after taking the drug, I was able to be alone in a room, and the mescal world was receding. True, an unexpected sound in the alleyway would bring back delusions for a short time. I still felt that the windows opposite were strange: one in particular was shaped like a coffin lid. Once or twice in the next twenty-four hours I had brief recrudescences of psychosis. Colors seemed unusually bright, and the sun burned me. I was in a "touch me not" mood. I did not wish to discuss the experience with anyone. I tried not to think about it, although I could not avoid doing so. I did not read the notes which I had made for nearly a fortnight —I had no wish to revive what had happened too soon.

What can we learn from this and similar accounts? What might we hope to learn from enduring such an experience ourselves, omitting the possibility of philosophical and psychological discoveries about the nature of mind, its range, and the way it works? There is much, I believe, that can be applied to everyday work. We can recognize that the schizophrenic person is not imagining or fantasizing when he says that the world has changed and looks different: it is different for him and there is an end of it. We must accept what he says as true, and try only to persuade him that the remarkable changes in the world are due to his illness. Those of us who are fortunate enough to be well should make it our business to help when we can, or at least harm the sick person as little as possible. The madman, in the face of the overwhelming assault of the illness, frequently behaves childishly and in so doing is subjected to hatred, ridicule, and often contempt from his healthy fellows. This provokes a vicious circle of fear and guilt that leads to more hallucinations and delusions. In this black world, the greatest comfort and help will come from nurses, doctors, and friends who, although recognizing that the patient's fears are real for him, nevertheless refuse to be dismayed by them or by anything he may do or say. This calls for understanding and courage, for which there is no counterfeit. Schizophrenics, in some stages of the illness, are far more aware of other people's real feelings toward them than we have been inclined to believe.

We should listen seriously to mad people, for, in phrases that are usually clumsy, ill-constructed, and even banal, they try to tell us of voyages of the human soul that make the wanderings of Odysseus seem no more than a Sunday's outing. They tell us of a purgatory from which none returns unscathed. They tell us of another world than this; but mostly we don't hear, because we are talking at them to assure them that they are mistaken. Sometimes, when they might make their escape, we do not heed, or even unwittingly drive them back into hell. The least we can do for these far voyagers is to hear them courteously and try to do them no harm.

EXPERIENCE AND REFLECTIONS

E. ROBERT SINNETT

In the fall of 1956 I participated in an experiment being conducted for a doctoral dissertation in psychology.[1] Three psychiatric residents and I were administered mescaline sulfate; the standard dosage used was two hundred milligrams. We were observed and supervised by a psychiatrist and a psychologist. The drug experience took place in a setting familiar to me: the old Topeka VA Hospital, where I had been a staff psychologist for approximately a year and a half at that time.

I was sitting in Hawley Auditorium about half an hour after receiving my mescaline, wondering if the drug would have any effect on me. I am not highly reactive to drugs or alcohol, and I am also a bit of a skeptic—inclined to wonder about the influence of expectations and placebo effects on the drug experience and reports of such experience. My first hint of an effect was a tingling sensation in my left hand, as if the circulation were poor; but instead of rubbing it, I pinched myself, and the mild pain had a strange, "not-me" quality to it. The pain did not seem diminished in intensity from what it would have been in my normal state, but it was almost as if I were pinching someone else.[2]

Soon we went outside, and with no provocation I became overwhelmed with laughter. Dr. M. grimaced and stared at me in such a way as to communicate that my behavior was very strange. I ceased laughing abruptly, and I felt pained, for there was no denying that my state of feeling was "crazy" and inappropriate. It was as if the greatest self-conscious fears

---

[1] Silverthorn, Lee J., Jr. "An Experimental Investigation of Some of the Psychological Changes Associated with the Effects of Mescaline Sulfate." Unpublished doctoral dissertation, University of Kansas, 1957.

[2] On reflection later, I could intuitively appreciate why psychedelic drugs might be useful in cases of intractable pain.

I had ever had (in adolescence) were transcended. This kind of outburst was quite alien to my ordinary state.[3] On a later occasion I felt an intense, almost uncontrollable need to laugh—as intense and organic in quality as a distended bowel or bladder. This time, however, my behavior was somewhat more adaptive: I ran into the room where the group was assembled, saying, "Quick, someone hand me a *New Yorker*— I feel a laugh coming on!" I then stopped fighting off my feeling, laughed vigorously, and my tension dissipated.

Although there were four of us participating together as subjects, the experience did not have the character of an ordinary small group. We seemed largely isolated from one another by the boundaries of our separate experiences. One subject was quite nauseated and dysphoric. Another kept denying that the drug had any influence on him when with us, but he was observed to leave the room, hallucinate outside, and re-enter denying that he was feeling any effects. For both of these individuals, the experience was predominantly an unpleasant one. I was surprised that even later they seemed to wish to avoid me and avoid reference to the experience. I had expected that scientific interest, if nothing else, would lead us to some informative, sharing exchanges. The remaining subject and I did share experiences later: for both of us, the session had been primarily positive in character.[4]

In the room where we gathered, there was a painting that I had seen numerous times before. It was a very bad, amateurish canvas that had been done by a patient. It was similar to the paint-by-numbers kind and had rather garish colors. Even though I remembered the quality of the painting, it took on a beauty that was striking and very absorbing. I don't know how long I must have stared at its whirling, luminous colors and into its cavernous depths. It seemed as though I

[3] I had not been able to intuitively understand the silly laughter of the hebephrenic or inappropriate affect until this time. Also, I was unaware of the social plight of the schizophrenic, who must receive feedback of his strangeness even from highly trained professional staff.

[4] Dr. Philip B. Smith has published an account of his experience: "A Sunday with Mescaline," *Bulletin of the Menninger Clinic* 23, 20–27, 1959.

might step through the frame into another world, in Alice-in-Wonderland fashion.

I checked my watch to see what time it was. I seemed unable to integrate the perceptions of the big hand and little hand into the meaning of time. Several times I cycled back and forth saying to myself, "The big hand is on 9, the little hand is on 4," before giving up. I hadn't realized before, the sequential nature of telling time—it is usually so instantaneous rather than process in character. I was later reminded of my early experience in beginning to learn to tell time.

Time sense itself seemed absent for me, and only that which was in my immediate field of experience was real.[5] My self seemed like a small sphere within the center of my head. The rest of my body seemed somehow peripheral and empty, as if my self were a pea-sized object in a shadowy, gray void enclosed by my body.

Because of my experience with psychological tests I was exempted from participating in the psychometric part of the study. As I observed one of the other subjects taking a psycho-motor performance test, I wondered if I would show a deficit: I felt that I would not. I did feel that, had I been asked to take the test, I might have knocked it off the table and laughed and been delighted to see the pieces fly about. I thought, too, that I might have told the experimenter, "Go fuck yourself!" and laughed uproariously at the funny, original joke I had made. I thought further that if I did show a decrement (basically I think that I was scared I would), it might be attributable to a lack of motivation.

Goal-oriented activity in general seemed alien to me, and I wanted to be absorbed in my fantasialike hallucinations without interruption. I am sure that I must have been very irritated with respect to any such intrusions. The hallucinations were indescribably beautiful and of such a raw sensory

[5] What profound implications this has for a rehabilitation program oriented toward planning! If relatives, the future, and the outside world do not exist, such planning activity would be meaningless and absurd to the patient. The hallucinations and perceptual distortions seemed decidedly more real than the non-immediate aspects of my experience.

character (moving, vivid colors without form) that I was surprised at my impotence in describing them later. The fantasia simile represents my most articulate attempt to convey my direct experience, but it seems quite pallid and inadequate as a representation or communication. After a time, when I tired of the hallucinatory experiences that would appear vividly on shutting my eyes, I felt them to be intrusive. Neither sleep nor rest was possible, and I had not realized before how much sleep is dependent on one's ability to exclude stimulation from within.[6]

As I walked down a corridor to another room, I had the distinct feeling that the wooden floors were like the canvas of a boxing ring; i.e., quite elastic, yielding, and bouncy. I also felt that, as my feet pressed into the floor, some other part of the floor must be rising. It was as if the whole floor were some sort of hydraulic system. The ordinary experience is that one's foot yields to something solid. Whether kinesthetic experience was attributed to an external state or whether the normal slight elasticity of a wooden floor was somehow given more weight in determining the experience, I don't know.

I entered the room, and after a short while I lay down on the floor with my head against the baseboard almost at a right angle to my body. One of the observers thought it odd that I didn't lie on the cot across the room. It was obvious that he felt uncomfortable seeing me in this somewhat contorted position. I felt no discomfort, and crossing the room didn't seem worth the effort. Later I moved over, lay on a cot, and tried to rest or sleep, but I hallucinated a grid on a luminous yellow background. The grid was somewhat like that of an oscilloscope or radar screen, and it seemed that some mathematical function might readily be graphed on it.

Afterward, when we went outside the hospital, it was evident that my space perception was greatly altered. Although I knew the flagpole was approximately fifty yards away, as I stretched my hand out it seemed that if I were to stretch

[6] It occurred to me later that the psychedelic drugs might be a powerful technique for brainwashing; I would suppose that after a period of being incessantly harassed by hallucinations, a person might promise anything for release from this state.

a bit farther I could touch its top. I stretched several times trying to reach it, knowing I couldn't, and feeling that I could with "just one more try." Repeated "one more tries" didn't negate my feeling that this feat was possible.

During a ride in a car, as we went down Huntoon Street it seemed as if we were in a tunnel and the surroundings were blurred as they are when one passes something very near at high speed (we were moving about twenty miles per hour). One of the experimenters told me that although reports of tunnel vision are not uncommon, actual measurements of visual fields on previous subjects had showed no measurable change from the normal, drug-free state. My illusion was not dispelled by this information.

After approximately four hours, the experience was terminated by Thorazine. The effects tapered off rather gradually. I wanted to leave, and although I was aware of my disorganization, I left the hospital ahead of the experimenters and was intent on driving my car home alone. However, I seemed also to realize that this was foolhardy and went slowly enough to be "caught." I was somewhat surprised that they weren't angry with me when they found me. In this instance, as in previous experiences, I was grateful that I could trust a professional staff to be kind and care for me.

At home I tried to tell my wife about the drug experience, but it was difficult to express myself, and I think, too, that I felt some guilt about having had such an intense experience without her—it was as if I had done something "bad." She seemed indulgent and less curious than I had anticipated.

For a time I sat outside on our front porch alone, opening myself once more to hallucinations, contemplation, and inner experiences of diminished intensity—wanting to prolong the experience. The most vivid hallucination I experienced at this time was of smelling burning oak wood. It was a very pungent olfactory experience. When I queried my wife in an attempt to determine whether this was a veridical perception or not, she said she could not detect any such odor.

What lingering effects has the mescaline experience had? In fleeting moments and with greatly diminished intensity, I have felt the tunnel-vision phenomenon and the elasticity of the floor beneath me that I described above. It is as though the perceptual constancies are themselves now seen as something of an illusion and an oversimplification of the sensory world. The best analogy I can make is that after once seeing the set for the Bonanza show on location, I have found the illusion of the Western adventure somewhat fragile and harder to maintain than it was prior to visiting the set, where the illusion-creating implements were visible and obvious.

The most important effect of the drug for me was directly experiencing a psychotic state. Although I had had much clinical experience working with schizophrenics as well as academic preparation in clinical psychology and two years of psychoanalytically oriented psychotherapy, new vistas and understanding were made available to me. Hebephrenic, hypomanic, delinquent, schizophrenic, and organic brain syndrome behavior and experiences became possible for me. The temporary exemption from the dictates of perceptual, cognitive, and habit structures also drew me into a vital experience of the world of childhood. It seemed to me that the implications for doing rehabilitation and psychotherapy with psychotic patients are far-reaching. With the impairment I felt, I am sure that I would only have been amenable to a verbal therapy that used simple vocabulary, short sentences, and redundant messages. My disorganization made me very dependent on the professional staff for my well-being. Differences in their personalities seemed insignificant as long as I could feel they were competent and kind and would set limits appropriately. I must admit that with only such simple conditions necessary for satisfactory treatment, my faith in the desirability of a sophisticated, psychodynamic treatment approach was somewhat shaken. There would be value in providing the student in the mental health professions with such an orienting experience. It occurred to me, too, that the experience might help relatives of psychotic patients achieve greater understanding in a way that explanations or information cannot. I look on the mescaline experience as having been a provocative, rich source of data for speculation—richer, I am embarrassed to say, than much of my formal scientific research and study. I am sure, however, that it differs in many respects from a schizophrenic state; e.g., the hallucinations seem to be of a more primitive sensory character than those of the schizophrenic, which may be organized and endowed with meaning.

AN ADVENTURE IN PSILOCYBIN

STANLEY KRIPPNER[1]

It began with a kaleidoscope of multihued swirling shapes taking form on the inside of my eyelids. It resulted from thirty milligrams of psilocybin plus thirty minutes of anticipation.

I opened my eyes to find the living room vibrating with brilliant colors. My first words to the others were that I seemed to be in the middle of a three-dimensional Vermeer painting. At this point, I was still aware of "the others"—Steve, Sam, and Alice, my guides in the "trip" I was taking as part of the Harvard University Psilocybin Research Project.

My limbs were trembling. I felt a tingling sensation in my fingers. I reclined on the sofa and closed my eyes again. I lost myself in the whirling colors funneling up like a huge mushroom spreading over me.

I could now make out numbers, letters, and words in vivid colors. These symbols were billowing up, branching out, and forming a glowing canopy. I had the impression that this swirling tornado was divesting me of verbal conventions, rules, signs, and everyday boundaries, leaving me naked and open to a more basic world of feeling and direct impression. I felt overwhelmingly tuned in to "the true nature of things."

An apple brought back awareness of my physical setting. It had been placed in my hand by one of the others. I bit into it and was astounded by the extraordinarily delicious taste, the perfection of it. "This is ambrosia, the food of the gods," I declared, urging the others to sample the apple.

The process of chewing seemed to go on forever. My

[1] The author expresses his appreciation to Robert D. Nelson for his help in the preparation of this report.

mouth was a mammoth cavern and I seemed to be able to visualize the mastication, the swallowing, and the descent of the apple pulp through the esophagus. Following a sudden urge to take advantage of this heightened sensory ability, I groped my way toward the kitchen. Strong waves of distinct aromas swept into my head through huge, yawning nostrils. Thyme, cloves, cinnamon, vanilla, all at once and yet separately, registered themselves upon my consciousness. Impulsively, I swallowed some vanilla. This was a mistake. "Vanilla is to be smelled, but not tasted," I announced with profundity.

I tested my tactile sensitivity. I worked my way back to the couch and found Alice. My exploration of the softness of the sweater and the warmth of her flesh was an ecstatic sensual experience. However, it was devoid of sexuality, devoid of passion. While on the couch, the stimulation of touch became less important to me as I began to experience the dichotomous sensation of sinking into the cushions and yet floating slightly above them.

It was at this point that I became aware of the music from the phonograph. I was hearing the music as I had never heard it before. The composer, the counterpoint, the arrangement were unimportant. Only the sheer beauty of each individual tone mattered. I was listening to the music vertically rather than horizontally.

The visual sense provided additional surprises. Virtually every item in range of my vision was transformed. The alarm clock was a work of art from a Cellini studio. Alice's gaudy jewelry was on loan from the Empress Josephine. The faces of my companions radiated light. Auras shone about their bodies. For just a moment I felt an inexpressible kinship with them.

Steve muttered something and broke the spell. His utterances seemed superficial and inappropriate. Words were useless; speech was a waste of time. I headed for an adjoining bedroom. I could not walk, as my large body muscles failed to respond to my orders. I found myself creeping along the floor into the dimly lit room.

My visual perception was still astounding me. Pieces of lint on my trousers sparkled like lustrous sequins. A painting on the wall began to move. The horses in the picture were stamping their hoofs and snorting about the canvas.

On my way to the bedroom, I passed by the kitchen. Remembering my great delight in eating the apple, I picked up a jar of cloves and some peppermint candy. I sniffed the cloves, and their fragrance seemed to envelop my whole being. I *became* the odor as I inhaled and exhaled. The candy was equally sensational; I *became* the taste.

I reached the bedroom and flopped down upon the bed. Rolling the candy about my monstrous cavern of a mouth, I held the cloves to my nostrils and let my eyelids fall.

The oriental Yin-Yang symbol emerged on the horizon of my consciousness. During this period of reverie, I felt as if I were slowly diving into the center of the Yin-Yang. Once immersed, I experienced a negation of time. Past, present, future all seemed the same—just as the Yin-Yang symbolized unity and oneness.

Now a series of visions began. The imagery appeared to synchronize with the phonograph music. To majestic orchestral accompaniment, I envisioned myself in the court of Kublai Khan. I admired the rich brocade of the emperor's gown, noted the finely detailed embroidery of the courtiers' cloaks, and was impressed by the brilliant colors and textures of the nobles' clothing. At that moment, a peacock strutted by and put the emperor's clothes to shame.

Suddenly, I was at a concert being held in an immense auditorium. It struck me that I was in some futuristic Utopia. The architecture exceeded the wildest geometric formulations of either Eero Saarinen or Buckminster Fuller. The Utopian orchestra was playing something by Debussy. Each member of the orchestra was dressed in an ostentatious scarlet uniform with gold braid that contrasted markedly with the violet and silver walls of the auditorium.

Within an instant I was at Versailles. Benjamin Franklin was in conference with the king and queen of France. The royal couple were elaborately gowned in crowns, jewels, satins, and furs. Franklin, however, had a better sense of humor, and the members of the entourage were giving him their attention.

I knew that the record on the turntable had been changed,

because France yielded to Spain. I was caught up in a frenzied whirl of flamenco dancers and gypsy guitars. One girl began throwing roses into the air. They exploded like firecrackers.

The scene shifted to the New World. I was with Thomas Jefferson at Monticello as he was explaining his newest invention to a group of friends. The newest product of Jefferson's fertile mind was a four-sided music stand, so designed that all four members of a string quartet could use the same device as they performed.

A somber note was interjected as I found myself with Edgar Allan Poe in Baltimore. Poe had just lost his young bride and was mourning her death. The sad eyes of the poet haunted and disturbed me.

From Baltimore, I traveled to the nation's capital. I found myself gazing at a statue of Lincoln. The statue was entirely black, and the head was bowed. There was a gun at the base of the statue and someone murmured, "He was shot. The President was shot." A wisp of smoke rose into the air.

Lincoln's features slowly faded away, and those of Kennedy took their place. The setting was still Washington, D.C. The gun was still at the base of the black statue. A wisp of smoke seeped from the barrel and curled into the air. The voice repeated, "He was shot. The President was shot." My eyes opened; they were filled with tears.[2]

Wiping the moisture from my eyes, I again dropped my eyelids, sniffed my cloves, and chewed my peppermint candy. Almost immediately, I felt myself engulfed in a chaotic, turbulent sea. The waves were pounding, the lightning was flashing, and the rain was tumbling in a steady torrent.

There were a number of small boats tossing on the raging sea. Alice, Sam, Steve, and I were in one of these vessels. We clung to the sides of the boat as it lurched with the waves. We had no paddles, no oars, no sail, nothing to direct our

[2] In 1962, when I had my first psilocybin experience, I gave this visualization of Kennedy relatively little thought, as so many other impressions came my way. However, it was the only one of my visualizations that brought tears to my eyes, so I described it fully in the report I sent to Harvard. Nineteen months later, on November 23, 1963, the visualization came back to me as I mourned Kennedy's assassination.

course. Our plight seemed hopeless. If the sea represented the universe, and if the boats represented life, what rational purpose could there possibly be to it all?

As our lifeboat tossed and turned from one wave to the next, we came upon a gigantic figure standing waist-deep in the churning waters. He was young, black-haired, bare-chested. His facial features were graced by an unforgettable look of compassion, love, and concern. We knew that this was the image of God.

We realized that God, too, was caught in the storm. To change the course of the storm was beyond God's power as well as beyond ours. Yet, just as he was compassionate toward all the passengers in all the lifeboats, so could we show concern and love to our fellow men.

We knew that, for the most part, our course could not be controlled, our destination could not be directed. However, we also knew that we were able to love, and that in the act of loving we could partake of divinity.

My eyes opened. The vision had been a vivid one, an experience with deep meaning and impact. I realized that I was still "bemushroomed," because the ceiling was still swirling.

I stared at the ceiling and christened it "the most beautiful plaster job in the world." I opened a bottle of 7-Up and became fascinated with the impact of the bubbles tickling my nose.

The phonograph was now playing a Beethoven symphony. Closing my eyes, I could see letters, numbers, and words cascading into place, once again superimposing themselves on the non-verbal world.

I returned to the everyday world with a sense of joy rather than regret. For a few hours, psilocybin (with the assistance of my guides) had permitted me to peek beneath the cosmic curtain to see what the universe was all about.

THE USE OF PSILOCYBIN IN A PRISON SETTING

JONATHAN CLARK

During 1961–62 and the following academic year, Timothy Leary and I worked rather intensively with a small group of inmates at The Concord Massachusetts Reformatory for Men, to see whether their use of psilocybin would help them negotiate the outside world upon their release from prison. In the course of our work with these men, I participated in three drug sessions, and shall here describe the first of these after outlining our work with the men.

The opportunity to take psilocybin was offered to the men as a vehicle for exploring the "hang-ups" that might prevent them from succeeding in the way they wanted. Tim compared our program with the New York Giants' film-watching sessions of the previous day's football game. Out of uniform and away from the tension and immediacies of the game, the players are able to observe their mistakes and take notes that will become the basis for changes in strategy the following Sunday. Like these film sessions, the drug experience was to be a non-game situation, in which each of the men could remove himself from the hotly contested and closely played games in prison and break through the rigid defensive structure that being a "con" seemed to engender.

Planning sessions were held before taking the drug to help each of the four inmates in the group chart as specifically as possible the problems that prevented him from playing his game as he would like, and the point in his development at which they emerged. The others in the group worked with the inmate in question on this project, reviewing the past and commenting on the way he was getting on in the prison. Thus each man constructed a map of his psychological terrain so that when the time for the trip arrived he could find his way to the areas he wished to understand more thoroughly. There was an air of expectation about these sessions, and for the most part each man seemed to be eager to help the others in their preparations for the voyage of exploration. After about three months of weekly meetings, all seemed ready, and the first drug session was held in the conference room at the antiquated prison hospital.

In two ways the drug session was a disappointment, both to me and, I feel, also to the inmates. First of all, there was a good deal of commotion throughout the session. Most of this was due to the many people, both other inmates and guards, who frequently peered in through the windows or even entered the room. This series of intrusions prevented the men from gaining much momentum in their own explorations, since they were largely at the mercy of whoever entered the room during the course of the day. All of us felt we had confronted many facets of ourselves during the session, but that there had not been the stillness and quiet necessary to extend an exploration beyond the initial encounter. Like Alice and the plum pudding, the introduction to a spirit conjured up by the drug all too often seemed to be the sign for its departure. While much of this rapid movement might have taken place under any conditions, many of us wondered afterward what the session would have been like if held outdoors, or at least away from the distractions of other inmates and guards.

The second source of disappointment during the day was the discovery that there was more hostility and mistrust among the men than the preparatory sessions had indicated. At that time, the men had worked co-operatively, brought together perhaps by their uncertainties about the forthcoming encounter with the drug, perhaps by their eagerness to behave as Tim and I wanted them to—as co-operating and mutually trusting human beings. The fact that each inmate was not taking the drug in the company of those with whom he felt comfortable produced tensions and seemed to prevent the kind of exploration and discovery that had been anticipated in the planning sessions.

Both these remarks must be modified by the reminder that the experience was a highly personal one for each man, and that our follow-up sessions were not of the kind that permit a full evaluation of what each experienced that day.

They are only general comments that follow from my own experiences, and discussions with others in the group afterward. Perhaps my own experiences on that day may be the most direct way of describing what the effects of the drug and the setting were like.

As we lay on our cots, which were arranged in a circle, the radio was playing, and the first feeling I remember after taking two pills (each containing twenty milligrams, I believe) was of elation. Music was emerging from the radio, undulating and uncoiling as it spread out across the room. Some of the notes seemed to float in the air, while others skittered about on the floor, and the sense of time moving forward in unison was immediately broken. The music with its autonomy of movement had shattered the orderly progression of events. Sometimes as air, sometimes as water, it swirled about us, creating a world in which everything was mobile, almost plastic.

This mobility was present throughout the session and constitutes one of the most remarkable experiences of the day. It was as if the whole world, including myself, were pliable, assuming any contour depending partially on external circumstance but essentially on the exercise of my own will power.

If I wished to be happy, I could be happy; if I was afraid, it was because I had chosen fear and welcomed it into my being. It might grow to greater proportions than I expected or desired, but the act of choosing was mine and reflected what I was. My choice set in motion great waves of feeling that frequently overwhelmed me, but throughout I sensed that the thrust of events within me was not merely a matter of mood or setting. Rather it was a response to my summons, as were the demons that surrounded Pandora when she lifted the lid of the mysterious and forbidden box.

Only two resources were available in the face of what seemed to be utter destruction, and, in a sense, each seemed diametrically opposed to the other. The first was an act of will, to choose to entertain other spirits than those about to engulf me. Since mine had been the choice to permit them entrance in the first place, I now had the freedom and the responsibility to banish them, to tell them that they had become too large and unruly to be welcome longer and that they must leave. During the first session I resorted to this method most frequently, and was surprised to find that these spirits left submissively.

Perhaps the most dramatic example of this came during the afternoon, when I became increasingly anxious over the fact that we would have to leave at four o'clock. It seemed as though I would never be able to meet the responsibilities of pulling myself together and of walking out of the prison. I was a patient and helpless. My feelings and thoughts were spread out over an immense terrain and could not be collected in time. I was a prisoner like the others, a slave rather than a master. I was surprised to find that, when the actual moment to leave came, I was quite able to rise to the occasion. I remember knotting my tie and feeling my powers of control and focus come marching back, as though summoned by this symbolic act. When I told myself that it was time to become well, to become active and to cope with the tasks at hand, matters changed almost instantly.

The other resource available to me in the face of helplessness and destruction was to place myself at the disposal of these feelings; to tell them that, if they wished, they could abduct and consume me, that I would follow their lead and would not do battle with them. During the second session I felt as though I were shooting up into the atmosphere in a rocket with no control over where it was going, and that my feet might never touch the ground again. I felt doubly miserable because I blamed myself for entering the rocket when I could have stayed away by not taking the drug. As I shot up through space, I was able to accept the fact that I was no longer in control of my destiny, and resigned myself to going wherever the rocket would take me. With that, the fear subsided and a feeling of great peace came over me, which remained for the rest of the session.

This account underlines the sharp break between the expectations of the planning sessions and the intense personal realities of the drug experience. It was as if we had all planned to climb a mountain together and had worked on maps that would help us on the expedition. We had started out together on the trip, but each man encountered such storms that there was little chance to consult the maps or the others in the group.

This is where we began in our work with the men at Concord—with a large gap between the plans we constructed with our minds in preparing for the drug session, and the immensity of the day itself. I believe it would have taken a long series of drug and follow-up sessions before we could have emerged with a fruitful combination of planning and drug sessions—with a sense of how rational thought and self-examination could have combined with the revelations of the drug session to prepare the men for re-entry into society.[1] Unfortunately, the development of such a program was impeded and finally stopped by the publicity surrounding the use of consciousness-expanding drugs.

WHAT I DESERVED

BERNARD S. AARONSON

While I shall try to be accurate, it is hard to be completely accurate. The events were in many ways hazy even as they took place, and the record of the first half of the session, including the beginning and the peak of the experience, was unfortunately destroyed, so I have nothing to refer to. Fortunately, H. kept some notes, so I have a rough chronology. Another problem is the difficulty in putting these experiences into words and having the words mean the same thing to the reader that they do to me. Perfect communication is probably never attainable. The approximation will have to be enough.

I received two hundred gamma of LSD-25 at 9:45 A.M. in distilled water. It tasted very salty and left a salty, bitter

---

[1] Records kept on the effectiveness of the work with the inmates at Concord indicate that, over a five-year period, more than twice the usual number of men have been able to stay out of prison after their release. The significance of these, however, is sharply reduced by the lack of a control group of inmates, which should have received an equal amount of attention from us while not using psilocybin.

taste in my mouth for a long time. I have since been able to ascertain that it was the water, not the LSD, that was responsible for the taste. The session was carried out in my laboratory, in very familiar surroundings.

At 9:55, I experienced a mild sense of ataxia as I walked along the hall. I gradually developed a sense of strangeness, and I felt stimulated and mildly drunk. Subsequently I felt muscle tension all over my body, but especially in the back and around the nape of the neck. My stomach felt queasy, as if with suppressed excitement, and I felt tenseness in the back of the throat. The floor seemed to be revolving in the room to some extent, and I seemed to lose sensation, in the cheeks and jaws especially but also all over my torso. The internal symptoms subsided, but the muscular symptoms in the back and neck and the loss of sensation around the jaws returned throughout the day and signaled my going in and coming out of the states.

The first visual experience was a series of transient palings of color all over the room, which began at 10:15. Periodically there seemed to be flashes of white lightning. In between, everything seemed very distinct and very beautiful. I became increasingly euphoric and laughed a great deal.

A bird flew toward the window of our room seeming to be flying abnormally slowly. We then heard a clatter from outside behind our building, and I went to the window that faced the rear of the building. B. was walking back toward the building with an empty trash can. His face seemed covered with white grease paint, and he seemed a sad clown. He smiled and waved up at me. We were listening to a record of Plains Indians songs and dances, and every time the drum beat, the light in the room would get brighter. I closed my eyes and saw lettering on stone in the shape of the Hebrew letters *shin* and *tsaddik*. As I think about it, these letters may represent portents of what I really wanted the experience to do for me. According to Feuchtwanger in his novel *Power*, *shin* is a symbol for wisdom and is represented by the pattern of lines over the bridge of the nose of the cabbalists. *Tsaddik* may be a pun on *tsadduk*, the holy, wise miracle workers of the Hassidic Jews. Starlings walking among the trees outside seemed to be touched with red at the tips of their beaks and the ends of their tails. I was reminded of the story of the phoenix and talked about it for a time.

At 10:35 my hands seemed to me to be shaking, although H. said they seemed unusually steady. I noted that I was short, and expressed resentment that I was not as tall as the rest of my siblings. I felt psychotic and was quite pleased. I began to laugh hilariously. I wanted to call my wife to ask her, "What's new, pussycat?" and also to call an absent friend, but H. would not give me permission to use the telephone and I had to grant that he was right. About this time I suddenly perceived H. as Old Scratch, and he seemed suddenly quite cruel for a brief moment. I was not frightened, for he was after all old H., whom I like and respect very much. I don't know why I should see my good English friend as an Early American devil. He denied the identification, and I believe I even had to explain to him who Old Scratch was.

H. and I talked a great deal throughout the day. He was always kind, forbearing, and understanding, even though I pointed out to him several times that he was such a compulsive talker that I was afraid he might interfere with my experience. He definitely did not talk too much, and was always tactful and sensitive, even when I made this rude remark. I remember discussing how comedy and tragedy were really the same and how a pie in the face might be funny to an uninvolved onlooker, but a calamity to the person it hit. Throughout the day I was involved with getting him to understand my exact nuances of meaning, and I felt hurt that he could not obtain more than an approximation of what I was saying.

At 11 A.M., with my eyes shut, I saw myself with a brown skin, walking in the market place of a strange city. Surrounded by brown-skinned people, I thought I was in a city in India or Portugal. It was obviously my city, and I knew my way around it. Most of the people around and I myself were wearing white clothing. Suddenly I heard a baby crying and commented, "Always there is a baby crying." I wondered to myself if this was a memory from a previous existence, and scolded myself for thinking such nonsense. I then had the first of many epiphanies, which I have forgotten, although have a sense that much was going on. I became determined to examine and triumph over my problems and especially to solve the riddle of life and death. At some point I viewed the world as a battleground between the Children of Light and the Children of Darkness, and identified myself with the former. I noted an absence of Buddhist sentiment, and H. pointed out that I had after all been reared in a Judaeo-Christian tradition. I noted that the cognitive changes that was experiencing were far more striking than the perceptual changes and wondered whether the drug acts to disarrange the controlling, essentially verbal formulae that govern the organism, rather than to affect perception directly.

We then went downstairs, out among the trees. It was 11:35. The stairway seemed unusually long and steep. I sat on the top step and contemplated it. We went down and I stood among the trees, wondering what it was like to be a tree. The M.'s drove by and stopped. I described N. M. as a vine tree, I am told. I remember being impressed by the fact that she was wearing brown shoes that were roots. M. seemed to move swiftly and gracefully, with many bowing and scraping movements. Their little boy was with them, and his eyes seemed to be at once shy, observant, and laughing. M. reminded me of an Arabian Nights djinn. After they drove away, I ran after their car, anxious to know whether they were going to Troy. I was especially anxious to know if N. M. was going to Troy, but although they stopped their car to hear me, N. did not seem to know what Troy was. Obviously not a part of the Achaean host!

H. and I then went back under the trees. I examined one tree with rather rough bark and was very impressed with its fantastic roughness. The trees did not seem altered in any way. Each was unmistakably a tree, full and sufficient unto itself, and nothing more. We sat on the bench under the trees and talked about the loneliness of being, and how people are forever needing things they expect you to provide. For what seemed a long time, I cried as I have not cried since I was a baby, for all the people in the world who need things and whose needs cannot be met. I cried, too, for all the people around me who need things from me that I botched in the giving or to whom I cannot give because I am depleted. I wept for my wife and for my son and was especially concerned about him because of a feeling of special responsibility springing from the fact that I generated him. I expressed great hostility toward both my parents, and with H.'s help analyzed my feelings as they derived from my relationship to each of them. I examined my relationship with my next older brother, and examined the meaning in my life of my relationship with that friend whom I love the most. Many times in the course of this I would be seized by an epiphany and I do not know where I went or what I did there.

At 12:45 we went back upstairs. H. felt that I should look at myself in a mirror, and I did, but I never changed, although I looked periodically for several hours. I was always myself. The only changes that I noted were the changes in my expression as a function of how I was feeling. I talked about how one had to give oneself up to experience and about the importance of being. I continued to express great sadness for others. H. mentioned my relationship with someone whom I hated, and I flew into a rage in which I identified that person as a Nazi. While I did this, I had a sense of, but did not see, stone, cement, and blood. I talked about the relation among past, present, and future, and recognized how each person is more than just a collection of needs. At 1:50 I read *Fern Hill* and was greatly moved. I talked about Homer, my own work, and the relation of poetry to science. I discussed my very early identification with Ulysses and my recent reading of Hermann Hesse. I asked H. to read to me from the *Manual of Psychedelic Experience* sometime here, but rejected it as irrelevant to what I was experiencing.

Depth seemed expanded during this part of the experience, but objects seemed closer. H. suggested that the perception of distance and the perception of depth might be separate things. The floor seemed to tilt markedly toward the side of the room in which we were sitting, and I wondered that I had not observed this before. I have checked this since the experience, and the floor does slope that way, but not nearly so markedly as I saw it. We went out on the porch, and I was impressed by how the tree that grows near the building seemed to float and how the road changed briefly after every car passing over it. I got hungry, and we ate some fruit, the first of many such adventures from this point on.

Later in the day there was again an increase in the profundity of the experience. From a discussion of parenting in general and mothering in particular, I went on to a discussion of my son and my relations with him, and finally cried for him for a long time. I did not want H. to help me through this situation, but I had to find my way myself. At the end of an epiphany of sorrow with my eyes closed, I saw a cave. I had a feeling of wings, and followed them up to the roof of the cave, which was like a basilica bathed in white light, which glowed through it. Gradually the light turned a bright yellow, and the light point was the sun, which moved back and forth like lightning. This vision ended and another vision replaced it in which I was moving toward the left along a series of intricately carved, horizontally placed poles. These suddenly parted and I looked into the face of The Dancer, who was wearing an Indian (Eastern) headdress, and then the poles closed. I was able to come out of the experience after this.

From this point on, the experience began to abate, although residuals of the experience remain even today as I write this. Later in the day I had a sense of bulls and stone porches, and read H. the entire *Lament for the Death of Ignacio Sánchez Mejías*, by Lorca, which moved me greatly and seemed in some way to be about and for me. We continued discussing the thoughts and ideas brought up by the day and dealt with some new issues as well. I noticed that whenever I dealt with questions that had emotional relevance for me, perceptual changes occurred. When I paid attention to the perceptual changes, they disappeared. There was a very interesting phenomenon, which lasted for a while, in which one particular patch of ground began to bubble and boil. This did not spread to any other part of the ground and was there to see whenever I chose to look at it.

We returned to my home at about 10 P.M. My wife looked healthy and sunburned, pretty and petulant. I sat up for a while reading. I read a book of Zen koans and they made a great deal of sense emotionally. Not all of them seemed applicable, but those that did, I understood intuitively, and I understood the events of the story even before I read the solution. When I finally went to bed, I had such brilliant hypnagogic visions of colored snapshots of children that it was difficult to fall asleep. I also had one vision of an African drummer.

My feelings of serenity continued on the next day and continue even today. I was very impressed by the unity in nature, down to the image of a tree reflected in the veins of a lettuce leaf. My general feeling of peace has continued to the present.

What have I learned? I died and I am here, and I shall never fear dying again. The experience was not what I had expected, but it was just as much as I deserved. I feel that I am quits with life. I know that I cannot give other people anything and that they cannot give me anything. Anything I give, I give not because it is needed but because I want to. Anything I get, I get because it is available and I want it. When you are born, no trumpets blow, because there are no trumpets. While we are each totally alone, it is an error to confuse this with being lonely. Each of us is himself and there is nothing better and nothing greater and nothing more. I no longer feel concerned with God, whether or not He exists (I used to feel sure He did). He takes care of His Self, and I take care of mine. I eat when I am hungry, I drink when I am thirsty, and, if I feel like it, I forgive when I am insulted.

WHO AM I, AND SO WHAT IF I AM?

JERRY RICHARDSON

The first noticeable effects of the drug were physical. At about 10:20, fifteen minutes after ingestion, I began to feel somewhat lightheaded and dizzy: I became overactive, fidgety, impatient, and irritable, waiting for something to happen.

The feeling of lightness gradually changed to heaviness; I was now becoming slightly numb. The room and the objects in it began to look tilted, and I seemed to be seeing with a new, living astigmatism. My body started to tingle, felt heavier and heavier, and my nervousness passed away. Things were beginning to happen.

The outlines of objects began to shimmer and quiver, as did the convolutions in Bernie's shirt, which made him appear to be breathing in a remarkable manner. He was sitting in his chair reading poetry and seemed to be having quite an experience. Looking through the window, I could see the bare branches of the trees outside. They were moving back and forth rhythmically to the music of Debussy's "La Mer," which was playing on the phonograph. As I looked harder, it seemed that the trees were framed in the window, depthless, as if painted in layer upon layer of diaphanous paper. If I concentrated on any one branch, it stood out and came toward me, giving the impression that I could almost touch it.

When I looked up at the neon ceiling light, it too was shimmering, not really attached to the ceiling, but floating overhead, suspended in an inky, yellowish fluid. I gazed at this for some time, and as the light became more detached from the ceiling, I became more and more dissociated from everyday concerns. When I turned back to the room, I found everything—chairs, tables, even Bernie—in constant motion, quivering and vibrating.

I walked unsteadily to the window. It was a magnificent scene: the movement of the trees, and the ground below, patches of brown and green, in swirling, snakelike motion. There were blackbirds hopping around on the grass, comically, looking for worms. It was all a living painting—and I was the artist.

After a few minutes of this, I began to feel sleepy and lay down on the cot for a while. "La Mer" had finished; Bernie put on a guitar solo by Montoya. I closed my eyes and began to experience strange internal visions.

At first I saw only vague shapes, which soon became brightly colored geometric patterns that spontaneously exploded into view, dissolved, and were replaced by others, similar, but never quite the same. Then came a splendid array of red, green, blue, yellow, and purple spirals sliding around inside my head, gold doorways opening out into infinity, and flashes of white lightning illuminating variously colored question marks, dots, and ribbons. Other forms appeared—vaguely defined and brightly colored animals and faces coming mysteriously and quickly, illuminating themselves, dissolving, and disappearing.

After a while I wondered if I could conjure up some images myself, so I tried to imagine something horrible. This time I saw goblins in green and yellow and blue; red devils with sinister, twisted faces; and then bodies, faces, ghostlike creatures in white, coming out of nowhere, rushing toward me, tumbling over each other, and disappearing into the back of my mind in a seemingly endless procession of ludicrously grotesque imagery.

It appeared ludicrous because none of this seemed particularly threatening. I'm not even certain why I wanted horrible forms instead of pleasant ones. I think it was probably because I had read and heard that these sessions can be quite nightmarish for some people. But in my case this was not so. These weird figures were only comical.

Opening my eyes stopped the mental imagery. Around the room, everything was now bathed in a curious yellowish-warm, glowing radiance. An ordinarily rather nondescript, somewhat messy, and ugly room had been transformed into something out of a fairy tale. In front of me, at the foot of the cot, two closet doors had assumed fantastic proportions, appearing much wider at the top and narrowing sharply toward the bottom, as though someone had painted them to emphasize and exaggerate the perspective. To give a comic effect, the artist had also drawn in a long, curving crack running lengthwise from the floor to halfway up one of the doors. It struck me as very humorous and appropriate.

Again I looked up at the ceiling light. It was now not a light, but a mass of fluctuating, vibrating, yellowish squares floating in, around, and in front of a yellow sky. The ceiling was all atmosphere—yellow, radiant, infinite, fascinating.

Through all of this, Bernie had been sitting with his back to me, reading. When I looked at him, he appeared to be some kind of elf, with slightly pointed ears and a wrinkled complexion. As I watched, thinking that in some ways he looked, with his pointed ears, very much like a wolf, he began to become more and more wolf-like. Then I thought, "Leprechaun," and again he changed. It was very peculiar;

what I had been able to do before with my eyes shut, I could also accomplish with my eyes open. I discovered that I could cause these distortions myself. It was a very strange world I was in, but when I attempted to tell Bernie something of what was going on, words were difficult to find. I felt almost completely incoherent, incapable of saying anything intelligible. All I could manage was, "Bernie, it's all gnarled . . . and you're the little old man sitting at the foot of the gnarled tree."

Ordinarily, I am not particularly susceptible to music. This time, lying on the cot, I became acutely aware of the Montoya record playing. This was more than music: the entire room was saturated with sounds that were also feelings—sweet, delicious, sensual—that seemed to be coming from somewhere deep down inside me. I became mingled with the music, gliding along with the chords. Everything I saw and felt was somehow inextricably interrelated. This was pure synesthesia, and I was part of the synthesis. I suddenly "knew" what it was to be simultaneously a guitar, the sounds, the ear that received them, and the organism that responded, in what was the most profoundly consuming aesthetic experience I have ever had.

As magnificent as this was, it seems less significant than what happened next. After I had lain on the cot for some time, enraptured by Montoya, Bernie suggested that I take a look at myself in a small mirror provided for the occasion. This seemed interesting, so I got up from the cot, took the mirror, and sat down again.

At first, nothing happened. The face in the mirror was just me, with a rather foolish grin. Not very impressive, I thought. As it was difficult to focus clearly, I looked harder, straining to fix the facial outlines. Then, as I stared at them, they began to change—like the way by which, in the movies, a man's face slowly becomes that of a wolf. But I never saw myself as any kind of animal; what I saw was my own face in transition: in rapid succession, there were all the expressions I had ever seen before in a mirror—and many that I had not. A quizzical gaze turned quite sad, contemplative, amused, broke into a broad grin, and then changed to mournful, tragic, and finally tearful (real tears, it seemed)—all these faces within just a few seconds, and never the same face for longer than a brief moment.

I spent some time looking at myself, and while I was doing so, I began to age. As the faces changed, I also became older, younger, and then older again, each face with a different expression and a different age.

This last was attributable, I think, to the questions Bernie was asking me as I contemplated myself. One of the purposes of the session was to give me an opportunity to identify myself better both personally and vocationally. I had been having some difficulty with these matters, and it was hoped that in this experience I could confront and perhaps resolve these problems.

After I had looked in the mirror for a while, Bernie asked me, "What is the face you see behind all the faces?" It was difficult to answer: there were so many faces, and none of them appeared to stand out against the rest—except perhaps the laughing one. I told Bernie this, but he kept asking the question until I felt obliged to give a better answer. So I looked harder, trying to project myself into the future to determine what I might be years hence. It was then that the faces began to age. But even with aging, there was no dominant face. Bernie asked the question again, and again I tried to find the face that might give the answer. Finally, I found one: "I see a kindly old judge," I said. This was true; however, I am not certain now, nor was I then, that this was the best answer—or even if it was any better than any other I might have given.

The problem here was that I had been in a dilemma as to whether to go to law school or not. I didn't particularly want to; yet, I could not really think of anything else more practical. This is one reason for the LSD session—to give this business of law school some deep thought. Hence, the reason for Bernie's questions and, I think, the reason for my seeing the "kindly old judge" among the many faces. He was there, all right, but I cannot honestly say that he arose because of any deep desire on my part to become a lawyer and a judge. I think I chose this figure because I felt that, given my shaky commitment to study law, it would be to my advantage to see such a face win out. However this may be, Bernie seemed satisfied (although I don't think he believed it any more than I did) and didn't pursue the matter further at the time.

After the question-and-answer period, while I was sitting there with the mirror, Bernie got up and came over and stood behind me. I noted before how he had changed into an elf and a wolf, but now, as I looked at him in the mirror, he became very, very sad. His mirror image became pained, as though he were suffering great mental anguish. It was an oriental face, grotesque and tragic, and stayed that way for several minutes. Then the sad and pained expression passed away, replaced by one of abstracted contemplation, like that of the Buddha. For some time he stood there Buddhalike; then he returned to his chair and sat down.

One theory of hallucinations elicited by drugs such as LSD holds that these visions reflect one's deeper feelings about both himself and the world. Bernie and I discussed this afterward as it related to the various ways in which I had seen him during the day. We felt that my seeing him as a wolf represented some apprehensions I have about him, but that because of my own particular way of dealing with potentially threatening people and situations, I chose to regard this as comical instead of dreadful. Similarly, the other changes I perceived in Bernie were also manifestations of my feelings about him, the sad and suffering oriental face being an especially good example of this, and the Buddha another. It is as though there is a self-programming device within each of us—a computer in the basement, so to speak—that causes us to react as we do, whether our actions are voluntary or involuntary, recognized for what they are or rationalized. Under LSD, however, one may not be so easily able to disguise his feelings—his real ones, not the rationalized product of several intervening stages of conscious and unconscious manipulation; with the result that *reality itself* emerges from the depths. This may explain why some people react quite negatively, even disastrously, to the encounter. Their mental and emotional processes cannot cope with the program they themselves, unwillingly or not, have set up.

In any event, Bernie's face altered once more. This time it turned to stone, cracked, and crumbled, Humpty Dumptylike. And no sooner had it finished crumbling, than it was back—Bernie together again! It was not that his face fell away completely; it seemed as though an outer layer of it cracked and fell off, leaving another in its place. This happened several times, and caused me to wonder whether it would happen to me, so I looked back in the mirror. The face there immediately turned ash-gray, cracked, and fell away, and then spontaneously regenerated itself. I watched myself do this several more times and then glanced at my hand holding the mirror. It, too, became stonelike and cracked.

As I sat there, contemplating this, I began to see, even though my eyes were open, a flood of human forms. They were a mournful lot, mostly women, children, and old men, all Eastern, and all despairing, chanting a long, silent wail. They were in a river—*were* a river—coming toward and passing through me, an endless stream of faces, mournful and pitiful, and yet somehow with a nobility that transcended their suffering.

Where all this came from, I'm not quite certain, but I suspect the record that was playing, "Japanese Koto" by Shinichi Yuize (Cook), had something to do with it. On this record is the voice of an old man whose chant is long and mournful, like a dirge, and to me it seemed that he lamented about life. When I tried to visualize him, I saw the old man in the river of mourners dressed in the plain, white garb of an Indian beggar; he was chanting with the rest, and he, too, possessed both sadness and nobility.

In addition to the music, which provided a theme (lamentation) and a setting, I think there was another reason for my experiencing this particular imagery: this river of pitiable creatures was almost literally a manifestation of my own stream of consciousness, which tends to borrow heavily from the morbid stuff of life. Just as my feelings about Bernie were brought out by seeing him change, so did my feelings about life in general materialize in this mournful procession.

At about three in the afternoon, the hallucinatory effects of the drug had almost completely subsided. After three, until about nine that evening, my general mood was one of quiet, anxiety-free contemplation. The entire day, in fact, had been quite unusual in that never once (after the initial nervousness) did I feel anxiety nor did I worry about the present, past, or future. Time in its usual sense had ceased to be, and with it my concern about temporal matters. With respect to time, I should add that I never completely lost my ability to estimate time intervals; however, I did feel that time was somehow unimportant to the world I was perceiving, in which a minute is an hour, an hour a minute. Time was not only relative; it was in fact irrelevant.

It is difficult to assess the long-range psychological effects of this session. I do not feel that I achieved any new and startling insights—at least not in the sense that I have any answers I did not have before. However, I do think that certain things occurred that have caused me to reflect more deeply upon the state of being alive and what to do about it. As a result, I am less confused by and about life than before, and have come to better terms with the questions "Who am I?" and "So what if I am?"

First of all, I am many different faces, confusing, contradictory, but never mutually exclusive. They all exist, and I must learn to live with them. Some are more dominant than others, but they are all nevertheless there. I have many identities, but to demand that one rise above all the others is to deny being human—it is as simple and as complex as that.

I am also the river, among the flood of images I saw during the koto music. The river is not kind; it is just there. It has no meaning; it is just there. Everything that exists, exists in the river, and each man is subject to all that the river is. Some men are carried along gently, in the shallows along the river's edge; some drown early, others late; some drown others in their attempt to survive, and some help others to survive. And after we are all gone, the river will still be flowing on.

None of this is especially profound or original, but thinking about it, I have decided to throw my lot where life appears to be most interesting and rewarding—not in the financial sense, but in those gray areas where things seem to be happening consonant with my own interests, which are somewhat offbeat and literary. Law probably would not allow me to pursue those interests outside the mainstream of life. I might, for example, want to go to China for a year or two, just to see what the river is like there. Or perhaps I might decide to teach or write or dig ditches, or do all these things simultaneously, or do nothing at all. In any manner, however, in which I ultimately choose to identify myself, I can be assured as long as I live that there is a place for me in the river.

YAGE IN THE VALLEY OF FIRE

PETER STAFFORD

The four of us, heading out to the desert to get high together, had little more in mind than a feeling that we'd enjoy sharing an intense experience. Ed had picked up some yage a few days before from a man of diverse interests. I don't think any of us knew much about this, other than that it was from an exotic plant—possibly even a bark or a vine—from somewhere in South America, and that it had psychedelic properties. Each of us had had experience with psychedelics and was confident about handling mind drugs. We knew little about this one, but anticipated an exciting time together, whatever its effects might be.

We chose Las Vegas because we had heard glowing reports about a beautiful desert setting nearby called the Valley of Fire. When we got there, we saw that it was much more fantastic than any of us had really expected. Everywhere were monuments of reddish-gold pumice, striated by blues and purples and scarlets. The volcanic formations rose abruptly from the level valley floor, scattered here and there as though cast by the wind. Every rock seemed hand-carved into animal or other suggestive shapes, which the highway department had marked by signs along the road. We found that several crags were decorated with ancient Indian hieroglyphics. We also stumbled upon a small adobe dwelling, empty and cool inside.

We had heard that yage made the user feel somewhat nauseous, so Ed suggested we start our trip on a small amount

This yage report is taken from a considerably longer account, which is available from the author at Box 285, Peter Stuyvesant Station, New York, New York 10009.

of LSD he had brought along. By beginning with the acid, we hoped to minimize the early disagreeable effects.

After taking the yage, I very quickly found myself deeply involved with paradoxical trains of thought, swirling through an immense grab bag of flowering, exploding ideas. I became completely absorbed by my past, by the past of the race, and went tumbling and tobogganing through the ages of man. Feelings of sadness, then great excitement and joy. Physically, about all I could do was to look over at the others and smile. They seemed to be having much the same thing happen to them.

We spent a good deal more time whirling about in our private thoughts. Then someone suggested that we go swimming at the deserted oasis we had located earlier that morning. With that, we all rushed to the car, eager to get moving. Reaching the open-topped car, I just jumped in. So did the others.

When we arrived at the water hole/oasis, we found some fifteen or twenty people at its edge, swimming, getting out of cars, picnicking. We waved to some of them, then dashed into the water. It was warm and languorous. Out in the middle, a couple of kids were swimming.

Returning to the car to assess the situation, we smoked a joint and decided that the other arrivals were all right. There was no cause to feel that they might mar our trip. The surface of the water shimmered and beckoned. Soon we went back down to the water's edge, eager to stretch and swim, to dive and swirl about.

The only real drag was keeping on a swimsuit. It seemed so unnecessary and unnatural! Especially since I had become a snake writhing about in the water. I maneuvered in and out of a swamp. Minutes later I found myself a frog and started propelling myself with long kicks. In both cases, water seemed my natural habitat, and land was distant, alien, somewhat terrifying.

After a while, my mind decided that I would like to climb a small mountain that looked down on this idyllic setting, but by now I was a sea lion, so it was difficult to get myself up and onto dry land. As I waded out, I felt awkward, silly, completely out of my element.

＊　　　＊　　　＊

When I say I felt as though I was first one water creature
and then another, what I mean goes far beyond merely "feeling slithery and reptilian." The experience had a different
feel to it, different from anything I had previously felt, both
physically and mentally. Under the drug, I was conscious of
having different types of memories, and I lost my normal
self-awareness. Rather than *empathy* with what I might imagine a snake or frog might feel, I was sufficiently absorbed in
snakeness and frogness as to wonder vaguely how the humans
around me might feel.

Drug-induced animal transformations can be very impressive. One such occurrence, recorded in *The Varieties of Psychedelic Experience* (Masters and Houston, 1966), involved
an anthropologist who considered himself a tiger. He had
long been interested in metamorphosis rites as practiced in
such places as Rhodesia and Haiti. In the course of an LSD
session, he became aware of himself moving across the floor
on his hands and knees. Coming up against a full-length
mirror, he suddenly discovered himself "confronted by a huge,
magnificent specimen of a tiger!" He spit, snarled, and tensed
for a fight. Though he retained some perception of himself
as a human, there is no doubt from his subsequent account
that in essence he considered himself to be a tiger.

My own experience began pretty much in the same way as
many LSD experiences—with the quick, detailed, intense examination of various manifestations of the classic dualities:
knowledge/intuition, science/religion, sex/love, beauty/good-
ness, reality/illusion, and so on. My early experience could be
considered typical in the limited sense that it was similar to
one class of response. But I don't think it could properly be
called "ego loss"; it belonged to another constellation. The
effects were most intense at the very start, remained at that
plateau for a while, then gradually tapered off.

The quality of experience changed, once we began moving,
from being primarily explorations of inner events, with almost
no environmental stimulus, to the experiencing of the external world colored by "inner" emotions and experiences. Internal and external realities coexisted, alternating somehow
in a pleasing and harmonious way. As for my "objectivity"

at this point, everything visible was also being seen as I might normally recognize it—but with the difference that I sorted out my perceptions according to an unfamiliar value system.

What does it mean, that while under the yage I did not merely *feel* "like a snake," but in some sense I *was* a snake, that somehow I had reached a level of experience where I could contact a potential "snakeness" residing within? What does it mean, that I felt my perceptions were being sorted in terms of new and different categories?

Throughout the psychedelic literature, there are accounts of people saying, "I didn't feel like myself. . . ." Generally, these statements are made in passing, and without much interest in examining their implications. This transformation experience is of vast psychological and philosophical importance. The user becomes enveloped within a smaller but more intensely felt universe (as generally occurs when falling in love). William Braden (1967) has written an entire book about this distinct transformation as it occurs when the experience is religious; he describes it as a switch from a Catholic or Protestant point of view to that of an Eastern mystic.

* * *

Once out of the water, I started climbing the mountain on a sacred pilgrimage. I stopped to examine small flowers and brightly colored rocks. I picked the flowers, putting them in my hair. The world shone with the joy of existence.

Again on level ground, I ran along, feeling Indian things. With virtually no plant growth in sight, I was hacking my way through jungles. I saw visions of snake gods, and received stories to take to my people. When I looked down to the oasis below, my friends, the others there, the wind caressing the water—all poignantly symbolized the human condition. Everybody should have a chance to see this vast panorama of man's existence on earth. To see the tides of nature, as I did then, seems an overwhelmingly marvelous thing in itself.

* * *

I wonder how psychedelics might measure up as one of the solutions to the problem of excessive spare time. Television is the major outlet for our increasing leisure. A relatively engrossing trivializer. Psychedelics, on the other hand, are tremendous energizers, which lead to greater participation. The use of psychedelics has lingering effects upon personality and life style. As time passes, the values heightened by LSD will slowly but definitely creep into and transform our daily habits.

A question of growing importance has to do with the effect the psychedelics might have upon family life. To date, their main influence has been to exaggerate the generation gap. Once parents have actually tried a psychedelic, the majority will continue, in time, to be interested in the drug's effects and the possibilities it opens, and many will come to take pot with some regularity. Since the family, a highly structured unit, is the foundation of society, regular psychedelic use within a family could have enormous social consequences. I think the traditional structure might change from its present patriarchal or matriarchal orientation to that found in a group of equals. The child would truly, then, become adviser to the man.

Such a restructuring of the family unit might shake society to its core. But such a shift may be neither traumatic nor even widely noticed. When we consider social restructuring, there is a tendency to forget just how absorbent and flexible the human animal can actually be.

*   *   *

I was impressed by simple sights: the rushes growing beside the water, a small gentian poking out from behind a rock, the patterns and swirl of the shale beneath me. As I approached the water to join the others, it suddenly seemed ludicrous to think of wearing a swimsuit. Up on the mountain, with no one around, I had taken my trunks off; on my descent, I had put the suit back on. I took the impediment off, feeling much better, and dove into the water.

No one, it turned out, seemed to care. As I floated, I mused about how long it might be before public parks and beauty spots like this would be opened and arranged for psychedelic exploration.

*   *   *

For some time yet, society is bound to experiment with the concept of prohibition—rather than control—of psychedelic drug use. In attempting to prohibit anything easily accessible that is at the same time greatly desired, what usually happens is that officials create an active underground move-ment which operates independently of them—and thus they gradually relinquish all controls. This is a serious problem in the case of psychedelics, since these drugs have to be used with intelligence and control if their delicate potentials are to be fully and safely realized.

The cost of the "hysterical ostrich" approach taken by of-ficials is almost sure to mount sufficiently to force society to set up LSD centers and reservations, where the psychedelics may be used legally, safely, and with a reasonable level of good sense and security. To the extent that officials see value in LSD, it is almost exclusively in terms of medicine and psychotherapy. Beyond this, allowance will gradually have to be made for the creative, religious, rejuvenating, and educa-tional uses of the psychedelics. The only effective ways for guaranteeing the non-destructive use of psychedelics are through widespread education in their positive use, the set-ting up of beneficial, appealing rituals for their use, and the establishment of centers where the drugs can be used safely, knowledgeably, and for the purposes of their users.

It seems to me that the eventual outcome will be the con-struction of psychedelic parks. In general, these will feature a large center for therapeutic, creative, and other uses, super-vised by medical men and guides, and a psychedelic chapel for religious and mystical experience. The most likely setting will probably be a park of artificial environments. The di-mensions of the park need not be very great, since space counts for little in the experience. A point of some impor-tance, however, is the matter of diversity, for one of the major characteristics of these experiences, after all, is flux.

As the psychedelics become more familiar, we can look for-ward to a growing awareness of the diverse values to be de-rived from their utilization. As they gradually exaggerate the already unprecedented diversity that currently exists in human society, we can predict a greatly increased impact on social interaction.

*   *   *

I swam toward the others and we smiled. Nothing needed to be said. By now we all felt that we really ought to get moving and possibly see the sights of Las Vegas. After much indecision, we managed to get out and jump into the car and take off, surely "on the road." The highway was a river, leisurely wandering among the contours formed by the rocks. The rich hues of the desert led us into a strange Midland of Mordor. As we drove along, we entered into the land of fantasy.

At sunset, we left the car and climbed a peak. There was talk about the marvels of natural history. Once we had clambered to the top, we decided to claim the peak in the name of yage. We managed to find wood and propped up a pole. George offered his shirt for a flag. There was a short ceremony.

But now a car slowly came into view and we saw it was . . . the sheriff. We waved to him. We thought it marvelous that there was someone around to see that no harm comes to this territory. The patrol car stopped at the summit below. We met the sheriff and stood with him silently, watching the sun set. He told us about Nevada history and pointed to the hills where the Basques are, "the best sheepherders in the world." As the sun disappeared, the desert was gradually transmuted into the austere cold of blue-gray stillness. We stood transfixed, silently taking in the magic of the approaching night.

When we got to Las Vegas, the main drag was so lit up, it was a real DMT hallucination. Buildings were outlined by neon, and everywhere there were garish colors, crowds, the din of horns. We began to feel the closeness of the city. We sought escape and took a glassed-in elevator to the top of one of the more modern buildings. The operator didn't know what to make of us. She seemed relieved that when we reached the top we immediately decided to go back down. Our conversation had obviously left her feeling rather odd.

Back on the casino floor, I winced as I watched compulsive slot-machine players. But craps and "21" are fascinating. I felt sure that, by following some strong hunches, I could win. Yet I didn't feel I had sufficient control of myself to risk actual play. After watching the floor action for a while, we decided to order dinner.

*   *   *

What I have been reporting so far has been my subjective reaction to my yage experience. I am not so naïve as to believe that these experiences aren't on occasion absolutely miserable. My experience was so positive because of the unusually good setting. In addition, we were left alone and knew it. I believe that one of the main reasons the psychedelics are dangerous stems from the fact that they can be used only surreptitiously at the present time. Generally what happens when things go underground is that they become perverted.

The psychedelic experience shared by increasing numbers of people may mean that we're now on the verge of an appreciative revolution. At the present time, there are few places on this continent where it's possible to participate in exciting, cosmopolitan "modern living." In a profound sense, the psychedelics may alter this situation, by virtue of their amazing ability to tune up the senses and realign value systems.

When you couple the psychedelics with today's technology, affluence, and the cultural revolution occurring now at the popular level, it is easy to understand why we are seeing utopian experimentation throughout the country. The psychedelics are boosting the natural desire for such experimentation precisely when that growth can easily find a supportive environment. They tend to redress the imbalance of our perceptions, emphasizing similarities rather than differences. Psychedelics and technology promise a proliferation of utopian thinking across the land that hasn't been seen since at least the middle of the last century.

*   *   *

Once we were served, the meal was a delight. We were sharing half a dozen dishes, all participants in a glutton's feast. The atmosphere in the gambling rooms had seemed to confine our yage flights, but as we ate, the magic returned. I had only to consider an image, and it would realize itself, blossoming of its own accord, coloring over the dining scene.

After our magnificent meal, we walked farther through the town. By now the carnival atmosphere, the chrome-plated soul of this cold, impersonal city was getting to us. Before long, we all agreed we'd rather return to the desert.

As warm air flowed over us in the open convertible, I felt serene and joyous as I thought back to the shimmering water, the beautiful pumice, my happiness up on the mountain. Parking just off the road, we unrolled sleeping bags. We had a smoke, saying very little. Within half an hour, we were asleep.

PART III

ANTHROPOLOGICAL CONSIDERATIONS

As one looks at the uses to which psychedelics are put among the peoples of the world, the extent to which their use is associated with religious practices is very striking. Although alcohol, a depressant, is also used sacramentally, it is probably not used for religious purposes in as many diverse cultures. The high frequency with which red wine is the chosen alcoholic sacrament raises the question of the extent to which "the blood of the grape" is memorial of human or animal sacrifice, rather than being used for its direct effects on consciousness.

Where psychedelics are involved in religious experience, they are more frequently used as the direct carrier of the experience. The California Supreme Court specifically recognized this characteristic of peyote when it struck down an attempt by the state of California to prevent members of the Native American Church from using peyote (Chayet, 1967). Wasson and Wasson (1957) have argued that the idea of God may have arisen from the accidental ingestion of mushrooms with psychedelic properties. This hypothesis is strongly supported by the recent discovery that the fly agaric mushroom may have been the legendary *soma* of the founders of Hinduism (Wasson, 1969). The role of psychedelics and other hallucinatory plant material in gaining religious experience and the psychic abilities necessary to carry out the functions of a medicine man is beautifully set forth by Castaneda (1968) as his experiences with a Yaqui diablero.

The first paper in this section, Osmond's "Peyote Night," is a reprint of an account of a peyote ceremony of the Native American Church. His participation in the sacrament and ritual changes him from an outside observer to an inside observer, and his observations develop an impassioned clarity.

in contrast, "The Conversion of Crashing Thunder" expresses what the peyote ceremonies mean to an Indian.

Linzer's paper on yage summarizes what is known about the ceremonies and purposes of taking yage. Metzner's paper deals in the same way with the mushroom, an important source of psychedelic chemicals. It should be noted that his paper was written before Wasson identified soma with *Amanita muscaria*, so his comments on this mushroom will have to be modified in the light of these new data.

The paper by Mikuriya is probably the first that described kif-growing in Morocco. The use of cannabis preparations is not prohibited in Islam, as alcohol is. The government has been forced into an unpopular and ineffective anti-cannabis stand by national and international considerations. Mikuriya closes by comparing customs around the use of hemp in Morocco with those in the United States, and finds many striking parallels as well as differences.

PEYOTE NIGHT

HUMPHRY OSMOND

The Native American Church is a religious movement which originated among the Indians of the Southwestern United States. Its main features involve the use of peyote, a psychedelic, or mind-manifester, drug obtained from the dried tops of a cactus that contains mescaline, in a ceremony combining Indian religious motifs with certain Christian themes. The drug and the ceremony are fused together in a manner acceptable to many Indians today. My interest in this church was a professional one, springing from my researches into psychedelics, the vision-producing drugs the Indians use in a group setting. So far as our research group could make out, the Indians were the first people who used these substances together with certain aspects of Christianity.

We had heard about them in different ways. Religious

This article originally appeared in *Tomorrow* magazine, Spring 1961.

people who wanted this sect suppressed had published complaints in various newspapers. In my country, Canada, there had been questions and statements from a Minister in the House of Commons at Ottawa. A police report we read suggested that peyote was both a dangerous poison and a drug of addiction. Professor Charles Seevers of Ann Arbor, one of the world's leading authorities on both peyote and mescaline, one of its active principles, has frequently stated that it was of low toxicity and that he had no evidence of anyone becoming addicted to it. The U. S. Public Health Service Narcotics Section at Fort Leavenworth have never treated a peyote addict.

One of the clearest and kindest accounts of them and their religion came from the late Professor J. S. Slotkin of the University of Chicago. He had visited the Canadian branches of the Native American Church of North America in the summer of 1956. He told us they were being persecuted, not very obviously, thoroughly, or determinedly, but although it was mild and intermittent, it was persecution all the same. Some of these persecutors did not deserve the label, for they were good people genuinely concerned about the Indians, who had been misinformed about the nature of the peyote rite. They were naturally worried by reports that the Indians were obtaining a dangerous and addictive substance and engaging in wild orgies. There was reason to be concerned after the damage liquor has done to some Indians in the past. Along with these people who had a real interest in the Indians, there were others who never lose an opportunity to meddle in other people's affairs. There is not too much scope for this hobby in western Canada today, but the Indians, being government wards and a special minority group, are particularly susceptible to this sort of interference. As the scholarly Slotkin explained to us, "Their conditions are wretched. They are demoralized. Many of them hate and despise farming. The Native American Church is something of their own, born of their misfortunes and developed from their pre-Columbian traditions. It has grown and flourished in spite of white men and this makes it even more precious to the Indians."

Slotkin thought we could do no harm by attending one of their services, and we might help. It would at least show them hat all white men were not hostile. Their services have een described as orgies only by those who have never attended them. It is curious that the early Christians had much he same accusations leveled at them by the Romans, whose taid, formalized, official religion had become little more than n annex to politics, devoid of enthusiasm and feeling. Any oung religion (Quakers in Fox's day or the Methodists in Vesley's are examples) usually manages to offend longerstablished churches, just as young lovers are something of a eproach to long-wed people, for they reflect a vision of love hat time has more or less dimmed. Long-married people in vhom time does not produce this dimming can be embarassing to their more habituated contemporaries.

We corresponded in a desultory way with the Indians of the Red Pheasant Band, from among whose members most of the ongregation of the Native American Church of Canada was lrawn. The Church had been duly registered as a religious oody and so was safe from direct persecution. But the supply f peyote, their ceremonial cactus, came from the United tates, and this made them vulnerable to administrative presure, as later events have shown.

In September 1956, we learned that Mr. Frank Takes Gun, President of the Native American Church of North America, was planning to come north from his home in Montana to see how his fellow church members were faring in Canada. Shortly after this, we were invited to North Battleford. We drove north, picking up Dr. Abram Hoffer in Saskatoon, armed with a tape recorder, blankets, and lots of notebooks. Two members of the Saskatoon *Star Phoenix* staff raveled with us. It was a glowing early fall day, and the stuble was still live enough to give the land a blond, crew-cut ook. We arrived in North Battleford late in the afternoon of the sixth of October, 1956. Mr. Takes Gun and his companion, Mr. Russell, came to see us in our hotel. They had had a harassing time getting the hard-pressed Red Pheasant Band to organize the ceremony. They are poor Indians. Mr. Takes Gun had helped them to get permission to pitch a tepee for the meeting in the grounds of old Fort Battleford. He was also inquiring into the legal help the Indians were getting in Canada. The Indians' way of conducting business is still not very like that of the white man, and there is much misunderstanding.

I was tired and a little apprehensive on at least two counts. My colleagues and I had decided that, while they would watch and record the ceremony, I should take part in it, and observe from the inside, as it were. I did not wholly enjoy the idea of taking peyote, although I have used a variety of mind changing substances in the past few years. These have included taking harmola, the seeds of Syrian rue, which has a disgusting taste; kavakava, the roots and leaves of a South Sea Island pepper plant; ololiuqui, the seeds of *Rivea corymbosa* a vinelike plant from Mexico, once the chief and sacred narcotic of the Aztecs. I had also taken chemically pure mescaline, one active principle of peyote, and the immensely powerful Lysergic Acid Diethylamide, both derived from plants. In addition, we had worked with a new group of substances derived from adrenalin, whose use in this field had been discovered in Saskatchewan. I had, however, never taken peyote before. I found its dried, shriveled, and furry appearance uninviting, and reports said it frequently produced nausea and vomiting. I did not relish the idea of vomiting in public. My second worry was a more serious one. I had much sympathy for the Indians and wanted to assist their cause, but as an honest observer I would have to report everything that happened. I was concerned lest the service should be ill conducted.

Mr. Takes Gun was clearly worried about me. He told me repeatedly that they would have good, clean city water and that the cups would be personal and hygienic. The peyote, he assured me, would not be difficult to take, but would be made soft with a coffee grinder and wrapped individually in Kleenex. He is of medium height and very solidly built, of that almost pure mesomorphy that one finds often among the Plains Indians. His face might have been carved from old, oiled, highly polished teakwood. He glistened in the afternoon sun—for he was nervous. His eyes and hair were black. He had the longest ears I have ever seen. His face was impassive. This made one notice the eloquence of his hands.

ll the more (one finger was missing from the left one); his
gestures were as expressive as a Latin's.

Mr. Takes Gun left us to make the final preparations for
he ceremony. We agreed to be at North Battleford a little
fter sundown, and, before he left, he gave me a final reas-
urance about the purity of the water. We crossed the golden
alley of the South Saskatchewan River and drove up the hill-
ide to the old fort. They had set the tepee on the short grass
inside the stockade. It was small and pale, its ventilator flap-
ing in the breeze. The clear night sky with the stars appear-
ng and the faint swirl of nothern lights seemed about to
engulf us. Outside the tepee there was a great stack of small
ogs.

The ceremonial fire in the center of the tepee was ready
or lighting. It was between the horns of the low, crescent-
moon altar shaped from molded earth. Only the fire tender
occupied this middle space. The rest of us, eight observers,
ncluding two journalists, and fourteen Indian worshipers,
were ranged around the circumference of the tepee. Apart
rom Mr. Takes Gun, and Mr. Russell, who had driven up
rom Montana, our hosts came from Saskatchewan, mostly
rom the Red Pheasant Band, though a few had driven
over from Alberta. The elders of this group were Mr. Nicotine and Mr. Stone. There were several younger men and
two Indian ladies. All looked spruce and neat. They had
clearly put on their best clothes for the service. I sat on Mr.
Takes Gun's left so that I could learn about the ceremony
from him. He was the leader, and Mr. Russell, on his right,
was his drummer.

In a tepee, one sits with one's back slightly bent and one's
head forward. However one places the legs, they get stiff, the
long hamstring muscles in particular. Cramping pains can be
a nuisance. Mr. Russell played the fire taps on his drum, and
the fire tender lit the prepared wood. Sparks rose up and
fluttered in the darkness above us before vanishing. The tepee
was filled with the pleasant, acrid smell of sage, thyme, and
burning logs. Mr. Takes Gun put a single leaf and then a
large peyote button on the moon altar. The rest of us remained seated, and he was silent. He consulted his watch
from time to time. At eight-thirty he began to read a writ-

ten address he had with him. He asked for "Religious freedom
for the Indian form of Christianity." He quoted the Declara-
tion of Independence with its inalienable rights, which include religious freedom and the pursuit of happiness. The
long Indian faces, dark in the fire glow, expressed melancholy,
dolor, tragedy. "We want to be let alone to worship our God
as we wish." He then addressed the observers directly: "I
trust you will tell the truth and nothing but the truth so help
us God." It is no easy matter even to observe accurately
enough to be sure what the truth might be, and having done
this, how should one convey the truth so that it will mean
something to someone else? I wondered how I would be able
to communicate the solemnity of that frail tepee. It was like
being inside a lighted Japanese lantern, suspended in eternity.

The smoke started the ceremony proper. The Indians are
masters of symbolism; a few eagle feathers, a pinch of sweet
herbs, a little water drum, a gourd rattle, a fire, and little
more, are all the aids they need for worship. For them, everything that is, is holy. They have no written prayers, but as
among the Quakers, everyone prays according to his conscience. So a cigarette made from cornhusks symbolizes for
them the purification and dedication of the human spirit to a
greater spirit. The tobacco was handed around in a soft
leather pouch. It was runny, with many small grains. I am
not a smoker. I fashioned my cigarette clumsily and the tobacco leaked out, and the result was rather emaciated. A glowing brand was passed around for lighting the cigarettes.
Shortly after mine was lit, I choked. The fire felt very hot on
my face, almost scorching, while behind I was chilly. It did
not seem a good start for the evening.

While Mr. Russell beat the drum, Mr. Takes Gun chanted
and shook the rattle. Sometimes he used English and sometimes his own tongue. The wind noises were lost in the chanting and the drumming. His voice rose effortlessly from a firm
baritone to a high, clear falsetto.

> Dear Heavenly Father,
> We are representing our folks under this tepee.
> Dear Heavenly Father, Dear Heavenly Father,
> Bless these men that are observers here.

> Dear Heavenly Father,
> These poor people surrendered all their lands
> To the Government of Canada—their conditions
> Are pitiful.
> Dear Heavenly Father—bless my people back home.

Then he continued in his own tongue, which seemed made for rhetoric, for declamation, and his voice rose in searching falsetto. The Indians maintained a low background of song in their three different languages. The faces of his fellow worshipers were angry, resigned, supplicating, shifting with the changes of rhythm and the flickering fire. The chorus ceased from time to time and the leader continued alone, his voice cascading and dying away, the song of a bird fluttering against a great storm. The fire glowed. An Indian wept. We placed our cigarettes around the base of the moon altar.

At about 9 P.M. the peyote was brought in. It was carried in a little white cloth sack, which was handed from person to person. Mine came separately; it had been macerated in a coffee grinder and each button wrapped in a white tissue, so courteous are the Indians. They themselves crunched the hard, dry, furry cactus tops determinedly, as one cracks nuts with one's teeth. I nibbled cautiously at my soft, damp residue. It has a sharp taste, which lingers in the mouth. It is bitter and sour on the stomach. It repeats on one. It is not as bad as ololiuqui, and is pleasant compared with the sour, oily, rancid seed of the Syrian rue. Mr. Takes Gun belched a little after swallowing his. Peyote takers, making a virtue of necessity, sometimes allege there is something especially valuable about the nausea it induces in some people. As in other religions, rationalizations are always ready to help out anything unpalatable. I was glad when I swallowed the last bit of peyote. My apprehensions about vomiting were unnecessary.

The drumming and singing continued. The water drum is made of blackened iron covered with hide. Seven knobs on the side represent the dipper stars. Behind the singing there is always drumming and rattling. The drum beat in the brain and wearied me; every drummer seemed much the same. The fire tender moved the ashes into the space between the horns of the moon, so that it gradually filled up with fine wood ashes. I had respect for the ceremony. It was reverent and well conducted. But I was still not of the group, even though I was among them. I scribbled away at my note pad and often watched my observing colleagues, who were at the other side of the tepee.

At about nine-fifteen I wrote, "The young man with the superb face, puzzled by his fate—he has a kingly face," and again, "if feeling gets to God, this must." By nine forty-five there was a ghost of brilliant color in my eye grounds when I closed my lids. I felt remote and slightly depressed. The roof flap fluttered like a lost soul. The tepee is a microcosm, a tiny mirror of the universe. The fire glowed red and smokeless; the fire tender handed around a smoldering brand for those who wanted to smoke. Mr. Takes Gun recited prayers in his language—as he smoked, his hands moved with extraordinary delicacy. It was an unorgiastic orgy. The Indians sing without opening their mouths much, and often they hardly move their lips. They sing with their sound box and chest, while we use our lips, tongue, and sound box. I was never quite sure where the singing was coming from, and it was sometimes almost impossible to decide who was singing and who was not.

By about ten I had become more aware of what was happening, and recognized that peyote was starting to affect me. My sight was sharper and my hearing more acute. Looking around the tepee, it struck me that we white men, outnumbered in this tiny world, were an even smaller fraction of the larger one. I found it hard to write and did so reluctantly because, as I noted, ". . . it broke the chain of feeling." I got nothing down on my pad for the next hour and a half. Visual changes continued and increased during this time. They never became very marked, but at times the Indians seemed hostile. Their faces became distorted with anger. I realized that this was probably the effect of peyote and so did not become panicky. I felt that I was an intruder whom the Indians did not trust—they had no special reason to. I did not seem close to them. Peyote works slowly and subtly. It is well suited for a gathering of this sort, where people of differing temperaments, who do not necessarily share a common language, worship together and explore reality without the cushion of words and supported mainly by ritual.

A photographer took some flash pictures at about ten or fifteen minutes before midnight, and then I started writing again. The Indians chanted, drummed, and used the gourd rattle. Only their faces were impassive. The ceremonial swept me along with it.

At midnight, water was brought in. This was the pure city water Mr. Takes Gun had promised me earlier. It was in a new, white enamel pail with a swan transfer on the outside. It was passed around, and we drank from individual paper cups. It could have been depressingly hygienic, but the intention was a generous one to put me at ease. He then said, "Pray to God and ask him to bless the water." He explained that the Indians held their services at night, while the white man sleeps, because God would have time to spare for his Indian friends. He urged his fellow Indians to bring up their children to be intelligent and progressive, adding, "We are representing our lives here." Then he left us and, walking around the outside of the tepee, blew piercing blasts on an eagle's-bone whistle at the four compass points. The sound shrilled through aeons of space and corridors of time. It echoed to eternity. When he came back to us, he prayed, ". . . that the Universe may prevail."

Shortly after this my fellow observers left for what must have been twenty minutes or so, but it could have been as many centuries. I stayed behind with the Indians, and I became part of the worshipers. I entered their world, where for generation upon generation they had hunted the buffalo. They had lived with and on the buffalo. They were of one piece. They were the buffalo. Their lives were part of those shaggy, lumbering herd beasts whose myriads roamed the great plains. On these wide prairies, where trees and hills are almost equally scarce, sound often conveyed as much as sight. So the Indians call up their past with song, with drum, and with rattle. For them, minute alterations of rhythm and pace evoke ever-changing images. Because we cannot hear as they do, the drumming and rattling seem endlessly repetitive to us. The drumming was the steady running of a man with his dog padding beside him. It was the pawing and thudding of buffalo hooves crescendoing in thunder. It was the gentle crumpling of dung falling or the soft plop of a calf dropping on turf, soundless, yet heard by the hunter. The gourd evoked the endlessly sifting wind, catching at scrub and grass as it passed. It was the hissing of an arrow as it leaves the bow or snakes by one's head in battle. It was the sizzling of buffalo meat grilling on the campfire and the creak of a hide tepee as the blizzard twists and whirls around it. The drumming was life and death, scarlet blood spurting from a stricken buffalo or from a fallen warrior. Yet it was also the first fluttering of a child inside its mother. As he sang, a young man wept, and Frank Takes Gun said, "Shed tears on mother earth that the Universal God may take pity on him."

When my friends returned, I felt that the Indians and I were one and that, for a little time, or more accurately, a different sort of time, I was of their world rather than that of my colleagues, their conquerors. It was not simply that I realized they had a point of view I could respect, but that I felt in my bones as they felt in theirs. Looking back, I do not believe that this was an illusion, for I continued to be much more aware of their way of looking at things. But how could one prove such an opinion—without fine instruments for measuring a man's system of values.

The women did not drum, sing or use the gourd rattle, but they smoked, took peyote, and played a large part in the morning ceremony. They also prepared the feast for the next day. Women only very rarely enjoy their highest status among nomadic people.

The Indians must have begun to filter down from Siberia about ten thousand years ago, and as they reached the great central plains they spread out in the wake of the buffalo. For some mysterious reason, horses, which had once lived in America, died out long before man arrived. So the newcomers hunted on foot. Unlike our forebears, who were harassed and pushed west by waves of horsemen from Central Asia, many tiny Indian societies grew up far apart from each other, isolated by vast distances. There were occasionally brief, savage, and ceremonious wars on the prairies, in which little groups of men raided the enemies. In these, courage counted more than killing. Apart from this, their whole lives, their very existence, was at the heels of those heavy monsters. Pursuing them, they had endured drought and cold, furious rainstorms and blinding blizzards. For a very short time, a few generations only, they had horses, which, escaping from the Spaniards, bred splendidly on the grasslands. Few people accept an innovation so quickly and successfully as the Indians took to the horse. They were centaurs. The drumming told of that age of glory when, to the beat of horses' hooves, they swept across the prairies like wildfire and hunted with a splendor never surpassed. Then the white settlers invaded the prairies, and the unequal struggle between hunting peoples who lived in space without time, and the season-bound rapacity of the cultivators of the soil, began. The hunting grounds were eroded. Finally the buffalo were slaughtered wantonly by the million. With that holocaust, their traditions, their way of life, their world, their universe collapsed, and the veil of their souls was rent. Braves became bums, for there was nothing manly left to do. Their women mourned for them.

I was drenched in that world of sound, of singing, drumming, and the subtly changing rhythms of drum, rattle, and voice. We are a more visual people than the Indians, and this is perhaps why they seem impassive to us. We watch, in particular, for changes in facial expression and do not notice the auditory signals with which the Indians communicate their feelings. Those long silences during which they let the unspoken flow between people simply make us tense, embarrassed, uneasy, and ready to burst into nervous chattering.

The blue-shirted young man who had been weeping said, "Frank, can I have some more medicine?" and the little sack was passed along to him. He crunched two more buttons and began to sing and use the gourd rattle while his companion drummed. His song rose above the drumming, was drowned by it, and rose again and again, faltering but struggling still. It was an agony. The drumbeats were strides of fate. Life must go on, pain or no pain. There could be no concessions. The young man wept and sang for himself, for his people, for every human being who has ever quailed before the harshness of life. After singing, he was easier, and the rhythm of his drumming reflected this. There was in it a little of that cosmic beat of Tchaikowsky's great Second Movement of the Fifth Symphony, when, for a brief while, he heard and transcribed what must surely be the pulsing of the galaxies. I watched the young man, and I think I experienced some of the queasiness that peyote induced in him. Like most young men, he longed for a life that meant something—a life of action, danger, pain, defeat, torture, and death at the hands of his enemies if necessary. A life like that of his ancestors who lived on the prairies for centuries before. Anything rather than the humiliating meaninglessness of the present. But the drumming told him, "You cannot go back. You can go forward. It will be rough, but it can be done." It is sad to be a warrior from generations of warriors with nothing warlike to do—an Achilles without Troy, staying at home among his mother's spinning women.

The fire tender kept the hearth meticulously, and the moon altar, which had started as a thin crescent, filled up steadily. When a singer had sung his song, the Indians sat in silence and absorbed it. They applauded with a low guttural noise that might be a hum. They were polite, sensitive, and seemed very courteous and alert toward each other and to their guests. By now it was almost three in the morning, and most of the observers were asleep; one snored loudly and had to be prodded by his neighbor. The visual imagery I usually experience with psychedelic substances was much reduced in this setting, and the auditory imagery very much increased. I responded to every nuance of their drumming. They use a tiny range of sound with which to express themselves, and this is saturated with emotion.

The sparks spangled the upper darkness of the tepee every time the fire was stoked. The tepee was the universe. It had not increased in size nor changed its shape, but the sound had expanded it beyond thought. The young man still cannot bear his fate. All the warrior in him is assailed by it and revolts against it. But he must listen to the voice of the music, which is greater than man. He sings again, this time in high falsetto. There is a note of triumph in it, and perhaps peyote has dissolved the aching in his heart—for a little while.

The tepee smelled of wood and wood smoke, burning herbs, sweat. I noticed the tanginess of the smoke, like in a kippering room. It clung to my hair and clothes for days afterward. The Indians are creatures of sound and smell, with auditory symbolism predominating. We are creatures of sight and sound, with visual imagery predominating. Every drum tap has a meaning for them.

Through the small hours they sang of fleet horses and tireless riders, of unwearying runners and faithful dogs padding beside them. The stories are woven into the drum rhythms. They fanned themselves with a few eagle's feathers, evoking arrow, war bonnet, and battle club—endless parleys, pow-wows, and ceremonial meetings. They had few songs of war, and they returned always to the death of the buffalo, their banishment from the prairies, and so their unmanning and loss of their warrior status. The buffalo hoofbeats are in them as the sound of the sea is in me from generations of seafarers. The Indians may be poor and defeated, but they are not contemptible. They reveal themselves to each other with peyote in humility, but also in pride. For although they revere the Universal Spirit, they do not cringe. They are not ashamed of being men, for so they were created. They do not ascribe their misfortunes to sin, and are thus saved from much futile self-blame.

Mr. Russell's drumming was splendid. Frank sang of the long winter nights and their hopes of endless buffalo herds. He sang, too, of that brief time when they tamed horses, molding long-maned and long-tailed wildings to their will. This reminded me that the Trojan hero Hector, tamer of horses, was exercizing with his chariots on the windy plain of Ilium when their ancestors were hunting the buffalo on foot, over these same prairies. The service was very simple and drew the participants into it. Once I lost my fear and unsureness, the Indians accepted me with dignity, as an equal. I was impressed by their economy of gesture, the faultless taste of their religious art; like a very dry sherry, it is not for every palate. The prairies have molded them over the centuries—they are a people of the open spaces; their God is an open one of the wide earth and the limitless sky—not a shadowy, hidden god of the forests and thickets. Their Universal Spirit is mysterious in its immensity and omnipresence. Man's problem is not to find God, for it is impossible not to be aware of Him, but to relate oneself to Him in the best possible way.

By four-thirty I was becoming more aware of my hosts as individuals. We had experienced something together that cannot be contained in language. Poetry or music would come closer, but I am not a poet or a composer. The wind fretted around the tepee. The singing was like voices calling in the dark, calling for dawn to come, for winter to go, for the buffalo to return, for a child to be born.

Mr. Russell had the black drum passed to him. He sucked a little water from it, tautened the hide, and smoothed it with a caress. Frank Takes Gun explained the next part of the ceremony. "You have only seen three last night—the leader, the drummer, and the fireman. Now you will see the fourth. Thank God we have lived to see another day. We represent our lives: we don't imitate anything. The foundations of human life rest with our mothers who delivered us into this world." The Mother stepped into the tepee through the door flap, announced by the shrilling of the eagle's-bone whistle. She sat down by the white enamel waterpot. The tepee was dim, the fire was low, but some wisps of smoke rising from it seemed to surround her. She had a red blanket around her shoulders, a blue dress, smooth black hair, and her face seemed very broad. She was greeted by a song of welcome with voices, drum, and rattle. With the singing, she became superb mother earth, mother prairie, grass, cow buffalo, mare, and doe, the epitome of motherhood. The drum beating was not restful or sleep inducing. It was the fecund pulsing of sex, passion, generation, and death, sung without guilt and without self-consciousness. The mother was weary, patient, tender, but enduring. She stood behind all the men—drummer, fire tender, leader. In front of her were the waters of life and death.

Frank addressed her in the highest falsetto, a tearing, almost noiseless scream, the cry of the tiniest baby or of an old man breathing his last. It was unbearable. The mother could have been any age—maid, mother, or crone, from sixteen to a hundred sixteen.

"You have been good to us while we were here. You worked

hard and made this possible. God knows we worship Him. God knows we respect the mothers of our children."

Mr. Dave Stone, the oldest man present, spoke to the mother in his high, light voice. His voice was very clear and would carry over great distances. The wind had risen, and the day was being born with a storm. The old man called upon the mother and sprinkled dried sage on the fire, sweetening the air in her honor. She took a cigarette and lit it from the fire tender's brand. The smoke she exhales is the life she gives. Above her head, the dawn lightened the tepee flap. The fire was low. She drew on a cigarette. Its glowing tip was as evanescent as a man's life, almost aflame one moment, out the next. She prayed and smoked.

This is the mother who bears the baby, who nurses and cossets the infant, who rears the child and watches him grow into a young warrior, drummer, fire tender, or leader, who is possessed by him and who laments him when he dies. She is indomitable. Warriors die, but the mother, slave or matriarch, she is always there. Her voice was low and clear. She dominated the tepee—the mother who bears and the mother who buries her children. Her prayers were followed by rumbles of agreement. She reaffirmed the will to endure, to live on. The worshipers were deeply moved. Frank whispered to me, "That is how much they respect their mothers." But it was more than respect. It was awe. She conveyed the sorrow of a woman's lot in a destitute people. The dawn caught the pointed top of the tepee, but below where we were sitting, the fire was so low that I could hardly see to write.

Mr. Russell whispered to me, "Praying with the smoke— something good—something lasting forever." The Plains Indians were a Dionysian, an apocalyptic people, frugal but generous; no middle way existed for them—conquerors or conquered, no in-between, no compromise. The smoke breath was caught up with the warm air over the fire and twisted up into dawnlight. It struck me that with another turn of the wheel of history we Caucasians who, by means of gunpowder and printing, have gained so much authority in the world, might find ourselves subject to peoples who possess skills we do not have. No one who had been with the Indians as I had been could feel superior to them. The blue-shirted warrior is almost reconciled to living an unheroic, undionysiac life. It is against his whole being. But the drumming, the singing, and peyote have worked their magic. The buffalo are no more; the dawn is coming; there is a life to face now.

The observed were awake and alert, the observers mostly sleeping. At six, dawn came to us as the tepee flap was opened. We had wrestled with the angel. We had grappled with the Heavenly Father.

Water was poured into the hygienic cups again, and a little more was put into the drum. I was asked to say a few words, the stranger whom they had made welcome and allowed to enter into their mystery. I thanked them for their kindness to me and told them that I would do my best to tell people about their worship clearly and honestly. I also said that it would be no easy matter to convey to those who had not shared our experience and who do not have the Indian sense of oneness with life.

A child had come into the world again. Dawn lit the stockade, and the wind was chilly. Life had begun again and must be faced. The voice of the singers rose clear and high—a child's cry of delight at buffalo hooves thundering far away. The fire flared a little as if trying to hold back the morning, but it failed. The center of the tent floor was covered by a great, grayish-white half-moon of charred wood ashes. The mother left us. The barrier of everyday life began to return.

Aftermath

The sun was just coming up when we left them at about half past six. We felt that our Indian hosts would be easier if they could have their morning feast without us. There were handshakes and promises that we would do our best to tell our people about their religion. As I left the tent, I took a last look at the whitish-gray expanse of the moon altar: the three young men, including blue-shirt, were singing and drumming together by the door flap. They were very blithe. Outside, Mr. Nicotine and Mr. Stone stood by the mother and waved to us as we left. The tepee seemed too small and frail to have contained so much, but the drumbeats surged out of it as evidence of the extraordinary power concentrated there. I slept a little and thought much when I returned to the hotel. I felt relaxed and happy. I felt that I had seen the Indians, and what I had seen had cheered me. I wrote at this time, only a few hours after the ceremony, "We cannot ape them, but we can learn from them and perhaps gradually adapt their religion to our needs, as they have adapted ours—feel tired, at peace, an enlarging of the spirit." A little later, on my way back from North Battleford, I noted, "Peyote simply reveals what is the potential in all of us. The Indians, whose gifts have for so long been run down by the whites, have found that in spite of being poor Indians, the spirit of God is still with them. This is an immense advance. It is a new hope, a new humility, a new pride."

A day later I wrote, "Indian singing is incomprehensible to most white men simply because they have never learnt the fine discrimination of the Indian in matters of sound. Clearly a people who have lived in an almost soundless country (and the prairies are almost soundless to the city ear even now) would learn to pick up a different range of sounds and would use these sounds in their music. Grasses, grasshoppers, dust sifting, the wavelets on little rivers splashing, the shushing of wind among low bushes, and wind sounds infinitely varied with the seasons. Then, in great contrast, the very loud sounds —the sounds inside one, the heart thudding, etc., particularly loud when one is surrounded by great stillness; hooves stamping or clopping regularly; the drubbing stampede of the buffalo—again infinitely varied by terrain and weather, and the crash of thunder reverberating over the endless prairies. Birds few in number compared with the space, and therefore all the more memorable. Color on the prairies in great general masses with very small changes. The Indians would be used to the very large and the very small. Also the effect of six months or so of snow."

Then there was the matter of the resemblance between liquor and peyote that has been raised so often in the press. I made a special note about this: "Alcohol and peyote (psychedelics generally) *are* antithetical. Alcohol produces a downward transcendence, peyote an upward one—the difference between leveling up and leveling down. Alcohol allows one to relate to others by being more sure of one's self. This in small doses, is much better than not being able to relate at all, but it is a very precarious business, and selfishness may soon end in brawling and ill temper. Peyote acts not by emphasizing one's own self but by expanding it into the selves of others, with a deepening empathy or in-feeling. The self is dissolved and, in being dissolved, enriched. It becomes aware of the nobility of other selves and so of itself."

I tried repeatedly in the next few months to organize my experience, but it would not be organized. I carried my notes around with me and made many drafts of papers that were never completed, because they did not seem to carry out my obligation to Frank Takes Gun and my fellow worshipers of that little band. It was not until three years later, when I was quite unexpectedly asked to give a short broadcast about the peyote ceremony, that I began to see how I might be able to convey something of that night in the tepee to people who had not been there and who had never taken peyote or other psychedelics.

How does it look three years later? Has the wonder and beauty of those astonishing ten and a half hours receded so that they now seem unreal? Did my difficulty in writing about the experience of that strange night arise from a growing feeling that my notes were muddled and that I was as muddled as they? I do not think so.

That night in the tepee has resulted in many studies by my colleagues and me. We have observed the effects of psychedelic substances on groups of people taking them together —for various reasons, we did not use peyote. The Indians have been very skillful in structuring their ceremony so that it best meets their needs. They are such masters of symbol, ceremony, and ritual, that this is hardly surprising. It would be unwise and impertinent to ape their religion, which developed from their agony when they lost their hunting grounds at the end of the nineteenth century. Our needs are very different from theirs. So we must follow a different route.

We have suggestive evidence that psychedelics, properly used, can increase communication and understanding between those who take them together, and this is not simply a drug-induced delusion. It seems to persist long after the effects of the chemical have disappeared. This has not yet been proved. Proof in such a matter is not easy, and so for the moment we have to rely on personal opinion. We have to find some way of showing these effects so that they can be easily understood. But we have to recognize that we are dealing with aspects of the human mind that are even more elusive and mysterious than the depths of space and time.

Due to the interest and generosity of Mrs. Eileen Garrett, President of the Parapsychology Foundation, several of us have taken part in two international conferences about psychedelics. One was held in New York in November 1958 and the other in Le Piol, France, in July 1959. Both these conferences were attended by scientists of international repute. At both of them there was general agreement that these experiences induced by psychedelics, which fall into the category of what William James called "unhabitual perception," call for sustained inquiry and research. It was encouraging that the impetus for these meetings, which drew contributors from many countries, arose in a frail tepee raised by members of the Native American Church, mostly from the Red Pheasant Band, above the South Saskatchewan River three years ago.

In one respect, however, we have failed, at least so far. We have not been able to help members of the Native American Church of Canada to obtain peyote, which is the sacrament of their faith. Its importation is banned by the federal government department concerned with these matters, by means of a legal technicality. So far as we know, this has never been disputed in a court of law or debated in Parliament. The attitude of government, "We are doing this for your own good; we can't explain why because you wouldn't understand," is infuriating, unwise, and unnecessary. Among its other objectives, we hope that this article will lead others to question seriously such well-meaning but arbitrary attempts to do good. The Native American Church and the religion its members practice, far from demoralizing them, is likely to help them in their struggle to adapt to a very unfamiliar world.

Surely we can be fair-minded enough to pay respectful attention to this bold attempt by the Indians to develop a new way of coming closer to the source of all things. They do not want to convert us to their ways. They do not claim that the peyote road is the only way of reaching out toward their Great Spirit and Heavenly Father. In Frank Takes Gun's words, "We just want to be let alone to worship our God as we wish." Must we obstruct and attempt to crush a new religion, which is beautiful and has never been shown to do any harm, simply because it is unfamiliar and because we can't imagine that it would work? Can we not let them tread their peyote road and see what happens—provided they conduct their services decorously and account properly for the peyote used? They would, I believe, welcome observers from time to time. Those observers could see and experience for themselves the form of worship that the aboriginal inhabitants of these lands developed when their world was tottering. The loss of the hunting grounds and the slaughter of the buffalo was for them an even greater catastrophe than that appalling event one early morning at Hiroshima in August 1945.

I shall not forget my Indian hosts, who took me back to a life through which all mankind has passed. A harsh, fierce, dangerous, passionate life where hunter and hunted are one. A life rich in beauty and meaning. Little more than eighty years ago, this was their life and had been so beyond the memory of man. In a few short, terrible years it was torn from them, and they are still bewildered at the world in which we are clumsily trying to find a place for them. But then perhaps we share some of that bewilderment, for our new world is unimaginably strange. Should we not join them in their prayer that ". . . the Universe may prevail"?

REPORT OF THE MESCALINE
EXPERIENCE OF
CRASHING THUNDER

PAUL RADIN

(Crashing Thunder is a Winnebago Indian whose autobiography describes in detail his initiation to the peyote worship.

Long persecuted by the guilt of having once fraudulently told his people that he had had a vision, and of having made a shambles of his life through drunkenness, living with various women, and even implication in a murder, Crashing Thunder sets out for a peyote meeting with some reluctance. In this first experience, not too much happens except, he reports, "I felt different from my normal self." Several further meetings follow, and then the one reported below.)

When we arrived, the one who was to lead asked me to sit near him. There he placed me. He urged me to eat a lot of peyote, so I did. The leaders of the ceremony always placed the regalia in front of themselves; they also had a peyote placed there. The one this leader placed in front of himself this time, was a very small one. Why does he have a very small one there? I thought to myself. I did not think much about it.

It was now late at night and I had eaten a lot of peyote and felt rather tired. I suffered considerably. After a while, I looked at the peyote, and there stood an eagle with outspread wings. It was as beautiful a sight as one could behold. Each of the feathers seemed to have a mark. The eagle stood looking at me. I looked around, thinking that perhaps there was something the matter with my sight. Then I looked again, and it was really there. I then looked in a different direction, and it disappeared. Only the small peyote remained. I looked around at the other people, but they all had their heads bowed and were singing. I was very much surprised.

Some time after this, I saw a lion lying in the same place where I had seen the eagle. I watched it very closely. It was alive and looking at me. I looked at it very closely, and when I turned my eyes away just the least little bit, it disappeared. I suppose they all know this and I am just beginning to know of it, I thought. Then I saw a small person at the same place. He wore blue clothes and a shining-brimmed cap. He had on a soldier's uniform. He was sitting on the arm of the per-

This article is taken from *The Autobiography of a Winnebago Indian*, by Paul Radin, originally published by the University of California Publications in American Archaeology and Ethnology, Vol. 16, No. 7, 1920.

son who was drumming, and he looked at everyone. He was a little man, perfect in all proportions. Finally I lost sight of him. I was very much surprised indeed. I sat very quietly. This is what it is, I thought; this is what they all probably see and I am just beginning to find out.

Then I prayed to Earthmaker (God): "This, your ceremony, let me hereafter perform."

As I looked again, I saw a flag. I looked more carefully and I saw the house full of flags. They had the most beautiful marks on them. In the middle of the room there was a very large flag and it was a live one; it was moving. In the doorway there was another one not entirely visible. I had never seen anything so beautiful in all my life.

Then again I prayed to Earthmaker. I bowed my head and closed my eyes and began to speak. I said many things that I would ordinarily never have spoken about. As I prayed, I was aware of something above me, and there he was; Earthmaker, to whom I was praying, he it was. That which is called the soul, that is it, that is what one calls Earthmaker. Now this is what I felt and saw. The one called Earthmaker is a spirit, and that is what I felt and saw. All of us sitting there we had all together one spirit or soul. At least that is what I learned. I instantly became the spirit, and I was their spirit or soul. Whatever they thought, I immediately knew it. I did not have to speak to them and get an answer to know what their thoughts had been. Then I thought of a certain place far away, and immediately I was there. I was my thought.

I looked around and noticed how everything seemed about me, and when I opened my eyes I was myself in the body again. From this time on, I thought, thus I shall be. This is the way they are, and I am only just beginning to be that way. All those that heed Earthmaker must be thus, I thought. I would not need any more food, I thought, for was I not my spirit? Nor would I have any more use for my body, I felt. My corporeal affairs are over, I felt.

Then they stopped and left, for it was just dawning. Then someone spoke to me. I did not answer, for I thought they were just fooling and that they were all like myself, and that therefore it was unnecessary for me to talk to them. So when they spoke to me, I only answered with a smile. They are just saying this to me because they realize that I have just found out, I thought. That was why I did not answer. I did not speak to anyone until noon. Then I had to leave the house to perform one of nature's duties, and someone followed me. It was my friend. He said, "My friend, what troubles you that makes you act as you do?" "Well, there's no need of your saying anything, for you know it beforehand," I said.

Then I immediately got over my trance and again got into my normal condition, so that he would have to speak to me before I knew his thoughts. I became like my former self. It became necessary for me to speak to him. . . .

Now since that time (of my conversion), no matter where I am, I always think of this religion. I still remember it, and I think I will remember it as long as I live. It is the only holy thing that I have been aware of in all my life.

After that, whenever I heard of a peyote meeting, I went to it. However, my thoughts were always fixed on women. If I were married (legally), perhaps these thoughts would leave me, I thought. Whenever I went to a meeting now, I tried to eat as many peyote as possible, for I was told that it was good to eat them. For that reason, I ate them. As I sat there, I would always pray to Earthmaker. Now these were my thoughts. If I were married, I thought as I sat there, I could then put all my thoughts on this ceremony. I sat with my eyes closed and was very quiet.

Suddenly I saw something. This was tied up. The rope with which this object was tied up was long. The object itself was running around and around in a circle. There was a pathway there in which it ought to go, but it was tied up and unable to get there. The road was an excellent one. Along its edge, blue grass grew; and on each side, there grew many varieties of pretty flowers. Sweet-smelling flowers sprang up all along this road. Far off in the distance appeared a bright light. There a city was visible, of a beauty indescribable by tongue. A cross was in full sight. The object that was tied up would always fall just short of reaching the road. It seemed to lack sufficient strength to break loose of what was holding it. Near it lay something that would have given it sufficient strength to break its fastenings if it were only able to get hold of it.

I looked at what was so inextricably tied up and I saw that it was myself. I was forever thinking of women. This is it with which I was tied, I thought. Were I married, I would have strength enough to break my fastening and be able to travel in the good road, I thought. Then daylight came upon us and we stopped. . . .

[He did marry, and "together we gave ourselves up at a peyote meeting. From that time on we have remained members of the peyote ceremony."]

On one occasion while at a meeting, I suffered great pain. My eyes were sore and I was thinking of many things. Now I do nothing but pay attention to this ceremony, for it is good. Then I called the leader over to me and said to him, "My elder brother, hereafter only Earthmaker shall I regard as holy. I will make no more offerings of tobacco. I will not use any more tobacco. I will not smoke and I will not chew tobacco. I have no further interest in these. Earthmaker alone do I desire to serve. I will not take part in the Medicine Dance again. I give myself up to you. I intend to give myself up to Earthmaker's cause." Thus I spoke to him. "It is good, younger brother," he said to me. Then he had me stand up, and he prayed to Earthmaker. He asked Earthmaker to forgive me my sins.

Thus I go about telling everyone that this religion is good. Many other people at home said the same thing. Many, likewise, have joined this religion and are getting along nicely. . . . Before my conversion I went about in a pitiable condition, but now I am living happily, and my wife has a fine baby.

MUSHROOMS AND THE MIND

RALPH METZNER

Was the Buddha's last, fatal supper a mushroom feast? Was *soma*, the mystery potion at Eleusis, a mushroom? Why are mushrooms linked to thunder, and to toads? Why does Hieronymus Bosch have a gigantic mushroom standing at Hell's entrance? Why have they been called "God's Flesh," and "Devil's Bread"? Men have used mushrooms to murder, to worship, to heal, to prophesy. Some fear and abominate all fungi as "dirty" and "dangerous." Others use discrimination—enjoy them as food and as mediators to divine vision.

Two classes of mushrooms are of primary interest to the anthropologist and psychologist studying the ritual use of fungi. One, the fly agaric, *Amanita muscaria*, is the "drug of choice" among certain Siberian tribes. It is apparently hallucinogenic, though not psychedelic in the sense of inducing transcendent experiences, experiences of *expanded* consciousness. The other group, the *Psilocybe* mushrooms and related species of the Mexican mountains, are both hallucinogenic and psychedelic. They are the "God's Flesh" of the Aztecs.

The Fly Amanita

The fly agaric has a whitish stalk, swollen at the base, a lacerated collar about three quarters of the way up the stalk, and a gorgeously colored umbrellalike cap from three to eight inches wide. In North America the cap will be mostly whitish, yellowish, or orange-red, but in Europe or Asia bright red or purple. In all regions the cap is covered with many whitish, yellowish, or reddish warts.[1]

Tribes using the fly agaric include the Kamchadals, Kerjaks, and Chukchees living on the Pacific coast, from Kamchatka to the northeastern tip of Siberia; the Yukaghirs, farther to the west; the Yenisei Ostjaks; and the Samoyed Ostjaks, in the valley of the upper Ob. These Siberian tribes have become famous for the practice of drinking the urine of mushroom-intoxicated persons, in order to get a prolongation of the effect. Oliver Goldsmith, in 1762, described a "mushroom party" thus:

The poorer sort, who love mushrooms to distraction as well as the rich, but cannot afford it at first hand, post themselves on these occasions around the huts of the rich and watch the ladies and gentlemen as they come down to pass their liquor, and hold a wooden bowl to catch the delicious fluid, very little altered by filtration, being

[1] Norman Taylor, *Narcotics: Nature's Dangerous Gifts*. Delta Books, New York, 1963, p. 154.

still strongly tinctured with the intoxicating quality. Of this they drink with the utmost satisfaction and thus they get as drunk and as jovial as their betters.[2]

Whether the fly agaric is involved in the "berserkgång" of the Vikings is a debated point. Norman Taylor's book *Narcotics: Nature's Dangerous Gifts*, claims that "in proper amounts it promotes gaiety and exuberance among a morose people, while leading, in large doses, to berserk orgies."[3] R. Gordon Wasson, however, has dissented from this view, pointing out that no plant was ever mentioned in the Viking accounts.

In their monumental book *Mushrooms, Russia and History* (1957), the Wassons, Robert Gordon and Valentina, draw parallels between the beliefs of the Siberian tribes about the mushrooms and those of the Mexican mushroom-using peoples:

With our Mexican experiences fresh in mind, we reread what Jochelson and Bogoras had written about the Korjaks and the Chukchees. We discovered startling parallels between the use of the fly amanita (*Amanita muscaria*) in Siberia and the divine mushrooms in Middle America. In Mexico the mushroom "speaks" to the eater; in Siberia "the spirits of the mushrooms" speak. Just as in Mexico, Jochelson says that among the Korjaks "the agaric would tell every man, even if he were not a shaman, what ailed him when he was sick, or explain a dream to him, or show him the upper world or the underground world or foretell what would happen to him." Just as in Mexico on the following day those who have taken the mushrooms compare their experiences, so in Siberia, according to Jochelson, the Korjaks, "when the intoxication had passed, told whither the 'fly-agaric men' had taken them and what they had seen." In Bogoras we discover a link between the lightning bolt and the mushroom. According to a Chukchee myth, lightning is a One-Sided Man who drags his sister along by her foot. As she bumps along the floor of heaven, the noise of her bumping makes the thunder. Her urine is the rain, and she is possessed by the spirits of the fly amanita.[4]

Much is made by Wasson of the connection between mushrooms and thunder; we will return to this later.

Dr. Andrija Puharich, whose work has chiefly concerned itself with the experimental investigation of telepathic and

[2] Quoted in Taylor, op. cit., p. 156.
[3] Taylor, op. cit., p. 157.
[4] R. Gordon Wasson and Valentina P. Wasson, *Mushrooms, Russia and History*, Pantheon Books, New York, 1957, p. 211.

related phenomena, has also done some studies of mushroom use among the Chatino Indians of Mexico, and claims that amanita is used by them. Wasson, whose knowledge of the Mexican mushrooms is probably unequaled, disputes this:

For ten years we combed the various regions, and we have invariably found that it played no role in the life of the Indians, though of course it is of common occurrence in the woods. We had visited the Chatino country, where we were accompanied by Bill Upson of the Instituto Lingüístico de Verano, who speaks Chatino. Later he likewise helped Puharich, but he informs us that no *brujo* in his presence testified to the use of a mushroom answering to the description of *Amanita muscaria*.[5]

The three principal ingredients of *Amanita muscaria* apparently are muscarine, atropine, and bufotenine.[6] *Muscarine* is a cholinergic drug, which stimulates the parasympathetic system, causing sweating, salivation, pupil contraction, slowed cardiac rate, and increased peristalsis. These effects are counteracted by *atropine*, which was long used as an antidote to amanita poisoning until it was discovered that the mushroom itself also contained this. The effects of a particular ingestion of the mushroom would depend on the relative quantities of the two substances. Atropine alkaloids are found in many plants, including deadly nightshade, henbane, mandrake, thorn apple, and Jimson weed. They are generally believed to have been involved in the European witches' cults, definitely to cause hallucinations, as well as either excitement or depression. On the basis of my own experiments with *Ditran*, a hallucinogenic drug similar in its action to atropine, I would suggest that the anti-cholinergic agents are definitely consciousness-altering, since they produce thought disorientation and visions, but I would doubt that they are psychedelic, or consciousness-expanding. They may be more truly psychotomimetic than LSD or psilocybin.[7]

[5] R. Gordon Wasson, "Notes on the Present Status of Ololiuhqui and the Other Hallucinogens of Mexico," *Psychedelic Review*, #3, 1964, p. 301.
[6] Robert W. Buck, M.D., "Mushroom Toxins—A Brief Review of the Literature," *New England Journal of Medicine*, 265, 1961, 681–86.
[7] Ralph Metzner, "Subjective Effects of Anti-cholinergic Hallucinogens" (to be published, *Psychedelic Review*, #10).

The third ingredient of the amanita mushrooms, *bufotenine*, probably is psychedelic, since chemically it is 5-hydroxy-dimethyltryptamine, i.e., closely related to both DMT and psilocin. Bufotenine is also found in the South American snuff *Piptadenia peregrina* and in the sweat gland of the toad *Bufo marinus*, which sheds new light on the witches' brews containing toads. However, the quantity of bufotenine in *Amanita muscaria* is very small, so the principal visual effects of the mushroom are probably due to its belladonna (atropine) alkaloids. This is confirmed by the stories of the Siberian tribesmen who, having imbibed the mushrooms, jump very high over small objects; visual size distortions are common with Ditran-type drugs, though rare with tryptamine psychedelics.

Although to some people the drinking of muscarinic, atropinized urine may be a repulsive way to get high, as Norman Taylor points out, "Who are we to deny them this revolting pleasure? To these dull plodders of the arctic wastes, the fly agaric may well be their only peep into a world far removed from the frozen reality of their wretchedness. That such people found the fly agaric is merely another illustration of the worldwide hunt for something to break the impact of everyday life."[8]

The Sacred Psilocybes

The story of the *Psilocybe* mushrooms, the *teonanacatl*, or "God's Flesh," of the Aztecs, is one of the most dramatic episodes in modern anthropology. When the Spaniards arrived in Mexico, their clerics immediately labeled the mushrooms (and the other hallucinogens in use—*peyotl* and *ololiuhqui*) as products of the devil and did their best to stamp out this "idolatry." Brother Toribio de Benavente, a Spanish monk better known as Motolinia, in a work on pagan rites and idolatries, described their "vice" as follows:

They had another drunkenness which made them more cruel: which was of some small mushrooms . . . and after a while they were seeing a thousand visions, especially of snakes, and as they went completely out of their minds, it seemed to them that their legs and

[8] Taylor, op. cit., p. 158.

bodies were full of worms which were eating them alive, and thus, half raving, they went out of the house, wishing that somebody would kill them, and with that bestial drunkenness and the trouble they felt, it would happen sometimes that they hanged themselves. And they were also against others much more cruel. They called these mushrooms *teonanacatl*, which means flesh of the God (the Demon they adored), and in that manner, with that bitter food, their cruel god held communion with them.[9]

A Mexican historian writing in the 1870s, Orozco y Berra, stated that the mushrooms produced "a state of intoxication with frightening hallucinations." Friar Bernardino de Sahagún, a Franciscan monk who preserved texts written in the preconquest Nahuatl language, in writing of the mushrooms often referred to disconsolate, dissolute, disintegrating states of personality; the members of society using the mushroms were "the deranged one," "the angry young man," "the noblewoman without shame," "the prostitute, the procurer, the enchanter."[10]

This language is the sixteenth-century equivalent of the modern psychiatric approach to hallucinogens. AMA President Roy Grinker, M.D., in an editorial in the *Archives of General Psychiatry*, warns that ". . . latent psychotics are disintegrating under the influence of even a single dose; long-continued LSD experiences are subtly creating a psychopathology."[11] Dana Farnsworth, M.D., Harvard health officer, in another editorial refers to drug-induced "nightmares" such as thinking one is only six inches tall, and "horrid, involuntary hallucinations."[12]

The pattern is the same: the representatives of the current psychological power system—the clerics then, the psychiatrists now—react to the new "detonator of the soul" with puritanical paranoia and fearful fantasies of sin, degradation, disintegration. Since anxious suspicion does not allow them to become acquainted with the real nature of the alleged

[9] Quoted from "Historia de los Indios de la Nueva España," by Lothar Knauth, in *Estudios de Cultura Nahuatl*, Vol. III, 1962, p. 263.

[10] Knauth, op. cit., p. 266.

[11] Roy Grinker, M.D., "Lysergic Acid Diethylamide, Editorial," *Archives of General Psychiatry*, 8, 1963, p. 425.

[12] Dana Farnsworth, M.D., "Hallucinogenic Agents, Editorial," *Journal of the American Medical Association*, 185, 1963, pp. 878–80.

demonic plant or substance, ignorant misrepresentations soon shroud any mention of them, and repressive measures are vigorously pursued.

The historian Lothar Knauth has gathered further references which shed a somewhat different light on the Aztecs' use of the mushrooms. For example, Orozco y Berra, in his account of the coronation of Motecuazoma II, says,

The religious festivities ended, the lords gathered to eat woodland mushrooms, which contain that which confuses the mind, as if they were intoxicating drinks; while their minds were confused they saw visions, believed they heard voices; therefore they took these hallucinations as divine notices, revelations of the future, and augury of things to come.[13]

Another writer, Tezozomoc, has this to add:

. . . the strangers gave them mushrooms found in the mountain woods so that they would get intoxicated, and with that they began to dance; others went inside the room to rest. Then they took the big lights of the patio and every time they started the song the strangers began to dance and to sing, and so that they should not be known they dressed themselves with false hair.[14]

For another description of a mushroom ceremony among the Aztecs, Lothar Knauth draws again on a Nahuatl text preserved by Sahagún. It is part of the *fiesta* that the *pochteque*, the great merchants of the Aztec empire, gave the night before they sent their trading caravans to the distant, foreign commercial center of the Gulf and Pacific coasts.

There arrived those that were going to dance, . . . and those that were going to abandon themselves. Those of the merchant leaders who were not going to dance were the strait-laced, chaste ones, who thought themselves somebody. And the old merchants met them with flowers, with tobacco, with brilliant green paper collars and bunches of quetzal feathers, glistening in the moonlight.
Right at the beginning, as a refreshment, they ate the mushrooms. They felt with it a burn, a red-hot blown fire inside, and not from hot food they were eating. Therefore they drank hot cacao that was kept warm for the night. Thusly they ate the intoxicating mushrooms. When they had finished eating them, they danced and they cried. Meanwhile some of them felt the effect: they went inside, they

---

[13] "Historia Antigua y de la Conquista," in Knauth, op. cit., Vol. III, p. 267.
[14] "Crónica Mexicana," in Knauth, op. cit., LXXXVII, p. 267.

sat down, with their backs against the wall. They didn't dance any more. They sat by themselves, in the same place and let their heads hang.[15]

The preceding description of the festivities sounds not too unlike a modern description of a "psychedelic celebration," at, for example, the Avalon Ballroom in San Francisco.

On Friday and Saturday nights they swarm into the Avalon and Fillmore Ballrooms . . . to be bathed in constantly changing projections of liquid colors and films, to dance in the dancing light of their ecstatic costumes and faces and feelings, and to drench themselves in the saturating rock 'n' roll of the Grateful Dead. . . . The whole environment, in short, is turned on and total immersion is expected.[16]

The description of the Aztec mushroom celebration goes on in a more somber key as the participants apparently become involved in visions of the manner of their death. Whether these were genuine clairvoyant experiences or shared hallucinations induced by the high suggestibility of the be-mushroomed state, it is impossible to tell at this remove.

In that stupor, some imagined they were going to die, and they cried; some were to perish in the war; some were to be eaten by wild beasts; some were to be taken prisoners of war; some were to be somebody rich, very rich; some were to buy and be owners of slaves; some were to be adulterers, were to be stoned to death; some were to be taken for thieves and be stoned to death; some were to become dissolute, were to end as drunkards; some were to drown; some were to be somebody peaceful, peacefully living to themselves and dying the same way; some were to fall from the roof and die suddenly.[17]

The negative view of the mushrooms prevailed. Spanish mycophobia succeeded in stamping out the mushroom cult as a major force in Mexican culture. Only a handful of remote mountain tribes preserved the customs and rituals of what must once have been a splendid and powerful system of worship and magic. So complete was the neglect and ignorance in the Western world of this botanical aspect of Mexican religion, that in 1915 a reputable American botanist, William E. Safford, read a paper before a learned society claim-

---

[15] Facsimile editions by Paso y Troncoso, ff. 37 and 37 vo. in Knauth, op. cit., p. 269.

[16] William K. Zinsser, "The Love Hippies," *Look*, April 18, 1967.

[17] Knauth, op. cit., pp. 269–70.

ing that the so-called sacred mushroom of Mexico did not exist and never had.

In 1936, the Mexican engineer Roberto J. Weitlaner became the first white man in modern times to obtain or even see the sacred mushrooms, in the tiny Oaxacan village Huautla de Jiménez. Two years later, his daughter Irmgard, her anthropologist fiancé, and two friends became the first Westerners to witness a mushroom ceremony. In the same year, the Harvard botanist Richard E. Schultes made a trip to Huautla, obtained some specimen mushrooms from informants, and sent them to the Harvard Botanical Museum, where they were identified as the species *Panaeolus campanulatus*, sphinctrinus variety. Schultes published reports on his finds, but his own work took him to the Amazon jungles to investigate the fabled *caapi* or *yagé* vine, and he did not return to Mexico. The war years intervened, and the Mexican mushroom slipped again into the shadows of history.

On June 29, 1955, Robert Gordon Wasson and his wife, Valentina, became the first white persons in modern times to actually participate in and partake of the sacred mushroom ceremony, again in the tiny village of Huautla de Jiménez, under the wise guidance of the now famous *curandera* María Sabina. The news of their discovery became public with the publication in 1957 of *Mushrooms, Russia and History*, and with a May 13, 1957, article in *Life*. This magazine has often since that time been the first to signal, and perhaps in some "mediumistic" way to bring about, new developments in the growth of the "psychedelic movement."

The intriguing story of how Robert Gordon Wasson, a professional banker, partner and vice-president of the Morgan Guaranty Trust Company of New York, found himself ingesting the sacred mushroom on a remote Mexican mountaintop, is worth repeating in his own words:

(My wife) was a Great Russian and, like all of her fellow countrymen, learned at her mother's knee a solid body of empirical knowledge about the common species (of mushrooms) and a love for them that are astonishing to us Americans. . . . Their love of mushrooms is . . . a visceral urge, a passion that passeth understanding. . . . I, of Anglo-Saxon origin, had known nothing of mushrooms. By inheritance, I ignored them all; I rejected those repugnant fungal growths, expressions of parasitism and decay. . . . Such discoveries as we have made, including the rediscovery of the religious role of the hallucinogenic mushrooms of Mexico, can be laid to our preoccupation with that cultural rift between my wife and me, between our respective peoples, between mycophilia and mycophobia . . . that divide the Indo-European peoples into two camps. . . . I suggest that when such traits betoken the attitudes of whole tribes or peoples, and when those traits have remained unaltered throughout recorded history, and especially when they differ from one people to another, neighboring people, then you are face to face with a phenomenon of profound cultural importance, whose primal cause is to be discovered only in the wellsprings of cultural history. . . .

Our method of approach was to look everywhere for references to mushrooms. We gathered the words for "mushroom" and the various species in every accessible language. We studied their etymologies. . . . We were quick to discern the latent metaphors in such words. . . . We searched for the meaning of these figures of speech. We sought mushrooms in the proverbs of Europe, in myths and mythology, in legends and fairy tales, in epics and ballads, in historical episodes, in the obscene and scabrous vocabularies that usually escape the lexicographer. . . . Mushrooms are widely linked with the fly, the toad, the cock, and the thunderbolt; and so we studied these to see what associations they conveyed to our remote forebears. . . .

I do not recall which of us, my wife or I, first dared to put into words, back in the 40s, the surmise that our own remote ancestors, perhaps four thousand years ago, worshiped a divine mushroom. It seemed to us that this might explain the phenomenon of mycophilia versus mycophobia, for which we found an abundance of evidence in philology and folklore. . . . I remember distinctly how it came about that we embarked on our Middle American explorations. In the fall of 1952 we learned that the sixteenth-century writers, describing the Indian cultures of Mexico, had recorded that certain mushrooms played a divinatory role in the religion of the natives. Simultaneously we learned that certain pre-Columbian stone artifacts resembling mushrooms, most of them roughly a foot high, had been turning up, usually in the highlands of Guatemala, in increasing numbers. . . . We spoke up, declaring that the so-called "mushroom stones" really represented mushrooms, and that they were the symbol of a religion, like the Cross in the Christian religion, or the Star of Judea, or the Crescent of the Moslems. . . . This Middle American cult of a divine mushroom, this cult of "God's Flesh" . . . can be traced back to about 1500 B.C. . . . the earliest period in which man was in sufficient command of his technique to be able to carve stone. Thus we find a mushroom in the center of the cult with perhaps the oldest continuous history in the world. . . . The cult still existed in the Sierra Mazateca, in Oaxaca. And so we went there, in 1953. . . . We found a revelation, in the true meaning of that abused word, which for the Indians is an everyday feature, albeit a Holy Mystery, of their lives.[18]

The Wassons made many trips to Mexico, to the different regions, studying the various aspects of the use of the mushrooms. They enlisted eminent collaborators. One of these was Professor Roger Heim, the French mycologist, Director of the Musée National d'Histoire Naturelle, who visited Mexico with the Wassons on several occasions in order to make on-the-spot studies of the sacred mushrooms. The following species of mushrooms, many of them new to science, made up the Wasson-Heim list of hallucinogenic mushrooms used in Mexico: *Cantharellaceae-Conocybe siliginoides*, growing on dead tree trunks; *Strophariaceae-Psilocybe mexicana*, a small, tawny inhabitant of wet pastures, apparently the most highly prized by the users; *Psilocybe aztecorum*, called "children of the waters" by the Aztecs; *Psilocybe zapotecorum*, of marshy ground and known by the Zapotecs as "crown of thorns mushroom"; *Psilocybe caerulescens* var. *mazatecorum*, the so-called "landslide mushroom"; *Psilocybe caerulescens* var. *migripes*, which has a native name meaning "mushroom of superior reason"; and *Stropharia cubensis*.[19]

While we are on the subject of botanical identities, we might mention the later work of Singer and Guzman, who in 1957 found several additional species of *Psilocybe* used. As noted before, Wasson disputes Puharich's assertion that *Amanita muscaria* is used at all by the Mexicans. It will be recalled that *Panaeolus sphinctrinus* was identified as one of the *teonancatl* mushrooms by Schultes in 1938. Hallucinogenic activity was reported for a related species, *Panaeolus papilionaceus*, found in Oxford County, Maine. A note in *Science* reported that unsuspecting ingestion of this mushroom by two persons resulted in visual and hallucinatory effects comparable to hashish, opium, and "mescal." The mushroom was said to be "common on cultivated land."[20] More

[18] R. Gordon Wasson, "The Hallucinogenic Fungi of Mexico." *Psychedelic Review*, #1, 1963, pp. 27–42.

[19] Richard E. Schultes, "Botanical Sources of the New World Narcotics." *Psychedelic Review*, #2, 1963, p. 161.

[20] A. E. Verrill, "A Recent Case of Mushroom Intoxication." *Science*, XL, 1029, 1914, p. 408.

recently, Maurice B. Walters reported hallucinogenic activity for *Pholiota spectabilis*, a mushroom unrelated to the psilocybes. It is also fairly common in North America.[21] This writer had the experience of ingesting ground-up mushrooms, which had been collected in the Denver, Colorado, City Park, whose identity the finder refused to divulge for fear that spreading this knowledge would lead to legal restrictions on the noble fungus. The effects of this mushroom were completely hallucinogenic, comparable in all ways to the effects of synthetic psilocybin, with which I was very familiar. We may expect a rich, growing harvest of psychedelic fungi (as well as higher plants) as dedicated and ingenious amateur "theobotanists" investigate the vegetable kingdom for other active species during the next fifty years or so.

Those who are inclined to dismiss Wasson's theory of mycophobia versus mycophilia need only consider the fact that hallucinogenic mushrooms grow wild and are common on the North American continent, yet have never been used for religious or psychic purposes. Our distrust of fungi makes us surround them with so many taboos that we end up, like Professor Safford, even denying their existence in other lands. The mycophilic Mexicans, on the other hand, quietly use our imports, whose value we don't even realize: *Stropharia cubensis*, which is hallucinogenic, was not known in preconquest Mexico, because it grows in cow dung, and cows came to the New World with the Spanish. The Indians discovered the properties of the mushroom while the whites were busy denying it existed.

Wasson's other main collaborator on the chemical aspects of the mushrooms was the renowned Albert Hofmann of the Sandoz Laboratories in Basel, whose accidental discovery of the psychedelic properties of LSD in 1943 may well be regarded by future generations as one of the turning points of Western civilization, and who has devoted much of his professional life to the extraction of the active principles of various native hallucinogens, and their subsequent synthesis. Hofmann soon identified psilocybin as the main active principle in the mushrooms, along with smaller quantities of psi-

[21] Maurice B. Walters, "Pholiota Spectabilis, a Hallucinogenic Fungus." *Mycologia*, Sept./Oct. 1965.

locin. Psilocin is 4-hydroxydimethyltryptamine; psilocybin is the same, with an added phosphor group. Both are indole alkaloids, like LSD, and are related chemically and in activity to the neural transmitter substance serotonin. Psilocybin is probably converted to psilocin in the body. The effects of these tryptamines are roughly comparable to LSD, differing primarily in the duration of the effect, which is about half as long as LSD. Numerous studies have been done on the pharmacological and psychological effects of psilocybin. Wasson's 1962 bibliography listed a total of 362 technical and lay items;[22] since that time the number has probably passed 1000. These lie outside the scope of this article.

The use of the sacred mushrooms is heavily concentrated on Oaxaca, where it is used by the Mazatecs, Chinantecs, Chatinos, Zapotecs, Mixtecs, and Mijes. In each tribe the preferred species of mushroom and the particular rituals used vary somewhat. Secrecy about the mushrooms toward foreigners is the general practice. Puharich wrote, "The first thing one learns from the Chatinos is that no one of them will publicly admit that the sacred mushroom exists, that a rite involving its use exists, or that any practitioners of the rite exist."[23] Wasson makes a great deal of the religious motivation of the *curanderos*. "Performing before strangers is a profanation," and "the curandero who today, for a big fee, will perform the mushroom rite for any stranger is a prostitute and a faker."[24] Yet Wasson's own original *curandera*, the famous María Sabina, does perform rituals for strangers, sometimes for a fee, sometimes not.[25] It is hard for an outsider to evaluate the motivations of a Mexican *curandera*. According to recent reports, there are now always a dozen or so Americans in Hu-

[22] R. Gordon Wasson, "The Hallucinogenic Mushrooms of Mexico and Psilocybin: A Bibliography." *Botanical Museum Leaflets*, Vol. 20, No. 2, Harvard University, 1962.

[23] Andrija Puharich, M.D., "The Sacred Mushroom and the Question of its Role in Human Culture." Unpublished research memorandum, 1962.

[24] Wasson, op. cit. (18), pp. 34–35.

[25] Frederick Swain, "The Mystical Mushroom," *Tomorrow*, Autumn 1962. Also in *Psychedelic Review*, #2, 1963, pp. 219–29. See also Nat Finkelstein, "Honghi, Meester?" *Psychedelic Review*, #10, 1967.

autla during the mushroom season, June through August, looking for the inevitable *"honghi."* Some obtain the mushrooms and take them on their own. One American flipped out and tried to eat a live turkey while on such a trip, causing María Sabina great difficulties with local authorities. One need reach for no deeper reason than historical experience to explain the reticence of mushroom cults toward outsiders. As in America today, they have always been persecuted and vilified. Their very survival has depended to a large extent on secrecy.

We find that the mushrooms are referred to by various terms of endearment, such as *los niños,* "the children," or *las mujercitas,* "the little women," or most romantically, "the noble princes of the waters." In some areas, the *mujercitas* have to be eaten along with some *hombrecitos,* "little men," a different species of mushroom easily identified by its virile shape. But this is consumed for ritual purposes only, since only the "little women" give the psychic effect.

Wasson has taken photographs of a young girl grinding the mushrooms (also the *Ipomoea* seeds or the leaves of *Salvia divinorum*) on a grinding stone, in a posture identical to that found on the famous Guatemalan "mushroom stones," dating back twenty-five hundred years.

Not all the tribes have *curanderas* as such. The Mazatecs do, and usually the *curandera* takes twice as many mushrooms as the other voyagers. She decides who else takes them, and her energies dominate the session. In the Mije country, on the other hand, there are no *curanderas* as such; most of the families know how to use the mushrooms. One person takes them alone, with another present as observer. The reasons for consulting the mushrooms are medical and divinatory: to find a diagnosis and cure for an otherwise intractable condition; to find lost objects, animals, or people; or to get advice on personal problems or some great worry.

The use of the mushrooms for purposes of divination is accepted as a matter of fact. Demonstrations of its capacity to bring about states of higher vision have been convincingly made. A double telepathic experience was reported by the psychiatrist Dr. Margaret A. Paul under the mushroom *Aman-*

ita pantherina, a close relative of *A. muscaria.*[26] Wasson has described his own experience with María Sabina on his first session with the psilocybe mushroom.

Well, the *Curandera* María Sabina asked us what the questions were that were troubling us in the afternoon before the session. We were at a loss, because we had no questions that were troubling us, we just wished to see the ceremony. But, naturally, we had to comply with her request, and I said: "We have not heard from my son who is working in Cambridge, Massachusetts, and we are worried about him (which was not true) and we would like to know how he is faring." Now for an Indian in that country this means that you are really worried about the person, and so she went to work, and in the course of the evening she told us three things about him. She said: "He's not in Cambridge." (She didn't know what Cambridge was.) "He's in your home." I wrote notes down—and it's all in my contemporary notes—she said: "He's in your home. He's not in that other place." (It seemed awfully odd that she should volunteer this —there was no reason for it, but anyway we wrote it down.) And then she said: "He has an emotional disturbance, he reaches even to tears and it's over a girl." Well, we wrote this down—we didn't know anything about it and then finally she said: "I see the Army reaching out for him, I don't know whether the Army will get him." Well, we dismissed it. We didn't think at all about it. Then I got back to New York and was busy in banking, and then I went to Europe on a banking trip, and in Geneva a cablegram reached me from my wife saying that Peter insists on enlisting, and please to cable him not to do so. Well, I sent him a cable and it was too late and he had enlisted in the Army. Then, why had he enlisted in the Army? A letter followed and I learned that he had been in terrible emotional turmoil over a girl about whom he had never spoken to us. Oh, the first thing we discovered on returning to our apartment in New York —it was in an awful turmoil—there had been a party thrown there [laughter] and the bills of the purveyors were all accumulated for the very week-end that we had had this session with María Sabina And Peter made no bones about it—"Oh yes, I went down with three or four friends from Cambridge." And they had staged a party there Then the next thing was this Army business and then the next thing was that he had been in an awful turmoil over a girl who was living in New Haven. I have no explanation for that at all.[27]

Wasson's answer, when asked if he believed in ESP, was, "I don't believe; and I don't disbelieve. It's not my line." Re-

[26] Margaret A. Paul, "Two Cases of Altered Consciousness with Amnesia Apparently Telepathically Induced." *Psychedelic Review,* #8, 1966, p. 48.

[27] R. Gordon Wasson, Transcript of Discussion, held in Montreal, November 23, 1961.

search on supernormal perceptual processes, as demonstrated here and in Doctor Paul's cases, is sadly lacking and definitely indicated by the evidence brought up so far.

Where a *curandera* is present, she carries a thread of song almost continuously throughout the session, for many hours on end, with brief intermittent rests. The words vary slightly from session to session; the melodic line stays the same. Recordings have been published of the Mazatec ceremony, and anyone can hear for himself the forces that are collected and transmitted through these chants. Mixing Christian and Indian mythology, they run the whole conceivable range of incarnations and emotions. In addition, the *curandera* may emit a complex percussive beat, slapping thighs, forehead, arms. "The Mazatec communicants are participants with the *curandera* in an extempore religious colloquy. Her utterances elicit spontaneous responses from them, responses that maintain a perfect harmony with her and with each other, building up to a quiet, swaying, antiphonal chant. In a successful ceremony this is an essential element."[28]

In considering the Mexican ritual, we cannot forget that this is what remains among a primitive, illiterate people of a practice once widespread throughout the powerful Aztec empire. The ritual does not have the integrative synthetic qualities of the American peyote ritual, though most firsthand accounts agree that, depending, no doubt, on the wisdom and experience of the *curandera*, it can definitely induce a total transcendent experience.

Another and complex chapter in the checkered and colorful history of the divine mushroom was initiated in August 1960, when, in a villa near Cuernavaca, Dr. Timothy Leary, a Harvard psychologist, ate seven of the mushrooms given him by a scientist from the University of Mexico. "I was whirled through an experience which could be described in many extravagant metaphors but which was above all and without question the deepest religious experience of my life."[29] The experience triggered off over the next seven years a series of events that have been amply described and debated in the

[28] R. G. Wasson, op. cit. (18), p. 41.
[29] Timothy Leary, "The Religious Experience: Its Production and Interpretation," *Psychedelic Review*, #3, 1964, p. 324.

popular press and that have played a central role in the re-emergence on the North American continent of a religious revival using psychedelic plants and drugs as sacraments.

Etymology and Prehistory

The word "mushroom" is derived from the old French *mouscheron*, which in turn is based on *mousse*, moss. "In popular use," according to Webster, "mushroom denotes any edible variety, as opposed to the poisonous ones (*toadstools*)." Immediately we are back in a circle of associations of mushrooms with toads, bufotenine, the witches. Perhaps, as the Wassons argued, toadstool, like the French *crapaudin*, was originally the specific name of the demonic fly amanita, the German *Fliegenschwamm*. Flies, bugs, maggots are popular mythic embodiments of madness and possession (e.g., "la mouche luimonte à la tête"), as readers of Sartre and William Golding well know.

Another interesting line of inquiry opens up when the association of mushrooms with thunder is explored. We have already mentioned the Chukchee tale of lightning dragging his mushroom-possessed sister thunder across the floor of heaven by her foot. In ancient Greece and Rome, as well as in Mexico, it was believed that the growth of mushrooms is directly related not only to rain, but to thundery weather. Similar etymological and folkloric links can be found in Japan, the Philippines, Malagasy, Tadzhikistan, and among the Maoris, where *whatitiri* means both "thunder" and "mushroom." The Mazatec Indians call the mushroom *nti si tho* and the Mije Indians *tu muh*. In both languages the word means "that which sprouts by itself," i.e., without seed. The Zapotec Indian *curandero*, after gathering the mushrooms, invokes the "Powers" that control the mushrooms: the Earth, God the Father, the Trinity, the "Great Lightning Bolt that bred the mushrooms," and the "Great Lightning Bolt that injected blood into the mushrooms." Does this mean that the lightning bolt, "the strength of the earth," as the *curandero* called it, is thought of as impregnating the earth, and their offspring is the divine mushroom, without seed? Father Sky

nd Mother Earth form a mythic polarity common to many
American Indian tribes.

Wasson's theory is that at some preliterate stage in man's
early history, the mushrooms with extraordinary powers were
discovered and "served as an agent for the very fission of his
soul, releasing his faculty for self-perception, as a stimulant
for the imagination of the seer, the poet, the mystic. . . .
May not the hallucinatory mushrooms have been the most
holy secret of the Mysteries?"[30]

Puharich also has argued for the existence of a cult of the
divine mushroom in the early Eurasian cultures centered
around the powerful Sumero-Akkadian city-states of the third
millennium B.C. And in 1926 Henri Frankfort reported the
discovery of an ancient Egyptian temple in Byblos (on the
Mediterranean coast of Lebanon), dating back to the middle
of the third millennium B.C., in which a green jasper seal was
found. This seal shows a Horus priest giving two mushrooms
to a supplicant. Over the mushroom is a hare, which is the
sacred symbol of the Hittite god of rain, thunder, and lightning.

Such archaeological, etymological, and mythological frag-
ments must at present be regarded as mere tiny pieces of
the history of man's strange ambivalent relationship to the
hallucinogenic, psychedelic plants and drugs. It may be
decades before the missing pieces are placed together to give
a coherent picture. For the present we cannot much improve
on the poetic formulation of Wasson's Indian guide, who
when asked why the mushroom was called "that which
springs forth," replied:

El honguillo viene por sí mismo, no se sabe de donde,
como el viento que viene sin saber de donde ni porqué.

The little mushroom comes of itself, no one knows whence,
like the wind that comes we know not whence nor why.[31]

[30] R. Gordon Wasson, "Lightning Bolt and Mushrooms, An Essay in Early Cultural Exploration," in *Roman Jakobson: Essays on
the Occasion of His Sixtieth Birthday*, The Hague, Mouton & Co.,
1956, p. 610.
[31] Henri Frankfort, quoted in Puharich, op. cit., (23).

SOME ANTHROPOLOGICAL
ASPECTS OF YAGE

JEFFREY LINZER

Alfred Metraux (1948) relates a Cashinawa tribe story of th
origin of yage, called *ayahuasca* by these South American I
dians:

The intoxicating properties of *ayahuasca* were revealed to men by
water spirit. A man who had observed her intimate relations with
tapir, managed to capture her. She took him under the water an
gave him a decoction of *ayahuasca*, which provoked strange troubl
in him, but also made him see wonderful visions. He returned to th
world and revealed the secret to his fellow tribesmen. He was swa
lowed successively by several serpents, but still had time to teac
men how to use *ayahuasca*.

While the legend suggests that yage has roots in the myth
past, its use remained unknown to Western scientists unt
little more than a century ago. According to Schultes (1965
the earliest mention of yage seems to be that of Villavicenci
in his geography of Ecuador, written in 1858. Since that tim
numerous anthropologists and pharmacologists have invest
gated the drug, and what must be regarded as a composit
picture of its nature and use has taken shape.

Known by various indigenous names, such as *ayahuasc
natéma, caapi,* and others, yage is used regularly by the I
dians of the regions along the affluents of the upper Orinoc
and upper Amazon rivers (Cooper, 1948). In northwester
Brazil and in adjacent parts of Colombia, it is termed *caap
in Amazonian Bolivia, Peru, and Ecuador, *ayahuasca*; alon
the eastern foothills of the Andes in Colombia and Ecuado
it is yage (Schultes, 1965).

Yage is cultivated over most of the area, but it is als
gathered wild. In 1908, Spruce identified the source of th
drug as *Banisteria caapi*, a woody vine of the family Ma
pighiaceae. More recently, Schultes (1965) reports that yag
is now known to be a decoction or infusion prepared basical

rom species of *Banisteriopsis*, mainly *B. caapi*, *B. inebrians*, nd *B. rusbyana*.

In 1928, Lewin, among the first to investigate the active rinciples of *Banisteria caapi*, found that the alkaloid iso- ated from this plant, named "telepathine," "yageine," or "banisterine," was identical with harmine, an alkaloid from he seeds of wild rue. In the molecule of harmine is the ndole nucleus found in serotonin, which is also present in eserpine and LSD-25. Recent chemical investigations by Iochstein and Paradies (1957) suggest that, in addition, the lkaloids harmaline and d-tetrahydroharmine, discovered in 3. *caapi*, "may have substantial psychotomimetic activity n their own right."

Prepared as a boiled decoction or a cold-water infusion, the age drink may require repeated doses and comparatively arge quantities to be effective, depending on the potency f the particular preparation. Its immediate effect, according o Karsten (1935), Taylor (1963), and Lowie (1948), is lmost instantaneous vomiting, both by the experienced In- lians and by the explorers who have tried it. This was not loted by Harner (1966) or Schultes (1965). Norman Taylor 1963) has written of this facet of yage:

his vomiting, in fact, is apparently Nature's method of preparing he user for the final effects. Pharmacologists have described the ini- ial reactions as giving rise to "coarse tremors and colonic convul- ions." Following this purification, yage begins the work for which the ndians have cultivated it for centuries.

Lowie (1948) reports fantastic, hashish-type hallucinations mong the yage experiences of the Tucano tribe of the north- vest Amazon region. Visions appear, huge and brilliantly olored; multihued snakes are frequently encountered. The nost common effects of yage among the Tucano are vomiting, ollowed by trembling and giddiness. Giddiness leads to xhaustion and deep sleep, in which occur visions of intense ividness, imbued with a bluish light. Perhaps the most inique of the yage effects reported by Lowie is the presence f clairvoyance and the capacity for communication with the spirit world." Claims for such powers are considered to be nfounded by Schultes (1965).

Harner (1966), who first encountered yage among the

Jivaro Indians in eastern Ecuador in 1956, notes this sense of clairvoyance among the features common to the experience. He reports the experience of the soul as separate from the body; the viewing of one's own death; the feeling of flying sometimes as a great bird; the seeing of cities as from a great height; and sharper vision in the dark. A common vision, noted by Harner, is the encounter with jungle animals, such as tigers, jaguars, and snakes.

In a study on the effects of yage on volunteers at the University of Chile, Dr. Claudio Naranjo (1966) found that a number of the experiences were remarkably similar to those reported to Harner (1966) by the Indians of Ecuador and Peru. Encounters with predatory animals were reported, although none of the urban volunteers had been told that the drug came from the Amazon, nor had they ever visited a jungle where such animals lived. Harner states (1966): "Just what causes the similarities is an entirely open question. It would be a mistake just to ascribe it to a biochemical reaction without more research being done."

Karsten (1935), working in Ecuador, remarked:

White settlers at Canelos and Macas who have tried yage have in part had the same experiences as the Indians, seeing wonderful landscapes, hills, and rivers, beautiful birds, etc. Those particular "spirits," on the other hand, whom the Indians profess to see, do not of course present themselves to a person who does not share their religious ideas and superstitions.

The most comprehensive account of the "religious ideas and superstitions" of the Indians of the upper Amazon region is Karsten's description of the Jivaro traditions in *The Head-Hunters of Western Amazonas* (1935).

The Jivaros believe that *only* in dreams is true reality revealed. Normal, waking life is held to be a delusion. In dreams, the truth is told through the agent of spirits and demons, who act as friends and advisers. There are no enemies in the dream visions, for it is the impersonal soul that speaks.

While dreams occurring in natural sleep do have prognostic significance, it is only in yage-induced dreams that the spirits are compelled by conjuration to give information about future events. It is this precious power of divination that is

specially prized by the Indians. The spirits consulted in the
yage dream state are essentially ancestors, but are also considered to be the souls of the banisteria vines.

Among the Jivaros, the state of intoxicated revelation is
called *wuímektinyu*, which means "to see." They see fantastic landscapes, with their representative spirits. Hill spirits are especially important, because these are the souls of
dead sorcerers, who hold a position of special importance in
Jivaro society. In general, visions appropriate to the occasion
appear, in the form of ancestors, personified objects, and
other spirits, which are consulted for advice.

The Jivaro warrior is able to benefit from the appearance
in his yage dream of these spirit forms because of a whole
background of mythological and cultural beliefs. When he
meets the spirits, the "Old Ones," he is not surprised or hor-
rified, as we might be, for he is familiar from childhood with
the spirit mythology. The tribe has two mythic ancestors; both
are warriors, who give advice in matters of war. Most of the
other spirits take the form of animal demons, mainly of three
categories.

First are the feline animals, "soacha"—tigers, cougars, those
jungle beasts that haunt the yage hallucinations of so many
white explorers.

The second category of animal demons includes the Giant
Snake, the great mythical water monster, "pangi," whose symbolism extends far beyond the realm of the Jivaro yage dream.

The other group of dream animals met under yage are the
jungle birds, which are large birds of prey.

Concerning these standard yage images, Naranjo has written (1966): "It seems that the kind of experience a person
has with the tiger or dragon—the potentially hostile creature
—depends on his way of experiencing himself." As in Jungian analysis, wherein one becomes acquainted with the dark
aspects of the unconscious, the Jivaro does not fear the demon
or animal he has dreamed about if he meets him later in
waking form. Karsten writes (1935): "In the dream he has,
once and for all, become acquainted with these phenomena,
normally so terrible to the Indians; he knows their true nature and has been hardened against them."

If in yage sleep no dreams occur, it is regarded as a bad

omen; the elders concur that the dreamless individual "is no
a real man." Thus there is sociocultural pressure upon the
Jivaro to dream and to face the demons of the dream uncon
scious. If the yage taker sees demons and becomes fright
ened, this too is adjudged a bad omen by the elders.

Because of the effects and mythological significance of yage
a number of ritual occasions and annual feasts have deve
oped that center around the drug. One of the most importar
of these is the victory feast of the Jivaro head-hunters, de
scribed by Karsten (1935), which follows the conquest of a
enemy. On the first day, no drugs are used, and the ritua
consists of singing and dancing from evening to mornin,
culminating in a beautiful ritual, the bath in the river. All the
ceremonies connected with this feast have the object of pre
tecting the victor from the spirit of his defeated enemy.

The second day of the victory feast is called "the drinking
of the *natéma*," *natéma* being the Jivaro word for yage. Ritua
preparation includes the crushing, boiling, and mixing with
tobacco of the banisteriopsis vine. An ornate ceremonia
schedule attends this preparation of the yage.

The object of the initial ceremony is to establish a spir
tual connection between the slayer, who is supposed to b
filled with supernatural power, and the yage drink itsel
with its attendant spirits. The drinking is ceremonial; every
one "who wants to dream," including every member of the
slayer's family, partakes. The victory feast is indeed a com
munity project, a form of ritual group ecstasy.

Two rows of beautifully ornamented clay dishes contribut
to the formal setting within the house of the slayer. Befor
each of the repeated drinkings, a long conjuration is sung b
the drinker, summoning the yage spirits. Ritual vomiting,
such a term is conceivable, follows each drink. As the drink
ing ceremony has been preceded by ritual fasting, it is on'
the yage that is vomited up. When the drinking has bee
repeated a sufficient number of times, the slayer and h
family remain in their house and lapse into the dream stat
while the other participants retire to the forest to dream.

Later, the dreams are told to and interpreted by the elder
The object of yage drinking at the victory feast is to asce
tain whether everything will turn out favorably for the slay

-whether he will have a long life, attain material prosperity, nd be lucky in his undertakings. These are revealed symboli-ally in the dreams of the slayer and his nearest relatives. t the same time, the other drinkers who have partaken of he sacred drink are personally benefited by being purified rom impure and disease-bringing matter, and gaining strength or their respective occupations.

In the early evening, ritual dancing begins, and is con-inued through the entire night until sunrise, ending in he ritual river bath.

The victory feast and similar celebrations are special yage vents. A much more regular use of the drug, involving a itual of a very different nature, is involved in its use by the haman, or medicine man. This specialist is consulted in ll matters of particular importance, and, by drinking an es-ecially strong decoction of yage, he confers with the spirits. he preparation of the drink is different from that employed t festivals; a whole day of boiling the vine, accompanied y intensive ritual chanting, produces a very strong decoction.

The procedure followed by the medicine man in the proc-ss of divination and curing follows a prescribed ritual pat-ern (Karsten, 1935). Following the preparation of the age, in the evening, the curer drinks a quantity of the trong decoction, then visits the home of the person seeking elp. Working in complete darkness, the medicine man drinks obacco water and chants a long conjuration imploring the pirit of tobacco to take possession of him to aid in the diag-osis. After another cup of yage, he leans over the prone pa-ient and begins to sing prescribed conjurations. In the course f chanting, he may drink more yage. In fact, he may take s many doses as are necessary for him to achieve the de-red level of intoxication. If this level were not attained, he ould not conjure forth the required demons, and the treat-ent would be to no avail. Yet this state must be provoked radually, in order to avoid overly violent outbursts of spiritual cstasy. It is for this reason that the drink is taken repeatedly small doses.

One of the main principles in Indian conjuration is that he remedy must be sought where the evil or disease has its rigins; the same spirits that have caused the illness must also be compelled to cure it. The medicine man sends the conjuring words through his hand to that part of the patient's body believed to be the seat of the evil. He chants, for example:

I, myself [conjure you demons],
the water boa, possessing the arrow,
and the anaconda, the anaconda,
you that were once men,
and whose "arrows" I have seen when
intoxicated by yage,
you that are full of arrows;
the tiger, sending the arrow,
[may you come] to draw out the arrow! (Karsten, 1935)

Ackerknect (1948) has pointed out that divination, involving contact with the supernatural, often in conjunction with a trance, is the usual diagnostic method among primitives. The South American medicine man, however, has specialized in the *artificial* trance; nowhere else are drugs so consistently used to induce this state.

Among the Jivaros and Canelos tribes, divination consisting of yage trance is continually practiced by the medicine man or shaman, chiefly in connection with the treatment of illnesses. The shaman is considered a physician, not a priest his chief business is to kill or harm other people, enemies with sorcery, and to cure the evils sent by enemy sorcerers

To become a member of this very respected craft requires a solemn and challenging period of initiation, involving stringent ascetic practices and serious study. Just as drinking yage is essential in the practice of South American sorcery, so it plays a vital role in the training process. The novice shaman drinks this drug every morning to familiarize himself with the demons who will serve as his medical assistants in the future. In ritual dreams under yage, he goes to the riverbank and summons the anaconda demon, who rises from the river speaks to him as a friend, and gives him the *tunchi*, the important Magic Arrow, symbolic of the sting of the venomous snake. The shaman, in his operation, behaves like a poisonous snake poised for action. He is supposed to carry the poison in his mouth; when he shoots his "arrow," he whistles and hisses.

The office of shaman is not without its disadvantages. A Jivaro or Canelos medicine man is reserved and taciturn, states Karsten (1935); his eyes are dull and veiled, a consequence of his permanent habit of yage drinking.

In the Jivaro traditions, representative of the ritual use of yage among the many tribes of the upper Orinoco and upper Amazon rivers, we see the use of a psychedelic drug as an integral part of community life. The extent to which yage plays a role in the culture of South American Indian tribes is indicated by Villavicencio in his geography of Ecuador, written in 1858. Yage is used, he reported,

to foresee and answer accurately in difficult cases, be it to reply opportunely to ambassadors from other tribes in a question of war; to decipher plans of the enemy through the medium of this magic drink and take proper steps for attack and defense; to ascertain, when a relative is sick, what sorcerer has put on the hex; to carry out a friendly visit to other tribes; to welcome foreign travelers or, at least, to make sure of the love of their womenfolk.

(Schultes, 1965)

MARIJUANA IN MOROCCO

TOD MIKURIYA

Morocco, on the north coast of Africa directly across the Strait of Gibraltar from Spain, is the closest country to Western Europe where marijuana is extensively grown and used by the inhabitants. It is a poor country, with the per capita income less than $200 per year. Morocco obtained its independence from Spain and France only in 1956. Marijuana is grown in quantity by the mountain-dwelling "unacculturated" Berber tribes in the Rif Mountains and is sold in the partially Westernized coastal plains.

Kif is the Moroccan word for marijuana. It is a general name that covers all preparations smoked. These preparations are different from those encountered in North America in that only the blossoms of the mature female plant are used. Another difference is that the blossoms are always mixed with an equal amount of tobacco. Its use is widespread through out the country among adult males, as it has been for cen turies.

From August 20–23, 1966, I had the opportunity to trave in the Rif Mountains area in the province of Alhucemas Morocco. During this period, I had the opportunity to ob serve the cultivation of kif, particularly near the towns o Ketama, Taksut, Taberrant and Tleta Ketama. Introduction and translations were facilitated by the Director of the Na tional Co-operative of Artisans for the Province of Alhucemas He is responsible for supervising the operations of handi craft manufacture for this province. As handicraft manu facture happens to take place in the kif-growing area, I coul observe the traditional activity as well.

With proper introductions by an individual occupying position of some importance locally, I found the people quit hospitable and friendly. During my visit I had the oppor tunity of sharing various native dishes from the communa bowls in the center of the traditional circle. The people wer quite open about answering any of my many questions. A the same time, they were fully aware of the "illegality" of kif Even the children that I met knew that it is forbidden t take kif into the lowlands. During this visit, I talked with law-enforcement officials and local farmers, as well as with village officials.

The Rif are a chain of mountains stretching across th northernmost area of Morocco. Except in the highest eleva tions (7000–8000 feet), they are generally hot and dry. Th terrain is quite rugged. The slopes are steep and rocky an often drop several thousand feet to the narrow canyons be low. In the central region of the mountains there is a smal plateau. The village of Ketama is located at its western edge

The area surrounding this central plateau is strongly remi niscent of many areas of the western United States, such a northern California and Colorado. There are small, rathe scanty strands of fir trees on the upper elevations. In th lower areas, the vegetation is mostly low shrubs and grasses During the short winter, from November to March, ther may be as much as two or three meters of snow at the highe elevations.

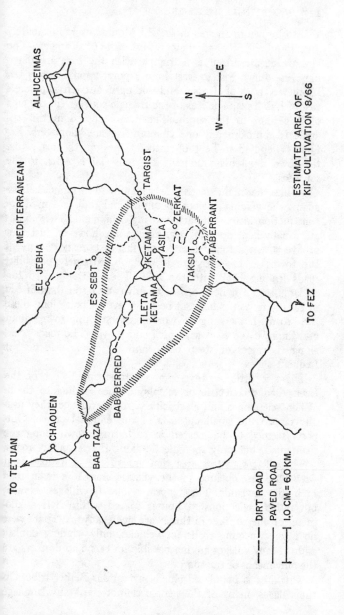

Kif is grown in an area in the Rif Mountains approximately one hundred fifty kilometers northeast of Tangier. The kif-growing area itself is a triangle with the base an imaginary line drawn east to west from a point approximately ten kilometers west of Targist and ending about ten kilometers east of Bab Taza. The legs of the triangle converge in the area of Taberrant to the south. The area included in this triangle is approximately one thousand square kilometers. Ketama is reputed to be the center of the growth area, while the town reputedly producing the most kif is Asila, to the southeast.

While the main roads are generally well-surfaced macadam, the grading is poor, because hand tools are used for construction instead of earth-moving equipment. These roads are usually kept open all year. There are, however, just four or five towns actually located on first-class roads. Many of the towns in the area are located on extremely poor dirt roads leading back into the hills. These latter are so formidable that it is not possible to drive any faster than fifteen or twenty miles per hour, at best. At several spots along these rural roads, I saw gangs of workmen attempting to maintain and improve the road with pick and shovel. The roads wind along the faces of steep cliffs, and there was evidence of frequent slides.

There is little, if any, rural electrification. Most of the towns had no electric or telephone lines leading to them. When telephones and electricity were in evidence, they usually ran to the small outposts of the national police. Outposts seemed to be located in each small town along the main road, but only sporadically along the secondary roads. The villages in this area that are off the main road bear very little resemblance to the villages along the main road or in the lowlands. They appear not to be villages as such, but rather collections of houses spaced within half a kilometer of one another in these very steep canyons. There were no interconnecting roads for vehicles, only winding donkey paths. Many villages are inaccessible for cars, and donkeys are the only means of transport.

This area is populated chiefly by various Berber tribes. In the villages, many of the people cannot speak any language ther than their native dialects. They often cannot speak Arabic. In most towns, however, Arabic is spoken, and occasionally French or Spanish is used as a secondary language. The language barrier may be the reason that they are a people not easily assimilated into the cultures of the "European" cities of the coast or the "Arabic" cities of the plains and foothills.

For perhaps a thousand years the tribes have rather successfully resisted outside influences from a succession of invaders that range from the ancient Phoenicians and Romans to the modern French and Spanish.

The Berbers seem to have a strong sense of private property and know exactly whose field is whose. The various families through the generations have taken much effort to build and maintain the neatly terraced fields that sit precariously on the steep, rocky slopes.

Throughout North Africa, these people are referred to as "The Berber Problem" because of their resistance to assimilation. Often along the road and again in the isolated villages, I saw men carrying ancient rifles on their backs. When I asked about this, I was told that they weren't really rifles, but were "just part of tradition."

Taksut is located in one of the myriad steep, craggy canyons so characteristic of the central Rif Mountains. The barren, gray mica-schist walls tower around the narrow, steep floor of the canyon. The fields are terraced with local stone in order to create level land for the cultivation of crops. Small, flat-roofed adobe houses are spaced several meters apart and surrounded by the family fields.

Taksut is not on the rather complete Michelin road map. It is located about seventy kilometers southwest of the town of Targist. The town is at the end of a spur of a road so primitive that only large trucks and four-wheeled vehicles can pass safely. During snowfall in the winter, it is isolated from the rest of the world. The road comes to an abrupt rocky end on the outskirts of this town. There are no streets—only donkey paths.

The center of town is just across a footbridge and up through some large boulders. This is just a small, unpaved space around which there is a little cluster of houses and two tiny general stores. Throughout the town, the buildings ar often built around the boulders or perched on top. Ther is a small stream nearby. There is no city hall, post offic or other evidence of government services in this town. Ther is no telephone or electricity and no evidence of a moder sewage system. No health services are provided.

As one goes from the center over the tortuous trails, th outlying houses are surrounded by larger plots of ground. Th fields are more rock than dirt, although much work has gon into clearing the rocks. The terraces of these fields are mad from the cleared rocks.

The fields around Taksut are planted about 50 per cent ki The remaining crops are corn, wheat, legumes, and truc garden products such as tomatoes and melons. Besides agr culture, the town is supported by artisans working in th home. Taksut has no one specialty in handicrafts, but rath depends on the work of several individuals who specialize i making such items as leather hassocks, leather purses an handbags, rugs, pseudoantique firearms, and hand-tied rug The population of this little town/valley was estimated l some of its residents to be between three and five hundre

The economy of this area is almost solely supported b the cultivation of kif. In the central areas of growth, it is th only crop. The individuals involved in kif production in thes areas must even purchase staple goods rather than grow the themselves. In the peripheral areas, however, more of th other crops are in evidence. These are apparently both f local consumption and limited cash crops. Although no a curate estimate can be made of the total area and yield, th area planted in kif is probably in the thousands of squa kilometers, with an output in the range of thousands of kil grams per square kilometer of marketable product.

The corn and wheat crops are quite poor in quality, wit yields of perhaps less than one bushel per acre. Concernin the yield of kif, the average is estimated by the local farn ers as being two kilograms per square meter of marketab product (dried tops and stems; the leaves are not included The farmers receive five dirham (one dirham equals twen cents) per kilogram of this product from the individuals wh come up from the lowlands with trucks to take the produ for distribution in the cities. The selling price in the cities jumps to between fifteen and fifty dirham per kilogram. Products refined further, those in which the blossoms have been separated from the stems and seeds, may bring up to two hundred dirham per kilo. These blossoms are mixed with an equal amount of high-grade tobacco, grown primarily in other sections. I did not see any cultivation of this tobacco in the area I visited.

Kif is planted in this high, mountainous region early in March, shortly after the spring snows have thawed. Male plants are culled when the plants are old enough for sex to be determined. It is harvested during the month of August and in early September, when the blossoms are ripe but before their plants go to seed.

The government attempts to practice a policy of containment. While it prohibits new areas of kif production, it allows those already in production to be maintained. The nature of this control is shown by the fact that in Taberrant, a comparatively inaccessible town, the national gendarmery had destroyed several unauthorized acres of kif growing there shortly before my visit.

Along the main road, at least at Bab Taza, Bab Berred, Ketama, and Targist, there are barricades and national gendarmery outposts. These outposts have telephones and sometimes short-wave radios for intercommunication. When I inquired what these were for, I was told that at night all trucks that pass through this area are searched. I was also told that most of the Moroccans who pass through the area have their luggage inspected at various bus stops. In my travels, however, I never saw this happen.

Along one of the dirt roads, I saw a weighing station, where some farmers had brought the dried kif to be picked up for shipment to the cities of the lowlands. I was not, unfortunately, able to find out more about the transportation arrangements. The regulation of kif is apparently a very complicated matter, handled by the Moroccan government in a way that seemed incomprehensible to me. It is apparent that large vehicles must be used for transporting the large amount of kif grown to the areas of consumption, but the exact arrangements for getting the kif to market were unclear. There

apparently must be some way of obtaining government "ap
proval" to enable these vehicles to take the crops to the citie
of the plains. The cultivation of kif in Morocco has gon
on for hundreds of years. Thousands of kilograms are con
sumed each year.

A situation of chronic unemployment in Morocco has bee
aggravated by the migration of Berbers with no industria
skills and who are not assimilated into either the Arabic o
the European culture. In 1965, Casablanca experienced riot
that necessitated seven days of martial law. These riots too
place primarily in the slum areas on the edge of the city
which are populated mostly by "displaced" Berbers.

I was told that five years ago there was an attempt to bur
kif fields in the mountains, but that this government effor
was met with armed opposition. The government ceased it
effort when it became apparent that this would be a lon
and costly struggle. The rugged terrain and the poor com
munications made effective resistance to the government cam
paign quite easy. In addition, pressures from people in th
cities who traffic in the huge quantities of kif were no
insignificant.

The government also realized that depriving the Berbers o
their chief, and often sole, cash crop would drive them from
their marginal rocky land, further inflaming the unemploy
ment problems in the cities.

The above observations and inferences illustrate the con
plexity of the problem of kif production in Morocco. The bar
ren marginal soil on which little else can be grown, combine
with the rugged terrain, poor roads, poor communica
tions, and the tradition among these people of resisting ou
side influence, interact with the pressure of large vested inter
ests in the transportation and distribution of kif as well as wit
a chronic unemployment situation. It is therefore unlikel
that any significant reduction of kif cultivation can be effecte
The situation of stalemate between the central governmen
and the Berbers of the Rif will probably continue for the fore
seeable future.

Kif is widely smoked by males throughout Morocco. It ma
have been introduced by one of the succession of Arab con
querors from the eastern Mediterranean countries durin

the seventh century A.D. Despite the efforts of various Arab, Spanish, and French rulers to suppress kif or at least tax it, its growth and use have continued to flourish.

Prohibitions against kif, according to some of the older kif users, or *kiefe*, were fewer during the Spanish-French partitioning of Morocco. For many years, it was taxed and concessions were allotted for growth and sale. As late as 1954, it was prepared in the form of packaged cigarettes by government-approved manufacturers. The efficacy of control by taxation and monopoly was not too effective, as seizures of contraband kif amounted to between one fifth and one half of the total legal output. The use of kif was finally made illegal in 1954.[1]

The fact that kif smoking is now illegal in Morocco has the effect of preventing the user from ostentaciously selling or smoking kif in the European sections of the larger coastal cities. Lack of respect for this recent law is hardly surprising, since the custom of kif use in Morocco has been present for centuries. The use of kif violates no Muslim holy law, which would provide another possibility of social control. By contrast, Muslims patronizing European bars are liable to summary arrest and incarceration; there seems to be a rising concern for the growing number of young men who are becoming alcohol users.

Unfavorable attitudes of the Moroccan Government seem not to stem from a general moral concern, but rather from a point of view that kif smoking may create more economic hardship in a people whose existence is marginal. The use of kif is also a symbol of the traditional order, which must be changed if the goals of Moroccan industrialization and self-sufficiency are to be achieved. Another factor may be pressure on the government from Western European and United States narcotics-law enforcement agencies to stop the growth and use of kif. It is said that the present king is not as well liked as his father, because he is attempting to suppress or discourage the use of kif.

As in Western Europe, England, and the United States,

[1] Benabud, A. "Psycho-pathological Aspects of the Cannabis Situation in Morocco: Statistical Data for 1956," *Bulletin on Narcotics*, 1957, 9 (4), 1–16.

the present incidence of kif smoking is impossible to estimate, due to the fact that it is illegal. Another stumbling block to estimation may be a reluctance to admit to a Westerner that one is at variance with practices of an alcohol culture that has (and economically still does) occupied a position of dominance. In addition, there are a substantial number of Moroccan men who have tried it at some time in the past, but have never become regular users. A group of users in the small town of Targist claimed that 20 per cent of the males are currently regular users, and that 90–95 per cent of the men have used kif at some time in that town. When asked about use among women, the answer almost universally elicited, both in rural Targist and urban Tangier, was, "No women use it around here, but I have heard that some use it in _____ [some other town or area]." In the rare contacts with Moroccan women, they answered that it was forbidden to them and that if they were caught using kif they would be beaten.

In Tangier, there was little evidence of kif smoking in the European sections of town, but within the Arab quarter (kasbah or medina), there was little to suggest non-use. Most stores selling handicraft sold the traditional pipes. Several small shops sold just pipes and pouches for the use of kif.

As one might expect, contacting Moroccan users is simple compared with a similar task in the United States, as it is far less dangerous to smoke kif in Morocco than to smoke marijuana in the United States. One need only ask about kif in a general way. If the man is a user, the chances are that he will smilingly proffer the traditional *supsi* pipe, which has a long wooden stem and a small clay bowl, happy to meet a foreigner who shares this common interest. If he is not a user, his reply carries with it the effect of one who does not use tobacco in the United States. He will usually admit to having tried it at one time, but not finding it to his liking.

The customs surrounding the use of kif in Morocco appear to be of a secular-social nature in contrast with those of the Hindu holy men of India described by Carstairs[2] as using

[2] Carstairs, G. M. "Daru and Bhang: Cultural Factors in the Choice of Intoxicant," *Quarterly Journal of Studies on Alcohol*, 1954, 15 (2), p. 228.

cannabis as a religious sacrament. In Arab sections of the cities, kif smoking is almost as ubiquitous as the highly sugared, mint-flavored tea that accompanies all but the most perfunctory of conversations.

The methods of kif smoking are quite different in Morocco from the ways in which marijuana is used in the United States. In the United States, use patterns, described by Becker[3] and Walton[4], are based on fear of discovery and avoiding waste of this precious commodity. By contrast, the Moroccan user is not concerned with waste, because kif is cheaper than tobacco. It is the custom to have the person who offers a *supsi* pipe load it, light it, and wipe the mouthpiece before handing it to the recipient. The recipient inhales the smoke deeply, but promptly exhales. He does not pass the half-smoked pipe to another, but continues to smoke leisurely until the first crackle is heard, as the heated ash approaches the bottom of the bowl. He then expels the remaining burning plug by blowing into the pipe. He either cleans, refills, relights, and passes the cleaned pipe to the next person, or passes the cleaned pipe and allows the recipient to use his own supply. In a group, often more than one pipe is used.

A similarity between the practices of United States marijuana smokers and the Moroccan kif smokers is the physical arrangement of the groups. Both groups tend to sit in circles, either around a table or else lounging about on the floor on cushions. This circular configuration may be to facilitate the passing of the pipe from one to another, or, wildly speculating, perhaps is a surviving vestige of the archetypal tribe around the communal fire. This may, however, be only coincidence, since lounging about on low cushions in a circle is usual practice in the Moroccan household.

Also similar was the content of the conversation during sessions of kif smoking. As with the United States user, his Moroccan counterpart often spins stories of legendary types and preparations of kif he has sampled, seen, or heard about. There were tales of oral preparations of cannabis combined

[3] Becker, H. S., *Outsiders; Studies in the Sociology of Deviance.* New York: The Free Press of Glencoe, 1963, pp. 47–48.

[4] Walton, R. P., *Marihuana: America's New Drug Problem.* Philadelphia: J. B. Lippincott, 1938, pp. 47–48.

with other substances purportedly given to children of mountain tribes to assuage the cold of night and help sedate them for the evening. A potent substance for eating, called amber, was described. A recipe for a special kif sweetmeat, majoon, was described. Majoon is usually compounded from powdered blossoms, sugar, honey, cinnamon, and almonds. It is baked in the hot sun until it reaches the consistency of a moist fudge. It is eaten by the "fingersful." The use of oral preparations was not observed.

Hashish, a more concentrated preparation, is much less common, but nevertheless widely known. Unfortunately, there was no opportunity to observe its manufacture during my short stay. One man in a village seems to be the local expert in its manufacture. Such a man exists in Ketama, the town in the middle of the growth area, but when I was there, he was out of town attending his wife, who expected to give birth to a child shortly. From descriptions by the residents, hashish is made from the blossoms and the leaves of the plant and takes at least two days to make, with many stages of cooking. This process differs from Norman Taylor's description of the manufacture of charas by harvesting pollen and resin by beating the blossoms on leather aprons.[5]

Terminologies for the effects and use of cannabis seemed to be relatively simple, considering its high incidence of use and long history of consumption. *Hashashut* means to feel the full effects of the cannabis. This term also appears to mean overdose. Moroccan users recognize both pleasurable and unpleasant effects of cannabis. *Fehrán* denotes having a pleasurable effect, a "good trip" in contemporary United States terms. *Teirala* means an unpleasant result, or unpleasant side effects, a bad trip. Unpleasant effects are described as related to overdosage. *Nashat* is a group of kif smokers. Few solitary kif users were seen. Its use appears to be primarily of a social nature, as it is in the United States. *Nashatu* refers to such a group lasting twenty-four hours. *Douach* means to become intoxicated with kif, or to "turn on."

The complexity of attitudes toward kif was illustrated by

[5] Taylor, N., *Narcotics: Nature's Dangerous Gifts*. New York: Dell Publishing Co., 1963, p. 14.

the behavior of my host and guide. This man, of some local importance in the province of Alhucemas, showed quite varying responses to the topic in different circumstances. When with men who were his social inferiors but not his subordinates, he would smile and speak affably of kif as if it were a fine wine, an experience that all should enjoy. He would refer to himself as a heavy user and describe the pleasure he derived. By contrast, when he was with people of like or superior station, he would minimize, but not deny, his use of kif. He would then portray himself as a light or intermittent user. One of his friends, a *caid* (mayor or chief) of a small village, showed a similar "selective" attitude. During lunch with him and the lesser officials of the town, the lesser officials smilingly admitted to regular smoking of kif, but the *caid* denied any use at all. After lunch, as we drove over the winding mountain roads to the next town, the *caid*, who accepted the proffered ride, volunteered that he used it at home regularly. He said it would not be proper to speak of such things in front of his employees. A parallel might be seen in the attitudes in contemporary America toward alcohol.

The chief differences in the use of cannabis between the United States and Morocco are smoking technique, pharmacology, and formality. Although kif is more readily available and cheaper in Morocco, it appeared from sessions with the Moroccan users that while much more is smoked than in the United States, much less is actually ingested. The practice of inhaling but *not* holding the breath might decrease significantly the amount of active principle absorbed. Combination of kif with tobacco would also decrease the amount of cannabis actually ingested. These differences in technique make comparison of dosage difficult.

Tobacco itself seems to play an important role in the smoking of kif. In several of the kif sessions, I would substitute pure kif blossoms for the standard mixture when the pipe passed my way. The response was fairly uniform. The recipient would take a few puffs, wait until he felt that I wasn't looking, discreetly discard the contents, and reload the pipe from his own supply. The respondent indicated only that he preferred kif-and-tobacco. It is hard to know whether or not it was the taste or the psychic effects that determined his preference more. It is certainly possible that the kif-tobacco mixture has different psychic effects from pure kif, as the pharmacological effects of nicotine are not without consequence.

Use of kif in Morocco is certainly less formal than "pot parties" in contemporary United States. In the back of any shop or cafe, the ubiquitous *supsi* pipe can be seen. The Moroccan does not suffer from fear of discovery and prosecution as does his American counterpart.

Although commonly confined to non-European settings, the musicians and dancers in an expensive restaurant for tourists on "packaged" tours would pass the *supsi* pipe from member to member. They made no effort to conceal their activity from the audience. The audience was oblivious to this performing *nashat*. The proprietor, when asked about this practice, first acted as though he could not understand the question. Persistence yielded the reply that the musicians were Berbers, but that "none of the people around here do that."

Several small cafes were observed that sold only the familiar sugared green mint tea, local cakes, and sweets. The patrons devoted themselves to smoking kif and participating in instrumental/vocal renditions of familiar songs. The atmosphere was relaxed and congenial, but not lethargic, in contrast with the familiar noisy ebb and surge of the average United States neighborhood bar.

Morocco is a country in which modern efforts to suppress an ancient habit have only succeeded in making it mildly unrespectable without really inhibiting the use of kif or seriously affecting the customs around its use. It continues to be one of the major socialization devices of the people. Given the Islamic prohibition against alcohol, the character of the Berbers who grow kif, and the economic situation of the country, it seems unlikely that its use will ever be eradicated or even seriously curtailed.

PART IV

EFFECTS OF PSYCHEDELICS
ON RELIGION
AND RELIGIOUS EXPERIENCE

The intrinsic association of psychedelic substances with religious experiences has been previously discussed. Organized religion may be conceived as a communication channel through which man and God talk to one another. Beneath the panoply of ritual designed to foster such communication and control is the individual experience, "the still small voice" of the Bible, the confrontation between Arjuna and Krishna in his universal form described in the *Bhagavad-Gita*, Huxley's (1945) *Perennial Philosophy*. The *Mandukya Upanishad* (Mentor Edition, 1957) specifies that, beyond the three attributes of being that each of us displays (waking, dreaming, and dreamless sleep), there is a fourth way, described as not subjective or objective experiences nor intermediate to these, nor reducible to any conceptualization or sense datum, but "pure unitary consciousness, wherein awareness of the world and of multiplicity is completely obliterated. It is ineffable peace. It is the supreme good. It is One without a second. It is the supreme Self."

Marsh (1965) lists seven major categories of effects of the drug experience that seem relevant to this fourth way. These are (1) the release of the symbolizing function, in which "we come up against that part of our inner world where meanings are made"; (2) the experience of unity, in which the unity of all things is perceived and "opposites rush together like a clap of thunder"; (3) the realization that there is more to us than a set of cultural expectancies; (4) receptivity to stimuli without preconceptions; (5) awareness of the Jungian shadow, the dark side of ourselves that we identify as not-self; (6) the discovery of love, which is perceived as

coterminous with hate; and (7) the discovery of the true
Self behind the personas of our daily lives.

Alan Watts finds that psychedelic experience has similar
properties to those described by Marsh and by the *Upanishads*, and deals with the implications of the attitude produced by psychedelics for Western religion. The conclusions
he comes to are not unlike those described by Braden in
The Private Sea (1967).

The testimonials for the production of religious experience
by psychedelics include Watts (1962) in the Christian
tradition, Blofeld (1968) in the Buddhist, and Schacter
(1968) in the Jewish. The experimental demonstration that
psychedelics can produce deeply felt mystical experiences is
contained in Walter Pahnke's famous "Good Friday Experiment," which he describes briefly here. Reports of religious
experience occur in all contexts of psychedelic experimentation (Masters and Houston, 1966); only Pahnke has demonstrated it experimentally.

When religious experiences of a certain kind are produced,
those who share the experience tend to band together. From
this tendency has emerged the denominations of Protestant-
ism. The same phenomenon has taken place among those
whose religious horizons have been altered by their drug
experiences. Timothy Leary founded the League for Spiritual
Discovery, Art Kleps founded the Neo-American Church, and
John and Louisa Aiken founded the Church of the Awakening.
The Church of the Awakening is the oldest psychedelic
church. In presenting the account of its founding and development, John Aiken presents a contemporary account of
an age-old problem common to all who develop a new religious vision. Parts of the account are reminiscent of some of
the accounts of the difficulties of the early Christians and of
the early history of any new sect. This is probably no accident,
but is rather part of the sociological consequence of trying to
alter the fabric of accepted belief in any organized fashion.

Walter Houston Clark deals with the over-all consequences
for Western religion of the psychedelic vision. A specialist
in the psychology of religion, his observations point to some
of the problems in contemporary theology arising from hav-

ing to deal with the authenticity of psychedelic experience from a religious point of view.

PSYCHEDELICS AND RELIGIOUS EXPERIENCE

ALAN WATTS

The experiences resulting from the use of psychedelic drugs are often described in religious terms. They are therefore of interest to those like myself who, in the tradition of William James,[1] are concerned with the psychology of religion. For more than thirty years I have been studying the causes, the consequences, and the conditions of those peculiar states of consciousness in which the individual discovers himself to be one continuous process with God, with the Universe, with the Ground of Being, or whatever name he may use by cultural conditioning or personal preference for the ultimate and eternal reality. We have no satisfactory and definitive name for experiences of this kind. The terms "religious experience," "mystical experience," and "cosmic consciousness" are all too vague and comprehensive to denote that specific mode of consciousness which, to those who have known it, is as real and overwhelming as falling in love. This article describes such states of consciousness induced by psychedelic drugs, although they are virtually indistinguishable from genuine mystical experience. The article then discusses objections to the use of psychedelic drugs that arise mainly from the opposition between mystical values and the traditional religious and secular values of Western society.

The Psychedelic Experience

The idea of mystical experiences resulting from drug use is not readily accepted in Western societies. Western culture has, historically, a particular fascination with the value and vir-

Originally appeared in the *California Law Review*, Vol. 56, No. 1, January 1968, pp. 74–85. Reprinted by permission of the publisher and the author.

[1] See W. James, *The Varieties of Religious Experience* (1902).

tue of man as an individual, self-determining, responsible
ego, controlling himself and his world by the power of conscious effort and will. Nothing, then, could be more repugnant to this cultural tradition than the notion of spiritual or
psychological growth through the use of drugs. A "drugged"
person is by definition dimmed in consciousness, fogged in
judgment, and deprived of will. But not all psychotropic
(consciousness-changing) chemicals are narcotic and sopo-
rific, as are alcohol, opiates, and barbiturates. The effects of
what are now called psychedelic (mind-manifesting) chemicals differ from those of alcohol as laughter differs from
rage, or delight from depression. There is really no analogy
between being "high" on LSD and "drunk" on bourbon. True,
no one in either state should drive a car, but neither should
one drive while reading a book, playing a violin, or making
love. Certain creative activities and states of mind demand a
concentration and devotion that are simply incompatible
with piloting a death-dealing engine along a highway.

I myself have experimented with five of the principal
psychedelics: LSD-25, mescaline, psilocybin, dimethyl-tryptamine (DMT), and cannabis. I have done so, as William
James tried nitrous oxide, to see if they could help me in
identifying what might be called the "essential" or "active"
ingredients of the mystical experience. For almost all the
classical literature on mysticism is vague, not only in describing the experience, but also in showing rational connections between the experience itself and the various traditional
methods recommended to induce it—fasting, concentration,
breathing exercises, prayers, incantations, and dances. A traditional master of Zen or Yoga, when asked why such-and-
such practices lead or predispose one to the mystical experience, always responds, "This is the way my teacher gave it
to me. This is the way I found out. If you're seriously interested, try it for yourself." This answer hardly satisfies an
impertinent, scientifically minded, and intellectually curious
Westerner. It reminds him of archaic medical prescriptions
compounding five salamanders, powdered gallows rope, three
boiled bats, a scruple of phosphorus, three pinches of henbane, and a dollop of dragon dung dropped when the moon

was in Pisces. Maybe it worked, but what was the essential ingredient?

It struck me, therefore, that if any of the psychedelic chemicals would in fact predispose my consciousness to the mystical experience, I could use them as instruments for studying and describing that experience as one uses a microscope for bacteriology, even though the microscope is an "artificial" and "unnatural" contrivance which might be said to "distort" the vision of the naked eye. However, when I was first invited to test the mystical qualities of LSD-25 by Dr. Keith Ditman of the Neuropsychiatric Clinic at UCLA Medical School, I was unwilling to believe that any mere chemical could induce a genuine mystical experience. At most, it might bring about a state of spiritual insight analogous to swimming with water wings. Indeed, my first experiment with LSD-25 was not mystical. It was an intensely interesting aesthetic and intellectual experience that challenged my powers of analysis and careful description to the utmost.

Some months later, in 1959, I tried LSD-25 again with Drs. Sterling Bunnell and Michael Agron, who were then associated with the Langley-Porter Clinic, in San Francisco. In the course of two experiments I was amazed and somewhat embarrassed to find myself going through states of consciousness that corresponded precisely with every description of major mystical experiences that I had ever read.[2] Furthermore, they exceeded both in depth and in a peculiar quality of unexpectedness the three "natural and spontaneous" experiences of this kind that had happened to me in previous years.

Through subsequent experimentation with LSD-25 and the other chemicals named above (with the exception of DMT, which I find amusing but relatively uninteresting), I found I could move with ease into the state of "cosmic consciousness," and in due course became less and less dependent on the chemicals themselves for "tuning in" to this particular wave length of experience. Of the five psychedelics tried, I found that LSD-25 and cannabis suited my purposes best. Of these two, the latter—cannabis—which I had

[2] An excellent anthology of such experiences is R. Johnson, Watcher on the Hills (1959).

to use abroad in countries where it is not outlawed, proved to be the better. It does not induce bizarre alterations of sensory perception, and medical studies indicate that it may not, save in great excess, have the dangerous side effects of LSD.

For the purposes of this study, in describing my experiences with psychedelic drugs I avoid the occasional and incidental bizarre alterations of sense perception that psychedelic chemicals may induce. I am concerned, rather, with the fundamental alterations of the normal, socially induced consciousness of one's own existence and relation to the external world. I am trying to delineate the basic principles of psychedelic awareness. But I must add that I can speak only for myself. The quality of these experiences depends considerably upon one's prior orientation and attitude to life, although the now voluminous descriptive literature of these experiences accords quite remarkably with my own.

Almost invariably, my experiments with psychedelics have had four dominant characteristics. I shall try to explain them —in the expectation that the reader will say, at least of the second and third, "Why, that's obvious! No one needs a drug to see that." Quite so, but every insight has degrees of intensity. There can be obvious$_1$ and obvious$_2$—and the latter comes on with shattering clarity, manifesting its implications in every sphere and dimension of our existence.

The first characteristic is a slowing down of time, a *concentration in the present*. One's normally compulsive concern for the future decreases, and one becomes aware of the enormous importance and interest of what is happening at the moment. Other people, going about their business on the streets, seem to be slightly crazy, failing to realize that the whole point of life is to be fully aware of it as it happens. One therefore relaxes, almost luxuriously, into studying the colors in a glass of water, or in listening to the now highly articulate vibration of every note played on an oboe or sung by a voice.

From the pragmatic standpoint of our culture, such an attitude is very bad for business. It might lead to improvidence, lack of foresight, diminished sales of insurance policies, and abandoned savings accounts. Yet this is just the corrective that our culture needs. No one is more fatuously impractical than the "successful" executive who spends his whole life absorbed in frantic paper work with the objective of retiring in comfort at sixty-five, when it will all be too late. Only those who have cultivated the art of living completely in the present have any use for making plans for the future, for when the plans mature they will be able to enjoy the results. "Tomorrow never comes." I have never yet heard a preacher urging his congregation to practice that section of the Sermon on the Mount which begins, "Be not anxious for the morrow. . . ." The truth is that people who live for the future are, as we say of the insane, "not quite all there"— or here: by overeagerness they are perpetually missing the point. Foresight is bought at the price of anxiety, and when overused it destroys all its own advantages.

The second characteristic I will call *awareness of polarity*. This is the vivid realization that states, things, and events that we ordinarily call opposite are interdependent, like back and front, or the poles of a magnet. By polar awareness one sees that things which are explicitly different are implicitly one: self and other, subject and object, left and right, male and female—and then, a little more surprisingly, solid and space, figure and background, pulse and interval, saints and sinners, police and criminals, in-groups and out-groups. Each is definable only in terms of the other, and they go together transactionally, like buying and selling, for there is no sale without a purchase, and no purchase without a sale. As this awareness becomes increasingly intense, you feel that you yourself are polarized with the external universe in such a way that you imply each other. Your push is its pull, and its push is your pull—as when you move the steering wheel of a car. Are you pushing it or pulling it?

At first, this is a very odd sensation, not unlike hearing your own voice played back to you on an electronic system immediately after you have spoken. You become confused, and wait for *it* to go on! Similarly, you feel that you are something being done by the universe, yet that the universe is equally something being done by you—which is true, at least in the neurological sense that the peculiar structure of our brains translates the sun into light, and air vibrations into sound. Our normal sensation of relationship to the outside world is that sometimes I push it, and sometimes it pushes me. But if the two are actually one, where does action begin and responsibility rest? If the universe is doing me, how can I be sure that, two seconds hence, I will still remember the English language? If I am doing it, how can I be sure that two seconds hence, my brain will know how to turn the sun into light? From such unfamiliar sensations as these the psychedelic experience can generate confusion, paranoia and terror—even though the individual is feeling his relationship to the world exactly as it would be described by a biologist, ecologist, or physicist, for he is feeling himself as the unified field of organism and environment.

The third characteristic, arising from the second, is *awareness of relativity*. I see that I am a link in an infinite hierarchy of processes and beings, ranging from molecules through bacteria and insects to human beings, and, maybe to angels and gods—a hierarchy in which every level is in effect the same situation. For example, the poor man worries about money while the rich man worries about his health, the worry is the same, but the difference is in its substance or dimension. I realize that fruit flies must think of themselves as people, because, like ourselves, they find themselves in the middle of their own world—with immeasurably greater things above and smaller things below. To us, they all look alike and seem to have no personality—as do the Chinese when we have not lived among them. Yet fruit flies must see just as many subtle distinctions among themselves as we among ourselves.

From this it is but a short step to the realization that all forms of life and being are simply variations on a single theme: we are all in fact one being doing the same thing in as many different ways as possible. As the French proverb goes, *plus ça change, plus c'est la même chose* (the more it varies, the more it is one). I see, further, that feeling threatened by the inevitability of death is really the same experience as feeling alive, and that as all beings are feeling this everywhere, they are all just as much "I" as myself. Yet the "I" feeling, to be felt at all, must always be a sensation relative to the "other"—to something beyond its control and experience. To be at all, it must begin and end. But the intellectual jump that mystical and psychedelic experiences make here is in enabling you to see that all these myriad I-centers are yourself—not, indeed, your personal and superficially conscious ego, but what Hindus call the *paramatman*, the Self of all selves.[3] As the retina enables us to see countless pulses of energy as a single light, so the mystical experience shows us innumerable individuals as a single Self.

The fourth characteristic is *awareness of eternal energy*, often in the form of intense white light, which seems to be both the current in your nerves and that mysterious e which equals mc^2. This may sound like megalomania or delusion of grandeur—but one sees quite clearly that all existence is a single energy, and that this energy is one's own being. Of course there is death as well as life, because energy is a pulsation, and just as waves must have both crests and troughs, the experience of existing must go on and off. Basically, therefore, there is simply nothing to worry about, because you yourself are the eternal energy of the universe playing hide-and-seek (off-and-on) with itself. At root, you are the Godhead, for God is all that there is. Quoting Isaiah just a little out of context: "I am the Lord, and there is none else. I form the light and create the darkness: I make peace, and create evil. I, the Lord, do all these things."[4] This is the sense of the fundamental tenet of Hinduism, *Tat tvam asi*—"THAT (i.e., "that subtle Being of which this whole universe is composed") art thou."[5] A classical case of this experience, from the West, is in Tennyson's *Memoirs*:

A kind of waking trance I have frequently had, quite up from boyhood, when I have been all alone. This has generally come upon me

[3] Thus Hinduism regards the universe not as an artifact, but as an immense drama in which the One Actor (the *paramatman* or *brakman*) plays all the parts, which are his (or "its") masks or *personae*. The sensation of being only this one particular self, John Doe, is due to the Actor's total absorption in playing this and every other part. For fuller exposition, see S. Radhakrishnan, *The Hindu View of Life* (1927); H. Zimmer, *Philosophies of India* (1951), pp. 355–463. A popular version is in A. Watts, *The Book: On the Taboo Against Knowing Who You Are* (1966).

[4] Isaiah 45: 6, 7.
[5] Chandogya Upanishad 6.15.3.

thro' repeating my own name two or three times to myself silently till all at once, as it were out of the intensity of the consciousness of individuality, the individuality itself seemed to dissolve and fade away into boundless being, and this not a confused state, but the clearest of the clearest, the surest of the surest, the weirdest of the weirdest utterly beyond words, where death was an almost laughable impossibility, the loss of personality (if so it were) seeming no extinction but the only true life.[6]

Obviously, these characteristics of the psychedelic experience, as I have known it, are aspects of a single state of consciousness—for I have been describing the same thing from different angles. The descriptions attempt to convey the reality of the experience, but in doing so they also suggest some of the inconsistencies between such experience and the current values of society.

Opposition to Psychedelic Drugs

Resistance to allowing use of psychedelic drugs originates in both religious and secular values. The difficulty in describing psychedelic experiences in traditional religious terms suggests one ground of opposition. The Westerner must borrow such words as *samadhi* or *moksha* from the Hindus, or *satori* or *kensho* from the Japanese, to describe the experience of oneness with the universe. We have no appropriate word because our own Jewish and Christian theologies will not accept the idea that man's inmost self can be identical with the Godhead, even though Christians may insist that this was true in the unique instance of Jesus Christ. Jews and Christians think of God in political and monarchical terms, as the supreme governor of the universe, the ultimate boss. Obviously, it is both socially unacceptable and logically preposterous for a particular individual to claim that he, in person, is the omnipotent and omniscient ruler of the world—to be accorded suitable recognition and honor.

Such an imperial and kingly concept of the ultimate reality, however, is neither necessary nor universal. The Hindus and the Chinese have no difficulty in conceiving of an identity of the self and the Godhead. For most Asians, other than Muslims, the Godhead moves and manifests the world in

[6] Alfred Lord Tennyson, A Memoir by His Son (1898), 320.

much the same way that a centipede manipulates a hundred legs—spontaneously, without deliberation or calculation. In other words, they conceive the universe by analogy with an organism as distinct from a mechanism. They do not see it as an artifact or construct under the conscious direction of some supreme technician, engineer, or architect.

If, however, in the context of Christian or Jewish tradition, an individual declares himself to be one with God, he must be dubbed blasphemous (subversive) or insane. Such a mystical experience is a clear threat to traditional religious concepts. The Judaeo-Christian tradition has a monarchical image of God, and monarchs, who rule by force, fear nothing more than insubordination. The Church has therefore always been highly suspicious of mystics, because they seem to be insubordinate and to claim equality or, worse, identity with God. For this reason, John Scotus Erigena and Meister Eckhart were condemned as heretics. This was also why the Quakers faced opposition for their doctrine of the Inward Light, and for their refusal to remove hats in church and in court. A few occasional mystics may be all right so long as they watch their language, like St. Teresa of Ávila and St. John of the Cross, who maintained, shall we say, a metaphysical distance of respect between themselves and their heavenly King. Nothing, however, could be more alarming to the ecclesiastical hierarchy than a popular outbreak of mysticism, for this might well amount to setting up a democracy in the kingdom of heaven—and such alarm would be shared equally by Catholics, Jews, and fundamentalist Protestants.

The monarchical image of God, with its implicit distaste for religious insubordination, has a more pervasive impact than many Christians might admit. The thrones of kings have walls immediately behind them, and all who present themselves at court must prostrate themselves or kneel, because this is an awkward position from which to make a sudden attack. It has perhaps never occurred to Christians that when they design a church on the model of a royal court (basilica) and prescribe church ritual, they are implying that God, like a human monarch, is afraid. This is also implied by flattery in prayers:

O Lord our heavenly Father, high and mighty, King of kings, Lord of lords, the only Ruler of princes, who dost from thy throne behold all the dwellers upon earth: most heartily we beseech thee with thy favor to behold. . . .[7]

The Western man who claims consciousness of oneness with God or the universe thus clashes with his society's concept of religion. In most Asian cultures, however, such a man will be congratulated as having penetrated the true secret of life. He has arrived, by chance or by some such discipline as Yoga or Zen meditation, at a state of consciousness in which he experiences directly and vividly what our own scientists know to be true in theory. For the ecologist, the biologist, and the physicist know (but seldom feel) that every organism constitutes a single field of behavior, or process, with its environment. There is no way of separating what any given organism is doing from what its environment is doing, for which reason ecologists speak not of organisms in environments but of organism-environments. Thus the words "I" and "self" should properly mean what the whole universe is doing at this particular "here-and-now" called John Doe.

The kingly concept of God makes identity of self and God, or self and universe, inconceivable in Western religious terms. The difference between Eastern and Western concepts of man and his universe, however, extends beyond strictly religious concepts. The Western scientist may rationally perceive the idea of organism-environment, but he does not ordinarily *feel* this to be true. By cultural and social conditioning, he has been hypnotized into experiencing himself as an ego—as an isolated center of consciousness and will inside a bag of skin, confronting an external and alien world. We say, "I came into this world." But we did nothing of the kind. We came *out* of it in just the same way that fruit comes out of trees. Our galaxy, our cosmos, "peoples" in the same way that an apple tree "apples."

Such a vision of the universe clashes with the idea of a monarchical God, with the concept of the separate ego, and even with the secular, atheist/agnostic mentality, which derives its common sense from the mythology of nineteenth-century scientism. According to this view, the universe is a

[7] A Prayer for the King's Majesty, Order for Morning Prayer, Book of Common Prayer (Church of England, 1904).

mindless mechanism and man a sort of accidental micro-organism infesting a minute globular rock that revolves about an unimportant star on the outer fringe of one of the minor galaxies. This "putdown" theory of man is extremely common among such quasi scientists as sociologists, psychologists, and psychiatrists, most of whom are still thinking of the world in terms of Newtonian mechanics, and have never really caught up with the ideas of Einstein and Bohr, Oppenheimer and Schrödinger. Thus to the ordinary institutional-type psychiatrist, any patient who gives the least hint of mystical or religious experience is automatically diagnosed as deranged. From the standpoint of the mechanistic religion, he is a heretic and is given electroshock therapy as an up-to-date form of thumbscrew and rack. And, incidentally, it is just this kind of quasi scientist who, as consultant to government and law-enforcement agencies, dictates official policies on the use of psychedelic chemicals.

Inability to accept the mystic experience is more than an intellectual handicap. Lack of awareness of the basic unity of organism and environment is a serious and dangerous hallucination. For in a civilization equipped with immense technological power, the sense of alienation between man and nature leads to the use of technology in a hostile spirit—to the "conquest" of nature instead of intelligent co-operation with nature. The result is that we are eroding and destroying our environment, spreading Los Angelization instead of civilization. This is the major threat overhanging Western, technological culture, and no amount of reasoning or doom-preaching seems to help. We simply do not respond to the prophetic and moralizing techniques of conversion upon which Jews and Christians have always relied. But people have an obscure sense of what is good for them—call it "unconscious self-healing," "survival instinct," "positive growth potential," or what you will. Among the educated young there is therefore a startling and unprecedented interest in the transformation of human consciousness. All over the Western world publishers are selling millions of books dealing with Yoga, Vedanta, Zen Buddhism, and the chemical mysticism of psychedelic drugs, and I have come to believe that the whole "hip" subculture, however misguided in some of its manifestations, is the earnest and responsible effort of young people to correct the self-destroying course of industrial civilization.

The content of the mystical experience is thus inconsistent with both the religious and secular concepts of traditional Western thought. Moreover, mystical experiences often result in attitudes that threaten the authority not only of established churches, but also of secular society. Unafraid of death and deficient in worldly ambition, those who have undergone mystical experiences are impervious to threats and promises. Moreover, their sense of the relativity of good and evil arouses the suspicion that they lack both conscience and respect for law. Use of psychedelics in the United States by a literate bourgeoisie means that an important segment of the population is indifferent to society's traditional rewards and sanctions.

In theory, the existence within our secular society of a group that does not accept conventional values is consistent with our political vision. But one of the great problems of the United States, legally and politically, is that we have never quite had the courage of our convictions. The Republic is founded on the marvelously sane principle that a human community can exist and prosper only on a basis of mutual trust. Metaphysically, the American Revolution was a rejection of the dogma of Original Sin, which is the notion that because you cannot trust yourself or other people, there must be some Superior Authority to keep us all in order. The dogma was rejected because, if it is true that we cannot trust ourselves and others, it follows that we cannot trust the Superior Authority which we ourselves conceive and obey, and that the very idea of our own untrustworthiness is unreliable!

Citizens of the United States believe, or are supposed to believe, that a republic is the best form of government. Yet vast confusion arises from trying to be republican in politics and monarchist in religion. How can a republic be the best form of government if the universe, heaven, and hell are a monarchy?[8] Thus, despite the theory of government by con-

---

[8] Thus, until quite recently, belief in a Supreme Being was a legal test of valid conscientious objection to military service. The implication was that the individual objector found himself bound to obey a higher echelon of command than the President and Congress. The

sent, based upon mutual trust, the peoples of the United States retain, from the authoritarian backgrounds of their religions or national origins, an utterly naïve faith in law as some sort of supernatural and paternalistic power. "There ought to be a law against it!" Our law-enforcement officers are therefore confused, hindered, and bewildered—not to mention corrupted—by being asked to enforce sumptuary laws, often of ecclesiastical origin, that vast numbers of people have no intention of obeying and that, in any case, are immensely difficult or simply impossible to enforce—for example, the barring of anything so undetectable as LSD-25 from international and interstate commerce.

Finally, there are two specific objections to use of psychedelic drugs. First, use of these drugs may be dangerous. However, every worth-while exploration is dangerous—climbing mountains, testing aircraft, rocketing into outer space, skin diving, or collecting botanical specimens in jungles. But if you value knowledge and the actual delight of exploration more than mere duration of uneventful life, you are willing to take the risks. It is not really healthy for monks to practice fasting, and it was hardly hygienic for Jesus to get himself crucified, but these are risks taken in the course of spiritual adventures. Today the adventurous young are taking risks in exploring the psyche, testing their mettle at the task just as, in times past, they have tested it—more violently—in hunting, dueling, hot-rod racing, and playing football. What they need is not prohibitions and policemen, but the most intelligent encouragement and advice that can be found.

Second, drug use may be criticized as an escape from reality. However, this criticism assumes unjustly that the mystical experiences themselves are escapist or unreal. LSD, in particular, is by no means a soft and cushy escape from reality. It can very easily be an experience in which you have to test your soul against all the devils in hell. For me, it has been at times an experience in which I was at once completely lost in the corridors of the mind and yet relating that very lostness to the exact order of logic and language, simultaneously very mad

---

analogy is military and monarchical, and therefore objectors who, as Buddhists or naturalists, held an organic theory of the universe often had difficulty in obtaining recognition.

and very sane. But beyond these occasional lost and insane episodes, there are the experiences of the world as a system of total harmony and glory, and the discipline of relating these to the order of logic and language must somehow explain how what William Blake called that "energy which is eternal delight" can consist with the misery and suffering of everyday life.[9]

The undoubted mystical and religious intent of most users of the psychedelics, even if some of these substances should be proved injurious to physical health, requires that their free and responsible use be exempt from legal restraint in any republic that maintains a constitutional separation of church and state.[10] To the extent that mystical experience conforms with the tradition of genuine religious involvement, and to the extent that psychedelics induce that experience, users are

[9] This is discussed at length in A. Watts, *The Joyous Cosmology: Adventures in the Chemistry of Consciousness* (1962).

[10] "Responsible" in the sense that such substances be taken by or administered to consenting adults only. The user of cannabis, in particular, is apt to have peculiar difficulties in establishing his "undoubted mystical and religious intent" in court. Having committed so loathsome and serious a felony, his chances of clemency are better if he assumes a repentant demeanor, which is quite inconsistent with the sincere belief that his use of cannabis was religious. On the other hand, if he insists unrepentantly that he looks upon such use as a religious sacrament, many judges will declare that they "dislike his attitude," finding it truculent and lacking in appreciation of the gravity of the crime, and the sentence will be that much harsher. The accused is therefore put in a "double-bind" situation, in which he is "damned if he does, and damned if he doesn't." Furthermore, religious integrity—as in conscientious objection—is generally tested and established by membership in some church or religious organization with a substantial following. But the felonious status of cannabis is such that grave suspicion would be cast upon all individuals forming such an organization, and the test cannot therefore be fulfilled. It is generally forgotten that our guarantees of religious freedom were designed to protect precisely those who were *not* members of established denominations, but rather such (then) screwball and subversive individuals as Quakers, Shakers, Levellers, and Anabaptists. There is little question that those who use cannabis or other psychedelics with religious intent are now members of a persecuted religion which appears to the rest of society as a grave menace to "mental health," as distinct from the old-fashioned "immortal soul." But it's the same old story.

entitled to some constitutional protection. Also, to the extent that research in the psychology of religion can utilize such drugs, students of the human mind must be free to use them. Under present laws, I, as an experienced student of the psychology of religion, can no longer pursue research in the field. This is a barbarous restriction of spiritual and intellectual freedom, suggesting that the legal system of the United States is, after all, in tacit alliance with the monarchical theory of the universe, and will, therefore, prohibit and persecute religious ideas and practices based on an organic and unitary vision of the universe.[11]

DRUGS AND MYSTICISM

WALTER N. PAHNKE

The claim has been made that the experience facilitated by psychedelic drugs, such as LSD, psilocybin, and mescaline,

[11] Amerindians belonging to the Native American Church, who employ the psychedelic peyote cactus in their rituals, are firmly opposed to any government control of this plant, even if they should be guaranteed the right to its use. They feel that peyote is a natural gift of God to mankind, and especially to natives of the land where it grows, and that no government has a right to interfere with its use. The same argument might be made on behalf of cannabis, or the mushroom *Psilocybe mexicana Heim*. All these things are natural plants, not processed or synthesized drugs, and by what authority can individuals be prevented from eating them? There is no law against eating or growing the mushroom *Amanita pantherina*, even though it is fatally poisonous and only experts can distinguish it from a common edible mushroom. This case can be made even from the standpoint of believers in the monarchical universe of Judaism and Christianity, for it is a basic principle of both religions, derived from Genesis, that all natural substances created by God are inherently good, and that evil can arise only in their misuse. Thus laws against mere possession, or even cultivation, of these plants are in basic conflict with biblical principles. Criminal conviction of those who employ these plants should be based on proven misuse. "And God said, 'Behold, I have given you *every* herb bearing seed, which is upon the face of all the earth, and every tree, in the which is the fruit of a tree yielding seed; to you it shall be for meat. . . . And God saw every thing that he had made, and, behold, it was very good." Genesis 1:29, 31.

can be similar or identical to the experience described by the mystics of all ages, cultures, and religions. This paper will attempt to examine and explain this possibility.

There is a long and continuing history of the religious use of plants that contain psychedelic substances. Scholars such as Osmond (1957b), Schultes (1963), and Wasson (1961) have made valuable contributions to this intriguing field. In some instances, such natural products were ingested by a priest, shaman, or witch doctor to induce a trance for revelatory purposes; sometimes they were taken by groups of people who participated in sacred ceremonies. For example, the dried heads of the peyote cactus, whose chief active ingredient is mescaline, were used by the Aztecs at least as early as 300 B.C. and are currently being employed by over fifty thousand Indians of the Native American Church as a vital part of their religious ceremonies. Both ololiuqui, a variety of morning-glory seed, and certain kinds of Mexican mushrooms (called *teonanacatl*, "flesh of the gods") were also used for divinatory and religious purposes by the Aztecs. These practices have continued to the present among remote Indian tribes in the mountains of the state of Oaxaca, in Mexico. Modern psychopharmacological research has shown the active chemicals to be psilocybin in the case of the mushrooms, and several compounds closely related to LSD in the case of ololiuqui. *Amanita muscaria*, the mushroom that has been used for unknown centuries by Siberian shamans to induce religious trances, does not contain psilocybin. The most important psychologically active compound from this mushroom has not yet been isolated, but promising work is in progress. Other naturally occurring plants, which are used by various South American Indian tribes in a religious manner for prophecy, divination, clairvoyance, tribal initiation of male adolescents, or sacred feasts are: cohoba snuff, made from the pulverized seeds of *Piptadenia*; the drink *vinho de Jurumens*, made from the seeds of *Mimosa hostilis*; and the drink *caapi*, made from *Banisteriopsis*. These last three products contain various indolic compounds that are all closely related to psilo-

Reprinted from *The International Journal of Parapsychology*, Vol. VIII, No. 2, Spring 1966, pp. 295–313. By permission of the author and the publisher.

cybin, both structurally and in their psychic effects (bufotenine, dimethyl-tryptamine, and harmine, respectively). Both
LSD and psilocybin contain the indolic ring, and mescaline
may be metabolized to an indole in the body.

An Experimental Examination of the Claim that Psychedelic Drug Experience May Resemble Mystical Experience

Some of the researchers who have experimented with synthesized mescaline, LSD, or psilocybin have remarked upon
the similarity between drug-induced and spontaneous mystical
experiences because of the frequency with which some of their
subjects have used mystical and religious language to describe
their experiences. These data interested the author in a careful examination and evaluation of such claims. An empirical
study, designed to investigate in a systematic and scientific
way the similarities and differences between experiences described by mystics and those facilitated by psychedelic drugs,
was undertaken (Pahnke, 1966, 1967). First, a phenomenological typology of the mystical state of consciousness was
carefully defined, after a study of the writings of the mystics
themselves and of scholars who have tried to characterize
mystical experience. [For example, William James (1935)
was an invaluable pioneer in this area.] Then, some drug
experiences were empirically studied, not by collecting such
experiences wherever an interesting or striking one might have
been found and analyzed after the fact, but by conducting a
double-blind, controlled experiment with subjects whose religious background and experience, as well as personality, had
been measured *before* their drug experiences. The preparation
of the subjects, the setting under which the drug was administered, and the collection of data about the experience
were made as uniform as possible. The experimenter himself
devised the experiment, collected the data, and evaluated the
results without ever having had a personal experience with any
of these drugs.

A nine-category typology of the mystical state of consciousness was defined as a basis for measurement of the phenomena
of the psychedelic drug experiences. Among the numerous
studies of mysticism, the work of W. T. Stace (1960) was

found to be the most helpful guide for the construction of this typology. His conclusion—that in the mystical experience there are certain fundamental characteristics that are universal and not restricted to any particular religion or culture (although particular cultural, historical, or religious conditions may influence both the interpretation and description of these basic phenomena)—was taken as a presupposition. Whether or not the mystical experience is "religious" depends upon one's definition of religion and was not the problem investigated. Our typology defined the universal phenomena of the mystical experience, whether considered "religious" or not.

The nine categories of our phenomenological typology may be summarized as follows:

Category I: *Unity*

Unity, the most important characteristic of the mystical experience, is divided into internal and external types, which are different ways of experiencing an undifferentiated unity. The major difference is that the internal type finds unity through an "inner world" *within* the experiencer, while the external type finds unity through the external world *outside* the experiencer.

The essential elements of *internal unity* are loss of usual sense impressions and loss of self without becoming unconscious. The multiplicity of usual external and internal sense impressions (including time and space), and the empirical ego or usual sense of individuality, fade or melt away while consciousness remains. In the most complete experience, this consciousness is a pure awareness beyond empirical content, with no external or internal distinctions. In spite of the loss of sense impressions and dissolution of the usual personal identity or self, the awareness of oneness or unity is still experienced and remembered. One is not unconscious but is rather very much aware of an undifferentiated unity.

External unity is perceived outwardly with the physical senses through the external world. A sense of underlying oneness is felt behind the empirical multiplicity. The subject or observer feels that the usual separation between himself and an external object (inanimate or animate) is no longer present in a basic sense; yet the subject still knows that on another level, at the same time, he and the objects are separate. Another way of expressing this same phenomenon is that the essences of objects are experienced intuitively and felt to be the same at the deepest level. The subject feels a sense of oneness with these objects because he "sees" that at the most basic level all are a part of the same undifferentiated unity. The capsule statement ". . . all is One" is a good summary of external unity. In the most complete experience, a cosmic dimension is felt, so that the experiencer feels in a deep sense that he is a part of everything that is.

Category II: *Transcendence of Time and Space*

This category refers to loss of the usual sense of time and space. This means clock time but may also be one's personal sense of his past, present, and future. Transcendence of space means that a person loses his usual orientation as to where he is during the experience in terms of the usual three-dimensional perception of his environment. Experiences of timelessness and spacelessness may also be described as experiences of "eternity" or "infinity."

Category III: *Deeply Felt Positive Mood*

The most universal elements (and, therefore, the ones that are most essential to the definition of this category) are joy, blessedness, and peace. The unique character of these feelings in relation to the mystical experience is the intensity that elevates them to the highest levels of human experience, and they are highly valued by the experiencers. Tears may be associated with any of these elements because of the overpowering nature of the experience. Such feelings may occur either at the peak of the experience or during the "ecstatic afterglow," when the peak has passed but while its effects and memory are still quite vivid and intense. Love may also be an element of deeply felt positive mood, but it does not have the same universality as joy, blessedness, and peace.

Category IV: *Sense of Sacredness*

This category refers to the sense of sacredness that is evoked by the mystical experience. The sacred is here broadly defined as that which a person feels to be of special value and capable of being profaned. The basic characteristic of sacredness is a non-rational, intuitive, hushed, palpitant response of awe and wonder in the presence of inspiring realities. No religious "beliefs" or traditional theological terminology need necessarily be involved, even though there may be a sense of reverence or a feeling that what is experienced is holy or divine.

Category V: *Objectivity and Reality*

This category has two interrelated elements: (1) insightful knowledge or illumination felt at an intuitive, non-rational level and gained by direct experience; and (2) the authoritative nature of the experience, or the certainty that such knowledge is truly real, in contrast to the feeling that the experience is a subjective delusion. These two elements are connected, because the knowledge through experience of ultimate reality (in the sense of being able to "know" and "see" what is really *real*) carries its own sense of certainty. The experience of "ultimate" reality is an awareness of another dimension unlike the "ordinary" reality (the reality of usual, everyday consciousness); yet the knowledge of "ultimate" reality is quite real to the experiencer. Such insightful knowledge does not necessarily mean an increase in facts, but rather in intuitive illumination. What becomes "known" (rather than merely intellectually assented to) is intuitively felt to be authoritative, requires no proof at a rational level, and produces an inward feeling of objective truth. The content of this knowledge may be divided into two main types: (a) insights into being and existence in general, and (b) insights into one's personal, finite self.

Category VI: *Paradoxicality*

Accurate descriptions and even rational interpretations of the mystical experience tend to be logically contradictory when strictly analyzed. For example, in the experience of internal unity there is a loss of all empirical content in an *empty* unity which is at the same time *full* and complete. This loss includes the loss of the sense of self and the dissolution of individuality; yet something of the individual entity remains to experience the unity. The "I" both exists and does not exist. Another example is the separateness from, and at the same time unity with, objects in the experience of external unity (essentially a paradoxical transcendence of space).

Category VII: *Alleged Ineffability*

In spite of attempts to relate or write about the mystical experience, mystics insist either that words fail to describe it adequately or that the experience is beyond words. Perhaps the reason is an embarrassment with language because of the paradoxical nature of the essential phenomena.

Category VIII: *Transiency*

Transiency refers to duration, and means the temporary nature of the mystical experience in contrast to the relative permanence of the level of usual experience. There is a transient appearance of the special and unusual levels or dimensions of consciousness as defined by our typology, their eventual disappearance, and a return to the more usual. The characteristic of transiency indicates that the mystical state of consciousness is not sustained indefinitely.

Category IX: *Persisting Positive Changes in Attitude and Behavior*

Because our typology is of a healthful, life-enhancing mysticism, this category describes the positive, lasting effects of the experience and the resulting changes in attitude. These changes are divided into four groups: (1) toward self, (2) toward others, (3) toward life, and (4) toward the mystical experience itself.

(1) Increased integration of personality is the basic inward change in the personal self. Undesirable traits may be faced in such a way that they may be dealt with and finally reduced

or eliminated. As a result of personal integration, one's sense of inner authority may be strengthened, and the vigor and dynamic quality of a person's life may be increased. Creativity and greater efficiency of achievement may be released. An inner optimistic tone may result, with a consequent increase in feelings of happiness, joy, and peace. (2) Changes in attitude and behavior toward others include more sensitivity, more tolerance, more real love, and more authenticity as a person by virtue of being more open and more one's true self with others. (3) Changes toward life in a positive direction include philosophy of life, sense of values, sense of meaning and purpose, vocational commitment, need for service to others, and new appreciation of life and the whole of creation. Life may seem richer. The sense of reverence may be increased, and more time may be spent in devotional life and meditation. (4) Positive change in attitude toward the mystical experience itself means that it is regarded as valuable and that what has been learned is thought to be useful. The experience is remembered as a high point, and an attempt is made to recapture it or, if possible, to gain new experiences as a source of growth and strength. The mystical experiences of others are more readily appreciated and understood.

The purpose of the experiment in which psilocybin was administered in a religious context was to gather empirical data about the state of consciousness experienced. In a private chapel on Good Friday, twenty Christian theological students, ten of whom had been given psilocybin one and one half hours earlier, listened over loudspeakers to a two-and-one-half-hour religious service which was in actual progress in another part of the building and which consisted of organ music, four solos, readings, prayers, and personal meditation. The assumption was made that the condition most conducive to a mystical experience should be an atmosphere broadly comparable to that achieved by tribes who actually use natural psychedelic substances in religious ceremonies. The particular content and procedure of the ceremony had to be applicable (i.e., familiar and meaningful) to the participants. Attitude toward the experience, both before and during, was taken into serious consideration in the experimental design. Preparation was meant to maximize positive expectation, trust, confidence, and reduction of fear. The setting was planned to utilize this preparation through group support and rapport; through friendship and an open, trusting atmosphere; and through prior knowledge of the procedure of the experiment in order to eliminate, if possible, feelings of manipulation that might arise.

In the weeks before the experiment, each subject participated in five hours of various preparation and screening procedures, which included psychological tests, medical history, physical examination, questionnaire evaluation of previous religious experience, intensive interview, and group interaction. The twenty subjects were graduate-student volunteers, all of whom were from middle-class Protestant backgrounds and from one denominational seminary in the free-church tradition. None of the subjects had taken psilocybin or related substances before this experiment. The volunteers were divided into five groups of four students each on the basis of compatibility and friendship. Two leaders, who knew from past experience the positive and negative possibilities of the psilocybin reaction, met with their groups to encourage trust, confidence, group support, and fear reduction. The method of reaction to the experience was emphasized (i.e., to relax and co-operate with, rather than to fight against, the effects of the drug). Throughout the preparation, an effort was made to avoid suggesting the characteristics of the typology of mysticism. The leaders were not familiar with the typology that had been devised.

Double-blind technique was employed in the experiment, so that neither the experimenter nor any of the participants (leaders or subjects) knew the specific contents of the capsules, which were identical in appearance. Half of the subjects and one of the leaders in each group received psilocybin (thirty milligrams for each of the ten experimental subjects and fifteen milligrams each for five of the leaders). Without prior knowledge of the drug used, or of its effects, the remaining ten subjects and the other five leaders each received two hundred milligrams of nicotinic acid, a vitamin that causes transient feelings of warmth and tingling of the skin, in order to maximize suggestion for the control group.

Data were collected during the experiment and at various times up to six months afterward. On the experimental day, tape recordings were made both of individual reactions immediately after the religious service and of the group discussions that followed. Each subject wrote an account of his experience as soon after the experiment as was convenient. Within a week all subjects had completed a 147-item questionnaire which had been designed to measure the various phenomena of the typology of mysticism on a qualitative, numerical scale. The results of this questionnaire were used as a basis for a one-and-one-half-hour, tape-recorded interview which immediately followed. Six months later each subject was interviewed again after completion of a follow-up questionnaire in three parts, with a similar scale. Part I was open ended; the participant was asked to list any changes that he felt were a result of his Good Friday experience and to rate the degree of benefit or harm of each change. Part II (fifty-two items) was a condensed and somewhat more explicit repetition of items from the postdrug questionnaire. Part III (ninety-three items) was designed to measure both positive and negative attitudinal and behavioral changes that had lasted for six months and were due to the experience. The individual descriptive accounts and Part I of the follow-up questionnaire were content-analyzed with a qualitative, numerical scale by judges who were independent of the experiment and who knew only that they were to analyze twenty accounts written by persons who had attended a religious service.

Prior to the experiment, the twenty subjects had been matched in ten pairs on the basis of data from the predrug questionnaires, interviews, and psychological tests. Past religious experience, religious background, and general psychological make-up were used for the pairings, in that order of importance. The experiment was designed so that by random distribution one subject from each pair received psilocybin and one received the control substance, nicotinic acid. This division into an experimental and a control group was for the purpose of statistical evaluation of the scores from each of the three methods of measurement that used a numerical scale:

he postdrug questionnaire, the follow-up questionnaire, and
the content analysis of the written accounts.

A summary of percentage scores and significance levels
reached by the ten experimentals and ten controls, for each
category or subcategory of the typology of mysticism, is presented in Table I. The score from each of the three methods
of measurement was calculated as the percentage of the maximum possible score if the top of the rating scale for each
item had been scored. The percentages from each method of
measurement were then averaged together. A comparison of
the scores of the experimental and control subject in each pair
was used to calculate the significance level of the differences
observed by means of the non-parametric Sign Test. As can
be seen from Table I, for the combined scores from the three
methods of measurement, p was less than .020 in all categories
except deeply felt positive mood (love) and persisting positive changes in attitude and behavior toward the experience,
where p was still less than .055.

TABLE I

SUMMARY OF PERCENTAGE SCORES AND
SIGNIFICANCE LEVELS REACHED
BY THE EXPERIMENTAL VERSUS THE
CONTROL GROUP FOR CATEGORIES MEASURING
THE TYPOLOGY OF MYSTICAL EXPERIENCE

Category	% of Maximum Possible Score for 10 Ss		
	Exp.	Cont.	P*
1. Unity	62	7	.001
A. Internal	70	8	.001
B. External	38	2	.008
2. Transcendence of time and space	84	6	.001
3. Deeply felt positive mood	57	23	.020
A. Joy, blessedness and peace	51	13	.020
B. Love	57	33	.055
4. Sacredness	53	28	.020
5. Objectivity and reality	63	18	.011

TABLE I (continued)

Category	% of Maximum Possible Score for 10 Ss		
	Exp.	Cont.	P*
6. Paradoxicality	61	13	.001
7. Alleged ineffability	66	18	.001
8. Transiency	79	8	.001
9. Persisting positive changes in attitude and behavior	51	8	.001
A. Toward self	57	3	.001
B. Toward others	40	20	.002
C. Toward life	54	6	.011
D. Toward the experience	57	31	.055

* Probability that the difference between experimental and control scores was due to chance.

Although this evidence indicates that the experimentals as a group achieved to a statistically significant degree a higher score in each of the nine categories than did the controls, the degree of completeness or intensity must be examined.

In terms of our typology of mysticism, ideally the most "complete" mystical experience should have demonstrated the phenomena of all the categories in a maximal way. The evidence (particularly from the content analysis and also supported by impressions from the interviews) showed that such perfect completeness in all categories was not experienced by all the subjects in the experimental group. In the data, the various categories and subcategories can be divided into three groups in regard to the degree of intensity or completeness, as shown in Table II. Criteria were the percentage levels and the consistency among different methods of measurement. The closest approximation to a complete and intense degree of experience was found for the categories of internal unity, transcendence of time and space, transiency, paradoxicality, and persisting positive changes in attitude and behavior toward self and life. The evidence indicated that the second group had almost, but not quite, the same degree of completeness or intensity as the first group. The second group consisted of external unity, objectivity and reality, joy, and

TABLE II

RELATIVE COMPLETENESS* OF
VARIOUS CATEGORIES IN WHICH THERE WAS
A STATISTICALLY SIGNIFICANT DIFFERENCE
BETWEEN EXPERIMENTAL AND CONTROL GROUPS

(1)	(2)	(3)
Closest approximation to the most complete and intense expression	Almost, but not quite, as complete or intense as (1)	Least complete or intense, though still a definite difference from the control group
Internal unity	External unity	Sense of sacredness
Transcendence of time and space	Objectivity and reality	Deeply felt positive mood (love)
Transiency	Alleged ineffability	Persisting positive changes in attitude and behavior toward others and the experience
Paradoxicality	Deeply felt positive mood (joy, blessedness, and peace)	
Persisting positive changes in attitude and behavior toward self and life		

* Based on qualitative score levels and agreement among the three methods of measurement in comparing the scores of the experimental versus the control group.

alleged ineffability. There was a relatively greater lack of completeness for sense of sacredness, love, and persisting positive changes in attitude and behavior toward others and toward the experience. Each of these last eight categories and subcategories was termed incomplete to a greater or lesser degree for the experimentals, but was definitely present to some extent when compared with the controls. When analyzed most rigorously and measured against all possible categories of the typology of mysticism, the experience of the experimental subjects was considered incomplete in this strictest sense. Usually such incompleteness was demonstrated by results of the content analyses.

The control subjects did not experience many phenomena of the mystical typology, and even then only to a low degree of completeness. The phenomena for which the scores of the controls were closest to (although still always less than) the experimentals were: blessedness and peace, sense of sacredness, love, and persisting positive changes in attitude and behavior toward others and toward the experience.

The design of the experiment suggested an explanation for the fact that the control subjects should have experienced any phenomena at all. The meaningful religious setting of the experiment would have been expected to encourage a response of blessedness, peace, and sacredness. In the case of love and persisting changes toward others and toward the experience, observation by the controls of the profound experience of the experimentals and interaction between the two groups on an interpersonal level appeared, from both postexperimental interviews, to have been the main basis for the controls' experience of these phenomena.

The experience of the experimental subjects was certainly more like mystical experience than that of the controls, who had the same expectation and suggestion from the preparation and setting. The most striking difference between the experimentals and the controls was the ingestion of thirty milligrams of psilocybin, which it was concluded was the facilitating agent responsible for the difference in phenomena experienced.

After an admittedly short follow-up period of only six months, life-enhancing and -enriching effects similar to some of those claimed by mystics were shown by the higher scores of the experimental subjects when compared to the controls. In addition, after four hours of follow-up interviews with each subject, the experimenter was left with the impression that the experience had made a profound impact (especially in terms of religious feeling and thinking) on the lives of eight out of ten of the subjects who had been given psilocybin. Although the psilocybin experience was unique and different from the "ordinary" reality of their everyday lives, these subjects felt that this experience had motivated them to appreciate more deeply the meaning of their lives, to gain more depth and authenticity in ordinary living, and to rethink their philosophies of life and values. The data did not suggest that any "ultimate" reality encountered had made "ordinary" reality no longer important or meaningful. The fact that the experience took place in the context of a religious service, with the use of symbols that were familiar and meaningful to the participants, appeared to provide a useful framework within which to derive meaning and integration from the experience, both at the time and later.

The relationship and relative importance of psychological preparation, setting, and drug were important questions raised by our results. A meaningful religious preparation, expectation, and environment appeared to be conducive to positive drug experiences, although the precise qualitative and quantitative role of each factor was not determined. For example, everything possible was done to maximize suggestion, but suggestion alone cannot account for the results, because of the different experience of the control group. The hypothesis that suggestibility was heightened by psilocybin could not be ruled out on the basis of our experiment. An effort was made to avoid suggesting the phenomena of the typology of mysticism, and the service itself made no such direct suggestion.

Implications for the Psychology of Religion

The results of our experiment would indicate that psilocybin (and LSD and mescaline, by analogy) are important tools for the study of the mystical state of consciousness. Experiences previously possible for only a small minority of people, and difficult to study because of their unpredictability and rarity, are now reproducible under suitable conditions. The mystical experience has been called by many names suggestive of areas that are paranormal and not usually considered easily available for investigation (e.g., an experience of transcendence, ecstasy, conversion, or cosmic consciousness); but this is a realm of human experience that should not be rejected as outside the realm of serious scientific study, especially if it can be shown that a practical benefit can result. Our data would suggest that such an overwhelming experience, in which a person existentially encounters basic values such as the meaning of his life (past, present, and future), deep and meaningful interpersonal relationships, and insight into the possibility of personal behavior change, can possibly be therapeutic if approached and worked with in a sensitive and adequate way.

Possibilities for further research with these drugs in the psychology of religion can be divided into two different kinds in relation to the aim: (1) theoretical understanding of the phenomena and psychology of mysticism, and (2) experimental investigation of possible social application in a religious context.

The first, or theoretical, kind of research would be to approach the mystical state of consciousness as closely as possible under controlled experimental conditions and to measure the effect of variables such as the dose of the drug, the preparation and personality of the subject, the setting of the experiment, and the expectation of the experimenter. The work described above was a first step in the measurement of these variables, but more research is needed. The results should be proved to be reproducible by the same and by different experimenters under similar conditions. Such work could lead to a better understanding of mysticism from physiological, biochemical, psychological, and therapeutic perspectives.

Several experimental approaches can be envisioned for the second kind of research—to determine the best method for useful application in a religious context. One suggestion would be the establishment of a research center where carefully controlled drug experiments could be done by a trained research staff which would consist of psychiatrists, clinical psychologists, and professional religious personnel. Subjects, ideally, would spend at least a week at the center to facilitate thorough screening, preparation, and observation of their reactions, both during and after drug experiments. Another suggestion would be the study of the effect of mystical experience on small natural groups of from four to six people who would meet periodically, both prior to and after a drug experience, for serious personal and religious discussion, study, and worship. The reactions of a varied range of subjects with different interests could be studied, but perhaps a good place to start would be with persons professionally interested in religion, such as ministers, priests, rabbis, theologians, and psychologists of religion.

Such research may have important implications for religion. The universal and basic human experience that we have called mystical is recorded from all cultures and ages of human history, but mysticism has never been adequately studied and understood from physiological, biochemical, sociological, psychological, and theological perspectives.

Perhaps there is more of a biochemical basis to such "natural" experiences than has been previously supposed. Certainly many ascetics who have had mystical experiences have engaged in such practices as breathing and postural exercises, sleep deprivation, fasting, flagellation with subsequent infection, sustained meditation, and sensory deprivation in caves or monastic cells. All these techniques have an effect on body chemistry. There is a definite interplay between physiological and psychological processes in the human being. Some of the indolic substances in the body do not differ greatly from the psychedelic drugs.

Many persons concerned with religion are disturbed by drug-facilitated mystical experiences because of their apparent ease of production, with the implication that they are "unearned" and therefore "undeserved." Perhaps the Puritan and Calvinistic element of our Western culture—especially in the United States, where most of the controversy about psychedelic drugs has centered—may be a factor in this uneasiness. Although a drug experience might seem unearned when compared with the rigorous discipline that many mystics describe as necessary, our evidence has suggested that careful preparation and expectation play an important part, not only in the type of experience attained but in later fruits for life. Positive mystical experience with psychedelic drugs is by no means automatic. It would seem that the "drug effect" is a delicate combination of psychological set and setting in which the drug itself is the trigger or facilitating agent—i.e., in which the drug is a *necessary* but not *sufficient* condition. Perhaps the hardest "work" comes after the experience, which in itself may only provide the motivation for future efforts to integrate and appreciate what has been learned. Unless such an experience is integrated into the ongoing life of the individual, only a memory remains rather than the growth of a unfolding renewal process which may be awakened by th mystical experience. If the person has a religious framewor and discipline within which to work, the integrative proces is encouraged and stimulated. Many persons may not need th drug-facilitated mystical experience, but there are others wh would never be aware of the undeveloped potentials withir themselves, or be inspired to work in this direction, withou such an experience. "Gratuitous grace" is an appropriate theo logical term, because the psychedelic mystical experienc can lead to a profound sense of inspiration, reverential awe and humility, perhaps partially as a result of the realizatio that the experience *is* a gift and not particularly earned o deserved.

Mysticism and *inner* experience have been stressed mucl more by Eastern religions than by Western. Perhaps Western culture is as far off balance in the opposite direction—with it manipulation of the *external* world, as exemplified by th emphasis on material wealth, control of nature, and admira tion of science. Mysticism has been accused of fostering es capism from the problems of society, indifference to socia conditions, and disinterest in social change. While the pos sibility of such excesses must always be remembered, ou study has suggested the beneficial potential of mystical ex perience in stimulating the ability to feel and experienc deeply and genuinely with the full harmony of both emotio and intellect. Such wholeness may have been neglected ir modern Western society.

The participants in our experiment who were given psilocy bin found the religious service more meaningful, both at th time and later, than did the control subjects. This findin raises the possibility that psychedelic drug experiences in religious setting may be able to illuminate the dynamics an significance of worship. Increased understanding of the psy chological mechanism involved might lead to more-meaning ful worship experiences for those who have not had the drug experience. The analogy with the efficacy of the sacrament is one example of what would have to be considered for better psychological understanding of what goes on during worship. Such considerations raise the question of the place of the emotional factor, compared to the cognitive, in religious worship. An even more basic question is the validity of religious experience of the mystical type in terms of religious truth. Reactions to such religious implications will vary with theological position and presuppositions, but one value of our study can be to stimulate thoughtful examination of the problems.

Although our experimental results indicated predominantly positive and beneficial subjective effects, possible dangers must not be underestimated and should be thoroughly evaluated by specific research designed to discover the causes and methods of prevention of physical or psychological harm, both short-term and long-term. While physiological addiction has not been reported with psychedelic substances, psychological dependence might be expected if the experience were continually repeated. The intense subjective pleasure and enjoyment of the experience for its own sake could lead to escapism and withdrawal from the world. An experience which is capable of changing motivation and values might cut the nerve of achievement. Widespread apathy toward productive work and accomplishment could cripple a society. Another possible danger might be suicide or prolonged psychosis in very unstable or depressed individuals who are not ready for the intense emotional discharge. If it can be determined that any of these forms of harm occur in certain types of individuals, research could be directed toward the development of pretest methods to screen out such persons. Our evidence would suggest that research on conditions and methods of administration of the drugs might minimize the chance of harmful reactions. Spectacular immediate advance must be sacrificed for ultimate progress by careful, yet daring and imaginative, research under adequate medical supervision.

The ethical implications also cannot be ignored. Any research that uses human volunteers must examine its motives and methods to make certain that human beings are not being manipulated like objects for purposes they do not understand or share. But in research with powerful mental chemicals that may influence the most cherished human functions and values, the ethical problem is even more acute. The mystical experience, historically, has filled man with wondrous awe and has been able to change his style of life and values; but it must not be assumed that greater control of such powerful phenomena will automatically result in wise and constructive use. Potential abuse is just as likely. Those who undertake such research carry a heavy responsibility.

This is not to say that research should be stopped because of the fear of these various risks in an extremely complex and challenging area that has great promise for the psychology of religion. But while research is progressing on the theoretical or primary level and before projects for testing useful social applications in a religious context become widespread, serious and thoughtful examination of the sociological, ethical, and theological implications is needed without delay.

Not the least of these implications is the fear that research that probes the psyche of man and involves his spiritual values may be a sacrilegious transgression by science. If the exploration of certain phenomena should be prohibited, should the mystical experiences made possible by psychedelic drugs be one of the taboo areas? Such restrictions raise several relevant questions: Who is wise enough to decide in advance that such research will cause more harm than good? If such restrictions are applied, where will they end, and will they not impede knowledge of unforeseen possibilities? This attitude on the part of religion is not new. Galileo and Servetus encountered it hundreds of years ago. The issue should not be whether or not to undertake such research, but rather how to do so in a way that sensitively takes into consideration the contribution, significance, and values of religion. A better scientific understanding of the mechanisms and application of mysticism has the potential for a greater appreciation and respect for heretofore rarely explored areas of human consciousness. If these areas have relevance for man's spiritual life, this should be a cause for rejoicing, not alarm. If the values nurtured by religion are fundamental for an understanding of the nature of man, then careful and sensitive scientific research into the experiential side of man's existence has the potential for illumination of these values. The importance of such research should be emphasized, especially because of its possible significance for religion and theology.

At present we are a long way from legitimate social use o

such drugs in our society. We do not yet have nearly enough adequate knowledge of the long-term physiological or psychological effects. It is true that thus far no organ or tissue damage has been reported in the usual dosage range, and physiological addiction has not occurred. But as in the case of any new drug, deleterious side effects sometimes do not become apparent until years after a drug has been introduced. The social suffering caused by the misuse of alcohol is a major public health problem throughout the Western world. We certainly need to hesitate before introducing a new agent, much more powerful than alcohol and perhaps with a potential for the development of subtle psychological dependence. And yet, paradoxically, these very drugs may hold a promise for the treatment of chronic alcoholism by way of the psychedelic mystical experience (Kurland, Unger, and Shaffer, 1957; Unger et. al., 1966; Unger, 1965). Such questions can be satisfactorily answered only by thorough scientific research of the possibilities and by sober evaluation of the results.

Many unknown conscious and unconscious factors operate in the mystical experience. Much investigation is needed in this area, and drugs like psilocybin can be a powerful tool. Experimental facilitation of mystical experiences under controlled conditions can be an important method of approach to a better understanding of mysticism. Better understanding can lead to appreciation of the role and place of such experiences in the history and practice of religion.

If parapsychology is concerned in an interdisciplinary way with the question of the potentials of human experience, then the controlled exploration of experimental mysticism, facilitated by psychedelic drugs, is an important parapsychological research area, where psychopharmacology, psychiatry, psychology, and theology can meet to mutual advantage.

THE CHURCH OF THE AWAKENING

JOHN W. AIKEN

The Church of the Awakening is a fellowship of those who are dedicated to conscious participation in their own spiritual evolution and who are aware of the importance of the proper use of psychedelic plants or chemicals as a factor in that growth. We believe that the real purpose of life is growth in awareness, or the unfolding, the actualizing, of our inner spiritual potential. The word "spiritual" is used in this discussion to refer to that non-material reality that underlies material reality; the depths of our being, as distinguished from the surface manifestation; the awareness of ourselves as Being or Life, rather than as the body or the personality in which that life is expressing itself.

In the process of spiritual growth, many techniques have been used, such as prayer, fasting, study of scriptures, meditation, mantras, surrender to a Higher Power, and service to others. As far back in history as we can probe, the ingestion of various plants, such as the peyote cactus in America, certain mushrooms in many areas, and soma in India, has also been a means of promoting growth in awareness, called by some "Self-realization."

The Church of the Awakening, then, is not a psychedelic church in the sense that its only or even its chief function is to promote the use of psychedelic chemicals. It is, however, a psychedelic church in the wider meaning of the word "psychedelic," which is "mind-manifesting" or "consciousness-expanding."

The Church originated in a group that has been meeting in Socorro, New Mexico, since 1958 for study and discussion, exploring ways in which life might be made more meaningful.

My wife Louisa and I, both osteopathic physicians engaged in general medical practice since 1937, moved to Socorro in 1948. We continued practice there, she majoring in obstetrics, until our retirement in 1964. We were active members of the Presbyterian Church and participated in community affairs. I served one term as president of the Rotary Club and ten years as a member of the City Council.

In 1951 we were severely jolted by the death by drowning of our younger son, David, in the crash of a U. S. Navy plane in the Mediterranean Sea. In 1957 our older son, Don, also a physician, drowned in a sailboat accident in Lake Huron. These events stimulated us to engage seriously in the search for the meaning of life. The answers provided by our church failed to satisfy us, for an admonition to intellectual belief could not meet a deep emotional need.

We found a few other people who had similar interests and needs, and the first meeting of the group was held on October 12, 1958, with six persons attending. Meetings were held weekly, and attendance grew to thirty. The basic interest was in the exploration of man's potential. Many questions were asked with deep sincerity, and we experienced the truth of Jesus' statement, "Seek, and you will find."

Because of our personal bereavement, we began with the question of death. We were acutely aware of Job's yearning when he wrote, "Man that is born of woman is of few days and full of trouble. He comes forth like a flower, and withers. . . . Man breathes his last, and where is he? If a man die, shall he live again?" This question is in the back of everyone's mind, but it had suddenly become the most important question in our lives, with immediate and personal urgency. The answers we found through our study and experience assure us that, if a man dies, he *does* live again (Ford and Bro, 1958). It is more accurate, however, to say that death is not an ending, but only a continuation of life, with expression in a different form.

Our experiences led to further questions: Is consciousness confined to this physical body and its very limited senses? Are there other, "extra" senses? We know that a dog can hear sounds pitched too high for the human ear, and I know that many people can hear sounds that are inaudible to me. May it not be that there are some who are sensitive to entirely different types of frequencies that are unrecognized by most of us, and who may have "extrasensory perception" (ESP)?

The British and the American Societies for Psychical Research have accumulated much evidence that indicates that ESP is a fact that must be taken into consideration if we are to have a truer view of life. With this ESP, some can become aware of events taking place at a distance in space (clairvoyance). Some can become aware of events that will occur in the future (precognition). Some even seem able to communicate with the so-called dead (mediumship). Russian researchers have referred to persons with this extrasensory capacity as "biological radios," for they are able to "tune in" to these frequencies, unsensed by most of us, and to convert them to a type of stimulus to which we can respond. In this way, through one of these "biological radios," a man named Arthur Ford, we first received evidence that our sons were dead only in the physical sense. We found that they are still very much alive as personalities, functioning in a different way. This seemed to be evidence that the world of the physical senses is only the surface of a reality that is actually much more vast.

We next became intrigued by reports of seemingly miraculous healing, which resulted when certain individuals or groups prayed for, or in some cases placed their hands on, the sick. (We should recognize that so-called miracles are only the manifestation of laws we do not as yet understand.)

We read reports by Rebecca Beard, M.D. (1950) of a personal healing and of other cases she observed, indicating that there is a healing force beyond that produced by medications, or even by the co-operation of the subconscious mind of the patient. Dr. Alexis Carrel witnessed almost unbelievable healings at Lourdes, in France (1950). Ambrose and Olga Worrall, of Baltimore, are two among many who seem to be channels for this healing power today (1965). Other strange manifestations of this power are reported by Harold Sherman after careful and extensive observation of "wonder" healers in the Philippines (1967).

In our own experience, one evening as we were praying for healing, and focusing our love on various people present, I felt impelled to put my hands on a woman present, named Natalie, who had a serious heart ailment. As I placed my hands on her, my left on the upper chest, the right on the upper back, I felt a surge of power, much like a strong electrical current, flowing through my right arm and hand. There remained a sensation of numbness in the arm and hand for some fifteen minutes afterward.

I had X-rayed Natalie previously and found her heart enlarged to almost twice normal size. Upon re-X-ray a month later, the heart size was normal, and her symptoms greatly improved. What happened, or whether this incident had anything to do with the healing, I do not know. I do know that something unusual happened, and that many others have had more-striking experiences of a similar nature. In the New Testament, James says, "The prayer of faith will save the sick man, and the Lord will raise him up." We studied, we experimented, as many others are doing, and we found that it is so.

It seemed that we had no choice but to continue to explore the depths of the mind and of consciousness. As we did so, we found ourselves coming face to face with life itself. We began to be dimly aware that our own true nature *is* this depth, which is life, or consciousness, and which is universal, omnipotent, and omnipresent. Many call it God. To discover that this is what we really are, rather than the body, the mind, or the personality, involves a radical shift in perspective. There are many who fear to experience this shift.

Many of the questions we were asking, and the areas of our explorations, seem to be off limits in most religious and scientific circles. Those who begin such "metaphysical" (beyond the physical) seeking are likely to become suspect by their friends who have chosen to accept the teachings of orthodoxy, whether scientific or religious. New ideas are regarded by many as threats to the ego, to personal security. Perhaps this is a part of the instinct for self-preservation, which we all have. When our mental structure of ideas is threatened, we become as defensive as when the physical body is in danger, for much effort has been invested in each case.

There were many in Socorro who felt that the members of our group were engaged in a very dangerous enterprise, and many warnings were given that we should return to the fold. The minister of one local church, several of whose members were attending our meetings, warned that such groups could be useful, but that a minister (presumably of his particular denomination!) should always be present to be sure that we did not go too far afield. The minister of another church, when invited to discuss with our group what his religion meant to him, declined the invitation. He said that the explorations in which we were engaged were not approved by the community, and he did not care to risk his reputation by meeting with us. A patient told one of our group that the Aikens had seemed to be fine people, and good doctors, but now that they had developed such strange ideas, they could no longer be trusted.

This, of course, was a threat to *our* security! Some of the members of the group could not stand the pressure of this negative public opinion, and withdrew. The majority remained, and we continued to inquire into the nature and purpose of life. One finds a great challenge in this quest, and a very deep inner satisfaction in the results. When one has *experienced* reality, there is little interest in mere *beliefs about* reality. When one has seen the ocean, he no longer has any need to "believe in" its existence. It is almost impossible to return to any orthodox teachings that seem inconsistent with one's own personal experience. We could only continue on the path we had chosen, even in the face of public disapproval.

At first, as has been said, we investigated the phenomena of ESP and the findings of parapsychology. As the interests of the group expanded, we became aware of the writings and experiences of the mystics of the world, including such people as Meister Eckhart, Thomas Kelly, Evelyn Underhill, Ramana Maharshi, Huang Po, the Hindu rishis, and the Sufis. They were of various cultures and religions. They seemed to have explored the deepest mysteries of life and experienced reality in depth. Many of the things that they have to say seem very strange from an intellectual point of view but strike a note of deep understanding from the perspective of experience. From this perspective also, the life and teachings of Jesus took on more-challenging and more-vital significance. For the little group in Socorro, the search was becoming more and more rewarding.

In 1959 we had our first information on the psychedelic substances, through reading an article in a scientific journal by Dr. Humphry Osmond, then medical director of the Saskatchewan Provincial Hospital, in Canada (1957b). Dr. Osmond reported on research dealing with the effects produced by the ingestion of such substances as LSD, mescaline, and peyote. He pointed out that new depths of awareness seemed to develop during this drug-induced state, and in this article proposed the word "psychedelic" for these substances, as being more accurate than the word "hallucinogenic," which was then in common use.

More important than the state of awareness that many developed, it seemed that insights attained during this experience could be applied to the problems of everyday life and their solution. Most interesting to us was Dr. Osmond's observation that the psychedelic state seemed often to be very similar to the mystical state, in the study of which we were at that time engaged.

Correspondence with Dr. Osmond brought additional information and the names of others who were doing research with these psychedelic substances. All were most helpful in sharing with us the results of their work and advising us as to the best ways in which to proceed with our own investigations. At that time we found that we could obtain peyote, a cactus that grows in the southern Rio Grande Valley. It seemed effective in inducing, in much greater depth, a type of awareness or mystical experience that some of us had already experienced, to a lesser degree, as a result of using other spiritual disciplines.

By "mystical experience" is meant here a state of consciousness in which the individual finds a oneness with the universe, and feels unconditional love for God, his neighbor, and himself. All are realized as One. It is not unlike the state of one who is deeply in love. In Eastern terminology this is called Self-realization, liberation, enlightenment, or satori. The Christian may call it a vital experience of God, or coming to know Christ. The psychologist may call it the creative integration of the personality around a deep center. By whatever name it may be called, it seems to those who have experienced it to be the way toward the actualization of our ultimate potential as human beings, toward the identification *as* that Life, or Divinity, which is the reality of each living being.

In the early days of our exploration of these deeper levels of consciousness, one of our group experienced a very marked change in his outlook as a result of the peyote sacrament. Prior to this he had been an atheist, but after his participation in the sacrament he said, "I have experienced God! I know that reality is there, that it is desirable above all things, and that it is attainable. Now I am willing to take the path of effort, to earn the right to have and to keep this reality. I know that I, too, may become the way, the truth, and the life."

To many it seems strange that the ingestion of a cactus can change one's outlook on life so dramatically, but modern chemistry has produced many compounds that modify the mind of man by changing the chemistry of the body. Tranquilizers—chemicals that relieve tensions, neuroses, and even psychoses—are well known. The psychedelics, however, when properly used, have a more constructive effect in that they may help produce *understanding*, and thus, unlike the tranquilizers, can remove the *cause* of the tensions, occasionally in a single dose. They have the unusual effect of opening wider the doors of perception and self-understanding. On the physical level, they enable one to see with new vision and to hear with new appreciation. A great many who have been through this experience find a much keener enjoyment of nature, of flowers, trees, mountains, and a greater appreciation of the arts. On an extended level, one may develop an awareness of an all-inclusive spiritual reality, which, the masters have told us, is the substance, the Ground of Being, that underlies the world of both the senses and the "extra-senses."

Our explorations with peyote went on, and we were more and more impressed with the importance of the effects of this substance when taken by people with a motivation toward better understanding of themselves and of life, and when given by one with similar motivation and an awareness of the hazards of improper use. Later we experimented with the use of mescaline, the psychedelic alkaloid present in the peyote cactus, and found the effects to be identical with those we had obtained through the use of peyote itself.

We were not alone in our explorations, and soon found others with similar interests in the religious use of these substances. In 1962 and 1963 the public was beginning to develop a very negative image of the psychedelics, especially LSD, as a result of sensationalism in the news media when reporting some of the unfortunate results of their unsupervised use. We were disturbed by the possibility that indiscriminate use for sensational purposes was likely to bring about restrictive legislation that would interfere with their use for religious purposes. My wife and I made two trips to Los Angeles to discuss this matter with interested friends there, and it was suggested that our group should incorporate as a non-profit organization or church, in which the use of psychedelics as a religious sacrament might be legally continued.

The idea seemed to have merit, and continued to develop. On October 14, 1963, the Church of the Awakening was incorporated under the laws of the state of New Mexico as a non-profit religious organization. The psychedelic experience was named as a sacrament of the Church, to be available only to those who have been members of the Church for a minimum period of three months, and whose readiness for the sacrament is approved by the Board of Directors. It is recommended that the experience not be repeated more frequently than every three months, for it seems to us that frequent use of these substances is likely to result for some in a desire for the experience for its own sake, rather than in the more important application of insights achieved to the development of a better way of life.

Our limitations on the use of the sacrament were also imposed in order to avoid some of the unfortunate results that were being reported in the news media from frequent and unsupervised use of large amounts of LSD by those who had little idea of what might result. When one takes a psychedelic "for kicks" and suddenly finds himself confronting what seems like Ultimate Reality, it is then too late to retreat, and panic frequently develops. It seems to us highly important to protect the proper religious use, and also to protect novices from unnecessary hazards.

Our goal has been to attract members who are interested primarily in spiritual growth and who are willing to follow the usual disciplines and practices for such growth both as a preparation for the sacrament and as a continuing follow-up. We are well aware of the importance of other methods of Self-realization. We have found, however, that the psychedelic sacrament, when added to the spiritual armamentarium, can be of great value in the search for meaning.

In our use of the experience as a religious sacrament with many people, we have seen some unpleasant, but no harmful, effects. Many seem to be outstandingly constructive. The experience of the atheist who found God seemed to us to be constructive. Another, who had little or no appreciation of music, now delights in his collection of classical records. Another found a new understanding and acceptance of her husband. Another has been able to relate more lovingly to her children. We are always pleased with the attitude that many express after their participation in the sacrament by saying, I have seen so many things in myself that need changing that I am sure I will not want another experience for at least a year!

Other experimenters, using these substances in ways somewhat similar to ours, have reported similar results. The work in progress at the Spring Grove Hospital since 1963 on the treatment of alcoholism indicates that many alcoholics, when they attain this degree of self-understanding, are able to recover from alcoholism, sometimes after only a single experience. This is in accord with the statement of Bill Wilson, the founder of Alcoholics Anonymous, that the most important factor in recovery from the disease of alcoholism is ". . . a deep and genuine religious experience." We have found that, for many, a properly oriented psychedelic experience can be a deep and genuine religious experience.

Religious or spiritual experience, like any other, is intensely personal and cannot be conveyed in words to one who has not had something similar. We cannot convey even the taste of a strange fruit to one who has not tasted it. The closest we can come to it is to say that it is "something like" the taste of another which we have both experienced. Again, how could we describe the color red, or any color, or even the sense of vision, to one who was born blind?

When one explores this inner space, the depths of consciousness (Jesus called it "the Kingdom of Heaven which is within you"), he finds experiences that have no counterpart in ordinary life, and so is at a loss as to how he can explain it to one who has not explored. All that he can say is, You must experience it for yourself before you will really understand.

There seems to be no way in which legislators, or the general public to whom they are sensitive, can be made directly aware of the religious benefits of a properly directed psyche-delic sacrament except through having the experience. There is still, however, some degree of respect, both among legislators and the general public, for religious sacraments, even those that may seem rather strange to some. The right of the Indians of the Native American Church to continue the use of peyote as a sacrament, as it has been used for hundreds of years, has been recognized by governmental agencies, in spite of all efforts of fanatics to deny them this right. The Code of Federal Regulations states, in Section 166.3 (c) (3) of Title 21, "The listing of peyote in this sub-paragraph (as being restricted or forbidden) does not apply to non-drug use in bona fide religious ceremonies of the Native American Church." We feel that other races should have equal rights before the law and that the Church of the Awakening should be able to continue its use of peyote as a religious sacrament. While the use of peyote or other psychedelics is not our primary purpose, we have found it to be a highly important aid to spiritual growth or "awakening." No one of the sacraments of the Christian churches is the primary purpose of any church, but each is an important aid to spiritual growth.

The name *Church of the Awakening* was selected after careful consideration of our orientation and motivation. The explorations in awareness, of "inner space," such as those we have described, result for many in a new perspective. It is a new state of consciousness, in which all things are perceived as One. This state cannot be comprehended intellectually, but it can be experienced by those who are ready for it. Readiness seems usually, though not always, to be a result of serious dedication to the inner quest.

When one has achieved this new perspective, his former state seems like a dream by comparison, in which he was unaware of many of the facets and relationships of life. David, in Psalm 17, says, "When I awake, I shall be satisfied with beholding Thy form." When Gautama Siddhartha, some twenty-five hundred years ago, achieved this mystical insight, he was asked what it was that made him view life so differently. He replied, "I am awake!" In his language, the word was "buddha," and so he came to be called "The Buddha," or "The One Who Is Awake." The Church of the Awakening is intended to be a fellowship of those who are seeking for this experience in depth, for this *awakening*.

Our purpose is not to present a body of doctrine for the acceptance of members, nor to furnish ultimate intellectual answers to the basic questions of life. The purpose of this fellowship is to encourage growth and awakening on the part of each member, to stimulate him to ask questions, to develop insights, and to encourage the sharing with others of such insights as a loving service.

Belief is a first stage in the religious life, but when we are ready to question, then we can begin to grow into the more mature stage of *experience*. Is this not true also in science? The student believes what his books and teachers tell him, but he is expected to prove it for himself in the laboratory, and in life. True doubt, then, is a constructive force, for when we question earnestly, we begin to experiment, and experiment leads to experience. We know then, from deep within ourselves, because of our own experience, what we formerly only believed because someone else had said that it was so. Our use of the psychedelic sacrament is an important factor in growth from the stage of belief to that of experience of spiritual truths.

The Church of the Awakening, therefore, encourages doubt, questioning, and experiment as the way of growth, the way of life. This process must begin at a different point for each individual. Each one is unique; each is the result of past causes —thoughts, feelings, and actions. Each is encouraged to participate in his own growth, to promote his own spiritual evolution, to be, as St. Paul says, ". . . a cocreator with God." We feel that such growth, such evolution, is the true purpose of all religion. In fact, such growth *is* religion!

Each of us must begin and continue the long, difficult— and joyous!—process of living life. There must be willingness to fail if there is to be any chance of success. There must be acceptance of ourselves and of others, with all our present defects and limitations. These defects and limitations are but the promise that growth and evolution can take place.

The Church of the Awakening is dedicated to this ideal of enhancing the growth of the inner life of each member, and also the expression of that growth through more-enlightened service. We note that the greatest service does not always consist in removing the problems of another, but more often in encouraging him to meet those problems as opportunities for growth.

Inner growth, or learning, and outer service, or sharing, can be encouraged in the traditional ways, but should be without the traditional bondage to forms and rituals. Forms and rituals may be used when desired, but should not become an end in themselves. Every means to the end of growth should itself be outgrown. When the growth has been achieved, the means should be discarded, as is the scaffolding used to erect a building. One may use a raft to cross a stream, but he is handicapped if he tries to carry it on his shoulders as he explores the other shore.

In addition to such traditional forms and rituals as may be used, which should change with the changing needs and desires of the group, we encourage the study of the writings of sages and mystics. We need to become acquainted with the lives and perspectives of those of past and present generations who have attained at least some measure of freedom from selfishness and egotism, which both the Christ and the Buddha pointed out were the cause of all our difficulties.

Another very important and useful means for sharing insights and for mutual help in the process of growth is the meeting of members and friends at stated times. In this group activity, two practices are helpful. One is sharing through discussion. The other is sharing through silence. By means of discussion, the sharing of ideas, we become able to change our old ways of thinking, to adapt to new ideas, to develop the intellectual aspect of life.

Sharing through silence, or meditation, however, is likely to be a greater stimulus to spiritual growth and the development of understanding. How can silence be so important in spiritual growth? We are usually led to believe that a powerful intellect, with a large supply of self-consistent concepts, is the supreme human achievement. We have even been taught that we *are* the intellect. But when one has been privileged to have a mystical experience, whether spontaneous, the result of spiritual disciplines, or induced by means of psychedelic substances, he experiences a Self of which the intellect is only a tool.

Like any other tool, the intellect is very useful for some purposes, but of little or no value for others. If we are to achieve this glimpse of the depths of awareness, or the "Awakening," the intellect must be quieted in order that we may go beyond it, to That which is its source.

Words are symbols of ideas, of concepts. Concepts, in turn, are symbols that point to an experience. When our attention is focused on words, or on concepts, we fail to achieve the depths of the experience they represent. Meditation or silence (inner as well as outer) is practice in going beyond concepts to the Self, which is the reality underlying all thoughts, feelings, and actions. "Be still, and know," the Psalmist says.

As one follows the path of inner exploration, it may happen that psychic powers develop. These powers include such abilities as clairvoyance, telepathy, precognition, healing, or communication with the after-death level of life. Such powers may, if properly used, be a help in turning our awareness from the outer to the inner life; "biological radio," as discussed earlier, was very helpful to me at one stage. However, if sought as ends in themselves, psychic powers can be a hindrance in our quest for That which is beyond all phenomena, whether physical, mental, or psychic. It is well, for example, that one should have a strong, properly functioning physical body; but to become an Atlas, to make physical strength an end in itself, is to be caught again in the trap of the ego. Psychic powers may be useful, just as physical strength is useful; but both are means rather than ends in themselves. The primary purpose of the Church of the Awakening has been stated to be the enhancement of growth in love and understanding, and the concurrent diminution of egotism and selfishness.

Our purpose may also be furthered by individual and group participation in the psychedelic sacrament or mystical initiation. We believe that this sacrament should be administered only to those who have prepared and qualified themselves for it, and only by properly trained monitors or ministers of the Church. Such administration should be in accord with the laws of the United States, and also of the state in which a particular Church group is located. If such laws seem restrictive of reasonable religious freedom, then when the time is appropriate the members may seek for an improvement in the legal situation.

In the life of the spirit, the psychedelic sacrament is also considered to be a *means* to growth, and not an end in itself. Of more importance is the development of insight, which results from participation in this experience, and the intelligent application of this insight in service to our fellow men and the improvement of our own character. It seems that we do have a choice as to whether we integrate or disintegrate, and that the investment of conscious effort toward integration is necessary and important in the development of character. Our goal for members of the Church is true integration, or Unitary Consciousness, which to us is the actualization through growth, aided by effort, of the highest potential inherent within each one.

We hope to develop ministers to serve the Church whose philosophy of life is in harmony with this outlook and who are also capable of administering the psychedelic sacrament. There are excellent monitors within the "psychedelic cult," but many are likely to regard the psychedelic experience as an end in itself, while others are careless of the legal situation. Among professional researchers in the psychedelic field, some do not have the religious or spiritual orientation we have attempted to express. Others, who may have this orientation, may not care to have their positions jeopardized by making it public. Our culture is heavily materialistic and is likely to reject any who attempt to follow another path. We are seeking men and women who can and will dedicate themselves to this type of growth and service.

We have emphasized the importance of the mystical experience as a means of spiritual growth, but whether it results from the psychedelic sacrament or from the practice of other spiritual disciplines, it is only the beginning, and not the end, on the path to Self-realization. It is evident that we should evolve beyond isolated moments of perception, or insight, or mystical experience. Our real growth consists in fusing such moments into the continuum of life. No doubt this is what St. Paul had in mind when he wrote, "Rejoice always, pray without ceasing, be grateful in all circumstances."

We would avoid, in the Church of the Awakening, the temptation to rely on the momentary experience and the desire to seek to repeat it frequently. We would encourage the application of insights and the development of new patterns of thought, feeling, and action more nearly in line with That which we have seen is our real Self.

Irving Babbitt, in his introduction to The Dhammapada (1936), comments that the readiness of men to succumb to schemes for acquiring sudden wealth is perhaps only a faint image of their proneness to yield to the lure of teachings that seem to hold out the hope of spiritual riches without any corresponding effort. Especially in America, he says, substantial material reward awaits any one who can devise some new and painless plan for getting "in tune with the Infinite."

There are many who are still hopeful that the use of LSD will prove to be such a painless plan; that it will save us, if not from our sins, at least from spiritual effort. Men seek to enjoy the fruits of renunciation, although renouncing nothing. They seek to achieve the ends, but to avoid the means, which seem difficult and arduous. The glimpse of reality achieved by psychedelic means or in other ways is only that—a glimpse. We have seen the mountain, and know the direction in which we must go. Repeatedly gazing at the mountain does not satisfy the mountaineer. He must place his own feet upon the path and climb it for himself. In fact, the greatest joy is found in the challenge of the climb. As one of our members, quoted earlier, said, "I have experienced God! Now I am willing to take the path of effort." So often we overlook the fact that one of the great satisfactions in life is found in overcoming, in meeting challenges. It is said in the Hindu scriptures that he who overcomes himself is greater than he who overcomes a multitude of the enemy. In the Christian scriptures, it is said, "He who overcomes shall have the fountain of the waters of Life."

Maturity teaches us that the reward is in the climbing, rather than in the arriving. The joy of life comes in living. Dr. Bernard Phillips, of Temple University, titled one of his lectures "The Search will make you free" (1964). Jesus said,

"Seek, and you will find." When we find the seeking, the search, we are free!!

It would seem that the state of expanded awareness and insight frequently achieved during the psychedelic state can be validated only by further effort in the following of spiritual disciplines in re-creating character. Mystical insight can make us aware of our own egocentricity and selfishness, and can challenge us to engage in the process of overcoming, of self-transformation and self-transcendence. It can challenge us to fulfill ourselves by "dying"; then, as St. Paul expressed it, "It is no longer I, but Christ that lives." A seed must give up its life as a seed, in order that it might become a channel for life.

The Church of the Awakening seeks to encourage this development of the inner life, not through imposing an authoritative teaching, but through voluntary choice and individual effort on the part of each member. We are learning that there are no recipes for life. Love is the law, of course, but each must choose how he will apply it, each instant. We cannot accept old doctrines that divide rather than unite, nor old shibboleths of nationalism when they demand unloving acts; nor can we unthinkingly accept old codes of conduct that we see have brought our world to the brink of chaos. Before rejecting the old, however, we must have sufficient spiritual maturity to choose new directions that will be in closer harmony with life.

The Church of the Awakening is not unique in facing these situations, and we also recognize that all problems, of whatever nature, are opportunities for learning, for growth, and for actualizing our potential. We know that a tree that is subjected to the buffeting of wind and weather can develop great strength in depth. We know also that it is life that is living us, that it is life that is doing all things that are done. We know that life holds the final answers. Each of us has only to do, to the best of his ability, that which is before him, and life will arrange all things well.

As we engage in these challenges of the outer world, we must not allow ourselves to be distracted from the inner quest, or we will have lost the way. We need to maintain our awareness of the inexhaustible mystery of life. We find it helpful to encourage this awareness in various ways: through association with mature people, through exposure to great literature, through the practice of meditation, and by means of the psychedelic sacrament.

Wordsworth, in *Tintern Abbey*, gives us the spirit of the inner life, on which a harmonious outer life can be built:

> I have felt
> A presence that disturbs me with the joy
> Of elevated thoughts; a sense sublime
> Of something far more deeply interfused.
> Whose dwelling is the light of setting suns,
> And the round ocean and the living air,
> And the blue sky, and in the mind of man:
> A motion and a spirit, that impels
> All thinking things, all objects of thought,
> And rolls through all things.

THE PSYCHEDELICS AND RELIGION

WALTER HOUSTON CLARK

The recent discovery of the religious properties of Lysergic Acid Diethylamide-25 is not such a wholly new phenomenon as some people seem to believe. There is some evidence to suggest that the secret potion that was part of the ordeal of initiation into the Eleusinian mysteries in ancient Greece contained a psychedelic drug. The somewhat mysterious drug called *soma*, used in India, sometimes for religious purposes, was psychedelic, while the Mexican mushroom whose active principle is psilocybin has been used by the Aztecs for centuries in their sacraments. Their word for it, significantly, meant "God's flesh."

The peyote button, the top of a certain spineless cactus plant, has been and is now used by some members of nearly all the American Indian tribes in cultic ceremonies. The peyote religion goes back nearly a century in historical records and certainly is even more ancient. At present it is represented by the Native American Church, a loose collection of some two hundred thousand members, according to its claim.

Peyote among the Indians has had a history of controversy not unlike LSD among whites. However, despite years of repressive laws and legal harassment, there has been little or no hard evidence of claims made as to its harmfulness, and some indication that it has done good. More importantly, laws made to repress its use have been declared unconstitutional in several states on the ground that they have violated constitutional guarantees of freedom of religion.[1]

Perhaps the most distinguished and eloquent advocate of the view that certain chemicals may promote religious states of mind was William James, who some seventy years ago inhaled the psychedelic of his day, nitrous oxide. He referred to this self-experiment, in *The Varieties of Religious Experience*, in his chapter on mysticism, where he wrote the often quoted words:

. . . our normal waking consciousness, rational consciousness as we call it, is but one special type of consciousness, whilst all about it, parted by the filmiest of screens, there lie potential forms of consciousness entirely different. . . . No account of the universe in its totality can be final which leaves these other forms of consciousness quite disregarded.[2]

But "religion" is an elusive term, and whether or not we can regard states associated with the psychedelics as religious depends on how we define it. Doubtless there are those who would regard any state initiated by the ingestion of a chemical as *by definition* non-religious. For such people, the reading of this chapter will be an idle exercise. Tillich defines religion as "ultimate concern," while both William James and W. R. Inge speak of the roots of religion as ultimately mystical. Rudolf Otto, in *The Idea of the Holy* (1958), speaks of the non-rational elements of the religious life in terms of horror, dread, amazement, and fascination as the *mysterium tremendum*, "the mystery that makes one tremble." Certainly, as I will point out in more detail later, the subject who has consumed the forbidden fruit of the psychedelics will often testify that he has been opened to his own "ultimate concern" in life and may even speak in terms reminis-

[1] See Aberle (1966) and Slotkin (1956) for full anthropological accounts.
[2] P. 298.

cent of the medieval mystics. Furthermore, one of the chief objections of the opponents of the psychedelics is that for many the experience may be "dread-full," as cogent an illustration of Otto's thesis as one could well expect to find.

Long before I took very seriously the claims that eaters of psychedelic chemicals made as to their religious experiences, I defined religion as "the inner experience of an individual when he senses a Beyond, especially as evidenced by the effect of this experience on his behavior when he actively attempts to harmonize his behavior with the Beyond."[3] Consequently, it would be to this standard that I would refer experiences triggered by the psychedelic drugs, in order to determine whether they should be called religious or not.

From the definition, it will be clear that the core of religious experience is subjective, therefore never to be fully shared with another person. Consequently, we are forced to rely to a large degree on the words of the religious person for any determination of religion. This necessity disturbs the modern psychologist, whose too-narrow conception of his discipline as a science bars him from probing the nature of the religious consciousness despite its cogency as a source of profound personality change. As he observes the conventional churchgoer and hears him glibly using such terms as "conviction of sin," "rebirth," "redemption," and "salvation," the psychologist may too hastily conclude that such terms are mere pious language that brings a certain sentimental comfort to the worshiper but hardly represents any marked change in his relations with his fellow men. The psychologist has forgotten, if he ever knew, that such terms are the echoes of experiences that, perhaps many years ago, but also today, have transformed the lives of prince and beggar, enabling them to unify their lives and attain heights that could have been possible in no other way. It is this effectiveness, *along with* the subjective reports by subjects of encounters filled with mystery and awe, for which we must be on the lookout as we try to appraise the religious significance and value of these strange chemicals.

But before we start our survey, I must say something about

[3] See my *The Psychology of Religion* (1958), Chapter 2, for a discussion.

the place of the non-rational in the religious life. Notice that I call it *non-rational,* not *irrational.* The religious life involves at least three basic factors: First is the life of speculation and thought, the expression of the rational function of the human mind. The second is the active expression of religious principles, the concern for others and the observance of ethics and other social demands that grow out of one's religious commitment. Religion shares these two functions with other interests and duties of humankind. But the third function is unique, and without it no other function or activity can be called religious in any but a very pale and secondary sense. This third function is the experience of the sacred, the encounter with the holy, which not so much logically, but intuitively, or non-rationally, the subject recognizes as that which links him with the seers and the saints of today and of yesterday. A non-drug example will be found in Arthur Koestler's autobiographical *The Invisible Writing* (1955), in the chapter entitled "The Hours by the Window." It is this non-rational perception of the holy that so moves the individual and interpenetrates both his thinking and his activity, infusing them with tremendous energy and giving to his whole life that stamp we call *religious.* We must ask whether in any sense the psychedelic substances arouse this factor, to determine whether we can characterize the result as religion.

If we can accept the direction of the argument thus far, that the essential core of religion may be found in the mystical consciousness and the direct experience of the holy, I can show considerable evidence that it is this aspect of the non-rational consciousness that the psychedelic drugs release. I consider my first example sufficiently persuasive to make the point.

Dr. Walter N. Pahnke of Spring Grove Hospital, Baltimore, in a doctorate study at Harvard, used twenty theological students in a double-blind study of the effects of psilocybin. All twenty were given similar preparations; half were given the drug and half placebos; then all attended the same two-and-one-half-hour Good Friday service. The experimental group reported overwhelming evidence of mystical experiences, while the control group reported next to none.[4] The reports included intuitions and encounters with ultimate reality, the holy, and God; in other words the "Beyond" of my definition. Furthermore, a six-month follow-up showed much evidence that the subjects felt they had experienced an enlivening of their religious lives, resulting in an increased involvement with the problems of living and the service of others.

The previous sentence supports that aspect of my definition that emphasizes the active functions of religion, the effect of the experience of the Beyond on the individual when he "actively attempts to harmonize his life with the Beyond." Western prejudices in religion favor the pragmatic test, so claims of encounter with God or ultimate reality are always more impressive when they can be supported by concrete evidence of benefit like this. Further cogent evidence is supplied us in studies of alcoholics treated with LSD by Osmond and Hoffer in the early 1950s in Saskatchewan. According to Dr. Hoffer's report, of sixty difficult cases, half were no longer drinking five years later, while there was a very high correspondence between success and the report of the subject that his experience had been transcendental in William James's sense of the term.[5]

Still more evidence pointing in the same general direction comes from work done by Dr. Timothy Leary when he was at Harvard. He received permission from the State Commission of Correction to give psilocybin to thirty-five inmates at Concord State Reformatory. Since Dr. Leary had reported that the convicts were having religious experiences and the work was controversial, I persuaded him to introduce me to some of them so that I could investigate at first hand. While unable to follow up all the subjects, I talked with those who were still in prison—by and large those who had committed the more serious crimes and so were serving long terms. I found that it was indeed true that these men referred to their experiences as religious in varying ways. One reported a vision

[4] For a fuller report, see the Pahnke article in this volume; also Pahnke, "Drugs and Mysticism" (1966).

[5] See remarks by Abram Hoffer in H. A. Abramson (ed.), *The Use of LSD in Psychotherapy* (1960), pp. 18–19, 114–15.

n which he had participated with Christ in His Crucifixion. Shortly after this, he had looked out the window. "Suddenly all my life came before my eyes," said this man, an armed robber of nearly forty who had spent most of his adult life behind bars, "and I said to myself, What a waste!" Since that time these men have formed, within the walls, an AA-type organization called the Self-Development Group, to rehabilitate themselves and others. I could not deny that there were profound religious forces at work among these men as the result of the drug treatment (Leary and Clark, 1963).

In their book *The Varieties of Psychedelic Experience* Masters and Houston present a wealth of cases illustrating psychedelic experiences of various kinds. Though nearly all their 206 subjects reported religious imagery of some kind, only a few demonstrated mystical experience of what the authors consider a transforming and integrating kind at the deepest level; but they believe that the drugs do facilitate the latter, making their belief clear chiefly through a remarkable illustrative case in their final chapter. The subject, a successful psychologist in his late thirties, had been irresistibly attracted to what society regards as "evil" from his earliest youth. He believed in nothing, was a militant atheist, was sexually promiscuous, and to his students "preached a gospel of total debauchery." The appearance of neurotic symptoms had led him into a process of self-analysis and therapy, which had been only partly successful. But only three sessions with LSD led this person, through an intricate series of shattering symbolic experiences, to an almost total transformation of self. A year afterward, this transformation was seen by the subject as an encounter with God that had been both religious and lasting. This fact was attested to by those who knew him.

The foregoing is just a sampling of many studies that report religious elements following the ingestion of psychedelic drugs. When the environment suggests religion, a higher proportion, up to 85–90 per cent, of the experiences are perceived as religious by the subjects. Those who resist the religious interpretation are much less likely to experience it, but even some of these, much to their surprise, may "experience God."

The following case is an illustration: As part of an experiment at a mental hospital, I had occasion to guide a young college graduate I will call Duncan Cohen. Brought up as a Jew, he had become a strong atheist and married outside his faith. The investigation required a number of sessions, and the study of its religious aspects was only an incidental aspect of the experiment. The setting aimed to be supportive, the surroundings softened with flowers and music, and the subjects were encouraged to bring with them into their private hospital rooms anything of significance to them, including their choice of music if desired. Duncan was given sixteen daily doses of 180 micrograms of LSD. He was initially irritated by me as a person who taught in a theological school; and, though he came to trust me more and more as the sessions continued, he steadfastly resisted any religious interpretation of the sessions, which, even from the first, he regarded primarily as experiences of rebirth. The early sessions involved a climactic series of symbolic encounters with various members of his family, followed by a dramatic enactment of his own death, in which he acted both as "corpse" and "funeral director," while I was asked to pray as the "officiating rabbi." Still the essentially religious nature of much of these proceedings was either denied or only dimly sensed. I tried to avoid pressing any religious interpretation on him, though my interests doubtless acted suggestively on him.

The climax came after the fifteenth ingestion. About four hours after taking the drug on that day, he had been sitting on the lawn outside the hospital watching two grasshoppers maneuvering in what he interpreted as a kind of cosmic dance. Suddenly, he felt at one with them and with the cosmos besides. I was aware of it only after he caught sight of me and came running over to me in great excitement calling, "Dr. Clark, I have had a mystical experience; I have met God!"

A nine-month follow-up indicated that Duncan regards the total experience as a most significant one. He has continued to grow and mature, as he sees it. There have been some difficult times. "What I regarded as the end of the experience when I left the hospital," he told me, "was simply the beginning of an experience of maturing which is still continuing." He reports more tolerance and open-mindedness, and he recoils when he thinks of what he now regards as his former narrow-mindedness. He has reflected with increased insight on the role of religion in history, history being a favorite subject. I do not know that he is any more hospitable to institutionalized religion, though now he is willing to accept a view of life that for him is more, rather than less, religious than that of the conventional churchgoer. At any rate, psychedelic religious cults, like the League for Spiritual Discovery, have an appeal for him that they did not have before. Religion in a profound sense, in human nature and in history, has more meaning to him.

In the middle 1950s Aldous Huxley published his influential The Doors of Perception, describing an experience with mescaline and advocating it as a means of vitalizing the religious life, with particular emphasis on its mystical aspects. R. C. Zaehner, in his Mysticism: Sacred and Profane (1957), takes issue with Huxley and points out that while mescaline may be able to release pantheistic or monistic types of religion, including those closely associated with psychosis, it cannot be said to stimulate a theistic religious experience. He does not see its use justified by Christian doctrine. Zaehner's reasoning is based partly on a self-experiment with mescaline, and so he cannot be classified with those many critics of the psychedelics anxious to make people's flesh creep without having any firsthand knowledge of what they are talking about. But, commendable though Professor Zaehner's effort may have been, he falls into a familiar fallacy common to all users and non-users of the psychedelics, including Huxley, namely, that of generalizing too widely on the basis of his own personal experience and point of view.

It is true that the religious experience of many of the drug users seems to them to fit more readily into pantheistic and Eastern religious patterns. But the experience itself is essentially non-rational and indescribable. In order that it may be described, one is forced to use concepts of one type or another, none of which seem to do justice to the experience. Consequently these are of great variety, and while some will agree with the Zaehner theological typology, others have no more trouble seeing their experiences as essentially Christian than did St. Teresa when she described one of her mystical visions as revealing to her the secrets of the Trinity. I have known those whose psychedelic experiences have returned them from atheism to the Christian tradition in which they had been brought up, and I have also known those who preferred Eastern concepts.

W. T. Stace, in *Mysticism and Philosophy* (1960), distinguishes between the mystical experience itself, which he finds to be universal in its characteristics, and the interpretation of that experience, which differs from faith to faith and from century to century. Thus the Christian will refer his experience to Father, Son, and Holy Spirit, while the Buddhist will explain an identical psychological experience in terms of Nirvana. Stace further aids us in clarifying the nature of a psychedelic experience in his "principle of causal indifference." This states that what makes an experience mystical is not what touches it off, whether drug or Christian sacrament, but its experiential characteristics. It may then be conceptualized in any way deemed suitable by the experiencer. I may add that, just as a Christian sacrament may or may not stimulate a mystical experience in any given worshiper, the same thing may be said of mescaline or LSD. Stace gives us an example of mystical experience meeting his specifications triggered by mescaline.[6]

In another part of his book, he discusses the experience of pantheism, which so often has gotten the mystic into trouble. Calling the experience "transsubjective," he points out its paradoxical character, in which the mystic may feel himself both merged with the Godhead and infinitely the creature of God at the same time. Consequently, we can understand how, in some sense, mysticism can be felt to be compatible with theism by one mystic and with atheistic Buddhism by another. The same argument will help to explain the variety of theological and philosophical concepts used to interpret the psychedelic experience.

There would be no greater mistake than to suppose, since the psychedelics are frequently accompanied by religious experience, that God, when He created these chemicals, baptized them and segregated them for religious purposes. In

[6] P. 71 ff. See p. 29 ff. for his "principle of causal indifference."

deed, had this been His purpose, it would seem that He has not kept up with His theological and medical reading, for He might have foreseen the difficulties He was preparing for their users. As I have already pointed out, there is no guarantee that a given person will have what satisfies him as a religious experience. However, certain conditions will favor this religious result, and I will indicate briefly a few of the most important.

First of all, there is the subject himself—his nature, and the desire he may have for the religious experience. A person already religiously sensitive is more apt to have a religious experience than one who is not, and one who deliberately prepares himself is more apt to be rewarded than one who is indifferent or unaware of the possibility. *Vide* the case of Duncan Cohen, who had ingested LSD fourteen times without a religious outcome; the only experimental subject in the Good Friday experiment who failed to report a mystical experience was one who did not believe it possible and deliberately set out to demonstrate this belief, partly by omitting the religious preparation engaged in by the other subjects.

The setting is another factor that favors or discourages religion. If the drug is taken in a church or the subject is surrounded by religious symbolism, he is more apt to obtain a religious result. Appropriate readings at strategic points during the period when the drug is active, say from the Bible or the Tibetan Book of the Dead, particularly when accompanied by religious music, are other favoring circumstances. If the guide is a deeply religious person and anxious to promote a religious outcome, this will be another plus factor. Subjects have reported feeling this with respect to Dr. Leary, and doubtless this helps to explain the high incidence of religious experiences reported in his experiments. It is obvious that all these factors depend for their influence on the suggestibility of the subject. However, it would be a mistake to think that suggestibility will explain it all, since, once the experience gets started, the unconscious of the individual subject seems to take over the direction of matters in large measure. But the initial suggestibility of the subject and the manner in which it is exploited, by himself or by others, will enhance the suggestibility that most investigators feel to be one of the salient characteristics of the psychedelic state.

Critics, to prove their point that psychedelic experiences are not truly religious, often cite the fact that beneficial results do not always last. But in this respect they are no different from other types of religious experience. Every evangelist is well acquainted with backsliders. If personality-changes brought about through psychedelic experience are to be made permanent, they must be followed up.

The issues that the psychedelics pose seem to most people to be in the realm of therapy, health, and the law. They may be more importantly religious. One of the functions of religion—perhaps its chief function—is that of supplying life with meaning. The most luminous source of this meaning, through the ages, has been the religious experience of religiously gifted leaders, the dreamers of dreams and the seers of visions, prophets, converts, evangelists, seers, martyrs, and mystics. According to their enlightenment, these men and women have stood before the Lord, some in joy, some in vision, some in transport, and some in fear and trembling. But however rapt, these are the people who have made their mark on that profoundest function of man's strange sojourn on this earth. Astonished, amazed, offended, and even horror-stricken, the present generation of responsible defenders of the *status quo* have seen many of those who have ingested these drugs present pictures of such conditions as capture the imagination of youth with a cogency that churches find hard to match. The psychedelic movement is a religious movement. The narrowly restrictive laws that have been passed have made it a lawless movement with respect to the use of the drugs, though generally it is not in other respects.

It has had its parallels in other ages, and it will be instructive for us to take a brief look at history. The early Christians were looked on with some alarm by that magnificent peace-keeping agency, the Roman Empire. Because they refused even that insignificant homage to the divine Emperor that would have satisfied the State, these dissenters were persecuted and led to death in the arena, their persecutors being among the more conscientious of their rulers. Heretics and Jews during the Middle Ages were burned at the stake for engaging in secret rites and the holding of views disapproved by the Church. Among the former were many mystics who had undergone experiences very similar to, and probably often identical with, those of many of the psychedelic hipsters of our times. Sitting in judgment on these sensitive religious spirits (such as Meister Eckhart) were not irresponsible sadists but sober clerics whose business it was to protect other souls from heresy. These judges had no firsthand knowledge of the mystic's vision. They were rational and conscientious men charged with the duty of saving their fellows from the flames of Hell, even as conscientious judges of our time enforce the modern equivalent of the stake as they sentence to long prison terms those whose visions and ecstasy they have never shared. They only know that laws have been broken, and they wish to protect society. They act according to their lights.

But religious people have never been notable for setting law above the dictates of their consciences, and it is this stubborn habit of the human mind that has brought us such protection as religious conviction has against the state. It will also make laws against the psychedelic drugs almost unenforceable. Yet it has been religious conviction hardened into legalism, whether theological or civil, that has led to intolerable controversy, self-righteous cruelties, and some of the most savage wars of history. This shameful record has led to the principle of religious freedom such as that written into the American constitution, which, nevertheless, only partially protects religious minorities from the tyranny of the majority. In general there is no type of religious experience for which the average American, high or low, has so little tolerance as that type fostered by the psychedelic drugs. The reason is that the mystical side of human nature has been so repressed that it is little understood. It has been looked on as esoteric and Eastern, therefore vaguely opposed to the American way of life. Society must be protected against it, say conservative churchgoers, Daughters of the American Revolution, rejected members of the academic community, and the American Medical Association.

In order to call attention to a neglected aspect of the controversy over the psychedelics, I have a little overstated a case in order to make my point clear. For certainly I recognize

the fact that the drugs have their dangers and need to be
controlled, though I wish that legislators and enforcement
agencies would make greatly needed research much easier.
Some of the world's most experienced and eminent investigators in this area find the drug denied to them.

But it is not surprising that cults that see in the psychedelics a sacramental substance of great potency have been
growing apace during the past few years, from the Neo-
American Church, whose leaders militantly stand on their
constitutional right to use the substances sacramentally, to
the Church of the Awakening, which is more conservative
but which nevertheless has applied to the FDA for the right
to use peyote as does the Native American Church. This right,
like other religious rights, has been hard won by the Indian,
through loyalty of cult members, self-sacrifice, and the willingness of individuals to go to jail if need be in support of
their convictions. If the Indians can use peyote, it is hard to
see why white churches cannot make good their right to do
likewise.

In the meantime, both legal and illegal use of the psychedelics goes on, sometimes religious and sometimes non-
religious, sometimes with irresponsible foolhardiness and
sometimes with the highest resolution that such promising
tools shall not be lost to society, at least until their most
cunning secrets be wrested from them through careful research and responsible practice.

But there is no doubt that the drugs and their religious use
constitute a challenge to the established churches. Here is a
means to religious experience that not only makes possible
more vital religious experience than the churches can ordinarily demonstrate, but the regeneration of souls and the
transformation of personality are made possible to an extent
that seems to be far more reliable and frequent than what the
ordinary churches can promise. LSD is a tool through which
religious experience may, so to speak, be brought into the
laboratory that it may more practically become a matter for
study. It is important that religious institutions face the issues raised so that any decisions they may have to make will
derive from sound knowledge rather than prejudice, ignorance, and fear. I do not have the wisdom nor does anyone

et have the knowledge to say in advance what the action of the churches will be or ought to be. But I do say that if such decisions are to be sound, they must be based on thorough information, freedom from hysteria, and above all, open-mindedness to what may reliably be learned both of the great promise and the dangers of these fascinating substances.

PART V

PSYCHEDELIC EFFECTS
ON MENTAL FUNCTIONING

The effects of psychedelics can be described at all levels of human functioning. On a physiological level, because comparatively small doses of LSD, for instance, produce relatively large effects on behavior, and because these effects last long beyond the time during which traces of them can be found in the body by any known methods, important questions about the nature of neural enzymes are raised, about their role in the ecology of the body, about the half lives of their components, and about how they interact to mediate our functioning. The fact that chemical interaction lies at the core of psychedelic experience poses in immediate terms the question of the relationship between mind and body. Is mind a separate substance encased in or manifesting itself through body, or is it just the live aspect of electrochemical changes in an electrochemical system? And what does it mean with regard to this question that we can even pose it? Considerations such as these led Leary (1966b) to pen hymns of praise to DNA, the central substance involved in heredity, but this is only one man's answer.

The variability of the effects of psychedelics makes it hard to come up with appropriate unifying generalizations about their action. Examination of the items constituting the LSD Scale in the ARC Inventory, an objective structured test built to measure drug effects (Hill, Haertzen, and Belleville, 1961) shows items affirming the presence of euphoria and depression, anxiety and calmness, heightened sensitivity and loss of sensation. The only uncontradicted factor in the item content is motor restlessness, but this is contradicted by other investigators in other studies. Set and setting are frequently adduced to account for this variability. The problem seems fundamentally one of tracking the effects on a complex system of on-specific stresser that operates at a fundamental level in he control mechanism of that system.

In this section, the paper by Koella brings together some of he effects of LSD on the functioning of the nervous system and attempts to draw from these data some generalizations about both drug and nervous system. Because minds are enerally found in bodies, it is important to understand how sychedelics affect the body and particularly those aspects of he body traditionally associated with mind. Other papers, y Giarman, Purpura, and Jarvik, dealing with problems aised here may be found in the excellent collection edited y DeBold and Leaf (1967).

There is no question but that psychedelics influence lanuage, although the manner in which they do so is unclear Amarel and Cheek, 1965). It is possible that they operate y increasing the associational content of speech (Cheek and marel, 1968). Language is, in fact, a very sensitive index of he effects of psychedelics (Cheek, 1963). In his paper, Kripper tries to analyze the effects of psychedelics in terms of the fferent and efferent functions of speech, and deals with lanuage on both a spoken and a written level.

In their paper, Harman and Fadiman offer highly suggesive evidence with regard to the effects of psychedelics on reativity. Krippner (1968) has reported a study on the efects of psychedelics on the creativity of professional artists; aronson (1967a) reported that a hypothesis in one of his xperiments derived from an LSD experience; Stafford and olightly (1967) have presented anecdotal evidence for the nhancement of creativity by psychedelics. Only Harman, adiman, and their colleagues have studied the effects of sychedelics on creativity in an experimental program. It is recisely this kind of program, which is most needed, that has een killed by current governmental hysteria against psyhedelics.

The paper by Mogar deals with the relationship between sychedelic and psychotomimetic experience. The relationhip between psychopathology and mysticism has long been rgued (Huxley, 1956; Landis, 1964), although it has been uggested (Aaronson, 1969a) that they may spring from opposite sides of the perceptual coin. In bringing together the similarities among these diversities, Mogar also brings together the organic and existential approaches to schizophrenia in a fundamental contribution to the understanding of the illness.

CENTRAL NERVOUS EFFECTS OF LSD-25

WERNER P. KOELLA, M.D.

In the majority of chapters of this book, the psychotomimetic, psychedelic, and hallucinogenic effects of LSD-25, and in this connection, the possible beneficial and damaging actions of this drug, have been described and discussed. Such considerations belong in the realm of the psychiatrist, psychologist, sociologist, geneticist, and possibly even the theologian and student of mysticism. In the present chapter, we shall look at LSD-25 from the point of view of the neurophysiologist and neuropharmacologist, investigators who are interested in understanding how the central nervous system (CNS) works and how drugs act on this substrate.

One can assume that every behavior of man and animal such as reflex movements, instinctive patterns, learned actions and reactions, voluntary behavior, various states of vigilance as well as thinking, moods, and recall of memory bits, is the manifestation of a particular and specific time-intensity-space pattern of activity in the nerve cells. About five to ten billion of these cells, together with an even greater number of supporting cells (the glial elements), make up the central nervous system of higher animals and man. During the past few years, neurophysiologists, using electrical recording techniques, have been able to detect, and to determine in their quantitative and qualitative aspects, correlates in nervous activity of such behavioral phenomena as sleep, resting, waking, arousal, the orienting reflex, memory traces, and many others.

It can be assumed further that abnormal behavior such as is encountered in mental disease is the manifestation of an aberrant time-intensity-space pattern of activity in the nervous system. One may then postulate that the abnormal behavior produced by such drugs as LSD-25, which in some aspects resembles the behavior exhibited by mentally ill people, is also the manifestation of similarly aberrant nervous activity, and that—to go even further—this abnormal activity is the direct consequence of the drug effect.

Finally, it is not unlikely that LSD-25 and similar drugs induce in the CNS of experimental animals such changes in nervous activity. Due to the certainly less complex "personality" of such animals, however, abnormalities in nervous activity may not manifest themselves by discrete abnormalities in behavior. But such abnormalities can, with some chance for success, be studied with the tools of the neurophysiologist.

The neuropharmacologists have in the past ten years or so intensively studied the effects of LSD-25 and similar drugs on various aspects of brain function. And indeed, in a number of instances, some insight has been gained into the way in which behavioral effects of the drugs may relate to abnormal nervous activity and reactivity. While this is just a beginning of a relatively new scientific field, it is hoped that, with an even greater effort and with refinement of our techniques, we shall, in not too many years, be able to state with some certainty what nervous circuits in the brain do deviate from their normal activity patterns to bring about behavioral disturbances.

In the following, we describe and discuss some of the work done in this field.

The Effect of LSD-25 on the Electroencephalogram

The electroencephalogram, or EEG, is the record of the electrical brain waves. It is obtained by means of electrodes (usually metal leads) placed on the surface of the brain, or aimed into particular structures of the interior of the brain. In routine clinical electroencephalography in man, the electrodes are attached to the scalp. The electrical potential-changes occurring in these recording sites are amplified about one million times and written out with ink on moving paper. The recorded EEG is a more or less irregular wavy line that allows us to distinguish oscillations of various frequencies. A discussion of the origin of these brain waves is beyond the scope of this chapter, and indeed, physiologists still do not understand this problem too well. It is of importance, though, to point out that these brain waves vary with the functiona state of the organism, and, of less importance here, that the signal, by abnormal wave forms and "spikes," pathologica processes in the brain. As to the former aspect, it was recog nized quite early in the development of the electroencepha lographic technique that fundamental changes occur in th appearance of the EEG, derived from the scalp in man an from the surface of the brain in animals, as the subjects shi from the aroused attentive state to quietly resting waking, t drowsiness, and to light and then deep sleep. In the arouse state, the EEG is characterized by an irregular low-voltag pattern exhibiting frequencies of about fifteen to thirty cycle per second, the so-called beta waves. In resting waking ther are, particularly in the posterior part of the brain, the typic: alpha waves, i.e., rather regular oscillations of about eight t twelve per second (of somewhat lower frequencies in th cat). During the drowsy, or "floating," state, the alpha gradually disappear and are replaced again by a beta patter With the onset of actual sleep, the EEG is characterize first by the occurrence of bursts of ten-to-fourteen-per-secon waves that wax and wane so as to produce a spindlelik envelope; hence we refer to these as sleep spindles. With th shift to deeper states of sleep, high-voltage, very slow wave (delta waves, one to three per second) dominate the pictur More recently it has been found that subjects can be soun asleep and still show at times episodes of arousal patterns i the EEG (i.e., low-voltage beta waves); these episodes a accompanied by rapid eye movements (REMs). Whe human subjects are awakened during these REM period they almost invariably report that they have been dreamin whereas they do not do so when awakened from a slow slee episode. It is for this reason that we think today that durin these REM periods, or periods of "paradoxical" or "activated sleep, we dream. These REM episodes occur in man abou every ninety minutes, in the cat about every thirty minute Figure 1 shows some typical records obtained from a "chronic freely moving cat. With the help of such tracings, togethe with continuous observation, the actual level of "vigilance can be diagnosed with a high degree of reliability. The ex periments discussed below are based on such techniques.

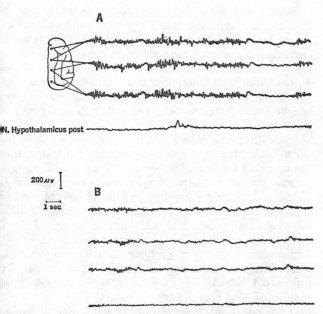

A

N. Hypothalamicus post

200 μv

1 sec

B

A, control record of normal conscious cat in quiet state; B, twenty minutes after an intraperitoneal injection of 15 u/k of LSD-25.

Figure 1. Records taken from a cat chronically prepared with electrodes to record: the eye movements (EOG), the electroencephalogram from both sides of the skull (EEG), and the activity of the neck muscles (NMG). The animal was kept in an air-conditioned, sound-attenuated room supplied with a one-way mirror for observation. The records were taken while the animal was awake and active (top left), awake and resting (top right—note alpha waves), just dropped off to sleep (middle left —note "spindles"), in deeper sleep (middle right—note slow waves in EEG); in still sounder sleep (bottom left—note very slow waves), and in paradoxical sleep (bottom right—arousal pattern in EEG). (Note eye movements in awake animal and in paradoxical sleep). Note also reduced electrical muscle activity in paradoxical sleep. Calibrations: vertical line at top middle = 100 microvolts (or 0.0001 volt), horizontal line = 1 second. Original from author's laboratory.

Bradley and Elkes (1953) worked in chronic cats an
monkeys, i.e., animals previously prepared with electrodes t
record the EEG from the cerebral cortex. For the actual e:
periments, the animals were placed in special chambers tha
allowed observation as well as electrical recordings. LSD-2
(given by intraperitoneal injection) in doses ranging fro
fifteen to twenty-five micrograms per kilogram of bod
weight (one microgram being one millionth of a gram) i
duced within a few minutes after administration a shift i
the EEG from the resting pattern to an arousal pattern tha
often lasted for several hours (figure 2). At the same time
the animals became restless and more alert, and their pupi'
became somewhat dilated. Similar effects were reported b
Takagi and co-workers (1958) and Schwarz and collaborato:
(1956). Some of these investigators also administered LSD-2
intraventricularly, i.e., into the brain cavities, and foun
again that low doses of LSD-25 produced the arousal reactio
Larger doses of this drug, up to several milligrams (one mi
ligram being one thousandth of a gram), however, tended t
bring about bursts of abnormal-looking slow waves (Passouan
et al., 1956; Vogt et al., 1957).

In the rabbit, low doses of LSD-25 also tended to produc
an arousal pattern and to eliminate all electroencephal
graphic features of drowsiness and sleep for several hours (R
naldi and Himwich, 1955). Again, elevation of the dose i
this species reversed the picture by bringing about the a
pearance of slow waves and sleep spindles.

Rinkel and his co-workers (1952) studied the effect c
LSD-25 on the EEG of human volunteers. They noted onl
slight changes, characterized by a small but distinct acceler:
tion of the alpha-wave rhythm.

From such experimental evidence one may infer that i
animals, and possibly in man, LSD-25 in low doses lea
to an arousal state that can last for several hours. In vie
of the more recent information about paradoxical sleep,
somewhat different conclusion may be justified. An "arousa
pattern in the EEG does not necessarily signal the onset c
arousal, but may just as well indicate the phase of paradoxic
sleep. This suggests that in dream sleep, or REM sleep, th
cerebral cortex is physiologically in a state similar to tha

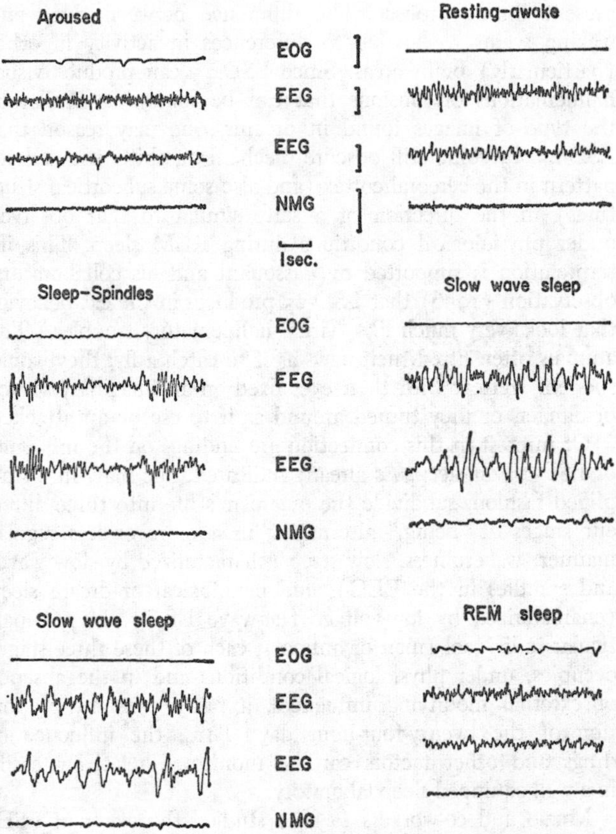

Figure 2. The effect of LSD-25 on the electroencephalogram of the normal unrestrained cat. Recording modes as indicated by connections and electrode position on cortex of cat brain in upper part of picture. Record 4 is derived from hypothalamus. A: (control) animal is in quiet waking state. Note alphalike waves in three cortical leads. B: records twenty minutes after LSD-25 (15 μg/kg) had been administered into peritoneal cavity, which leads to disappearance of alphas and to arousal pattern. Calibration in microvolts and seconds as indicated (From Bradley and Elkes, 1953). P. B. Bradley and J. Elkes, "The Effects of Some Drugs on the Electrical Activity of the Brain," *Brain*, Vol. 80, 1957. Reprinted by permission of the authors and the publisher.

present during arousal. The difference between sleep and waking seems to be due to differences in activity in other (particularly) brain areas. Since LSD-25 can produce visual hallucinations or illusions that can be somewhat similar to the type of images found in dreams, one may reason that LSD-25, by some still obscure mechanism, shifts the activity pattern in the cerebral cortex (and also some subcortical structures) in the direction of a state similar to that observed under physiological conditions during REM sleep. This interpretation is supported by Passouant and his collaborators' observation (1956) that LSD-25 produces in the cat behavior that looks very much like "visual hallucinatory troubles." The animals often lifted their paws as if to catch a fly; they would suddenly retreat with their eyes fixed on an imaginary source of danger, or they turned around as if to escape an attacker.

Of interest in this connection are findings on the influence of LSD-25 on sleep. As already indicated, one may, in a simplified fashion, subdivide the organism's life into three different stages of "being," alternating in a more or less regular manner: wakefulness, slow sleep (characterized by slow waves and spindles in the EEG), and paradoxical or dream sleep (characterized by low-voltage fast-wave EEG). In any particular individual (man or animal), each of these three stages occupies, under physiological conditions and in the absence of external modifying influences, a fairly constant proportion of the twenty-four-hour day. Thus, the influence of drugs and other factors can be monitored relatively easily in a well-equipped sleep laboratory.

Muzio and co-workers (1966) studied the effect of LSD-25 on the sleep of human volunteers. They found that with doses ranging from 6–40 μg total dose, the first two REM periods in the LSD-25 nights were prolonged, and that slow-wave sleep was often interrupted by brief REM periods. Hartmann (1967) also found an increase in total REM time and relative REM time (i.e., percentage of total sleep) in rats under the influence of LSD-25. These two experiments again support the idea that there is a relation between the functional changes that take place in the CNS during dream periods, on the one hand, and the changes induced by LSD-25, on the other.

Hobson (1964), on the other hand, found that LSD-25 in doses of 2 and 20 μg/kg of body weight reduced the paradoxical sleep in cats and made it less differentiated from slow-wave sleep. There were also more awakenings in these animals, and they tended to be more easily aroused by external stimuli. More work is needed on the fundamental mechanisms operating in the CNS both during REM sleep *and* during the particular state produced by LSD-25.

The Effect of LSD-25 on Sensory Transmission

Another method employed rather frequently by neuropharmacologists involves measurement of transmission in sensory systems by the so-called *evoked potential* technique. A sense organ, e.g. the eye or the ear, is stimulated by a light flash or a loudspeaker click, and an afferent volley of nerve impulses is produced. This volley travels first through peripheral sensory nerve fibers and then through the afferent systems in the CNS to reach finally the so-called projection area of the cerebral cortex.

In all sensory systems, this afferent pathway consists of at least three neurons (nerve cell and nerve fiber) arranged in a continuous chain. The transfer of nervous signals from one neuron to the next occurs in well-defined loci called synapses. The last subcortical synapse is located in the sensory relay nuclei of the thalamus, a part of the diencephalon located deep in the base of the brain.

When the volley of impulses reaches such relay locations or the projection area of the cerebral cortex, it leads to a more or less simultaneous transient excitation of a multitude of nerve cells. This excitatory focus manifests itself by an action potential or evoked potential that can be measured using electronic amplifiers and a fast-reacting recording device, usually a cathode-ray oscilloscope (similar in its technical principles to a TV set).

The amplitude of this evoked potential depends on the total amount of local nervous excitation. This, in turn, is related to the strength of peripheral stimulation and ease of transmission in the afferent channel. With a standard sensory stimulus applied to sense organs, or (as is done frequently) with a standard electrical stimulus applied to afferent nervous pathways, the amplitude of the evoked potential gives a measure of afferent conductance, or, to be more precise, of transmission at the synaptic sites of the afferent pathways including the synapses in the cortex of the brain. It is of importance to state that it is particularly these synaptic sites that are susceptible to drug action as well as to the modulating action of accessory neural systems.

Evarts and his collaborators (1955) investigated the influence of LSD-25 on transmission in the visual system of cats. These investigators not only were interested in the effect of this drug on the visual system as a whole, but, by an ingenious technique, they set out to study differential effects on the various synaptic sites in this afferent system.

To investigate drug action at the most peripheral sites, i.e., the light receptors and synapses in the retina, they stimulated the eyes of their (usually anesthetized) experimental animals with a light flash and measured the afferent volleys of nerve impulses by electrically recording from the optic nerve. They found that only very high doses of LSD-25 (5 mg/kg) were able to change these action potentials, which tended to become smaller. This indicated that the light receptors and/or the retinal synapses were relatively insensitive to this drug, and only under rather massive doses tended to react, and with decreased excitability.

The most pronounced effect of LSD-25 was found on the synapses of the thalamic relay, as demonstrated in the following way: These investigators stimulated the optic nerves of anesthetized cats with electrical shocks and recorded action potentials by means of metal leads, insulated except for their tips and placed in the lateral geniculate body, the thalamic relay station of the visual system. The signals they recorded revealed two different waves in response to each stimulus. These signaled, as shown in figure 3, respectively the nerve impulse traveling from the stimulus site in the optic nerve to the geniculate body (the presynaptic spike = T) and the synaptic excitation produced by that afferent volley in the nerve-cell bodies of the geniculate nucleus (the postsynaptic spike = S). As is evident from figure 3, LSD-25, in rather low doses injected into the carotid artery, markedly depressed the postsynaptic spike, whereas it left the presynaptic spike unaltered. This clearly indicates that the drug had profoundly impaired synaptic transmission in the thalamic relay

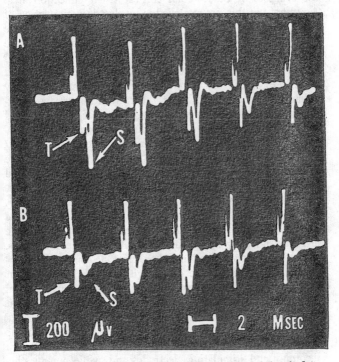

Figure 3. Influence of LSD-25 on synaptic transmission in lateral geniculate body of the cat. The optic nerve is electrically stimulated about 250 times per second, leading to the repetitive complex response seen in A and B. "T" points to the presynaptic wave arriving in the geniculate nucleus. After a delay of less than one millisecond, the nerve cells are synaptically excited and produce spike S. The deflections occurring prior to wave T are the so-called stimulus artifacts, i.e., the electrically conducted disturbance elicited by the electrical stimulus; they have no biological significance. A: control record of five responses out of a larger series. B: after 15 μg of LSD-25 had been given via the carotid artery. Note drastic reduction of postsynaptic spike, S, signaling impairment of synaptic transmission. (See Evarts et al., 1955.)

station but had not affected the excitability of the optic nerve fibers to electrical stimuli.

These scientists also investigated the effect of LSD-25 on the synapses of the cerebral cortical visual projection area. A response in this site was elicited by electrical stimulation of the optic radiation, i.e., the nerve fibers leading from the relay in the thalamus to the visual projection area in the posterior part of the cerebral cortex (figure 4). It was found that the response in the cortex to such stimuli even under high doses of LSD-25 was not depressed, but, rather, slightly enhanced. This indicated that the cortical synapses are relatively insensitive to the depressing effect of the drug and that they are made more, rather than less, excitable by LSD-25. In spite of the fact that LSD-25 in moderate doses failed to depress transmission in the retina and in the cortex, the drug-induced reduction in "gain" in the thalamic relay seemed to be sufficient to produce "behavioral blindness" in awake, freely moving cats (Evarts 1957) and monkeys (Evarts 1956).

The idea does not seem to be too farfetched to relate the impaired transmission in the visual pathway at the thalamic level, attended by increased excitability at the cortical sites, to the hallucinogenic action of LSD-25. One could indeed suggest that, in the absence of (or with reduced) visual input to the cortex, the somewhat more excitable visual cortical networks produce their own imagery, independent of what "meets the eye."

Purpura (1956) investigated the effect of LSD-25 on the visual and auditory system in cats that were supplied with recording and stimulating electrodes and, while non-anesthetized, were immobilized with curare-type drugs. He observed that LSD-25 in low doses (2–30μg/kg given intravenously) enhanced the response evoked in the cortical projection areas by light flashes and loudspeaker clicks. Of interest also is Purpura's observation that larger doses of LSD-25, while still facilitating the response to photic stimuli, tended to depress the signal evoked by loudspeaker clicks. The question, of course, arises of how this investigator's results can be brought into accord with Evarts' observation; one would have to assume that the increase in cortical excitability more than compensates for the reduced transmission at the thalamic relay.

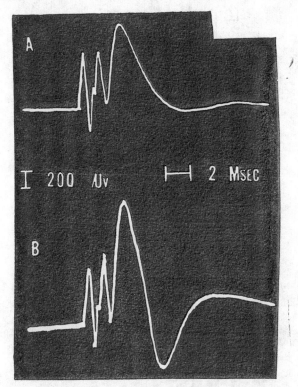

Figure 4. Effect of LSD-25 on synaptic transmission in the cerebral cortex of the cat. The response, recorded from the visual projection area, was produced by electrical shock to optic radiation. This response shows several typical deflections, the discussion of whose origin is beyond the scope of this paper. A: control, B: after injecting 1.5 mg of LSD-25 into the carotid artery. Note particularly the increase of late components after the drug (from Evarts et al., 1955).

It seems that more work is needed to clarify this and other questions arising from experimental data obtained so far.

Still, of interest in view of Evarts' results are the observations of Blough (1957). This author, using a rather intricate behavioral test arrangement, was able to measure the "absolute visual threshold" in pigeons. When the birds were given

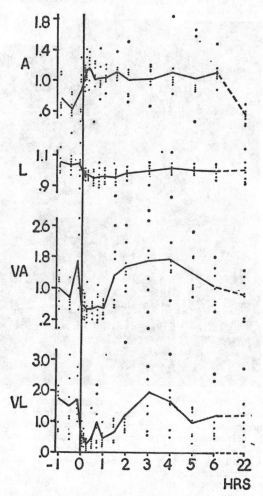

Figure 5. The effect of LSD-25 on the amplitude (A) and latency (L) of the cortical response to light flashes in the awake rabbit. Also shown are variability (expressed as variance) of the amplitude (VA) and of latency (VL). The measurements were done on the first downward component of the complex response shown in figure 6. Control (left of "o" hour) and effect of LSD-25 (50 μg total dose) were observed over several hours. The dots signify the readings (means of ten measurements of

LSD-25 (either by mouth or injected into the peritoneal cavity), he invariably noted an increase in threshold, i.e., an impairment of vision, whereas motor and discriminative functions were not grossly disturbed. The rise in threshold could again be related to the reduction in transmission in the thalamus, as noted by Evarts.

The present author studied the effect of LSD-25 on visually evoked responses in rabbits (Koella and Wells, 1959). The animals were supplied with chronically implanted electrodes to record the signals in the visual projection area of the cortex in response to repetitive (one every five seconds) light flashes. During the experiments the rabbits were semi-restricted in their movements by being wrapped in burlap sacking, but were otherwise unrestrained by either mechanical devices or drugs. We confirmed Purpura's observations that LSD-25 (25–50 μg total dose) increased somewhat the cortical evoked response (figure 5, A).

More significant, however, was an additional observation pertaining to variability of response. It is common knowledge that under physiological conditions and particularly in awake animals, indicators such as evoked responses vary greatly in amplitude when the stimulus is given repetitively to produce a whole series of evoked signals. In our experimental situation, the evoked responses (to constant, standardized stimuli) changed in amplitude over a range as great as 1:20 or more. LSD-25, in the dose mentioned, drastically decreased this variability down to about 25 per cent of the original value (figure 5, VA, and figure 6). The latency of the response (i.e., the time elapsed between the stimulus and the appearance of the response, signaling the transmission time from the retinal light receptors to the cortex) was somewhat decreased, and again its variability was greatly reduced under LSD-25 (figure 5, VL).

---

amplitude and latency) at each time for each of seven animals. In the case of variability, they indicate variance of the ten measurements. The full lines represent the means for all seven animals. Note slight protracted increase in amplitude and decrease in latency after LSD-25 (given at o hours). Note decrease and, after one to two hours, increase of variability of amplitude and latency. (From Koella and Wells, 1959; reprinted by permission of the *American Journal of Physiology*.)

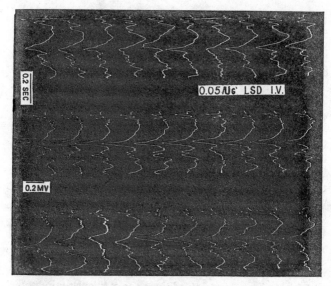

Figure 6. Ten consecutive responses to repetitive light flashes are recorded in the visual projection area of a rabbit. From such records the curves shown in figure 5 were constructed. Note the complex response, consisting of primary response (at about 20 milliseconds after stimulus, at extreme left of records) and series of later responses with large component about 200 milliseconds after stimulus. Left column before, middle column one minute after, and right column one hour after, LSD-25. Note marked decrease in variability of primary response and of later responses after LSD-25. (From Koella and Wells, op. cit.)

One may assume that the response variability is the manifestation of a spontaneous endogenous fluctuation in excitability of the various synaptic sites interposed in the afferent sensory pathways. One may go further by postulating that this variability is of importance for the well-being of the organism and that the psychotomimetic action of substances like LSD-25 is, in part at least, due to their ability to decrease this variability. In this connection, it is noteworthy to mention that Bergen and collaborators (1962), in rabbit preparations similar to those described above, demonstrated a variability-reducing effect, similar to that of LSD-25, as a result of administering plasma protein fractions from schizophrenic patients. Fractions from normal controls did not have such an effect.

Related to the findings of Koella and Wells are the observations of Goldstein and his co-workers (1963). These investigators have shown by means of automatic analyzing techniques that the alpha-wave output in the EEG varies in time. When they recorded the EEG over extended periods, they found that the number and amplitude of the alpha waves tended to increase and decrease in what was probably a random fashion. Goldstein and his colleagues demonstrated that this variability was reduced by LSD-25 and that it was also *a priori* smaller in schizophrenic patients as compared with normal control subjects.

Perhaps also related to these observations on variability of response and its reaction to LSD-25 are the findings of Witt (1951). This author, in his extended studies on the web-building ability of spiders, found that LSD-25 in low doses (less than 0.05 μg per animal) led to increased regularity of the web angles.

These few examples taken from the work of neuropharmacologists have shown that LSD-25 has a number of pronounced effects on the central nervous system. They also offered an opportunity to acquaint the reader with some of the techniques (though by no means all) used by the neuropharmacologist to study the effects of drugs on the nervous system. In some cases, it seems possible to relate the effects of LSD-25 to the behavioral and psychic actions of this drug. In other instances, we are still far from establishing such functional relations. It is hoped that renewed efforts with new and better techniques will enable us in the not-too-distant future to explain the whole "experience" produced by these substances, the whole "model psychosis," in terms of neural events. Should this be the case, one also would be a giant step closer to establishing a functional pathogenesis of endogenous mental disease; i.e., one would be able to explain some or all the behavioral symptoms of the mentally ill in terms of abnormal neuronal function. It seems that with such a prospect in mind one could not think of a nobler task for a substance like LSD-25.

THE EFFECTS OF
PSYCHEDELIC EXPERIENCE
ON LANGUAGE FUNCTIONING

STANLEY KRIPPNER, PH.D.

A. J. Ayer (1946, p. 65) once claimed, ". . . we are unable, in our everyday language, to describe the properties of sense-contents with any great precision, for lack of the requisite symbols. . . ." Ayer's statement about normal, everyday perception has even greater application when chemically altered perception is considered. The difficulties subjects have in describing their experiences are compounded by the difficulties experimenters often have in interpreting these reports in terms of some organizational structure.

One of the more successful attempts to organize subjective reports of psychedelic experience has been made by R. E. L. Masters and Jean Houston (1966). Having guided and observed 206 subjects through a large number of LSD and peyote sessions, Masters and Houston proposed the existence of four levels of mental functioning in the psychedelic state: sensory, recollective-analytic, symbolic, and integral.

At the first, or sensory, level, the subject may report a changed awareness of the body, unusual ways of experiencing space and time, heightened sense impressions, synesthesia ("feeling sounds," "hearing color"), and—with the eyes closed —vivid visual imagery. Experiences at the sensory level tend to "decondition" a subject, to loosen his habitual conceptions and to ease the rigidity of his past imprinting.

At the second, or recollective-analytic, level, the subject's reactions become more emotionally intense. He may relive periods of his life. He may formulate insights into himself, his work, and his personal relationships.

Only 40 per cent of Masters and Houston's subjects reached the third, or symbolic, level. At this level, visual imagery generally involves history and legend, or the subject may recapitulate the evolutionary process, developing from primordial protoplasm to man. He may also embark upon a "ritual of passage" and imagine himself participating in a baptismal ceremony or a puberty rite.

Eleven per cent of Masters and Houston's subjects reached the fourth, or integral, level, at which religious or mystical experiences occur. Masters and Houston have described the religious experience as a confrontation with "the Ground of Being"; they contrast it with mystical experience, which they see as a dissolution, as a merging of the individual with the energy field of the universe. One woman related, "All around and passing through me was the Light, a trillion atomized crystals shimmering in the blinding incandescence."

The Evolution of Language

Like psychedelic experience, human language processes may be studied at four different levels. The development of social language begins at the approximate age of nine months, with the acquisition of a simple listening vocabulary (Lewis, 1959). By one year, most children have spoken their first word. In the American culture, two other forms of language –reading and writing– are usually introduced when the child enters school, although some children acquire these before formal education begins. Speaking and writing are expressive, and involve encoding one's experiences; listening and reading are receptive, and require decoding of another person's attempts to communicate. Speaking and listening have developmental priority over the visual activities of writing and reading.

Language may be defined as a structured system of arbitrary vocal sounds and sound sequences, or a system of written or printed symbols that represent vocal sounds. A language system is used in social, interpersonal communication, and rather exhaustively catalogues the objects, events, and processes in the human environment.

The origins of oral language go back over a million years. Primitive man kept no written records and lost the words he uttered in time and space. Writing started only a few thousand years ago, when man developed hieroglyphics and ideographs to represent visible objects. Among the cultures bordering the Mediterranean, these standardized sets of pictures gave way to phonetic alphabets, in which the written symbol stands not for an object, but for a sound.

The alphabet restructured not only man's method of communicating, but also his very conception of the time-space milieu. The alphabet arrested words in spatial rather than temporal segments, and literate human cultures began to conceive of the universe in terms of linear space diagrams as well as temporal cycles. The day-night cycle, the life-death cycle, and other recurring events gave way in importance to conceiving events as historical, linear, and exhibiting cause-effect relationships.

For several centuries, the development of the alphabet affected most people indirectly in the cultures where it was used. Written language was difficult to master; its utilization was often reserved for scribes, philosophers, and priests. The invention of the printing press and movable type made reading a common skill and, according to Marshall McLuhan (1964), further exploded the tribal world and led to the fragmentation of society and to the specialization of mankind's functions. The priestly monopoly on knowledge and power came to an end.

The technical and cultural achievements resulting from movable type show the tremendous impact of literacy. However, the linear structuring of rational life forced the Western world to regard consciousness as sequential, and brought about its habit of investing events with cause-effect relations. As Western man became dissociated from the tribe and from direct experience, visual sequencing became the key skill used in examining and storing the symbolic record of his accomplishments.

Just as the voice-and-ear stage of language once gave way to what Walter Ong (1967) has referred to as the "chirographic-typographic" stage (dominated by the alphabet and the printing press), so this stage is now giving way to an electronic stage. Television, telephone, radio, phonograph, film, and recording tape have reinstated the importance of sound in communication. These media also convey a sense of simultaneity in time and space. A new aural structure is being superimposed upon the old visual structure of the chirographic typographic stage. As technology unites the scattered human cultures into a new solidarity, the contemporary individual must have all cultures present within him simultaneously in order to be realized as a human being.

At the same time that the electronic stage is extending man's exploration outside the body, it is creating a desire for exploration of the individual's inner world. One example is the widespread interest in psychedelic substances. Many Americans, having ingested these chemicals, echo McLuhan's and Ong's theories. They state that their psychedelic episodes bring about "a sense of simultaneity in time and space," and "a sense of solidarity with all the people in the world." Others gather into drug or "hippie" subcultures, in which tribal rites are enacted, in which bright Indian clothes and primitive body markings are worn, and in which an intense sense of community often develops.

A limited number of attempts have been made to investigate the effects of psychedelic experience on either receptive language (listening and reading) or expressive language (speaking and writing). The four levels of psychedelic experience (sensory, recollective-analytic, symbolic, integral) provide an organizational structure in which this area may be explored and discussed.

Receptive Language

Trouton and Eysenck (1961) have pointed out that psychedelic experience is influenced not only by factors related to drug administration, but by personality, physiology, set, and setting. In their account, they also mention "suggestion" and "reinforcement of responses by the experimenter," which suggests the importance of language in determining how a subject reacts.

The ritual developed by the Native American Church illustrates the use of language to produce a positive set and setting for the ingestion of peyote. A ceremonial leader, the head chief, initiates the singing of songs and co-ordinates requests by individuals for special prayers. The ritual is so arranged and so co-ordinated to the needs of the communicants that the maximum possible likelihood of a positive spiritual experience is enhanced (Flattery and Pierce, 1965).

Language, however, may also be used to develop a negative set and setting. Jean Houston (1967) has described one of her initial observations of LSD administration. The subject was told by the psychiatrist that he would have "a terrible, terrible experience" filled with "strong anxiety and delusions." The drug was administered in an antiseptic hospital room with several observers in white coats watching him. As the effects came on, the psychiatrist asked such questions as, "Is your anxiety increasing?" At the end of the experiment, the subject was in a state of panic. The psychiatrist announced to the group that LSD is indeed a "psychotomimetic" substance, which induces psychotic behavior.

Listening is the receptive process by which aural language assumes meaning. As listening involves attending to a stimulus, the act often includes a commitment to respond in some way to the messages that are received. The Native American Church communicants commit themselves to a positive experience while the unfortunate subjects of poorly handled LSD experiments commit themselves to a negative experience. In both cases, language plays a key role in determining which way the commitment will turn.

A vivid description of a psychedelic session has been given by Alan Watts (1962). This description demonstrates how the quality of what is listened to may change as the listener shifts from the sensory to the recollective-analytic, symbolic and integral levels.

I am listening to the music of an organ. . . . The organ seems quite literally to speak. There is no use of the *vox humana* stop, but every sound seems to issue from a vast human throat, moist with saliva . . . (p. 33)

This is the sensory level of the psychedelic experience. Perceptual changes have transformed the organ music into a human voice. Sense impressions other than aural take form as Watts speaks of "a vast human throat, wet with saliva."

I am listening to a priest chanting the Mass, and a choir of nuns responding. His mature, cultivated voice rings with the serene authority of the One, Holy, Catholic, and Apostolic Church, of the

Faith once and for all delivered to the saints, and the nuns respond, naïvely it seems, with childlike, utterly innocent devotion. But listening again, I can hear the priest "putting on" his voice, hear the inflated, pompous balloon, the studiedly unctuous tones of a master deceptionist who has the poor little nuns, kneeling in their stalls, completely cowed. Listen deeper. The nuns are not cowed at all. They are playing possum. With just a little stiffening, the limp gesture of bowing nuns turns into the gesture of the closing claw. With too few men to go around, the nuns know what is good for them: how to bend and survive. (p. 37)

This is the recollective-analytic level, at which memories and insights often occur. Watts is listening to a recording of the Mass, but suddenly perceives a pompous quality to the priest's tones. Going deeper into the analysis of what he hears, Watts discovers that the nuns' response displays more than obedience—it is their shrewd way of playing the game of survival.

But this profoundly cynical view of things is only an intermediate stage. . . . In the priest's voice I hear down at the root the primordial howl of the beast in the jungle, but it has been inflected, complicated, refined, and textured with centuries of culture. . . . At first, crude and unconcealed, the cry for food or mate, or just noise for the fun of it, making the rocks echo. Then rhythm to enchant, then changes of tone to plead or threaten. Then words to specify the need, to promise and bargain. And then, much later, the gambits of indirection. The feminine stratagem of stooping to conquer, the claim to superior worth in renouncing the world for the spirit, the cunning of weakness proving stronger than the might of muscle—and the meek inheriting the earth. (p. 38)

This is the psychedelic experience's symbolic stage. The priest's voice reflects the evolutionary process; the nuns' response echoes female archetypes.

As I listen, then, I can hear in that one voice the simultaneous presence of all the levels of man's history, as of all the stages of life before man. Every step in the game becomes as clear as the rings in a severed tree. . . . I, as an adult, am also back there alone in the dark, just as the primordial howl is still present beneath the sublime modulations of the chant. . . . Down and at last out—out of the cosmic maze . . . , I feel, with a peace so deep that it sings to be shared with all the world, that at last I belong, that I have returned to the home beyond home. . . . The sure foundation upon which I had sought to stand has turned out to be the center from which I seek. (p. 39)

This is the integral stage of the psychedelic experience. Watts sees himself in the voice of the priest and in all the precursors of that voice. His "home beyond home" and "sure foundation" is the very center of his being.

Reading, the assigning of meaning to perceived printed symbols, also plays a key role in some psychedelic sessions. In one experiment (Jarvik et al., 1955), subjects ingested one hundred micrograms of LSD and demonstrated an increase in their ability to quickly cancel out words on a page of standardized material, but a decreased ability to cancel out individual letters. The drug seemed to facilitate the perceptions of meaningful language units while it interfered with the visual perception of non-meaningful ones. Corroborative experimental data are lacking, but a number of clinical cases suggest that if the meaning of printed symbols happens to dovetail with the ongoing psychedelic experience, the symbols will be perceived quickly. If their meaning does not happen to tie in with the experience, the words may not be perceived at all.

One subject became fascinated by a newspaper headline and reportedly was able to read the entire article at a distance of thirty feet (Newland, 1962). Another subject, who became interested in studying famous paintings after ingesting thirty milligrams of psilocybin, assertedly lost his reading ability entirely while under the influence of the drug.[1]

In college, I had studied central nervous system dysfunction and knew that psycholexia is a condition in which a person has difficulty attaching meaning to printed symbols. I experienced a similar condition after the psilocybin began to take effect.

I glanced at my watch but could make no sense out of the numerical symbols. I looked at an art magazine. The pictures were beautiful, almost three dimensional. However, the script was a jumble of meaningless shapes.

The same subject, near the end of his "psilocybin high," reported still another alteration in the reading process:

Earlier, I had tasted an orange and found it the most intense, delightful taste sensation I had ever experienced. I tried reading a magazine as I was "coming down," and felt the same sensual delight in

[1] Except in those cases where a reference is cited, all first-person reports are from the files of the author.

moving my eye over the printed page as I had experienced when eating the orange.

The words stood out in three dimensions. Reading had never been such a sheer delight and such a complete joy. My comprehension was excellent. I quickly grasped the intent of the author and felt that I knew exactly what meaning he had tried to convey.

In the former instance, motivation for reading was low, since the subject was interested in studying art prints. In the latter episode, the pleasure of eating an orange permeated the act of reading a magazine, which then became a delightful experience.

The cases cited above both involved the sensory level of psychedelic experience. Masters and Houston (1966) presented an intriguing example of a subject who visualized a reading experience while at the recollective-analytic level of his LSD session:

I recalled detail that under ordinary conditions I could not possibly have remembered, including the address on an envelope of a letter that a friend had sent me some years before—an important letter, since it had great significance for me during my analysis. I saw the envelope in front of me, in my mind's eye, recalled the handwriting, and recited the street number and street. (A few days later I went to an attic where I had old letters put away, dug into a dust-laden box, and took out crumpled and yellowing old papers. There, among them, I found the envelope, just as I had recalled it, and the details of the address were correct, entirely correct.)

P. G. Stafford and B. H. Golightly (1967, pp. 140–41) have cited the account of a student who utilized the recollective-analytic level to practical advantage, learning enough German in a week to enroll for an advanced course in the subject:

I hadn't even gotten around to picking up a textbook, but I did have a close friend who knew German well and who said he was willing to "sit in" while I took the drug and try to teach me the language. . . .

The thing that impressed me at first was the delicacy of the language. . . . Before long, I was catching on even to the umlauts. Things were speeding up like mad, and there were floods of associations. . . . Memory, of course, is a matter of association, and boy, was I ever linking up to things! I had no difficulty recalling words he had given me—in fact, I was eager to string them together. In a couple of hours after that, I was even reading some simple German, and it all made sense.

By the time the student finished the LSD session, he had "fallen in love with German." He secured the original German text and an English translation of Mann's *Doctor Faustus*. By the time he had finished the novel, he found that he was scarcely referring to the English version. He also discovered that in having read *Doctor Faustus*, he had developed a feeling for grammar structure and word endings that was "almost intuitive."

When he registered for the second-year college course in German the following week, the instructor expressed skepticism when he heard that the student was self-taught. Upon testing him, however, it was evident that the student's German reading comprehension was more than adequate, and he was allowed to enroll for the course.

Also at the recollective-analytic level fall the examples of renewed spiritual inspiration from reading of sacred literature. Biblical passages or religious terms formerly meaningless sometimes acquire vivid meanings for many readers. Like the individual who through conversion experience suddenly finds himself in possession of the meaning of the term "salvation," so the LSD subject may find similar terms illuminated for him (Leary and Clark, 1963).

An example may be cited of an individual who found significant meaning in a biblical passage during a session with morning-glory seeds:

Upon opening my eyes, I found that I was facing the bookcase. The first book that I perceived was the Holy Bible. I seized it and flung it open. Strangely, the smooth, burnished pages felt like human skin. I fondled, kissed, and caressed the pages. For the first time in several hours, I had found some degree of tranquility.

I looked at the page I had selected and found that my finger was directly above Ezekiel 11:24. The words of this verse, as well as the one directly following it, described my liberation from the more terrifying aspects of the psychedelic experience as well as the importance of communicating my experience to others. They read, "Then the vision that I had seen went up from me. And I told the exiles all the things that the Lord had showed me."

As I read on, I found a new interpretation for the twelfth chapter of Ezekiel. The prophet spoke of a "rebellious house" and of people —perhaps in need of psychedelic substances—who have "ears to hear and hear not." The injunction of Ezekiel 12:13 is to "eat your bread with quaking, and drink water with trembling," an appropriate de scription of the consumption of psychedelics. Ezekiel 12:23–24 states that "the days are at hand and the fulfillment of every vision." Everything I read under the spell of the morning-glory seeds became directed toward the psychedelic experience.

Once again, in this instance, there was an integration of the act of reading into the ongoing psychedelic experience. As a result, a number of "connections" were discovered that would have eluded the subject had he not ingested morning-glory seeds. This phenomenon is surprisingly common among frequent LSD users; their belief in the direct interrelations among most of the events of their lives may well influence their behavior and their view of the universe.

The reading process is rarely associated with the third or fourth levels of psychedelic experience, but some individuals have been catapulted into a deeply moving symbolic or integral episode following a chance glimpse of a line of Hebrew script or of an Egyptian hieroglyphic. In other cases, a line of print has occurred at the end of a segment of the experience and has seemed to summarize it. One subject reported such an episode at the symbolic level during a mescaline session:

I was propelled back into time, back into the primeval jungle. I saw two savages stalking each other in the underbrush. Each savage carried a bow and arrow. Each was prepared to kill the other upon sight. Blood was on their minds; murder was in their hearts.

Suddenly, each saw the other. Each gasped in surprise. Each dropped his bow. The two bows fell together on the ground, forming a mandala. The arrows fell upon the mandala, dividing it into four sections.

The savages fell upon each other—but in an embrace rather than in an assault. As they strolled into the jungle to enjoy their newly discovered companionship, the mandala turned into a white button. Upon the button, in red and blue, appeared the words, "Make love, not war."

During one of my own psilocybin experiences I had an unusual visualization. I pictured a whirlwind carrying away all the words, letters, numbers, and verbal symbols that had acculturated and conditioned me throughout the years. One might say that my session was a form of non-verbal training, a dramatic confrontation with naked events that reminded me not only of the awareness encountered among preliterate tribes, but also of Alfred Korzybski's writings in the field of general semantics (1933).

Korzybski considered man's consciousness of the abstraction process to be the most effective safeguard against semantic problems (such as confusing words with objects) and the key to further human evolution. Consciousness of abstraction was defined by Korzybski as an "awareness that in our process of abstracting we have *left out* characteristics." An individual apprehends himself and his world fully and accurately to the degree that he continually translates higher-order abstractions back to the level of concrete experience. An individual is "sane" to the extent that he becomes experientially aware of the discrepancy between conceptualization and sense impressions. Developmentally, man (both as a species and as an individual) progresses from the preliterate stage (in which he is enmeshed in concrete experience) to the early literate stage (in which he confuses words with things and becomes split off from non-verbal reality) to a fully developed literate stage (in which he uses the printed word but does not confuse it with the object for which it stands).

Robert Mogar (1965c) has stated that, at its best, the psychedelic state can permit the individual to evaluate with some detachment both the structure of his semantic framework (i.e., its similarity to reality) and his semantic reactions. These two kinds of learning were strongly recommended by Korzybski as the most effective means of increasing one's consciousness of the abstracting process.

Richard Marsh (1965) has described how, under LSD, "we seem to come up against that part of our inner world where meanings are made, where the patterning process operates in its pure form." He has further noted that, semantically, the condition of being absolutely present to the outer and the inner reality has at least two advantages. First, it allows a person to tune in on that feedback, both external and internal, that enables him to correct his own errors in encoding. He is able to reduce the noise level in the various communication systems in which he is involved by re-encoding his message streams until they convey the meanings that he intends them to convey. Secondly, it allows a person to inhabit the world of the actual, the world of fact, instead of the unreal and empty world of the prefabricated abstraction. It allows him to experience the world instead of merely to think about it, and perhaps to begin to live in it at last.

Marsh's claim that a new level of reality is opened up by the psychedelics is a controversial one. It is a further step in the perpetual dialogue concerning language and reality. As long as men have reflected about their world, this basic issue has divided them. Some men have regarded man's language as a straightforward reflection of reality. Others have looked upon language as a reducing valve imposed by the limitations of man's consciousness upon the unlimited varieties of his internal and external world (Krippner, 1965). Aldous Huxley (1959, p. 22) has described the role that verbal and written symbols play in helping mankind to utilize this limited consciousness:

To formulate and express the contents of this reduced awareness, man has invented and endlessly elaborated those symbol-systems and implicit philosophies which we call languages. Every individual is at once the beneficiary and the victim of the linguistic tradition into which he or she has been born—the beneficiary inasmuch as language gives access to the accumulated records of other people's experience, the victim insofar as it confirms him in the belief that reduced awareness is the only awareness and as it bedevils his sense of reality so that he is all too apt to take his concepts for data, his words for actual things.

The psychedelic session as non-verbal training represents a method by which an individual can attain a higher level of linguistic maturity and sophistication. On the other hand, some psychedelic episodes have been reported in which an apparent regression took place, in which language was concretized—the letters becoming transformed into images and objects. One subject, while smoking marijuana, looked at a magazine cover and reported a concretization experience:

The magazine featured a picture story about Mexico, and the cover featured large letters spelling out the name of that country. As I looked at the letters, they turned into Aztec men and women. They retained their shape as letters, but subtle shades and shadows became eyes, heads, arms, and legs. That part wasn't so bad, but when Atzecs began to move across the page, I quickly turned the magazine over!

The concretization of letters has been put to artistic use by illustrators throughout the centuries (Mahlow, 1963). For example, Ferdinand Kriwet designed a mandala composed of nothing but several hundred capital letters. Joshua Reichert produced another mandala that consisted of several types of script. A number of contemporary poster artists have publicized "acid rock" musical performances by producing advertisements that fuse the letters with the pictures, making the names of such groups as "The Grateful Dead" and "The Byrds" an integral part of the over-all design, thus combining the "medium" and the "message." The "psychedelic poster" has, within a few years, become an original art form (Masters and Houston, 1968).

The variety of effects that psychedelics have upon receptive language functioning have at least one factor in common: they point up the role that language as a "connecting system" plays in verbal memory (Hastings, 1967). Electric brain stimulation and hypnosis have been able to retrieve long-forgotten memories; psychedelic drugs often produce similar effects, especially at those periods of time when subjects are at the recollective-analytic level.

Physical shock and psychic trauma often lead to the forgetting of verbal material or a regression in verbal functioning. In these cases, the "connecting system" breaks down, just as it does in certain episodes with psychedelics. Henri Michaux (1967) has stated, "After an average dose of hashish, one is unfit for reading." Other artists and writers, however, say that they appreciate receptive language (e.g., listening to poetry, reading novels) even more when they are "high." A great deal of research is needed to explore the variables that determine what effects psychedelics have upon language as it connects one's past memory with his present experience.

Expressive Language

A number of investigators have reported a reduction or even an absence of speech among LSD subjects. Some writers have suggested that these drugs suppress activity in the cortical levels of the brain, where the speech centers are located. J. H. Von Felsinger and his associates (1956), for example, noted that there was "a slowing down of speech and expression" with their LSD subjects, none of whom were psychiatric patients. On the other hand, Morgens Hertz, a Danish physician, described a patient whose long-standing stuttering condition disappeared following LSD treatment (Stafford & Golightly, 1967, p. 113). An American team of researchers found that schizophrenic children became more communicative following LSD treatment (Bender, Goldschmidt, and Siva Sankar, 1956). As with the other types of language, the alteration of expressive language under LSD can take a variety of forms, depending on how it happens to mesh with other aspects of the psychedelic experience.

One research team (Lennard, Jarvik, and Abramson, 1956) studied the effects of LSD on group communication, using both an experimental group of subjects and a control group. The subjects in the control group increased their verbal output during the observation period, while among those who had taken LSD there was a reduction in word output. In addition, the subjects who took LSD asked more questions and made more statements pertaining to orientation (e.g., "What's happening?" "Where am I?") than those in the control group. These findings are consistent with the typical reactions of subjects at the sensory level when traditional time-space orientation is lost.

Another reason for reduced verbalization during psychedelic sessions may be the presence of visual imagery. When an individual becomes involved in "the retinal circus," he often loses interest in speaking. Finally, relaxation and lethargy often mark a subject's first experiences with the psychedelics. In these instances, the speech muscles would be inoperative, and verbalization would be reduced still further.

E. S. Tauber and M. R. Green (1959) have discussed the difficulty in talking about visual imagery and trying to communicate it to someone else. Not only is there a difficulty in translating one's own private world into meaningful public symbols, but there is also a kaleidoscopic piling up of many different images and meanings. Speech is the vocal expression of one's experiences and feelings in verbal symbols; wherever communication involves much more than language can adequately express, there is a high probability of serious gaps, misunderstandings, and improper inferences. Tauber and

Green have stated, ". . . the communication of dream material perhaps most strikingly illustrates the weakness of the tool of language." Much the same could be said of psychedelic experience at the sensory level; this may be another reason why speech often is reduced during a subject's initial LSD experiences.

The description of visual imagery is not the only communication problem that faces the LSD initiate. At the sensory level, there is often an increased awareness of bodily feelings. Preliterate tribes paid great attention to these feelings, but the American culture generally ignores them, unless they are unpleasant. Those words that most quickly come to mind during periods of acute bodily awareness are "sick to my stomach," "pains in my back," and "nagging headache." Once these words become linked to what may be quite natural (and potentially pleasurable) sensations, an individual may very well get sick, regurgitate, and interpret the rest of his psychedelic session as unpleasant.

It is in this regard that the work of Russell Mason on internal perception (1961) assumes importance. Although Mason's experiments did not involve psychedelic drugs, they could serve as models for what can eventually be done with such substances. He asked subjects to specify where various kinds of feelings were located. Love and friendliness, for example, were associated with the central chest area, sexual feelings with the genital-pubic area. He concluded, ". . . the ability of the individual to permit *immediate awareness* of . . . non-cognitive internal perceptions appears to be necessary for healthy psychological adjustment." His data offer a possible physiological explanation for the body changes that take place when drug subjects report feelings of "oceanic love" or "strong sexual responses." They also suggest that persons who are unable to allow this immediate awareness to take place may be poor risks for LSD sessions.

Masters and Houston (1966) have reported statements from a number of subjects who purportedly "felt" the interior of the body during psychedelic experiments. One subject told about sensing his "interior landscape," describing the "trees, vines, streams, waterfalls, hills, and valleys" of the body. Another described the sensation of blood flowing through his veins as well as the receiving and transmitting operations of the nervous system. All these reports characterize the first, or sensory, level of psychedelic experience.

The verbal reports associated with the recollective-analytic and symbolic levels are somewhat different. For example, one subject at the recollective-analytic level reported the insight to Masters and Houston, "I have never been in love with my own body. In fact, I believe that a major emotional problem in my life is that I have always disliked it." At the symbolic level, a number of subjects experience bodily sensations in terms of a mythic drama. One anthropologist reported going through a Haitian transformation rite in which his body began to take on aspects of a tiger (Masters and Houston, 1966, pp. 76–78).

At the integral level, bodily sensations are also reported. One of Masters and Houston's subjects had a mystical experience in which he was ". . . overwhelmed by a bombardment of physical sensations, by tangible sound waves both felt and seen," after which he "dissolved." He later stated, "Now I understand what is meant by being a part of everything, what is meant by sensing the body as dissolving."

A great deal of research is needed to correlate the data on bodily sensations with the data on LSD. One important hypothetical formulation that would be helpful in effecting this correlation was presented by Gardner Murphy and Sidney Cohen in 1965. Murphy and Cohen suggested that psychedelic drugs lower the threshold for internal sensations, especially those from the digestive system, the sex organs, and the striped muscles. As a result, body feelings emerge into self-consciousness, and an individual may interpret the experience as one of "cosmic love." Murphy and Cohen also hypothesized that there was a direct relationship between certain physiological sensations and such verbal reports as "entrance into the void."

In considering the effects of psychedelic substances upon speech, attention could be paid not only to the physiological determinants but to the psychological concomitants of the experience. One of the most typical phenomena is the statement by the subject that his experience has been ineffable, that it cannot be communicated adequately to others. Some subjects assert that no words exist to describe internal events such as those they have felt, and that even if there were such words they would be devoid of significance unless the listener himself had gone through the same experiences. Richard Blum (1964) reported one man's reaction:

Really, when I first took LSD, I didn't know how to describe what had happened. It was intense and important, very much so, but there were no words for it. But after talking with others who had taken it, I could see that they were talking about the same thing. They did have words for it—"transcendental" was one—and so I started using those words myself. An interesting thing happened to my wife. After I gave her LSD she said very little about it. For a whole month she hardly said a word about her experience. But then I introduced her to some others who were taking the drug, and it wasn't more than a few days before she started talking a blue streak; you see, she'd learned how to talk about it from them.

This explanation describes how one learns a language that signifies to other users that one understands and has been through a psychedelic experience. According to Blum, the language is shaped by the culture of the speakers—in this case by the particular subgroup with which the LSD user is socially affiliated and under whose auspices he has taken the drug. This language is as much a sign of "togetherness" and "belongingness" as it is a device for communicating the content of an experience. It is not unusual that a number of people in drug subcultures become frustrated when talking with non-users; to the individual who has never undergone psychedelic experience, the user's words are not understood as affirmations that one is a particular kind of person or a fellow member of an important in-group.

Blum has maintained that learning the LSD language and vocalizing the philosophy of the psychedelic subculture are steps in the commitment of an individual to an identifiable group. Language, in this instance, becomes a device to provide structure and to create a community of experience among persons who have had LSD. Furthermore, whatever one expects from the psychedelics on the basis of prior information and personal predispositions strongly influences the choice of words later used to describe the experience itself.

The experience of being taught linguistic terminology by members of the drug subculture is more than instruction in communication. It is instruction in approved words and approved experiences; it is instruction in a point of view. The terms that are learned can be used to structure the pharmacological response to a drug, giving the experience sense and meaning that it may not otherwise have had. After his first trip, a novice might be told, "Oh yes, from what you say I can tell you really did have a transcendental experience." Such comments are not only instructive, helping the person define and describe his response, but they are also approving and rewarding. As experiments on conditioned behavior have demonstrated, rewarded behavior is generally repeated. In the case of illegal LSD use, the rewards—often linguistic in nature—are frequently great enough to overshadow such potential hazards as psychosis, suicide, and chromosomal damage.

Regarding legal experimental use of the psychedelics, it has often been observed that the language used by the guide will influence what the subject says later to describe his session. This observation is borne out by some of the early research studies. It was initially believed that LSD produced psychotic reactions, and the drug was termed "psychotomimetic" by psychiatrists and psychologists (Rinkel, 1956). LSD subjects were sometimes told by the physician administering the drug, "You probably will go out of your mind for several hours"; many subjects later reported terrifying experiences. One early experimenter took verbatim recordings of an interview with an LSD subject and of an interview with a schizophrenic subject, and outside judges could not distinguish which of the two was suffering from schizophrenia (Hoffer, 1956).

As research workers became more knowledgeable, the psychotomimetic label was discarded by many investigators. Pollard, Uhr, and Stern (1965) noted that psychotic disorders are characterized "by personality disintegration and failure to test and evaluate correctly external reality in various spheres." Following the conclusion of their work with LSD, they stated, "In none of the normal experimental subjects to whom we have given these drugs, nor in our own experience, could these criteria be satisfied."

The problem of scientific scrutiny of verbal reports made during psychedelic sessions persists. One promising tool for linguistic analysis is the measure devised by Bernard Aaronson (1955) for the examination of verbal behavior in psychotherapy. Using standardized measures of word complexity, Aaronson found that, as psychological stress is alleviated, word complexity increases. Another research tool is that used at the Maimonides Dream Laboratory to divide spoken dream reports into units of meaning (Malamud et al., 1967). As the typical subject in experimental dream studies has little concern for grammatical formalism when he makes his verbal report, this method determines units of meaning to be analyzed with regard to dream content.

Using the Cloze procedure to study grammatical predictability, Cheek and Amarel (1968) administered LSD to ten alcoholics, and analyzed their speech patterns. It was found that grammatical predictability tended to rise as the alcoholics continued to speak, both in the drug and non-drug conditions. A group of ten schizophrenics was also studied in the non-drug condition; their grammatical predictability tended to drop.

In another study (Katz, Waskow, and Olsson, 1968), a group of sixty-nine convicts were administered LSD, amphetamine, and placebos. The subjects receiving LSD were found to be significantly different from the other subjects regarding a number of effects, including language. LSD subjects in general were described as "giggly"; the more-dysphoric subjects spoke little and slowly, the ambivalent subjects spoke a great deal and rapidly, while the euphoric subjects fell in the middle regarding speech behavior.

Charles Dahlberg, Stanley Feldstein, and Joseph Jaffee (1968) are in the process of making a detailed analysis of the verbal reports of psychoneurotic patients during twenty-two therapy sessions. Before each session, the patient ingested between fifty and one hundred micrograms of LSD. The therapy sessions were spaced over a period of eighteen months.

The patients' verbal reports were transferred to IBM punch cards and are being submitted to several techniques of linguistic analysis. One such technique, the Role Construct Sorting Procedure, is a test to measure changes in the way patients conceptualize people who are important in their lives. Moreover, these measurements of change are themselves being nalyzed for indications of increased and expanded associations on the part of the patients.

In addition, the Cloze procedure, an index of redundancy, s being used as a measurement of the predictability of inerpersonal language in the patient-therapist interchange. The Type-Token Ratio is a measure of vocabulary diversity and, ndirectly, an indicator of the informational structure of peech. Finally, nurses who attended the patients after each ession have rated the patients as to speech patterns, periods f silence, periods of withdrawal, mood swings, etc.

Preliminary results indicate that LSD facilitates treatment f early experiences in patients by producing partial regresion. In addition, LSD appears to increase the patients' ability to evaluate their problems clearly and to communicate heir insights to the psychotherapist with facility.

Written language attempts to convey meaning through rinted symbols. Although S. Weir Mitchell (1896), one of he first to write a description of a psychedelic experience, tated that his peyote experience was ". . . hopeless to describe in language," he later managed to describe ". . . stars, elicate floating films of color, then an abrupt rush of countess points of white light [that] swept across the field of view, s if the unseen millions of the Milky Way were to flow in a parkling river before my eyes." His account was sufficiently ivid for Trouton and Eysenck (1961) to be able to suggest hat he substituted primitive thinking in the form of visual nages for conceptual thought.

While at the sensory level, during his first LSD experience, subject attempted to write an account of his subjective rections, but became fascinated with the very act of writing self:

mazing! Amazing! The fluidity of the panorama of the room! It ems like eons of time pass between each letter when I write it. As write, I see the loops, the dots, etc., spiral off the page in colors. ff to infinity!

At the recollective-analytic level, imagery persists but coneptualization is often possible as well. For example, Thomas ing and John Buckman (1963) have reported the case of a uropean writer who overcame "writer's block" through LSD

therapy. Prior to taking LSD, he had been unable to finis
a manuscript. After LSD therapy, he went on to become or
of the leading authors in Germany. His major work, cor
pleted during the time he was in therapy, was translated in
twelve languages and had a wide audience in the Wester
world. The writer concluded:

I am no longer afraid of putting one letter after the other to s
what I want. . . . I seem capable of expressing what many peop
would love to express but for which they cannot find the words.
did not find the words before, because I tried to avoid saying the
sential things.

Material that emerges at the recollective-analytic level do
not always lead to the well-being of the subject, especial
if the drugs are taken in unsupervised sessions and wi
an absence of preparation. Following an LSD session, a colle
student wrote the following account of his experience at tl
recollective-analytic level:

Apparently some sort of love-making was going on in the other roo
because the guide would not let me enter it. As it turned out, tl
was the wrong thing to do, because it started me on the road
paranoia, panic, and "the depths." His refusal to let me enter t
room aroused my suspicions of an ulterior motive. I picked o
which I have a curious fear of: homosexuality. I was unwilling
submit to what became suggestive words, lewd actions, and a
praved smile. I shudder when I recall it. My fear was not of the
but that if I submitted I would become "one of them"—"them" l
ing an indefinite but evil sort of being with a depraved smile—a
never able to "return." It reminds me of the movie "The Pod P
ple," where "people" are grown in pods and substituted for r
people. You don't know if your best friend is one of these "peopl
dedicated to your destruction or conversion until it is too late.

Because of the pathological elements in this written
scription, the student was advised by several people to do
more drug experimentation. However, about a year later, t
student accepted a friend's invitation to smoke marijua
The session began with a number of pleasant bodily feelin
and unusual perceptual impressions. Suddenly, the stude
became obsessed with the notion that his friend desired
have sexual relations with him. The student's friend call
the police, and the student was rushed to a hospital, havi

entered a serious psychotic episode.[2] In this tragic instance, the student's written account could have served as a predictor of what would likely happen during future sessions.

An individual attempting to write descriptions of psychedelic experience at the symbolic level has the difficult job of choosing verbal terms that convey some sense of his mythic encounters. This formidable task was well handled by an attorney in the following way (Masters and Houston, 1966, pp. 221–22):

I saw Jesus crucified and Peter martyred. I watched the early Christians die in the arena while others moved hurriedly through the Roman back streets, spreading Christ's doctrine. I stood by when Constantine gaped at the vision of the cross in the sky. I saw Rome fall and the Dark Ages begin, and observed as little crossed twigs were tacked up as the only hope in ten thousand wretched hovels. I watched peasants trample it under their feet in some obscene forest rite, while, across the sea in Byzantium, they glorified it in jeweled mosaics and great domed cathedrals.

The attorney's written description is imaginative, yet fairly concrete, just as the mythical world is concrete. The linguistic consciousness of primitive man is non-abstract; its concreteness is marked by a concrescence of name and thing as exemplified by the various types of name taboos). Ernst Cassirer (1955) has noted that in some primitive religions the worshiper did not dare to utter the name of his gods; in others, certain words were used for the purpose of hex and voodoo. This concrescence of name and thing is demonstrated by a subject's report of a peyote session:

The guide asked me how I felt, and I responded, "Good." As I uttered the word "Good," I could see it form visually in the air. It was pink and fluffy, like a cloud. The word looked "good" in its appearance and so it had to be "Good." The word and the thing I was trying to express were one, and "Good" was floating around in the air.

[2] When I interviewed the student, I discovered that no antidote had been given him once he entered the hospital. Instead, he was queried by policemen, who insisted on knowing the names of campus marijuana and LSD users. This type of treatment, in which the well-being of the patient is relegated to a secondary status by law enforcement personnel, has become very common as the general public's fear of psychedelics has increased.

Name and thing are often wedded at the recollective analytic and the symbolic levels. A subject will say the word "Mother" and feel that the word itself contains aspects of h own mother—or of his memories of her. A theology studer will say "Logos" and imagine that God and Christ are bot present within the word. Only after the drug's effects begi to wear off can these individuals tear the words apart from the experience.

As with other language processes, psychedelic substance can affect the act of writing by bringing about a regressiv type phenomenon (in which words and experience are united as they often are with the child and with the primitive tribe man) or else improve the process (by removing "writer block," facilitating verbal expression, etc.). In some cases bot occur, as when a writer engages in concrescence of word an thing at the symbolic or integral level and later presents vivid written description of that experience.

To assist the encoding of psychedelic experience, an "e perimental typewriter" has been invented by Ogden Lindsl and William Getzinger (Leary, 1966a). The typewriter ha twenty pens, any of which can be depressed by the subje to describe his ongoing experience. The subject must l trained in the use of the device and must learn the co that assists him to describe his psychedelic sensations an reactions. For example, the first key is depressed whenev bodily sensations are experienced; the third key is depresse when feelings about other people are experienced. Althoug further refinement of this device is needed, the researc possibilities seem extensive. A subject could tap out a secon by-second sequence of his experiences, and communica them at least in general terms. Experience patterns could l correlated with neurological recordings. A guide could ke a close watch on the subject's reactions should it be felt a visable to modify the experience.

In one first-person report (Roseman, 1966), a subje claimed that he learned how to become a skilled typist l means of psychedelic experience. Instead of emphasizing t more ideational aspects of the writing process, the subje concentrated on sheer motor activity. First, he familiariz himself with the keyboard and learned the proper fingeri echniques. To reinforce the matching of fingers and type-writer keys, he took LSD, began to type, and continued for several hours.

This subject's claims regarding a facilitation in motor function are provocative and need to be explored under controlled conditions. Peter Laurie (1967) has suggested that the act of writing may be feasible under light doses of psychedelic substances but, for most people, impossible under heavy doses. In the case of writing, therefore, one is struck by the same variety of reports as one encounters with other forms of language; certain people under certain conditions claim that their writing functions are enhanced, others assert writing is impaired, and still others report no discernible difference.

Conclusion

The emergence of professional and public interest in psychedelic substances coincides with the shift in human communication from the chirographic-typographic to the electronic stage. Just as electronic devices have begun to "re-tribalize" the world and convey a sense of simultaneity to human experience, so the LSD user often engages in mythic episodes, senses a "unity of all peoples," and has an impression that everything is happening "all at once"—in a non-linear manner.

Psychedelic substances, when they affect language processes, sometimes appear to assist an individual to observe the difference between the word and the object it represents. In this way, the drugs may serve as catalysts in a non-verbal training program, helping the subject translate verbal abstractions in terms of direct experience.

Psychedelic substances can produce the opposite result as well. The subject may revert to primitive thinking, his ability to conceptualize may decrease, and he may effect a union between the word and its object. This is exemplified by the concretization of letters into pictures and images, by the conrescence of verbalizations with the items they represent, and by the use of words in magical ways on the part of several LSD subjects.

In other words, any of the human race's communicative

stages—voice-and-ear, chirographic-typographic, electronic may be observed by the researcher during a round of psyche delic sessions. Therefore, psychedelic drugs offer an unpara leled opportunity for the investigation of human languag processes. The few experimental and clinical reports tha exist in the fields of listening, reading, speaking, and writin differ so greatly as to inspire curiosity as to the reasons tha the same drugs can produce varied effects at different dosag levels, with different individuals, and under different cond tions. An extremely important variable seems to be wheth or not language, either receptive or expressive, become integrated with the ongoing psychedelic experience. If the i tegration occurs, an improvement in function will often o cur. If the connection is not made, language functioning ma deteriorate or become blocked altogether.

At the sensory level, words are encoded and decoded i highly unusual ways. At the recollective-analytic level, la guage often serves as a "connecting system" in memory and i terpretation. At the symbolic level, words often becom part of a mythic or historical ritual. At the integral level, la guage rarely is a part of the immediate experience; howeve many writers and poets have effectively transformed the religious or mystical episodes into words.

A permanent state of altered consciousness is neither pra tical nor desirable. However, the individual may return the world of imprinting, conditioning, acculturation, and ve balization with new insights if his psychedelic session h been properly guided. The research possibilities in the fie of language and the psychedelics are immense. The da obtained by imaginative and responsible investigators ma well point the way to an enhancement of creative functio ing and a better understanding of the human potential.

SELECTIVE ENHANCEMENT
OF SPECIFIC CAPACITIES THROUGH
PSYCHEDELIC TRAINING

WILLIS W. HARMAN AND JAMES FADIMAN

This article discusses exploratory work that was interrupted
early in 1966 when the Food and Drug Administration, as a
strategy in combating the illicit-use problem, declared a
moratorium on research with normal human subjects. In view
of the preliminary nature of the work, it would not under ordinary circumstances have been submitted for publication.
However, because of the significance of the hypotheses, and
because they are consistent with experience gained in a previous study of four hundred subjects who received psychedelics in a therapy context, and because of the hope that when
it is again possible to resume psychedelic research the non-
medical applications will get long-overdue attention, the decision was made to release these results in their present, un-
finished form.)

Amid much controversy over the place of psychedelic chemicals in contemporary culture, we have quietly entered a third
phase of the research on human uses of these agents.

The first phase, typically identified in the literature by the
use of the adjective "psychotomimetic," was characterized
by dominance of *a priori*, structured models. Seriously under-
estimating the effects that such preconceptions might have on
the content and aftereffects of the subjective experience,
researchers variously reported that psychedelics mimicked
mental illness (when given in a setting that provoked it),
illuminated Freudian theory (when administered by a competent Freudian), evoked Jungian archetypes (when administered by a sensitive Jungian), substantiated the tenets of
behavior therapy (by increasing suggestibility and modifi-
ability), and demonstrated the soundness of the existential
approach.

The second phase, adopting Osmond's neologism "psyc
delic," was characterized by an emphasis on allowing
drug session to run its natural course, in an attempt to m
mize the influence of the conceptions and interpretations
the therapist or monitor. Care was taken to provide s
expectations, rapport, and environment that the experie
would be as non-threatening as possible. Opinions varied
to what constitutes optimum set and setting, and subje
and experimenters varied. As a consequence, reported eff
range from ecstasy to psychosis, from community to isolati
from greatly enhanced mental and perceptual abilities
greatly impaired abilities. From this work emerged a variety
psychotherapeutic applications, well summarized by Ho
(1965), as well as widespread, mainly illicit, use with sens
philosophical, and transcendental goals.

Growing out of this informal experimentation and clini
research, largely as a consequence of suggestive spontane
occurrences, the possibility gradually emerged that spec
kinds of performance might be selectively enhanced by
liberate structuring of psychedelic-agent administrations. T
a third phase of psychedelic research began. Whereas, in
first phase, experiences tended to be controlled and del
ited—never mind if inadvertently—by preconceptions of exp
menter and subject, and in the second phase they ten
to be more uncontrolled and wide-ranging in scope, now
emphasis was to be on deliberate selection of specific aspe
of the psychedelic experience and of specific parameters
functioning.

As these experiments on specific performance enhan
ment through directed use of the psychedelics have gone
in various countries of the world, on both sides of the I
Curtain, and as, furthermore, some, at least, of the infor
exploration has been in defiance of existing laws govern
use of the psychedelic agents, publicly available informat
on results is scant and scattered. In the remainder of t
chapter we shall discuss one pilot study in which the parti
lar type of performance chosen for attention was creat
problem-solving ability. The implications of the work are,
believe, much broader than this particular application. Inde
the basic assumption underlying setting up the project, a

ot negated by any of our observations during the course of
ie research, is that, *given appropriate conditions, the psyche-
elic agents can be employed to enhance any aspect of men-
il performance, in the sense of making it more operationally
fective.* While this research was restricted to intellectual
id artistic activity, we believe the assumption holds true
or any other mental, perceptual, or emotional process. The
sychedelic agent acts as a facilitator, an adjunct to the sit-
ttion it facilitates, and is by itself neither good nor evil,
ficacious nor powerless, safe nor dangerous.

ationale Behind the Creative Problem-Solving Study

Reports in the literature on psychedelic agents that deal
ith effects on performance are inconclusive or contradictory.
hanges in performance levels have been intensively investi-
ited, both during and after the drug session. Instrumental
arning has been found to be impaired during the drug ex-
erience in some studies, enhanced in others. Similarly,
ontradictory results have been noted for color perception,
call and recognition, discrimination learning, concentration,
mbolic thinking, and perceptual accuracy (Mogar, 1965a).

In some of the research, where impairment was reported,
ie drug was used as a stresser with the intention of simu-
ting psychotic performance-impairment. Practically all of
ie formal research in which improved performance was
aimed subsequent to the drug experience has been in a
inical context. Performance enhancement during the drug
xperience has been sporadically reported in both experi-
iental and clinical research, but not in general where the
sychotomimetic orientation was dominant.

Our experience in clinical research (Mogar and Savage,
964; Fadiman 1965; Savage et al., 1966) had been amply
onvincing with regard to the possibility of long-term per-
ormance enhancement through employment of the psyche-
elic agents in a clinical setting. We also had much evidence
ith regard to the subtlety and pervasiveness of the influence
f set and setting. Furthermore, although they had not been
eliberately sought, there were numerous spontaneous inci-
ents of what appeared to be temporarily enhanced perform-

ance during the drug experience itself. These observati
led us to postulate the following propositions:

1. Any human function, as generally elicited, can be
formed more effectively. This amounts to an acknowle
ment that we do not function at our full capacity.

2. The psychedelics appear to temporarily inhibit cen
that ordinarily limit the mental contents coming into
scious awareness. The subject may, for example, discover
latent ability to form colored imagery, to hallucinate, to
call forgotten experiences of early childhood, to gene
meaningful symbolic presentations, etc. By leading the
ject to expect enhancement of other types of performa
—creative problem solving, learning manual or verbal sk
manipulating logical or mathematical symbols, sensory or
trasensory perception, memory and recall—and by provic
favorable preparatory and environmental conditions, it
be possible to improve the level of functioning in any des
respect.

3. Both objective and subjective indicators of mental
formance are appropriate to use in establishing whether th
has indeed been an improvement (or impairment) of
formance.

As Table 1 indicates, commonly observed characteris
of the psychedelic experience seem to operate both for
against the hypothesis that the drug session could be u
for performance enhancement. In this research we attemp
to provide a setting that would maximize those characte
tics that tend toward improved functioning, while minir
ing those that might hinder effective functioning.

For several reasons we chose to focus our efforts on crea
problem solving. One was its obvious utility, an import
consideration at that juncture because of the increasing p
sure for stricter regulation of the psychedelics by those
doubted that they were good for anything at all. Ano
factor was that many of the observed spontaneous oc
rences had been of this sort. Finally, because of exten
recent research activity in the field of creativity, a numbe
relevant objective measures were available for use.

Interest centered on three questions:

1. Can the psychedelic experience enhance creative p

TABLE 1

SOME REPORTED CHARACTERISTICS OF THE PSYCHEDELIC EXPERIENCE
(as found in the literature and in subjects' reports)

Those supporting creativity	Those hindering creativity
1. Increased access to unconscious data.	1. Capacity for logical thought processes diminished.
2. More fluent free association; increased ability to play spontaneously with hypotheses, metaphors, paradoxes, transformations, relationships, etc.	2. Ability to consciously direct concentration reduced.
3. Heightened ability for visual imagery and fantasy.	3. Inability to control imaginary and conceptual sequences.
4. Relaxation and openness.	4. Anxiety and agitation.
5. Sensory inputs more acutely perceived.	5. Outputs (verbal and visual communication abilities) constricted.
6. Heightened empathy with external processes, objects, and people.	6. Tendency to focus upon "inner problems" of a personal nature.
7. Aesthetic sensibility heightened.	7. Experienced beauty lessening tension to obtain aesthetic experience in the act of creation.
8. Enhanced "sense of truth," ability to "see through" false solutions and phony data.	8. Tendency to become absorbed in hallucinations and illusions.
9. Lessened inhibition, reduced tendency to censor own by premature negative judgment.	9. Finding the best solution seeming unimportant.
10. Motivation heightened by suggestion and providing the right set.	10. "This-worldly" tasks seeming trivial, and, hence, motivation decreased.

lem-solving ability, and if so, what is the evidence of enhancement?

2. Can this result in enhanced production of concrete, valid, and feasible solutions assessable by the pragmatic criteria of modern industry and positivistic science?

3. Working with a non-clinical population and with a non-therapy orientation, would there nevertheless result demonstrable long-term personality changes indicative of continued increased creativity and self-actualization?

Procedure

The subjects in these experiments were twenty-seven males engaged in a variety of professional occupations (sixteen engineers, one engineer-physicist, two mathematicians, two architects, one psychologist, one furniture designer, one commercial artist, one sales manager, and one personnel manager). Nineteen of the subjects had had no previous experience with psychedelics. The following selection criteria were established:

1. Participant's occupation normally requires problem-solving ability.
2. Participant is found to be psychologically stable as determined by psychiatric interview-examination.
3. Participant is motivated to discover, verify, and apply solutions within his current work capacity.

Each group of four subjects met one another during an evening session several days before the experimental day. (In one of the groups, one subject had to be eliminated, which left only three.) The proposed sequence of events during the experimental session was explained in detail. This initial meeting also served the function of allaying apprehension and establishing rapport and trust among the members and the staff.

Subjects were told that they would experience little or no difficulties with distractions such as visions, involvement with personal emotional states, and so on. The instructions emphasized that the experience could be directed as desired. Direct suggestions were made to encourage mental flexibility during the session. An excerpt from those instructions is quoted below:

Some suggestions on approaches:

Try identifying with the central person, object, or process in the problem. See how the problem looks from this vantage point.

Try asking to "see" the solution, to visualize how various parts might work together, to see how a certain situation will work out in future, etc.

You will find it is possible to scan a large number of possible solutions, ideas, data from the memory, etc., much more rapidly than usual. The "right" solution will often appear along with a sort of intuitive "knowing" that it is the answer sought. You will also find that you can hold in conscious awareness a number of ideas or pieces of data processes simultaneously, to an uncommon extent.

You will find it is possible to "step" back from the problem and see it in new perspective, in more basic terms; to abandon previously tried approaches and start afresh (since there is much less of yourself invested in these earlier trials).

Above all, don't be timid in the ambitiousness with which you ask questions. If you want to see the completed solution in a three-dimensional image, or to project yourself forward in time, or view some microscopic physical process, or view something not visible to your physical eyes, or re-experience some event out of the past, by all means ask. Don't let your questions be limited by your notion of what can and what cannot happen.

Approximately one hour of pencil-and-paper tests were administered at this time. Subjects were told that they would take a similar battery during the experimental session. To insure that the problems to be worked on were appropriate for the purpose, each participant was asked to present his selection briefly. By the end of the preparation session, participants were generally anticipative and at ease. They had been given a clear picture of what to expect, as well as information on how to cope with any difficulties that might arise.

The session day was spent as follows:

8:30 Arrive at session room
9:00 Psychedelic material given[1]
9–12 Music played, subjects relaxed with eyes closed
12–1 Psychological tests administered
1–5 Subjects work on problems
5–6 Discussion of experience; review of solutions.

[1] Mescaline sulphate (200 mg). The mescaline was procured from F. Hoffmann-LaRoche Co., Basel, Switzerland.

Participants were driven home after this. They were given a sedative, which they might take if they experienced any difficulty in sleeping. In many cases, however, they preferred to stay up until well after midnight, continuing to work on insights and solutions discovered earlier in the day.

Each subject wrote a subjective account of his experience within a week after the experimental session. Approximately six weeks after the session, subjects were administered questionnaires that related to (1) the effects of the session on post-session creative ability and (2) the validity and acceptance of solutions conceived during the session. These data were in addition to the psychometric data comparing results of the two testing periods.

Subjective Reports

The literature on creativity includes analytical description of the components of creative experience, the personal characteristics of creative individuals, and the distinguishing features of creative solutions. From the participants' reports, it was possible to extract eleven strategies of enhanced functioning during the session. The relationship of these strategies to enhanced functioning should be self-explanatory. Those readers interested in the relationship of these aspects to current research and theory on creativity can refer to the detailed technical discussion in Harman, McKim et al. (1966).

The factors are listed below with representative quotations from the subjects' reports.

1. Low Inhibition and Anxiety:
"There was no fear, no worry, no sense of reputation and competition, no envy, none of these things which in varying degrees have always been present in my work."

"A lowered sense of personal danger; I don't feel threatened any more, and there is no feeling of my reputation being at stake."

"Although doing well on these problems would be fine, failure to get ahead on them would be threatening. However, as it turned out, on this afternoon the normal blocks in the way of progress seemed to be absent."

2. Capacity to Restructure Problem in Larger Context:

"Looking at the same problem with (psychedelic) materials, I was able to consider it in a much more basic way, because I could form and keep in mind a much broader picture."

"I could handle two or three different ideas at the same time and keep track of each."

"Normally I would overlook many more trivial points for the sake of expediency, but under the drug, time seemed unimportant. I faced every possible questionable issue square in the face."

"Ability to start from the broadest general basis in the beginning . . ."

"I returned to the original problem. . . . I tried, I think consciously, to think of the problem in its totality, rather than through the devices I had used before."

3. Enhanced Fluency and Flexibility of Ideation:

"I began to work fast, almost feverishly, to keep up with the flow of ideas."

"I began to draw . . . my senses could not keep up with my images . . . my hand was not fast enough . . . my eyes were not keen enough . . . I was impatient to record the picture (it has not faded one particle). I worked at a pace I would not have thought I was capable of."

"I was very impressed with the ease with which ideas appeared (it was virtually as if the world is made of ideas, and so it is only necessary to examine any part of the world to get an idea). I also got the feeling that creativity is an active process in which you limit yourself and have an objective, so there is a focus about which ideas can cluster and relate."

". . . I dismissed the original idea entirely, and started to approach the graphic problem in a radically different way. That was when things started to happen. All kinds of different possibilities came to mind. . . ."

"And the feeling during this period of profuse production was one of joy and exuberance. . . . It was the pure fun of doing, inventing, creating, and playing."

4. Heightened Capacity for Visual Imagery and Fantasy:

"Was able to move imaginary parts in relation to each other."

". . . it was the non-specific fantasy that triggered the idea."

"The next insight came as an image of an oyster shell, with the mother-of-pearl shining in different colors. I translated that in the idea of an interferometer—two layers separated by a gap equal to the wave length it is desired to reflect."

". . . As soon as I began to visualize the problem, one possibility immediately occurred. A few problems with that concept occurred, which seemed to solve themselves rather quickly. . . . Visualizing the required cross section was instantaneous."

"Somewhere along in here, I began to see an image of the circuit. The gates themselves were little silver cones linked together by lines. I watched the circuit flipping through its paces. . . ."

"I began visualizing all the properties known to me that a photon possesses and attempted to make a model for a photon. . . . The photon was comprised of an electron and a positron cloud moving together in an intermeshed synchronized helical orbit. . . . This model was reduced for visualizing purposes to a black and white ball propagating in a screwlike fashion through space. I kept putting the model through all sorts of known tests."

5. Increased Ability to Concentrate:

"Was able to shut out virtually all distracting influences."

"I was easily able to follow a train of thought to a conclusion where normally I would have been distracted many times."

"I was impressed with the intensity of concentration, the forcefulness and exuberance with which I could proceed toward the solution."

"I considered the process of photoconductivity. . . . I kept asking myself, "What is light?" and subsequently, "What is a photon?" The latter question I repeated to myself several hundred times till it was being said automatically in synchronism with each breath. I probably never in my life pressured myself as intently with a question as I did this one."

"It is hard to estimate how long this problem might have

taken without the psychedelic agent, but it was the type of problem that might never have been solved. It would have taken a great deal of effort and racking of the brains to arrive at what seemed to come more easily during the session."

6. Heightened Empathy with External Processes and Objects:

". . . the sense of the problem as a living thing that is growing toward its inherent solution."

"First I somehow considered being the needle and being bounced around in the groove."

"I spent a productive period . . . climbing down on my retina, walking around and thinking about certain problems relating to the mechanism of vision."

"Ability to grasp the problem in its entirety, to 'dive' into it without reservations, almost like becoming the problem"

"Awareness of the problem itself rather than the 'I' that is trying to solve it"

7. Heightened Empathy with People:

"It was also felt that group performance was affected in . . . subtle ways. This may be evidence that some sort of group action was going on all the time."

"Only at intervals did I become aware of the music. Sometimes, when I felt the other guys listening to it; and it was a physical feeling of them listening to it."

"Sometimes we even had the feeling of having the same thoughts or ideas."

8. Subconscious Data More Accessible:

". . . brought about almost total recall of a course that I had had in thermodynamics; something that I had never given any thought about in years."

"I was in my early teens and wandering through the gardens where I actually grew up. I felt all my prior emotions in relation to my surroundings."

9. Association of Dissimilar Ideas:

"I had earlier devised an arrangement for beam steering

on the two-mile accelerator which reduced the amount of hardware necessary by a factor of two. . . . Two weeks ago it was pointed out to me that this scheme would steer the beam into the wall and therefore was unacceptable. During the session, I looked at the schematic and asked myself how could we retain the factor of two but avoid steering into the wall. Again a flash of inspiration, in which I thought of the word "alternate." I followed this to its logical conclusion, which was to alternate polarities sector by sector so the steering bias would not add but cancel. I was extremely impressed with this solution and the way it came to me."

"Most of the insights come by association."

"It was the last idea that I thought was remarkable because of the way in which it developed. This idea was the result of a fantasy that occurred during Wagner [Note: the participant had earlier listened to Wagner's 'Ride of the Valkyries.']. . . . I put down a line which seemed to embody this [fantasy]. . . . I later made the handle which my sketches suggested and it had exactly the quality I was looking for. . . . I was very amused at the ease with which all of this was done."

10. Heightened Motivation to Obtain Closure:

"Had tremendous desire to obtain an elegant solution (the most for the least)."

"All known constraints about the problem were simultaneously imposed as I hunted for possible solutions. It was like an analog computer whose output could not deviate from what was desired and whose input was continually perturbed with the inclination toward achieving the output."

"It was almost an awareness of the 'degree of perfection' of whatever I was doing."

"In what seemed like ten minutes, I had completed the problem, having what I considered (and still consider) a classic solution."

11. Visualizing the Completed Solution:

"I looked at the paper I was to draw on. I was completely blank. I knew that I would work with a property three hundred feet square. I drew the property lines (at a scale of one inch to forty feet), and I looked at the outlines. I was blank.

Suddenly I saw the finished project [Note: the project was a shopping center specializing in arts and crafts]: I did some quick calculations . . . it would fit on the property and not only that . . . it would meet the cost and income requirements . . . it would park enough cars . . . it met all the requirements. It was contemporary architecture with the richness of a cultural heritage . . . it used history and experience but did not copy it."

"I visualized the result I wanted and subsequently brought the variables into play which could bring that result about. I had great visual (mental) perceptibility; I could imagine what was wanted, needed, or not possible with almost no effort. I was amazed at my idealism, my visual perception, and the rapidity with which I could operate."

Results: Subjective Ratings

As mentioned above, several weeks after the experimental session all participants were asked to complete a brief questionnaire. Here they rated their experience with respect to nine characteristics relevant to enhanced functioning. Items were rated on a five-point scale from MARKED ENHANCEMENT (+2) through NO CHANGE (0) to MARKED IMPAIRMENT (−2). The average ratings are listed in Table 2.

TABLE 2

MEAN SUBJECTIVE RATINGS
OF FACTORS RELATED TO ENHANCED FUNCTIONING
(*all ratings refer to behavior during the session*) n = 27

	Mean	S.D.
1. Lowering of defenses, reduction of inhibitions and anxiety	+1.7	0.64
2. Ability to see the problem in the broadest terms	+1.4	0.58
3. Enhanced fluency of ideation	+1.6	0.69
4. Heightened capacity for visual imagery and fantasy	+1.0	0.72
5. Increased ability to concentrate	+1.2	1.03

MEAN SUBJECTIVE RATINGS . . . (Continued)

6. Empathy with external processes and objects
   heightened   +0.8   0.97

7. Empathy with other people heightened   +1.4   0.81

8. Data from "unconscious" more accessible   +0.8   0.87

9. Enhanced sense of "knowing" when the right solution appears   +1.0   0.70

These data, too, seem to substantiate the hypothesis of
enhancement of both verbal and non-verbal skills.

Results: Psychometric Data

Test-retest scores on some of the measures used showed
dramatic changes from normal to psychedelic-session conditions. Most apparent were enhanced abilities to recognize
patterns, to minimize and isolate visual distractions, and to
maintain visual memory in spite of confusing changes of form
and color. Specific tests used included the Purdue Creativity,
the Miller Object Visualization, and the Witkin Embedded
Figures. This last test has been reported to be stable under
a variety of experimental interventions including stress, training, sensory isolation, hypnosis, and the influence of a variety of drugs (Witkin et al., 1962). With these twenty-seven
subjects, enhancement was consistent ($p < .01$), and in some
cases improvements were as great as 200 per cent. (For a
fuller description of the psychometric evaluation, see Harman et al., 1966.)

Long-term Results

The practical value of obtained solutions is a check against
subjective reports of accomplishment that might be attributable to temporary euphoria. The nature of these solutions
varied; they included: (1) a new approach to the design
of a vibratory microtome, (2) a commercial building design,
accepted by the client, (3) space probe experiments devised
to measure solar properties, (4) design of a linear electron
accelerator beam-steering device, (5) engineering improvement to a magnetic tape recorder, (6) a chair design, mod-

led and accepted by the manufacturer, (7) a letterhead design, approved by the customer, (8) a mathematical therem regarding NOR-gate circuits, (9) completion of a furniture-line design, (10) a new conceptual model of a photon, which was found useful, and (11) design of a private dwelling, approved by the client.

Table 3 outlines the initial results of attempting to apply the solutions generated in the experimental sessions back into the industrial and academic settings of the subjects. (These data were obtained by questionnaire and follow-up interview six to eight weeks after the session.)

TABLE 3

OUTCOME OF PROBLEMS ATTEMPTED IN EXPERIMENTAL SESSION ONE MONTH AFTER SESSION DATE

new avenues for investigation opened	20
working model completed	2
developmental model to test solution authorized	1
solution accepted for construction or production	6
partial solution obtained being developed further or being applied	10
no further activity since session	1
no solution obtained	4
*total number of problems attempted**	44

* Many subjects attempted more than one problem during the session.

A quote for a follow-up report written several months after the session is typical of the relative usefulness and validity of the session-day solutions: "In the area of ionospheric source location and layer tilt analysis, I was able in the weeks following the session to build on the ideas generated to the extent of working out the mathematics of the schemes proposed, and of making them more definite. The steps made in the session were the correct ones to start with . . . the ideas considered and developed in the session appear as important steps, and the period of the session as the single most pro-

ductive period of work on this problem I have had in the se
eral months either preceding or following the session."

Many subjects in the follow-up interview reported chang
in their modes of functioning that were continuous with t
enhancement reported for the session itself (e.g., continui
visualization ability). Table 4 lists the result of a questic
naire dealing with changes in work effectiveness.

TABLE 4

WORK PERFORMANCE SINCE SESSION ($n=16$)

	Marked Impairment	Significant Impairment	No Change	Significant Enhancement	Marke Enhan men
1. Ability to solve problems	0	0	8	8	0
2. Ability to relate effectively to others	0	0	8	5	3
3. Attitude toward job	0	0	7	8	1
4. Productivity	0	0	9	5	2
5. Ability to communicate	0	0	10	5	1
6. Response to pressure	0	0	7	8	1

The results given in Table 4 indicate that approximate
half the subjects reporting were still noticing some chang
in their performance level several months after the expe
mental session. These results are particularly interesting
view of the relatively low dosage and the fact that no su
gestion was made at any time that continuing changes of t
nature were expected. The deliberate anticipation of e
hanced performance level, the incitement to a high degr
of motivation, and use of a sheltered and non-critical
mosphere—none of these were directly suggestive of long-ter
personality changes or permanent therapeutic benefit. Yet
certain amount of such change seems to have occurred. O
implication is clear: We are dealing with materials and

erimental situations that have long-term effects; it would
e foolhardy and irresponsible to treat this kind of research
s if it were isolated from the fabric of the subjects' lives.

Comments and Speculations

We had originally intended to follow this pilot study with
controlled experiment employing a double-blind design, in
hich a fraction of the subjects receive an active placebo.
his would have addressed the question of whether sug-
estion alone could account for the performance enhance-
ent. Because of interruption of the research program by
overnment fiat, this extension was never carried out. The
eed for controlled hypothesis-testing research in this per-
lexing area of chemical facilitation of mental functioning
as become a common plea, and rightly so. But equally need-
l of furthering is the exploratory sort of research that
ms at invention of conceptual models and hypothesis con-
ruction. Because of the controversy surrounding use of the
sychedelic agents, this latter type of research is even more
kely to be slighted.

In the research described, we employed naïve subjects.
here are clear methodological virtues accruing from the
e of untrained subjects. However, when the central ques-
on is not one of pharmacological effects, but rather the
egree to which certain processes can be facilitated, the more
perience the subjects can gain the more we are likely to
arn about the process. Thus we would urge the desirability
further investigations employing a series of sessions for
ch subject.

A similar comment holds with regard to selection of sub-
cts. Clinical studies already referred to indicate that those
bjects who are more stable and productive beforehand
nd to "benefit considerably from the psychedelic experi-
ce along the lines of self-actualization, richer creative ex-
rience, and enhancement of special abilities and aptitudes"
avage et al., 1966). Subjects for this pilot study were delib-
ately selected to be persons with known reputations as
eative individuals. In general, we would expect the outcomes
this kind of research to be more fruitful with gifted rather
an "merely normal" subjects.

In contrast with reports of other researchers, we expe[rienced] little difficulty in getting subjects to work on psycholo[g]ical tests. Many studies seem to indicate a temporary debi[li]tating effect of psychedelics on higher cortical processes. [It] seems to us that variables that affect results on these kinds [of] tests include attitude and motivation as well as ability. W[e] found that discussing this problem with subjects in the p[re]paratory meetings eliminated any tendency in the expe[ri]mental session to shrug off the tests as meaningless or to [re]sist them as disconcerting. In short, on the tests, as well [as] in problem solving, by establishing an anticipation of i[m]proved performance, we seemed to obtain results that su[p]port it.

Assuming that these findings are eventually substantiat[ed] by additional research, they find their most obvious applic[a]tion to problem solving in industry, professional practice, a[nd] research. Here the procedure could play a role similar to th[at] played by consultants, brainstorming, synectics, and other [at]tempts to augment and "unstick" the problem solver's unsu[c]cessful efforts. A quote from one of our subjects illustrat[es] the possibilities:

"I decided to drop my old line of thinking and give it [a] new try. The 'mystery' of this easy dismissal and forgettin[g] did not strike me until later in the afternoon, because I ha[d] many times before this session indulged in this line of thin[k]ing and managed to work up the whole thing into an airtig[ht] deadlock, and I had been unable to break, much less d[is]miss, this deadlock. The miracle is that it came so easy a[nd] natural."

A much more important application in the long run, [we] believe, is the use of the psychedelic agents as training faci[li]tators to gradually upgrade the performance level of alrea[dy] effective personnel. This would require establishment of [ac]cepted training procedures and certification provisions f[or] those qualified to use them. This may seem to be a utopi[an] projection from our present state, but we live in an age [of] rapid change, and it is perhaps not out of the question with[in] a decade.

Among consequences of this line of exploration, the mo[st] significant of all, in our estimation, is the gaining of ne[w]

nowledge of the mysterious higher processes of the human
mind, the framing of new and more productive research ques-
ions, and the eventual effect on our image of man—of what he
an be, and of what he is, of the vast potentialities he has
eemingly only begun to tap.

PSYCHEDELIC STATES AND SCHIZOPHRENIA

ROBERT E. MOGAR

eason is only part of a man; when it usurps most of one's living
pace it becomes a tumor . . . a cancer gnawing away the other
arts of human nature. *John Langdon-Davies*

swear, gentlemen, that to be too conscious is an illness, a real,
noroughgoing illness. *Fyodor Dostoevsky*

ust as madness is the beginning of all wisdom, so is schizomania the
eginning of all art and fantasy. *Hermann Hesse*

Ve regard evolution as primarily psychical transformation . . . the
ory of life is no more than a movement of consciousness veiled by
norphology . . . as children of a transition period, we are neither
ully conscious of, nor in full control of, the new powers that have
een unleashed. *P. Teilhard de Chardin*

As long as a man can talk to himself about himself, he
etains some sense of personal identity and separateness.
Once he stops talking (self-reflective thinking) and begins
o listen "to the song going on within him," all boundaries,
nternal and external, cease to exist—including the internal-
xternal boundary itself. In some cases, this state is experienced
r interpreted as psychotic death; in others, as cosmic union.
f the song of silence becomes too loud and discordant or
alls on deaf ears when communicated, the individual is likely
o feel and act crazy. If, on the other hand, the song becomes
 compelling symphony that titillates the consensual thresh-
ld, the individual is more likely to be hailed as an artist
r prophet.

Throughout man's history, millions have been judged psy-

Originally published in *Journal of Existential Psychiatry*, Vol. 6,
Vinter 1968, pp. 401–20.

chotic, only a few prophetic. The incidence of manife
schizophrenia is estimated at a fairly constant 1 per cent i
all racial and ethnic groups (Huxley et al., 1964). Prophe
are estimated in numbers, not percentages, for ". . . few a
capable of holding themselves in the state of listening to the
own songs" (Henri, 1923); ". . . rare indeed are madme
equal to their madness" (Michaux, 1963); ". . . many su
cumb during the cure" (Kierkegaard, 1956); while ". . . on
the strongest of them force their way through the atmosphe
of the Bourgeois-Earth and attain to the cosmic" (Hess
1929).

Some investigators consider psychedelic drugs a potenti
key to understanding and thereby reducing schizophreni
Others welcome the new drugs as an unparalleled means
inducing transcendental states of consciousness. Few clai
both. To suggest that the same agent may induce or mim
psychosis *and* transcendence seems highly improbable a
contradictory. Both psychotomimetic and psychedelic resear
ers usually accept the traditional view of the two states
distinct and unrelated (Bucke, 1923). Those with a psych
delic approach to the drug experience readily embrace th
less-partisan analyses of William James, Anton Boisen, a
more recently Carl Jung, but fail to note that these wr
ers attempted to "study the experiences of inner defeat a
inner victory, the one in the light of the other" (Boise
1952). Also ignored is their conclusion that a strong associ
tion exists between the pathological and the mystical.

The reluctance to acknowledge a link between the norm
abnormal, and supranormal stems in part from the implic
belief (fear?) that similarities preclude essential difference
A corollary belief holds that *schizophrenic* and *mystic* deno
types of persons rather than qualities of experience and b
havior. Accordingly, to accept the cosmic revelations of p
tients as possibly valid and valuable would somehow d
credit normality and transcendence. Yet "psychotic insigh
is frequently a prelude to creative insight; religious co
versions often occur in the wake of psychotic episodes. I
Asian cultures, for example, the shaman's apprenticeship
usually marked by recurrent "hysterical crises" (Eliad
1964). The converse is also true. "Divine discontent" ma

alternately revitalize and paralyze its host. The line between "soul sickness" and mental illness oscillates with time and circumstance.

A wide variety of heightened states of awareness have important similarities and are continuous with normal waking consciousness. Whatever similarities exist do not preclude or minimize differences, either between individuals or within the same individual on different occasions. This contention is strikingly confirmed by the drug-induced experiences of normal subjects. Although characteristic features are prominent, individual differences in reactivity abound. Even within the same person, the experience vacillates widely along the psychotomimetic-normal-psychedelic continuum. These observations suggest that schizophrenic and psychedelic states are dynamic variates of a common core experience differing possibly in cause, emotional valence, or outcome. Discovering the determinants and personal meanings of variable response to psychedelic drugs would enhance our understanding of both psychotic and transcendental states.

Schizophrenic and Psychotomimetic Research

Since the discovery of LSD-25 in 1943, numerous comparative studies have been conducted to ascertain the relationship between naturally occurring and drug-induced altered states of consciousness. As indicated earlier, almost all this work hypothesized that psychotic and psychedelic states were either identical or mutually exclusive entities. In addition to this conceptual fallacy, a number of limitations and methodological flaws have characterized psychotomimetic research. It has become a truism that the nature, intensity, content, and aftermath of the drug experience are functions of complex transactions between biochemical changes, the subject's past history and personality, the expectancies of all persons involved, and the conditions surrounding the drug-induced state. Yet the influence of non-drug factors has generally been ignored or minimized rather than controlled and clearly specified. As a result, the collective findings are inconsistent and contradictory.

What Is Schizophrenia?

The problem of interpreting psychotomimetic research
compounded further by the enigma surrounding psychot
states. Etiology of the multiple overlapping groups of schiz
phrenic syndromes is presently obscure, and diagnostic c
teria are notoriously unreliable. Bleuler's (1965) recent c
tique of contemporary views ranged from biochemical to ps
chological, from genetic to environmental, from pragmatic
existential, from descriptive to dynamic orientations. His cor
prehensive review of the empirical evidence led to the co
clusion that no single specific cause of schizophrenia has be
found. Yet various theorists have reported findings indica
ing a genetic factor, biochemical irregularities, a distinct f
milial pattern, a characteristic personality structure of eith
the patient or his mother, an atypical social milieu, and
on. The multiple theories and seemingly conflicting eviden
can be reconciled if it is recognized that (a) an ever-increa
ing range of experiences and behaviors are currently label
schizophrenic, (b) there is nothing in schizophrenic ph
nomenology that would be quite strange to the healthy, i.
there is nothing intrinsically pathological in the experience
ego loss, (c) a variety of avenues can lead to a schizoid sta
and (d) various levels of interpretation of the empirical ev
dence may have entirely different individual and social co
sequences and yet be simultaneously valid and consistent.

These contentions may be strikingly illustrated by compa
ing two currently prominent but opposing points of vie
namely, the disease model and the social-existential perspe
tive. Representative of the disease model is the adrenochrom
metabolite theory proposed by Hoffer and Osmond (1960
These investigators present convincing evidence that a ten
ency to schizophrenia is inherited. According to this view,
genetic mechanism produces consistent physiological, bi
chemical, and clinical peculiarities, which result in perceptu
and affective changes that in turn determine the extensi
psychosocial consequences of the illness. The hypothesiz
genetic mechanism is assumed to increase the production
adrenochrome and adrenolutin, substances that are psychos

imicking in many animals, including man. In support of heir theory, Osmond and Hoffer (1966) review evidence rom a variety of sources that tentatively indicates excessive uantities of these substances in acute schizophrenics and ome subjects who have taken LSD-25.

These investigators also raise the interesting question of vhy a genetically determined condition that is so obviously naladaptive should persist in all mankind at such a stable ate. They suggest, ". . . schizophrenics have traits conerring Darwinian 'fitness' in a variety of environments." Reearch findings are cited indicating that schizophrenic patients ave a high tolerance for active chemicals, a low incidence f allergies, and are highly resistant to infectious diseases as ell as wound and surgical shock. In addition to their aparent biological advantages, Osmond and Hoffer point out hat the same psychological effects of schizophrenia that have uch painful, disruptive consequences in a highly urbanized ociety may have great personal and social value in lessechnological cultures. Furthermore:

brief scrutiny of the history of art, politics, philosophy, religion, id science itself shows that all these activities have from time to me been much influenced by those whose perceptions ranged from e unusual to the bizarre (p. 305).

Viewing the relationship between culture and psychopanology within an evolutionary framework, Hammer and Zuin (1966) also suggest some possible culturally adaptive unctions of schizophrenia. They point out that the characteristics of the mentally ill occur in most people, and symptoms uch as anxiety, guilt, shame, and depression are often haressed to socially useful purposes. Similarly, Bowers and reedman (1966) and Ludwig (1966) emphasize the healing unction of schizophrenic states and consider them a major venue of new knowledge and creative experience.

In sharp contrast to the genetic/disease theory, Szasz, Laing, nd the existential analysts stress the familial/social origins f schizophrenia, and its existential significance. Unlike hysical illness, Szasz (1961) considers "mental illness" a culurally relative myth that subtly strips the "patient" of perenal responsibility and basic human rights. He also em-

phasizes the strong tendency in a technological society towa
indiscriminate application of the mental-illness label wi
its pejorative connotations and unwarranted promise of "tre
ment" and "cure." Similarly, Laing (1967) asserts that th
is no such condition as schizophrenia, but that the label
a social fact and the social fact is a political event. He
scribes the schizophrenic simply as someone who has qu
experiences or acts in a queer way, from the point of vi
usually of his relatives and mental-health workers. Citing
large body of research findings, Laing goes on to state
equivocally, ". . . *no* schizophrenic has been studied wh
disturbed pattern of communication has not been shown
be a reflection of, and reaction to, the disturbed and c
turbing pattern characterizing his family of origin," a
". . . *without exception*, the experience and behavior tl
gets labeled schizophrenic is *a special strategy that a pers
invents in order to live in an unlivable situation.*" (ital
included in original)

Existential analysts such as Binswanger, Jaspers, and Stor
consider the virtues of so-called normality vastly overrat
in our culture, and emphasize the truth content of schi
phrenia and its potentially constructive aspects. The key f
tures of the existential position are well described by Ste
(1964):

The schizophrenic is the unwitting explorer and herald of unfathom
boundary areas of human existence. In his illness, uncanny pot
tialities, which lurk in the shadows of every human existence,
come real. He bears witness to an experience of universal impc
the confrontation with primordial fear, surrender to naked hor
where the normally veiled or hidden aspect of the fundamental
lornness of existence is revealed with shattering impact. Viewed
this fashion, the madness of the schizophrenic transcends the ca
gory of mere pathological accident, and becomes an existential mc
of being which puts into question the foreground of consensu
validated, 'objective' reality, and unveils the existence of other, ba
stage, realities which are no less real for being generally kept in
shadow (p. 168).

There is no essential conflict between the genetic/dise
and the social/existential conceptions of schizophrenia. Bc
positions recognize the potential benefits of schizophre
states, be they biological, psychological, or cultural. Also,

cial/existential writers do not rule out a possible evolutionary/
genetic factor but prefer to speak of schizophrenics as "children of a transitional period" (P. Teilhard de Chardin) or
an "experiment in nature" (Adolph Meyer), as "unwitting
explorers" or as having "one dimension too many" (Hermann
Hesse). Conversely, Hoffer (1966) has stated that, despite its
genetic origin,

[Schizophrenia] is also psychological, sociological, and even theological. For like the psychedelic reaction, the molecular abnormality
in schizophrenia merely sets off the train of events which are perceived and reacted to by a person in terms of his life's programming. . . . The same factors that lead to a psychotomimetic reaction
in normal people probably lead to the psychosis features of schizophrenia (p. 128).

As suggested earlier, diverse views of schizophrenia usually
reflect different levels of explanation or interpretation that
complement, rather than pose alternatives to, each other, i.e.,
both the disease and the existential positions are valid and
may be simultaneously endorsed. Another source of confusion is the vagueness and wide variety of conditions labeled
schizophrenic. In many cases of conflicting evidence, it is apparent that investigators are not studying comparable patient
groups, behaviors, or subjective experiences. Similarly, what is
delusional thinking to one observer may be novel insight to
a second observer.

The only substantive difference between contemporary
views of schizophrenia concerns the individual and social consequences of adopting one frame of reference to the exclusion of all others. Numerous writers have described in detail
the anti-therapeutic and often inhuman consequences of
treating unusual mental and perceptual experiences as by-
products of a disease process that lies outside the agency of the
person, i.e., as an illness "that the person is subject to or
undergoes, whether genetic, constitutional, endogenous, exog-
enous, organic, or psychological, or some mixture of these"
(Laing, 1967). Treating schizophrenia as "nothing but"
pathology defines the patient as a non-responsible object, re-
jects the validity of multiple realities, and ignores the potential value of altered states of awareness. If nothing else,
the advent of psychedelic drugs has given impetus to the

emerging view of schizophrenia as a potentially orderly, natural sequence of experiences that should be permitted to run its course rather than suppressed, arrested, or obliterated.

This sequence is very seldom allowed to occur, because we are so busy "treating" the patient, whether by chemotherapy, shock therapy, *milieu* therapy, group therapy, psychotherapy, family therapy . . . (p. 85).

No age in the history of humanity has perhaps so lost touch with this natural *healing* process that implicates *some* of the people whom we label schizophrenic. No age has so devalued it, no age has imposed such prohibitions and deterrences against it, as our own (p. 88). (italics in original)

In his recent book, Foucault (1966) traces the close historical parallel between the rise of the disease model of madness and the increasing dominance of reason and order as governing principles in Western civilization. He shows how madness gradually lost its rich metaphoric meanings, how it was progressively demystified. "What was once a dialogue between reason and unreason became a monologue in a language which exhausted itself in the silence of others." Reason has become almost totally cut off from one of its chief sources of vital strength, its dialectical counterpart. Foucault concludes that madness and unreason cannot be explained. "It is both a fundamental and ultimate category of human existence, and its utterances reveal ultimate truths."

The ambivalence expressed in these representative observations and allegations concerning contemporary approaches to schizophrenia also applies to drug-induced psychedelic states. The current fascination and controversy over LSD and similar compounds may be viewed as a counterreaction to our ultra-rational commitment to structured, controlled forms of experience, i.e., the restricted range of experience sanctioned by public consensus (Mogar, 1966). A corollary to this feature of modern culture is our inordinate investment in language and higher-order abstractions at the expense of non-verbal experience and empathic communication. Narrowing the scope of human awareness to manageable proportions has no doubt permitted man's remarkable technical progress and made his existence far less precarious. Unfortunately the toll exacted in sensibilities and imaginative thought has been excessive and, for some people, intolerable (Mogar, 1965a). No doubt many such individuals, with and without the aid of drugs, are currently labeled schizophrenic.

Psychotomimetic Research

Having described the enigma surrounding both schizophrenic and psychedelic states, and the cardinal importance of the cultural context in which they occur, it is not surprising that psychotomimetic research has yielded contradictory results. As suggested earlier, the intrinsic complexity of the phenomena involved has been compounded further by various conceptual and methodological flaws. In extensive reviews of LSD studies (Mogar, 1965c, 1967), it was shown that almost all the work conducted thus far fit two essentially different research paradigms that are mutually exclusive in every major respect and yield opposite findings. One approach, the the clinical investigation, views the drug as a liberator that facilitates accurate perception and insight (psychedelic orientation), pays particular attention to intrapersonal and interpersonal factors, optimizes the conditions under which the drug is taken, and obtains results indicating various kinds and degrees of performance enhancement. The other major approach, the laboratory investigation, usually views the drug as a stresser capable of simulating psychotic behavior (psychotomimetic orientation), ignores non-drug factors, employs impersonal, "objective" procedures, and obtains results indicating various kinds and degrees of performance impairment. Needless to say, almost all comparative studies of schizophrenic and drug-induced states have conformed to the laboratory paradigm. As a result, the major outcome of this work has been conflicting lists of superficial similarities and differences between diverse unspecified psychotic patients and diverse unspecified "normal" subjects given LSD under unspecified conditions.

There is general agreement that LSD can amplify and caricature schizoid deviations from conventional thinking and perception. Recent investigators emphasize, however, that the drug experience is at times similar, but not identical; that it can model, but not ape, a chronic psychotic state (Cole and Katz, 1964; Hoffer, 1965). It has been found, for example, that hallucinatory patterns and images are highly similar in schizophrenic patients and LSD subjects (Horowitz, 1964), but in the latter case visual changes are recognized by the subject as not being veridical perceptions (Sandison, 1959). A similar difference is usually reported with regard to "delusional" thinking (Manzini and Saraval, 1960). The relevance of the hallucinogenic properties of LSD to schizophrenia is further lessened by the finding that visual hallucinations seldom occur in schizophrenia, and conversely, auditory hallucinations are rare in LSD experiences (Buss, 1966).

Most investigators presently assume a basic similarity between the two states while attempting to identify essential differences and possible determinants of these differences. The basic similarity is variously termed a dissolution of the ego, an expansion of consciousness, a regression to infantile modes of functioning, a grossly impaired cognitive/perceptual "filter mechanism," a breakdown of self/world boundaries, or less judgmentally, a heightened state of emotional arousal, an increased sensitivity to stimuli in all modalities, a marked lowering of the threshold between conscious and unconscious activity, or a lessened capacity to think and perceive abstractly in conventional terms. These views of the communality among altered states of consciousness all imply a wider, more inclusive experiential mode—whether enlightening or chaotic. While some emphasize a greater access to intrapsychic activity, others stress an increased sensitivity to external events.

Individual reactions to comparable deviations from normal consciousness vary widely. Many researchers have concluded that schizophrenics and most LSD subjects differ consistently in their reactions to "disturbances" of consciousness. A number of reasons for differences in response have been suggested. The most obvious reasons given are that the LSD subject begins with an unimpaired character structure and knows that his unusual mental state is temporary and due to a drug. He is able to look upon the experience as a spectator, whereas the schizophrenic is, from the onset, an actor portraying a problem that affects him personally (Vinar, 1958). Other distinguishing features frequently reported include emotional lability, ecstasy, and laughter, unimpaired reality-testing, and outward passivity, in contrast to the schizophrenic's characteristic emotional flatness, periodic panic and anxiety, autism and dissociation, and occasional outbursts of hyperactivity (Cohen, 1964; Roubicek, 1958; Sandison, 1959).

In many studies, no one or combination of these features has been found to differentiate the two states (see, e.g., Trouton and Eysenck, 1961). Negative results have typically been attributed to mismanaged drug sessions (Masters and Houston, 1966) or personality factors. Cohen (1964), for example, reports that when the drug is given blind, response to it is much more overwhelming and anxiety-ridden, i.e., psychotomimetic. Similarly, Hoffer (1965) found that LSD produces a prolonged schizoid experience in prepsychotic subjects. The collective evidence strongly indicates that almost all adverse reactions to LSD are due to non-drug factors, namely, inadequate preparation, negative expectancies, character deficits, and poorly managed sessions. However, the same reasoning can be applied to psychotic states. Although not drug-induced, some schizophrenic reactions may have "adverse" effects because of personal limitations or an uncongenial environment. As suggested earlier, there is nothing intrinsically pathological about ego loss, regardless of its determinants—genetic, biochemical, familial, or social.

Reviewing psychotomimetic research, one is struck by the tendency in this work to indiscriminately view all unpleasant effects of the drug as "mimicking psychosis," and all positive effects as psychedelic or transcendental. Stated another way, LSD investigators have almost invariably showed a preoccupation with the schizoid features of psychedelic states and completely ignored any possible psychedelic features of schizophrenic states. As indicated earlier, the focus on disease entities rather than transactional processes obscures the nonpathological aspects of psychosis and fails to take into account the vague, wide variety of conditions currently labeled schizophrenic.

Differences in reaction to similar altered states of consciousness (e.g., pleasant-unpleasant; pathological-transcendental) and the determinants of these differences (e.g., character structure; interpersonal and social milieu) are essentially the same whether the experience is naturally occurring or drug-induced. That is, differences in reaction and their determinants do not clearly differentiate schizophrenic from psychotomimetic or psychedelic experiences. Both schizophrenic and drug reactions oscillate widely along pleasant-unpleasant, pathological-transcendental dimensions—and for the same reasons. Differential reactions such as those cited above do little more than define the extremes of an unpleasant/pathological–pleasant/transcendental continuum. Most reactions to an altered state of consciousness are probably dynamic mixtures of awe and dread, terror and ecstasy, delusion and revelation.

Two major hypotheses can be derived from this view that are consistent with current approaches to mental illness as well as the results of LSD research. First, the LSD subject can be clearly distinguished from the chronic schizophrenic patient who is hospitalized for prolonged periods. Second, unpleasant reactions and pathological reactions are not identical, nor do they necessarily covary. The same holds for the mistakenly assumed relationship between the pleasant and the transcendental. Hellish LSD experiences, no less than the joyously cosmic, may have a validity "that transcends mere pathological accident." Similarly, although most hospitalized patients seem aptly described as "unsuccessful mystics" (Eliade, 1964), some have experiences early in their illness that are indistinguishable from religious, creative, or transcendental states (Bowers and Freedman, 1966). These hypotheses warrant further elaboration.

Some Meaningful Distinctions

Like most research on schizophrenia, psychotomimetic studies have used chronic hospitalized patients almost exclusively (Higgens and Peterson, 1966). Patients recently admitted for the first time have seldom been included. As a result, these studies demonstrate marked differences between psychotic and LSD subjects but add little to our understanding of the schizophrenic process. Schizophrenia is a catch-all category in most hospitals for marginal members of society. After extensive investigation, Gendlin (1966) concluded that a large subgroup of patients were simply pushed out of the world very early and did not display the cardinal symptoms associated with schizophrenia. Consistent with this view, few hospitalized patients manifest depersonalization or disturbances of body and self image. Buss (1966) reports substantial evidence indicating that such "disturbances" are found *more* frequently among neurotic and healthy people.

A mass of projective-test data fails to provide evidence of greater imaginative richness in most schizophrenic patients, but instead reveals a poverty of associational material and fantasy activity (Beck, 1964; Rickers-Ovsiankina, 1960). Perhaps these results offer a tentative basis for explaining why schizophrenics, when given LSD, denied that the experience was anything at all like their psychotic episodes (Turner et al., 1959). A similar link is suggested by the findings of Osmond and Hoffer (1966) that only *acute* schizophrenics and *some* LSD subjects produce the excess of adrenochrome and adrenolutin predicted by their genetic theory of schizophrenia.

Parenthetically, these results are also consistent with differences between schizophrenic adults and schizophrenic children. While most adult patients are unresponsive to psychedelic therapy, a number of independent studies have reported dramatic alleviation of autistic symptoms in severely withdrawn children following LSD treatment (Mogar and Aldrich, 1967). This parallels the findings that adult schizophrenics, unlike autistic children, were generally extraverted and hyperactive during their childhood (Hoffer and Osmond, 1966b). Similarly, Wagner and Stegemann (1964) found that introverted children (emotionally inhibited, active fantasy life) were least likely to end up as schizophrenic adults.

This line of evidence suggests that a person under the influence of LSD may fit the traditional description of schizophrenia more closely than the majority of patients currently placed in this diagnostic category. On the other hand, there is a striking similarity between the *initial* experiences reported by some schizophrenic patients and drug-induced experiences. Partial recognition of these qualitatively different "schizophrenias" is implied in currently employed distinctions between chronic/acute, process/reactive, endogenous/exogenous schizophrenia, and between regressive/restitutive symptoms. These typologies are variously defined in terms of differences in etiology, successive stages of a unitary process, prognostic or treatment implications, and so on. Although such distinctions are seldom used consistently and have questionable validity, each implies an essential difference between an intense, temporary altered state and a relatively stable condition of long duration. On this point there is little disagreement.

Arieti (1955) makes a sharp distinction between the acute, or anxiety, stage and the chronic, advanced phase of schizophrenia. Many patients are frightened and perplexed when they first recognize cognitive/perceptual changes. They express a fear of going crazy, of being hospitalized, or of dying. During the advanced stage, "psychotic insight" occurs, followed by an enduring resolution of novel perceptions and unusual sensations. The patient becomes apathetic, withdrawn from social interactions, and finally comes to terms with his altered state by developing symptoms. During the acute phase (or type) of schizophrenia, many patients describe a profound inner state rich in imagery and meaning (Kaplan, 1964). Others report being swamped by an incoming tide of sensations (McGhie and Chapman, 1961). Whether the emphasis is on internal or external events, descriptions of this initial fluid state are indistinguishable from personal accounts of LSD experiences.

In a comparative study of subjective reports obtained from LSD subjects and incipient schizophrenics, Bowers and Freedman (1966) identified a common core experience characterized by a disquieting sense of dread coupled with intense happiness, a fear of breakdown together with an awareness of breakthrough. It was concluded that psychedelic and psychotomimetic phenomena were closely related, differing primarily in outcome; i.e., the consequences of a heightened state of awareness may be either harmful or beneficial. According to Bowers and Freedman, a complex interplay of intrapsychic and environmental factors determine and shape the final result. Particular emphasis is given to the degree that such experiences are delusional or adaptive, as a basis for judging their validity. Following William James, Bowers and Freedman assert that personal discoveries, insights, or new perspectives must "run the gauntlet of confrontation" with total experience before their significance can be determined.

After emphasizing the similarities between acute psychotic episodes and LSD experiences, Prince and Savage (1966) also conclude that the major differences between them lies in their consequences for the individual. These writers use the concept of regression to account for similarities between altered states as well as subsequent differences in outcome. Psychotic, mystical, and LSD experiences are characterized by common regressive features. These include a return to preverbal, magical modes of thought, renunciation of worldly interests, ineffability, the noetic quality, ecstatic feelings, and a sense of cosmic union or suspension of self-nonself boundaries. Such experiences may alternately impair and expand awareness. Although regressive in similar ways, Prince and Savage make a sharp distinction between an altered state having self-destructive consequences and one that facilitates self-realization:

A psychosis is a pressured withdrawal with—in many cases—an incomplete return. A mystical state is a controlled withdrawal and return; a death and rebirth, often a rebirth into a world with a radical shift in its iconography—a death and transfiguration (p. 74).

Turner (1964) makes a similar distinction between schizophrenia and what he terms "oneirophrenia." Schizophrenic states are preceded by a prolonged period of painful struggle with irrationality. Eventually, primary regressive activity breaks through the secondary ego-control system uninvited and unwanted. In oneirophrenic states such as those induced by psychedelic drugs, secondary control processes are willingly withdrawn, and feelings of exhilaration prevail. Turner emphasizes that the eruption of unconscious forces in schizophrenia is born of frustration (double-bind sort), a stress that cannot be solved by rational means. There remain three possibilities: murder, suicide, and psychosis. Consistent with this view, Aaronson (1966) found that by hypnotically eliminating and expanding a perceptual modality such as depth or time, he could simulate psychotomimetic phenomena. His studies indicate that schizophrenia is a psychic analogue for death, whereas psychedelic states are characterized by perceptual expansion and a commitment to living.

"The Supreme Fiction" and Other Realities

The distinctions made by these writers call attention to common features and meaningful differences between psychotomimetic and psychedelic states. To avoid semantic confusion, it should be emphasized that both "drug-induced" and "naturally occurring" experiences may have psychotomimetic or psychedelic properties. Drugs offer an unparalleled means of deliberately producing an altered state under controlled conditions. As indicated earlier, however, unique features of drug-induced states are superficial and relatively insignificant for comparative purposes; i.e., they are often indistinguishable from psychosis, on the one hand, and mystical states, on the other. Similarly, schizophrenia "is potentially liberation and renewal as well as enslavement and existential death" (Laing, 1967).

Although meaningful differences between psychotomimetic and psychedelic phenomena can be specified, it is presently impossible to predict the nature, course, and outcome of an anticipated altered state, except in very broad terms. It is hardly less difficult to identify an ongoing experience as psychotomimetic or psychedelic—either from an objective or subjective frame of reference. With the control afforded by mind-altering drugs, the ability to identify and predict specific reactions promises to increase greatly. To some extent, however, unpredictability is an essential ingredient of altered states. By their very nature, psychotomimetic and psychedelic experiences involve high risk, shock and surprise, venturing into unknown realms, and uncertainty concerning outcome. At the level of sensation and perception, the phenomena of altered states are characterized by oscillations, immediacy, and nearness, while practically devoid of objectification and invariance (Klüver, 1965):

Distinctions within this range are difficult to make, since on the perceptual, hallucinatory, imaginal, and other levels, different kinds of "reality" are continuously judged and experienced. Under pathological as well as normal conditions we operate on, or relate ourselves to, many different levels of "reality," and are able to shift, or are forced to shift, from one level to another (p. 24).

The fluidity and complexity of the phenomena involved seem to insure some measure of unpredictability, even though the key features of psychotomimetic and psychedelic reactions, as well as their determinants, have been identified. It is safe to assume that individual response is a function of ongoing transactions between a finite number of intrapsychic and environmental factors. The interplay of these variables results in an altered state that is brief or prolonged, pleasant or unpleasant, voluntarily or involuntarily regressive. The experience may represent self-abnegation or self-expansion, a complete or incomplete return, death with or without rebirth. Its consequences may be destructive or constructive, delusional or adaptive—today, tomorrow, or never—from the standpoint of either the individual or society. It seems apparent that these distinctions between psychotomimetic and psychedelic reactions offer meaningful guidelines for understanding, not programming (1) varieties of altered states.

In addition to their inherent unpredictability and the complexity of the process involved, no universal criteria exist for evaluating the validity or desirability of specific reactions and outcomes. Certainly the nature of a person's experience and his subsequent mode of being-in-the-world are meaningful ways of distinguishing psychotomimetic from psychedelic states. However, the current tendency to equate psychotomimetic with harmful, and psychedelic with beneficial, represents a gross oversimplification. What constitutes an "adverse" reaction or aftermath to variously induced altered states is extremely difficult to determine. As suggested earlier, the meanings of the experience may be equally valid whether joyful, dreadful, or both. What have been variously called psychotic episodes, mystical states, religious conversions, maturational crises, *nadir* and *peak* experiences, may at times lead to misery and helplessness and at others to personal growth and self-actualization (Maslow, 1964; Mogar, 1965b).

Long before the advent of synthetic mind-altering drugs, Anton Boisen suggested that acute mental illness and sudden transformations of character

. . both arise out of a common situation—that of inner conflict and disharmony, accompanied by a keen awareness of ultimate loyalties and unattained possibilities. . . . Where it is unsuccessful or inde-

terminate, it is commonly spoken of as "insanity." In those construc
tive transformations of the personality, the individual is relieved of
his sense of isolation and is brought into harmony with that which is
supreme in his hierarchy of loyalties. He succeeds in effecting a syn
thesis between the crisis experience and his subsequent life which
enables him to grow in the direction of inner unification and social
adaptation on a basis conceived as universal. In mental illness, no
such synthesis occurs. The patient may get well, but he may not
solve his problem (Boisen, 1952, p. viii).

Viewing psychosis as an indeterminate but potentially
problem-solving process (rather than a disease process) is
consistent with major trends in contemporary psychiatry
(Bleuler, 1965; Searles, 1961). As indicated earlier, the ef
fects of LSD on normal subjects has given impetus to the
emerging concept of schizophrenia as an orderly, natural se
quence of experience that should be permitted to run its
course rather than suppressed, arrested, or obliterated. Repre
sentative of this trend, Kaplan (1964) describes the outcome
of this process:

The cure or solution must be neither a return to the so-called nor
mality that preceded the illness nor a negation of the illness. The
new state must rather involve a genuine moving to a new solution, a
movement which would have been impossible without the illness
(p. xi).

Other investigators indicate that attitudes and practices
currently prevalent in our culture contribute greatly to the
illness by disrupting the death-rebirth sequence (Adams,
1963; Laing, 1967). In this respect, Bateson (1961) posed the
question of why so many who embark upon a voyage of dis
covery fail to return from it. "Do these encounter circum
stances either in family life or in institutional care so grossly
maladaptive that even the richest and best-organized hallu
cinatory experience cannot save them?" Similar sentiment
have been passionately expressed by Henri Michaux (1967).

Recent medications prevent the insane from following their aliena
tion through. They have thereby lost their own "liberation." Even
when they cannot really be cured, they are damped. Strange, dull
"improved" cases, which one encounters at present in the asylums
or outside, madmen frustrated of their madness . . . (p. 190).

It is noteworthy that Michaux's observations were

prompted by his personal experiences with mescaline. As suggested by Osmond (1965), the mind-altering drugs have great possibilities for training psychiatrists and other mental health workers, "who are then less likely to produce standardized answers for their patients' distresses." A similar application of LSD-25 has led to the design and construction of new hospitals for mental patients. By personally experiencing an altered state of space, time, color, and texture, it was possible to create architectural environments more congenial to the experiential worlds of schizophrenia (Osmond, 1965). These developments are consistent with Laing's plea for replacing "the *degradation* ceremonial of psychiatric examination" with "an *initiation* ceremonial, through which the person will be guided with full social encouragement and sanction into inner space and time, by people who have been there and back again."

As suggested previously, conventional "normality" and conventional "reality" have become increasingly narrow and exclusive in our ultrarational, technological society. Conversely, a progressively wider range of experiences and phenomena are currently defined as "abnormal" and "unreal." By present-day standards, both psychotomimetic and psychedelic states qualify as "loss of reality" experiences. This point of view is being challenged by social-existential and psychedelic approaches to altered states of consciousness, with their emphasis on multiple, equally valid realities, the sterility of conventional experience, and the continuum of normal, psychotomimetic, and psychedelic states.

No doubt, far more people today "suffer" from a lack of psychedelic experiences than from an excess. It is also likely that significantly fewer *aborted* personal tragedies and crises would occur in a genuinely humanistic society. Yet the possibility remains that, even in an optimal environment, few would be "equal to their madness" or capable "of listening to their own songs." Whether drug-induced, naturally occurring, psychotomimetic, or psychedelic, altered states are generally dreaded as much as they are desired, since, in Kurt Goldstein's terms, one can never be sure that his capacities are equal to the demands and discoveries of the experience. Particularly with drugs there is the ever-present danger of seeing too much, too clearly, too soon. William James cautioned that seraph and snake occupy the same transliminal region, to which Rilke might have replied, ". . . if his devils were to leave him, he was afraid his angels would also take flight."

Man's history has been characterized by a seemingly insoluble ambivalence toward altered states and intense experience. Freud said that in schizophrenia things become conscious that should remain unconscious. As Kierkegaard pointed out, however, "One cannot transcend one's self objectively. The existential realization of a unity of finite and infinite which transcends existence comes only in the moment of passion." Tolstoy had a similar view: "It is possible to live only as long as life intoxicates us; as soon as we sober again we see that it is all a delusion, and a stupid one!" Despite their emphasis on intensity, both men conceded that "It is perfectly true that only terror to the point of despair develops a man to his utmost—though of course many succumb during the cure" (Kierkegaard). Sartre's Roquentin in *La Nausée* realized this hazard all too well when he said, "The Nausea has not left me and I don't believe it will leave me so soon; but I no longer have to bear it, it is no longer an illness or a passing fit; it is I." Similarly, Hermann Hesse's *Steppenwolf* laments, ". . . a man cannot live intensely except at the cost of the self," and although he ". . . made sundry holes in the web of time and rents in reality's disguise, it held him a prisoner still."

Perhaps the main conclusion to be drawn from this critique is that we have been prematurely and overly judgmental toward modes of experience differing markedly from our own. We would do well to adopt the attitude expressed by the physicist-philosopher-psychologist Ernst Mach before science and humanism became hopelessly split:

The expression "sense illusion" proves that we are not yet fully conscious, or at least have not deemed it necessary to incorporate the fact into our ordinary language, *that the senses represent things neither wrongly nor correctly.* All that can be truly said of the sense-organs is that *under different circumstances they produce different sensations and perceptions* (1914, p. 10). (italics in original)

PART VI

NON-DRUG ANALOGUES TO THE PSYCHEDELIC STATE

Apart from spontaneous experience, the principal sources of analogues to the psychedelic state come from hypnosis and meditation. It has been argued that yoga arose in India as a means of altering consciousness after the legendary soma was no longer available. This is probably specious reasoning, for *charas*, the Indian equivalent of hashish, is used ritually to this day in Hindu temples. Nevertheless, experiences from hypnosis and meditation, including yoga, are comparable to those of the psychedelic states.

Hypnosis, meditation, and drugs are not the only way to obtain psychedelic experiences. In his fine anthology of papers dealing with altered states of consciousness, Tart (1969) also includes papers on hypnagogic states and dreaming. The physiological methods for producing such states range from fasting and special diets to specialized kinds of breathing and the creation of states of excessive fatigue. The behavioral methods range from perceptual deprivation and social isolation to specialized forms of concentration and movement, and even include the commission of horrendous acts. Wavell (1967) describes the universal conditions for group trance in highly diverse cultures around the world as involving "fasting, rhythmic music, deafening noise, incense, smoke, whirling prayer wheels, the constant reiteration of a word or phrase, three-night dances, candle flame, tobacco inhaled or swallowed and vomited." Castaneda's (1968) mentor, Don Juan, produced states of "non-ordinary reality" without drugs by forcing him to find a personally relevant solution to a crucial problem without specified limits or criteria for recognizing that solution, and, subsequently, by blurring the edges of reality like "the magus" in Fowles's novel (1965).

There is probably a strong relationship between hypnotic

states and drug-induced psychedelic states (Aaronson, 1967c). Not only have the aftereffects of each of these kinds of state been independently accounted for by invoking the concept of imprinting (Leary, 1964a, 1965; Spiegal, 1965), but Sjoberg and Hollister (1965) and, more recently, Netz and Engstam (1968) and Netz, Morten, and Sundwall (1968) have shown enhanced scores on a test of hypnotic suggestibility as a result of administering LSD. Fogel and Hoffer (1962b) have shown that a full-blown psychedelic experience could be suppressed and restored by hypnosis in a well-trained subject and subsequently recreated by hypnosis alone.

In a similar fashion, there is more than a strong family resemblance between hypnosis and meditation. Erikson (1965) has explored this question in a famous experiment with Aldous Huxley as his subject. A common approach to Zen meditation (Wienpahl, 1964) involves having the meditator breathe in a relaxed fashion and count his breaths from one to ten, after which he returns to one again. This differs from one of the classic autohypnotic inductions only in that in the autohypnotic induction one does not return to one, but continues to count upward (Weitzenhoffer, 1957). Kroger (1963) offers an extensive discussion of the similarities between religious practices in Buddhism, Judaism, and yoga, and in hypnotic and autohypnotic techniques.

The paper by Aaronson deals with hypnosis. It recounts a series of experiments in which posthypnotic suggestions of perceptual change are given to normal subjects, and the resultant alterations in their behavior are observed. Some changes produce schizoid behavior, others psychedelic experience. These data are analyzed to present a first approximation to a theory of what produces psychedelic reactions.

The paper by Deikman is one from his series of papers on the effects of meditation. These pioneering studies have not only suggested the value of meditation for psychotherapy, but have focused attention on the process of perception itself and on the laws governing the perceptual process in meditation and, perhaps, in the psychedelic state. This paper, like that by Aaronson, stresses the role of perception in accounting for these experiences. In particular, after reading Dr. Deikman's paper, one is moved to ask whether the effect of psychedelics is to shift thinking from the abstract, cognitive sphere to the perceptual.

SOME HYPNOTIC ANALOGUES TO THE PSYCHEDELIC STATE

BERNARD S. AARONSON, PH.D.

The effects of psychedelic drugs are many and varied. Masters and Houston (1966) have attempted to set down a partial list of the phenomena produced by these drugs that are of psychological significance, and have ended up with a catalogue of behavior changes that embraces almost the entire range of organismic functioning. The effects are often so profound, so protean in their manifestations, that it is difficult to decide which effects are primary and which changes are associated with other changes.

Nevertheless, inspection of accounts of psychedelic sessions (e.g., Metzner, 1968) suggests that they are not just random concatenations of effects, but follow an orderly process of unfolding. The influence of set and setting has been documented by many researchers (Hyde, 1960; Leary, Litwin, and Metzner, 1963; Krippner, 1965; Mogar, 1965a, 1965c; Alpert and Cohen, 1966). Klüver (1966) has reviewed the literature on hallucinations in general to show the underlying form-constants that set off the oscillating patterns of phenomenal experience.

The general tendency is to seek to explain these effects by appeals to neurophysiology, pathophysiology, or psychodynamics. As organisms, we seem to be constituted in such a way as to take our own perceptions of the world around us as veridical, without questioning our own contributions to what

Presented in part at the meetings of the American Psychological Association, San Francisco, California, 1968.

These studies were supported in part by grants from the Parapsychology Foundation, Inc., the Ittelson Family Fund, and U. S. Public Health Service Grant No. 1-SO1-05262-01.

and how we perceive (Aaronson, 1967b). Until fairly recently in the modern world, evidences of non-veridicality were attributed to magic, an outside force. As magic and supernatural explanation fell into disrepute, causations internal to the perceiving organism were posited for those situations in which external checks were not available to enable the classification of misperceptions as illusions. Psychodynamic causations are generally posited if the non-veridicality involves affective factors; pathophysiological explanations are favored if the non-veridicality is merely bizarre or if there are other, concurrent signs of biological disorder. Neurophysiological causation may be appealed to in either instance, and is usually regarded as involving a more neutral, more biological, and hence, more basic, level of explanation.

Neurophysiological explanations are especially favored in accounting for the effects of drugs. These are biochemical substances, and it seems somehow more appropriate to account for their effects in terms of changes in the humors and secretions of the body, and the responses of muscle and nervous tissue. Yet the reason these drugs are studied springs from the changes in behavior and the alterations in consciousness they produce. The best that can be obtained when correlating alterations in consciousness with neurophysiological changes is a correlation, not a statement of causation. Merleau-Ponty (1963) has shown the great variability of behavior mechanisms involved in producing even the simplest reflex. In addition, the mere fact that a person's report that he is perceiving the color red can be correlated with electrochemical changes in the topography of his brain tells us nothing about the phenomenal properties of his perception of red, nor the variety of mechanisms that may be involved in making that perception possible. When Milton Erikson (1939) wished to create color blindness hypnotically, he had to suggest a way not only the ability to see particular colors, but the memory of having seen them as well.

The primacy of the biological substrate is an assumption, and the opposite view, that biological changes are the dependent variable to more fundamental, behavioral changes can just as easily be taken. Indeed, we shift to this opposite view whenever we warn somebody not to do something because it might be injurious to his health. We are in effect saying that the behavior will produce physiological changes of an unpleasant kind. Behavior is considered to be more complex than physiology, and patterns of behavior change can be traced to changes in specific patterns of physiological function. Yet the entire field of psychosomatic medicine is founded on the effect of changes in psychological function upon physiological function. Krech, Rosenzweig and Bennett (1960) have shown that when rats are reared in enriched environments, their neurophysiology is vastly different from littermates reared in impoverished environments.

Perhaps the strongest basis for the emotional bias toward biological primacy is that while many of us may claim to have seen bodies operating without minds, few will claim that they have seen minds functioning without bodies. Although we are all aware of periods of unconsciousness, as in sleep, very few of us can recall a time in our lives when we functioned apart from our bodies. Leaving aside the claims of those who assert that they have indeed functioned outside their bodies (Tart, 1967), there is at least a strong supposition that we build our models of the universe on the way in which our bodies are constructed to receive information and act upon it (Aaronson and Mundschenk, 1968). The possibility remains that this may not be the way we think about it at all. McLuhan and Fiore (1967) have shown how our innate sensory capacities and abilities to act have been extended and enhanced by modern communications media. These authors have tried to indicate some of the ways in which our concepts of the world may be changing in consequence. Alan Watts (1966) has observed that if someone, knowing nothing at all about cats, were to watch through a chink in a fence a cat prowling back and forth past that chink, he might conclude that the cat's head was the cause of its tail. In the face of such arbitrariness, the only appropriate concern is the pragmatic one of what will solve a given problem most easily.

To solve the problem of how psychedelic states are produced, it is first necessary to specify which changes produced by these substances are primary and which secondary. This specification should be at the level at which these states are experienced: the level of consciousness itself. Klüver's (1966) fundamental work on form-constants in mescaline-induced hallucinations, Oster's (1964) work on Moiré patterns, and the work of Horowitz (1964) relating the phenomena of hallucination to physical anomalies in the perceptual apparatus, represent attempts in this direction. Once the primary and secondary changes and their interrelationships have been specified, it is possible to set forth some meaningful correlations between consciousness and physiological function. It will still not be possible to assert that either one is more conceptually primary than the other, but a more clear-cut picture will emerge.

The following set of experiments represents an attempt to clarify the variables involved in psychedelic experience at the level of the experience itself. The method has involved taking a single component perceptual variable involved in the psychedelic experience and examining what happens to the individual when this variable is altered. Because of limitations of space, not all the perceptual variables that have been studied will be reported here, but only some of the alterations in time and space deemed most pertinent to psychedelic experience.[1] Because these experiments are long-drawn-out, this chapter should be taken as a report on work in progress. The end of these experiments is not yet in sight.

Method

The sample comprised seven male subjects ranging in age from twenty to twenty-seven, who were attending local colleges and universities when the experiments were begun. Two were English majors, two psychology majors, one majored in pastoral counseling, one majored in art, and one had no major but chose psychology after leaving this laboratory. In personality, one was dependent and open, one was withdrawn and intellectualized, one was hypomanic and convivial, one was irritable and introspective, one was ambitious and serious, one was gentle and idealistic, and one was mystical and impetu-

[1] Other studies published elsewhere in this series and including these and other variables are shown in the Bibliography as Aaronson, 1964a, 1964b, 1965, 1966a, 1966b, 1967a, 1967b, 1967c, 1968a, 1968b, 1968c, 1969a, and 1969b.

ous. Because of the long duration of these experiments, and the time and expense involved in training subjects, each subject, once trained, was used as long as possible. For the same reason, not all subjects completed all conditions. In reporting these data, the total number of subjects involved in each condition will be noted.

Six of the subjects were true hypnotic subjects. One was a simulator, chosen for this after extensive attempts at hypnotizing him had failed to produce anything deeper than a light trance. The role of the simulator is to act out and try to "live" the suggestions according to his understanding of their implications. This provides a check on how much of what seems to be happening in these experiments is in the eye of the beholder, as well as a control for the process of hypnotizing itself. This subject did undergo marked mood and affect changes in the course of carrying out these instructions and often seemed to go into some kind of hypnoidal state, which was not quite like the state entered into by the hypnotic subjects.

As detailed accounts of the procedures involved in these experiments have been published elsewhere,[2] they will not be repeated here. The basic procedure for each subject involved first giving him a battery of tests, after which he was hypnotized and given the posthypnotic instructions of perceptual change. The subject was then allowed two hours of free time, after which he took a ride in a car over a standard course. He then wrote an account of what had been happening to him and how he felt up to that point. He was then interviewed by an outside clinical observer,[3] ignorant of what condition, if any, had been imposed. He then took a battery of personality tests, repeated the earlier battery, was interviewed by the experimenter, and was dehypnotized. He was once more interviewed by the experimenter, and then both subject and experimenter wrote separate accounts of

[2] More-detailed descriptions of the procedures will be found in the papers listed in footnote 1.

[3] The writer would like to thank Drs. A. Moneim El-Meligi, Frank Haronian, Harriet Mann, Humphry Osmond, Stanley R. Platman, Hubert Stolberg, and A. Arthur Sugerman for their assistance in this study.

their impressions of the day. Each such posthypnotic session lasted from five and one half to nine and one half hours, according to the speed with which the various tasks were completed.

Because the literature on the effects of psychedelics frequently notes alterations in spatial perception, in size, and in the speed with which time passes, the conditions of *no depth, expanded depth, blurred vision, clear and distinct vision, diminished size, enlarged size, fast time, slow time,* and *stopped time* have been selected for inclusion here. Each of the time conditions involves an alteration of time by keying it to a metronome, as well as a verbal alteration of time. Interspersed through all the other conditions are *control* conditions, in which the subject is hypnotized, but no suggestions of perceptual change are made. The control condition for the metronome involved keying the subject into the metronome, but letting the metronome continue to run at the rate of one beat per second.

The instructions for the *no depth* condition were that, when the subject opened his eyes, the dimension of depth would be gone. In the *expanded depth* condition, the subject was merely told that the dimension of depth would be expanded. In the *blurred vision* condition, the subject was told that everything he looked at would seem blurred; and in the *clear and distinct vision* condition, that everything he looked at would seem clear and distinct. In *diminished size*, the instruction was that everything would be one half its present size in each dimension; and in *enlarged size*, that everything would be twice its present size in each dimension.

The time instructions for the metronome series involved setting the metronome to a speed of one beat per second and telling the subject that the metronome was beating at the rate of one beat per second and that it would continue to beat at this rate. The metronome was then speeded up, slowed down, stopped, or left unchanged, as the conditions of the experiment dictated. The verbal instructions for *fast time* set the subject's personal time, as defined by Cooper and Erikson (1959), to world time in such a fashion that three seconds of the subject's personal time passed every time one second passed for anyone else. In *slow time*, the instructions made one second of personal time equivalent to three seconds of world time. In *stopped time*, the subject was told that time had stopped, there was no time.

The order of these conditions was different for each subject, and the order in which they are presented here is adopted arbitrarily, for purely heuristic reasons.

Results

SPATIAL SERIES

No depth. Five hypnotic subjects and the simulator completed this condition. All found it unpleasant, and the outside evaluator raised the question of schizophrenia in each instance. One showed disturbances of gait, posture, and movement, similar to that seen in catatonia; a second felt that the people around him were inhuman robots, plotting against him; one subject showed marked withdrawal and sleepiness, and two showed inappropriate emotional behavior along with regression. The simulator also became withdrawn and hostile.

Four subjects reported loss of sensation extending beyond the visual into other sensory modalities, but all the hypnotized subjects reported perceptual disturbances of some kind. All the hypnotized subjects showed some odd and peculiar difficulties in movement. Four subjects, including the simulator, withdrew from people and things around them, one to the point of compulsive sleeping, and five showed delusional thinking of a paranoid sort. All six reported feeling hemmed in, but only three reported that the walls and ceiling were closing in on them.

Expanded depth. The opposite instruction, that depth was expanded, produced positive and happy feelings in four hypnotic subjects and the simulator, and ambivalent feelings in the fifth. At the time the condition was induced, the fifth subject, unknown to the experimenter, had a slight stomach ache and other signs of a beginning illness. He reported that he felt that if he could only let go of his body, a beautiful experience was beginning to unfold around him, but the stomach ache kept bringing him back, and in the process, grew worse. A second attempt to produce this condition resulted in a positive, happy state, which was brought crashing down when the outside observer raised some issues about which the subject felt guilty.

The quality of the experience for the other subjects is best exemplified by the fact that one subject reported that everything was part of a divine order and he must spend his life serving God. A second subject described the world as ". . . at once a gigantic formal garden and an irrepressible wilderness of joyous space." A third subject titled his account of this session "And then there was Depth!" The two subjects with experience of a psychedelic (marijuana) reported the experience as being like "a pot high." The simulator became convinced that our usual perception of depth is an illusion, and was engrossed with the tridimensionality of space.

All six subjects responded to this condition with an expanded awareness of the world similar to the experiences described by Huxley in *The Doors of Perception* (1954). With the exception of the fifth hypnotic subject, all became and remained exuberantly happy. All but the simulator seemed to have experiences similar to what has been described under the rubric of "psychedelic experience." All the hypnotic subjects reported sensory enhancement, most marked in the visual area, but cutting across all sense modalities. The hypnotic subjects were also, as a group, impressed with the order inherent in the world about them, which three of them imbued with religious significance.

Blurred vision. Three hypnotic subjects responded positively to this condition; two hypnotic subjects and the simulator responded with schizoid withdrawal. Those that responded positively responded in terms of the primacy of color and light over form, and compared their perceptions of the world with impressionist paintings. One subject and the simulator responded in terms of an inability to make contact with anybody; the last subject responded with a blunting and dulling of thought processes. All subjects lost some sensation in non-visual modalities. When the perception of outlines alone was blurred, colors tended to stand out. Alan Watts (1962) has noted how the perception of form and the perception of color may really be the same, but the behavior patterns of these subjects do not support this point of view.

Clear and distinct vision. Four subjects and the simulator responded positively, and one hypnotic subject negatively, to this condition. The subject who reacted negatively reported that everything seemed too clear to him and stood out horribly in all its ugliness. The others became impressed with the beauty of small details such as the interweaving of the mesh of a screen and the pattern inherent in a cigarette ash. One subject was impressed by his own separateness and the separateness and self-existence of everything around him. The simulator reported an increased preoccupation with the environment around him, which made him happier as he moved away from himself.

All six subjects reported an increased preoccupation with the world. Five subjects and the simulator became energized and happy as a result; one subject was made anxious. This supports Palmer's thesis (1966) that some individuals may adopt nearsightedness as a defense against too much sensory input. Form and light seemed augmented for all the subjects, including the simulator. Four hypnotic subjects reported an increased intensity of color and also increased clarity of perception of stimuli in all sense modalities. All subjects but the one responding negatively reported a feeling of increased ability to think clearly.

Decreased size. Four hypnotic subjects and the simulator experienced this condition. Each of the hypnotic subjects responded initially with withdrawal, marked anxiety, and disturbance of relationships with the world around them. The simulator became happy and expansive. As the world was small and he was large, he felt that he now had nothing to fear from anyone. Two hypnotic subjects in the course of the day made their perceived selves physically smaller to bring themselves into scale with the world, and one made himself younger. The fourth hypnotic subject remained out of scale, isolated and unable to adapt to anything around him. To the extent that the subjects were able to bring themselves into accord with the perceived scale of the world, their moods lightened. Only one subject was able to make a complete translation of his perceived scale to that of the world about him. The other two subjects who attempted to make this kind of shift were only partially successful and so only partially alleviated their dysphoria.

Increased size. Three hypnotic subjects and the simulator reacted with fear to a world grown suddenly too large. The fourth hypnotic subject immediately perceived himself as large in a world suddenly immense, and reported a loss of a sense of reality. Two of the subjects were able to alter their perceived physical scale to that of the large world about them, and subsequently became very happy. One subject, who seemed to operate within a context of psychological rather than physical change, grew more mature and able to function with the people around him, whom he also perceived as mature. The simulator and the subject who immediately perceived himself as large did not try to grow larger.

Growing larger seems to have been a more successful maneuver for the subjects than growing smaller. This may arise from the fact that all of us have experience in growing larger. (While there is some tendency for us to lose height with advancing years, this is less obvious than the more-marked tendency to gain height in the early years, and certainly at the ages of the subjects in this study would not be noticed at all.)

Control. No changes were noted for any subject or the simulator under control conditions with regard to any personality or behavioral variable.

TIME RATE SERIES

For the sake of convenience, metronome and non-metronome inductions of the same condition will be treated under the same heading. The effects of each kind of induction will, however, be considered separately. The sample for all these time rate conditions consists of four hypnotic subjects and the simulator.

Fast time. When the metronome was speeded up, all the subjects and the simulator became hyperactive, tense, driven, and irritable. Three hypnotic subjects began to move rapidly, with a jerky quality similar to that seen in reruns of early silent films. All the subjects showed some annoyance at people about them who were functioning at lower rates of speed than they were.

All the hypnotic subjects reported their dominant mood as

happy, but all had very sweaty palms (a common sign of anxiety), and two showed marked behavioral evidence of anxiety from time to time. All the subjects, including the simulator, showed difficulties in speech and concentration. Three subjects and the simulator seemed to become rather grandiose in their manner and in their judgments about others, and two subjects showed mood swings from elation to rage.

When fast time was induced verbally, without the metronome, a similar set of changes in behavior seemed to occur. Without the ticking of the metronome in the background, however, the quality of being driven was absent from many of these experiences, and there was much more euphoria expressed. With or without the metronome, all subjects continued to report a heightened influx of stimulation, which was at times threatening. One subject reported a number of perceptual distortions and visual hallucinations, so that at one point it seemed to him that I was literally holding my head *in* my hand when, in fact, I was leaning my head *on* my hand.

Slow time. When the metronome was slowed, all the subjects but the simulator became depressed. In only two cases did this approximate a true depression; in the other two, it seemed to produce a more generalized kind of dysphoria. The simulator, who was a Southerner, related the condition to the pace of a southern day. (This suggestion was given on a hot day.) He felt that the metronome helped in this in giving a "reassuring sound of time slowed down."

All the hypnotic subjects reported boredom and apathy. Their voices became flat and their expressions listless. One subject became hostile and mildly sadistic. All hypnotic subjects reported difficulty in thinking, and two seemed to become paranoid in the trend of their thinking. One subject reported transient visual and auditory hallucinations, which he did not specify, and transient enhancement of visual and taste sensations. This same subject reported, ". . . distant objects seemed more distant and unreal than usual, while objects close to me were vivid and dazzling."

When time was slowed verbally, two subjects and the simulator became depressed. The third subject, also a Southerner given the suggestion on a hot day, related the condition to "a lazy southern day" and became calm and relaxed. Another subject, who tended to react to conditions of stress by sleeping, felt calm and unhurried, and spent the day in relaxed meditation. Under this condition, as well as under the metronome condition, all the subjects felt incompetent to handle situations that might arise that might call for quick judgments or action. Even those who responded with calm relaxation made the comment that they could not handle emergency situations feeling as they did, but reassured themselves that they didn't have to.

Stopped time. When the metronome was turned off, one subject and the simulator continued to behave as if hallucinating the metronome. One hypnotic subject claimed to move into a situation of timelessness, although he looked worried to me, and his psychological tests showed marked defensiveness and denial. Two subjects became depressed, withdrawn, and apathetic, and one of these became so sleepy that he would fall asleep even in the middle of a conversation. On a later occasion, the hypnotic subject who hallucinated the metronome beating became rigid and immobile when moved into a stopped-time situation by a gradual slowing of the beat of the metronome. This is similar to the previous case reported by Fogel and Hoffer (1962a).

Two of the subjects showed memory loss and difficulties in comprehension. Three subjects reported changes in the visual, auditory, and tactual spheres. Three subjects showed marked withdrawal from everyone and everything, and two reported body-image changes. Two subjects reported changes in space such that things seemed insubstantial and depth non-existent. This last is in keeping with the observation of a strong conceptual stereotype that seems to exist in our culture, at least, linking time and depth (Aaronson and Mundschenk, 1968).

When time was stopped verbally, all the hypnotic subjects reacted with depression and feelings of unreality. The simulator moved into a state of timelessness, where nothing bothered him. For those subjects who had negative reactions under the metronome condition, the negative reactions with the verbal instructions were even more profound. All hypnotic subjects became withdrawn, anxious, and yet apathetic.

Three subjects reported the destruction of depth, which also seemed to invade and distort the other visual dimensions of space.

All hypnotic subjects reported perceptual changes involving loss in all other sensory dimensions. One subject was appalled by the silence he felt around him. Another commented that he could move through a tree, and neither he nor the tree would feel it. Still another described a malted milk he was trying to drink as tasting like chlorine gas.

All the hypnotic subjects were fearful, and all showed confusion in their thinking. Three subjects became hostile, and two showed active paranoid delusions. All four hypnotic subjects had their sense of personal identity impaired, and one felt that the people in the laboratory were a collection of apelike robots plotting against him.

Controls. Under no control condition, with or without a metronome, were any changes observed in any subject either clinically or on any test.

Discussion

The data point clearly to depth-perception changes as being central to many of the changes reported as occurring as a result of the ingestion of psychedelics. The changes resulting from ablation of depth, which in other contexts have been identified as related to schizophreniform behaviors, are also related to many of the changes characteristic of "bad trips." Conversely, the changes that result from the expansion of depth are similar to the experiences recorded on "good trips." The relationship is like that postulated by Huxley (1956) in which he contrasted the perception of the "clear light" with a schizophrenic girl's perception of a landscape bathed in a horrible electric light.

If one makes the conservative assumption that any instance of behavior observed in response to the posthypnotic instructions has a 0.5 probability of having in fact occurred as a response to the instructions, at least five such instances are required to establish a correlation between the behavior and the instruction at the .05 level of probability, the standard cutting-off point generally used. Using this criterion, the ablation of depth is at least unpleasant and associated with behaviors that lead trained clinical observers to raise the question of schizophrenia. Generalized perceptual disturbances extending into other modalities, difficulties in movement and spatial orientation, withdrawal, delusional thinking with expectations of danger from others, and a feeling of being hemmed in, complete the picture. Expanded depth is pleasant and even joyous; attention is directed out into the environment. It is characterized by sensory augmentation and experiences of perceptual enhancement that may spring from the greater clarity of lines that demarcate forms. As Kant (Bleibtreu, 1968) has pointed out, "Space is merely the form of all appearances of the outward senses." In the absence of forms to contrast and compare, there can be no experience of depth. When Pollard, Uhr, and Stern (1965) administered LSD, psilocybin, and sernyl to subjects strapped down on beds, with their heads under milky plastic domes, with auditory and tactual stimulation also cut off, they found that most of the characteristic experiences reported with psychedelics failed to appear, although their subjects still tended to find their experiences with psilocybin and LSD pleasant.

Blurred vision and *clear and distinct vision* do not have the same effects as the changes in depth. The only changes significant by the criteria noted above under blurred vision was a general tendency for subjects to lose sensitivity in other modalities than the visual, and a general disinclination to read. *Clear and distinct vision* produced happy reactions with a heightened attention to the world and a preoccupation with small details. The perceptions of form and light were reported augmented, as well as the subjective sense of an ability to think clearly. The effects of *clear and distinct vision* are more like *expanded depth*, although they are not identical, than *blurred vision* is like *no depth*. The similarity may result from an augmentation of perceptual processing, so that more stimuli can be admitted and handled without overtaxing the capabilities of the organism.

While none of the changes with regard to size have as yet met the statistical criteria set forth here, they are in their broad outline similar to Swift's accounts, in *Gulliver's Travels*, of the effects of size on perception and behavior. Being out of scale with one's environment seems, in general, a negative stimulus. Being small in a large environment may produce feelings of being overwhelmed, while being large in a small environment may give a sense of power, but also a sense of isolation and insensitivity to others.

In the metronome-induced time rate changes, the sound of the metronome seems to be the adequate stimulus. There was less variability in the metronome versions of *fast* and *slow time* than in the verbally induced ones, but more variability in the *stopped-time* conditions, when the metronome was stopped. The verbal instruction that time was stopped seems to have been a stimulus the subjects other than the simulator could not evade.

Speeding time produced hyperactivity, tension, impatience, euphoria, sweaty palms, and reports of heightened stimulation. Slowing time produced a slowing down of rates of activity, thinking difficulties, and feelings of incompetence for quick action. Because of the difference in response between the simulator and the subjects, the stopped-time changes fail to reach our statistical criterion. However, stopping time verbally produced in all the hypnotic subjects depression, feelings of unreality, withdrawal, apathy, anxiety, thinking difficulties, and loss of perception in all sensory modalities. The effects of *stopped time* are similar to *no depth*, which is underscored by the tendency of subjects to report a loss of depth in this condition. *Fast* and *slow time*, however, are less like the other spatial conditions, except that fast time is associated with increased stimulation and positive feelings, while slow time seems the reverse.

The data suggest that psychedelic experience is associated with conditions that enhance the input of stimuli and augment the perceptual processing of that input. Bleibtreu (1968) has pointed out that in effect this perceptual processing is, on an experiential level, the time flow. In the time rate experiments here, altering time rates seems to change not only perceptual processing, but the rates at which responses are emitted as well. In the conventional psychedelic experience, however, an increase in the rate of perceptual processing does not seem to be accompanied by necessary changes in response output. It may be that there are two kinds of organismic time, one based on the rate at which input from the environment comes into the system, and the other on the rate at which responses are emitted into the environment. The individual's perception of time at any moment would represent the interaction between these two systems.

Not only is there an increase in perceptual processing, but in these data the increase seems most related to the dimension of depth. In considering this, it should be noted that our major senses and areas of sensitivity, including our major sense, vision, are located in that part of our bodies called "the front" and are best designed to provide information about an area parallel to the earth's surface. Because of the mobility of our necks, we have a situation that enables depth to be seen wherever we look, but our muscles soon pull us back to look in front of us again to the usual geometrical dimension of depth, which is generally defined along the line of the front-back dimensions of our bodies. If this is so, then the instruction for enhanced depth is really an instruction to augment perceptual processing. The intensification of stimuli and the sense of space and order reported by these subjects represent the consequences of admitting into consciousness stimuli that, in the normal course of events, are generally excluded. That this may be so is shown by the fact that the simple instruction to see things clearly and distinctly produces some of the same phenomena as *expanded depth*. In further support of this analysis, it should be noted that sernyl, which reduces sensory input, also seems to produce psychotic states (Lawes, 1963).

The augmentation of perceptual processing is not the only variable that enters into psychedelic experience, however, for the subjects here constantly testify that they have succeeded or failed to have such experiences to the extent that they have succeeded or failed in getting out of their bodies or in getting out of themselves. This suggests again the existence of two kinds of stimulus input: one relating to events in the world around us and the other to events occurring within ourselves. Given our preferences, and leaving aside the obvious exception of sexual feeling, we seem to prefer to invest ourselves in the kinds of stimuli that reflect changes in the world around us. The experience of the void, the highest expression of Eastern mysticism, involves a total absorption into the environmental stimulus system such that all sense of self, including the verbal labels with which the environment is ordered, disappears. In these data, it is suggested that psychedelic states seem to occur when the environmental perceptual system is augmented so that it dominates and includes the self- (or body-) perception systems. When the two systems are of equal valence, the organism may be experiencing conflict. When the self-perception system dominates the environmental perception system, the individual is exhibiting withdrawal, depression, or other signs of psychic or physical distress.[4]

The data gathered here suggest that psychedelic experiences come into being under conditions in which there is an enhancement of sensory input, an increase in the rate of perceptually processing that input, and a selective enhancement of perceptual processing of environmental or extraorganismic stimulation as opposed to intraorganismic stimulation. Psychedelic experiences should be obtainable under high-intensity stimulation of distance senses, such as vision, hearing, and smell, with comparatively low-intensity stimulation of the body senses, such as one might find in a typical rock band concert. It should not be assumed that these data exhaust the range of phenomena associated with the word "psychedelic." In a complicated area, this can stand at best as a first approximation.

[4] This last statement would seem to contradict what goes on in meditation, and the fascinating work of Charlotte Selver (1966) with sensory awareness. In meditation, however, one objectifies the inner world not by identifying with what one experiences, but merely by experiencing it as an experience. As soon as one identifies anything as an object of perception or conceptualization, it is excluded from the "I" system. We say "My elbow itches," not "I itch in the elbow." Selver's work seeks to bring self-awareness into relation with environmental awareness so that they function as a unified system.

IMPLICATIONS OF EXPERIMENTALLY INDUCED CONTEMPLATIVE MEDITATION

ARTHUR J. DEIKMAN, M.D.[1]

Introduction

Unusual perceptions have always been the subject of intense interest, desire, and speculation. In early history it was customary to interpret and seek such occurrences within a religious context. Even the gross disorders of epilepsy and psychosis were thought to be cases of supernatural possession, blessed or otherwise. Strange experiences were valued, and the use of fasting, drugs, ceremony, and dancing to induce a strange experience was common in cultures ranging from the Amazon Indians to ascetic European monks. Only with the rise of Western science did man become dissatisfied with theological inquiry and seek to understand strange experiences as a type of natural phenomena, to be explained by the same powerful mechanical and mathematical models that were conquering the planets and the chemical elements. Psychological science began studying conscious experience, and the advent of psychoanalysis ushered in the exploration of unconscious functioning. The problem of unusual perceptions, however, is still a puzzle, a challenge, and a matter of philosophical dispute.

The classical mystic experience is the prime example of an unusual perception still subject to conflicting interpretations. Both Eastern and Western mystic literature describe an

Reprinted from *The Journal of Nervous and Mental Disease*, Vol. 142, No. 2, February 1966. By permission of the author and the publisher.

[1] This investigation was supported by a Research Grant, MH07683, from the National Institute of Mental Health, USPHS; and by the Austen Riggs Center. The author is grateful to Dr. George S. Klein and Dr. Richard O. Rouse for their suggestions and criticism during the preparation of this manuscript.

xperience that goes beyond ordinary sensory impressions and
et is a perception, a perception of something so profound,
plifting, and intense as to lie beyond communication by
nguage and to constitute the highest human experience. It
ould appear that contemplative meditation is one instru-
ent for achieving such a state, although not necessarily suffi-
ent in itself.

This paper reports some results of a phenomenological in-
estigation of meditation phenomena and attempts to explain
e data and relate them to a broader context.

rocedure

In order to investigate the mystic experience, an experi-
ental procedure was devised based on classical descriptions
f contemplative meditation. This procedure can be described
s one of perceptual concentration. An initial short-term ex-
erimental study showed that very striking changes in the
erception of the self and of objects were possible through
e use of this procedure, and there were also indications that
alogues to the classical mystic experience could be achieved
well. The rationale, procedure, results, and conclusions of
is experiment have been reported elsewhere.

The same procedure, somewhat simplified, was then em-
oyed to study the effects of perceptual concentration over a
nger period of time. Although many of the phenomena that
sulted seemed readily explainable on the basis of after-
ages, autokinetic movement, phosphenes, and the like, cer-
in data did not seem adequately accounted for by reference
familiar perceptual phenomena or by the use of such
eoretical explanatory concepts as are currently available,
g., suggestion or projection. Additional hypotheses seem
ecessary, and it is the purpose of this paper to present these
ta and the postulates derived from them.

The original experiment involved a total of twelve "concen-
ation" sessions. It was hoped that four to six subjects could
en be studied over a total of seventy or more sessions. One
the subjects of the original experiment did continue for a
tal of seventy-eight sessions, at which point she changed
bs, moving to a distant area. Six subjects who began the

experiment did not proceed beyond ten sessions for a variety
of reasons ranging from job conflict (the procedure calls for
three experimental sessions per week, during the day) to an
inability to adopt the way of psychological functioning required. Four subjects continued for thirty to forty sessions.
One additional subject completed 106 sessions and is currently involved in a different experiment.

The data with which this paper is concerned came primarily from the two subjects, A and G, who completed the longest series of sessions. These subjects had the most intense and
unusual experiences of the group, approximately in direct relationship to the number of sessions. In this connection, it
should be noted that vivid experiences seemed, on the one
hand, to indicate a tolerance and compatibility with the procedure and, on the other hand, to motivate the subject to
continue over a long period of time. Subjects C, D, and E
(thirty to forty sessions) appeared to have gone part way
along the same paths as A and G in that they experienced the
beginnings of breakdown in the self/object distinction, and
had some experience of light, strange imagery, and the like.
However, they appeared less able to relinquish control and
"accept whatever happens."

Subject A was a thirty-eight-year-old psychiatric nurse who
was undergoing psychoanalysis at the time of the experiment.[2]
Subject G was a forty-year-old housewife. Both subjects were
personally known to the experimenter and were asked to participate in the experiment on the basis of their apparent intelligence, interest, and available time. Subject G was paid,
subject A was not. It seemed clear that money was not a crucial factor in their participation. There was evidence of neu-

---

[2] When questioned (at the end of the experiment) as to any interaction between her psychoanalysis and the meditation, A replied
". . . my guess would be that, had I not been in analysis, I would
have not had the same kind of experience that I did in this. I think I
would have been less prone to or I would have been far more restricted . . . there were two very special experiences going on at the
same time and there was interaction between them but they both
remained separate in their own ways and were special in their own
ways." She replied in the negative when the experimenter asked if
any of the things she had found out about herself in the analysis had
explained any of the experiences she had had in the experiment.

otic conflicts (by history and MMPI), but both subjects were functioning relatively normally in their environments.

The experiment was conducted in a comfortable, carpeted office, the lighting, colors, and atmosphere of which were subdued. The subject sat in an armchair about ten feet from a medium blue vase that rested on a simple brown end table; the experimenter sat to one side and behind the subject, at a desk on which there were two tape recorders. It was necessary to move to a different experimental room twice during the course of the experiment, but the general atmosphere was maintained and the change did not seem to affect the phenomena reported by the subjects.

Contemplative meditation requires that the subject relinquish his customary mode of thinking and perceiving. Thoughts must be stopped, sounds and peripheral sensations put out of one's mind, and the contemplation of the meditative object be conducted in a non-analytic, non-intellectual manner. This aim determined the composition of the instructions that were read by the experimenter to the subject immediately preceding the first few sessions. Subject A, who had begun the first experiment, received the following directions: "The purpose of these sessions is to learn about concentration. Your aim is to concentrate on the blue vase. By concentration I do not mean analyzing the different parts of the vase, or thinking a series of thoughts about the vase, or associating ideas to the vase, but rather, trying to see the vase as it exists in itself, without any connections to other things. Exclude all other thoughts or feelings or sounds or body sensations. Do not let them distract you, but keep them out so that you can concentrate all your attention, all your awareness on the vase itself. Let the perception of the vase fill your entire mind."

Subject G received a differently worded set of instructions, as an attempt had been made to present the required concept more clearly for the second experiment and thus decrease the need for additional explanations: "This is an experiment in how we see and experience things. Ordinarily we look at the world around us with only part of our attention; the rest is taken up with thinking about what we are seeing or with unrelated thoughts. This experiment will explore the possibilities of seeing and experiencing when you cease thinking altogether and concentrate your attention on only one thing: the blue vase on the table in front of you.

"Look at the vase intently; focus all your interest on it; try to perceive the vase as directly as possible but without studying or analyzing it. Have your entire mind concentrated on the vase; at the same time, remain open to the experience—let whatever happens happen.

"All thinking must come to a stop so that your mind becomes quiet. Do not let yourself be distracted by thoughts, sounds, or body sensations—keep them out so that you can concentrate all your attention on the vase."

The intent of both sets of instructions was the same, and the different wording did not seem to be significant; the same types of questions were raised by both subjects, and the experimenter was required to amplify and explain the instructions in the early sessions in approximately the same way. The principal difficulty encountered by subjects was grasping the concept of *not thinking*: to cease actively examining or thinking about the vase. The main problem that required additional explanation was the confusion about whether to try to block out all sensations arising during the session. They were told that insofar as the sensations were part of the experience of concentration rather than distraction or interference, they should accept them.

Both sets of instructions concluded with the directions: "While you concentrate I am going to play music on the tape machine. Do not let the sounds occupy your attention or disturb your concentration. If you find you have drifted into a stream of thought, stop and bring your attention back to the vase. At the end of _____ minutes I will tell you that the session is over, but take as much time as you like to stop."

After a few initial sessions of ten and fifteen minutes of concentration, with cello music played as a background on the tape recorder, the concentration period was extended to thirty minutes and performed in silence. At the end of the designated time, the experimenter gave the signal "thirty minutes" and the subject could stop or continue longer if he desired. All subjects were able to complete thirty minutes, but they seldom continued much longer.

After the subjects had finished concentrating, the experimenter conducted an inquiry based on the following questions: 1) "How did it go?" 2) "Describe the course of the session." 3) "How much of the time were you able to concentrate so that you were aware only of the vase and nothing else?" 4) "What means did you use to maintain concentration?" 5) "What thoughts did you have during the session?" 6) "What feelings did you have?" 7) "What was your experience of the vase?" 8) (Optional; introduced as sessions progressed) "What is your intent as you look at the vase?" 9) Subject is asked to go to the window.) "Look out the window and describe what you see and the way it looks." As the experiment progressed, the subjects tended to cover the main question areas spontaneously, so the experimenter asked questions mainly to clarify statements of the subject. The interview was flexible, designed to elicit whatever phenomena the subject had experienced and to follow up anything of interest to the experimenter. During the inquiry, the experimenter endeavored to be as neutral as possible, but from time to time it was necessary to reinstruct subjects in the procedure and to deal with a subject's anxiety when startling phenomena occurred. The latter was done by stressing that the experience was under the subject's control, and that the phenomenon was very interesting and, apart from its newness, need not be frightening. The inquiry lasted about twenty minutes and was tape recorded in its entirety.

Results and Discussion

In trying to understand the data that resulted from the experiment, a basic question was asked: What was the subject perceiving? The bulk of the percepts resulting from the experiment seemed readily explained in terms of such familiar concepts as afterimages, phosphenes, stabilized retinal images, projection, and distortion. The data selected for discussion below consist of perceptual phenomena whose explanation may require the construction of additional hypotheses. For the purpose of clarity, the data will be presented in three groups, each followed by discussion. It should be noted that these phenomena did not occur in every session, but once the subject experienced a percept it tended to recur in later sessions, usually with greater intensity.

LIGHT

G; *28th session:* ". . . the vase changes in concept for me; then shortly after that, suddenly, I begin to feel this light going back and forth. It's circular. I can't follow it all the way to my forehead but I can certainly follow it about as far as my hand . . . and I can feel it go the rest of the way."

G; *67th session:* ". . . somewhere between the matter that is the wall and myself, somewhere in between the matter is this moving, this vibrating light and motion and power and very real substance . . . it's so real and so vital that I feel as though I could reach out and take a chunk of it and hand it to you."

C; *41st session:* "It seems as if you were turning a light down, that you were turning the intensity of the light down and yet I still had this kind of shimmering sensation of very bright light simultaneously with the idea that everything is getting dark."

G; *87th session:* "This circle of light, this area that goes in and then out to encompass me . . . it's not like sunlight . . . it isn't even like moonlight, it's kind of cold light in a way . . . it's jagged in a way around the outside . . . it's a kind of compaction or compression and suddenly out of this compression comes a light. It's not like a searchlight, it isn't like a beacon, it's very irregular in its outline."

G; *104th session:* "You can't discern a shimmering in the room, can you, a color or bright shimmering in this whole area?"

(*Experimenter*): "No."

G: "Well, it's very real to me; it's so real that I feel you ought to be able to see it."

FORCE

A; *54th session:* "It was also as though we were together, you know, instead of being a table and a vase, and me, my body, and the chair, it all dissolved into a bundle of something which had . . . a great deal of energy to it but which doesn't form into anything; it only feels like a force."

G; 55th session: ". . . like a magnetic attraction as though
I had iron in me and there was a magnet pulling but you
would have to imagine that I had iron in every one of my
cells. . . ."

A; 53rd session: ". . . at the point when I felt as though
everything was coming from there directed against me . . .
some kind of force, I can't say what it was, as though a force
were enveloping me."

G; 93rd session: ". . . I felt this strong, strong pull in my
thoughts. I could feel it as I have never felt anything before
. . one instant there was this tranquil sort of thing and the
next minute there was this vital, pulling, pushing force . . .
it felt as though somebody had hooked up or made a connection with a vital thing that was real, that was pulling my
thoughts. Not only pulling them but compressing thoughts,
too."

MOTION

A; 17th session: ". . . the table and the vase were rocking.
Now I was conscious that they were not in any sense moving,
but the sensation of rocking, their rocking or rocking inside of
me back and forth, was quite prominent for quite some time."

C; 21st session: "I had the distinct impression . . . that
what I could see of the vase was drifting . . . it was in motion
just very slightly . . . it just seemed to be wavering somehow
. . the whole thing seemed to be moving."

(Experimenter): "You saw it move or you had the impression it was moving?"

C: "I had the impression that it was moving."

G; 5th session: "It's almost as though within that cone,
movement is taking place back and forth. I'm still not sure,
though, whether it's the motion in the rings or if it's the
rings. But in a certain way it is real . . . it's not real in the
sense that you can see it, touch it, taste it, smell it, or anything, but it certainly is real in the sense that you can experience it happening."

G; 8th session: "It's the feeling of something pulling your
whole being together to a point, and you can feel it in an
actual sensation of motion."

These perceptual experiences were characterized by: 1) an

unusual way of perceiving (e.g., light is *felt*; motion of the vase is felt but not seen; force envelops), although the usual perceptual routes are also employed; 2) the percepts are primitive and basic (i.e., force, light, and motion); and 3) the percepts are intensely *real*.

To answer the question, What was perceived? we must consider both the possibility that the relevant stimuli were of internal origin and the possibility that the stimuli orignated externally to the subject. In the discussion that follows, the assumption of internal stimuli and the possible explanations of suggestion, projection, dreaming, and hypnagogic state will be taken up first, followed by a consideration of the hypotheses of sensory translation and reality transfer. Then, assuming external stimuli, the hypothesis of perceptual expansion will be presented.

Internal Stimuli

SUGGESTION

"Suggestion" refers to a subject's reporting a perception corresponding to some previous overt statement by the experimenter pertaining to what the subject would perceive. This concept is often extended to include cues, given unconsciously by the experimenter, that indicate to the subject what phenomena are expected. The subject may make suggestions to himself, producing autosuggestion. In the perceptual concentration experiment, the experimenter's verbalizations were recorded, transcribed, and compiled under the category "Experimenter's Role." These records indicate that no direct verbal suggestion pertaining to expected phenomena was made by the experimenter, with the exception of such statements as "most people have found this (concentration) to be interesting and rewarding." In no case was a statement made indicating the actual phenomena reported by other subjects or reported in the classical meditation literature. None of the subjects had read about meditation phenomena, and all were instructed not to discuss the phenomena with anyone else. (One subject began reading mystic literature toward the end of the experiment and was excited to note the similarity between her experiences and those described by various auors.) None of the subjects were close friends, and the identities of the experimental subjects were unknown to each her. In one instance during the first experiment, when an change of information did take place between subject A d another subject, the phenomena reported were quite fferent and, indeed, subject A felt very disappointed that, th prior to the conversation and afterward, she was not le to have the experiences reported to her by the other bject. In addition, this subject and most of the others demstrated on many occasions their resistance to statements ade by the experimenter that did not seem accurate to them hen he attempted to paraphrase their own reports.

There were some indications of the experimenter supplyg covert cues. From time to time, subjects remarked that ey felt he expected them to report *new* phenomena as the periment progressed. In one case, subject A felt aware, corctly, of the experimenter's interest in a particular phenomon (disappearance of the vase) and remarked that she erefore thought that he wanted such phenomena to occur. e stated in this connection that this was the only cue she d detected in the course of the experiment. There was also me opportunity for extraexperimental covert influence, nce all the long-term subjects were personally known to the perimenter, and G, C, and D were social acquaintances d friends of his. The possibility for covert suggestion cant be eliminated and, to some extent, was always present. If e experimenter gave covert cues to the subjects as to what enomena delighted and fascinated him, this would unbtedly result, at the least, in a biased selection by the bject of the phenomena reported. In a broad sense, this ay well have taken place, since the interview did not consist systematic questioning of all areas of perceptual phenoma but was largely a following up of the subject's report plus estions directed at main subject categories. As sessions proessed, fewer such questions were asked of the subjects as ey reported striking phenomena that spontaneously covered e areas of questioning themselves. There was no evidence of ccessful autosuggestion. On different occasions, subjects ould try to repeat an experience they had had, and usually und this very difficult, if not impossible. Indeed, such attempts were found to be an interference in the concentration process.

Perhaps the most important argument against suggestion being an important determinant is the fact that, on the one hand, the very striking phenomena reported were quite unexpected and surprising to the experimenter, who had not believed that classical phenomena such as "merging" or unity experiences could occur without years of practice but, rather had expected the phenomena to be mostly that of image breakdown. Further evidence against suggestion or autosuggestion is the fact that phenomena such as animation of the vase and currents of force are not part of classical meditation reports. (It should also be mentioned that there are almost no published accounts of the day-by-day phenomena of long-term "meditation" practice, and none that I know of dealing with long-term concentration upon an object such as a vase.) Also very significant in this connection was the subjects' experience of anxiety and disbelief at the *initial* appearance of a phenomenon. The subjects often stopped the process quickly the first time it occurred. Only as they became more familiar with it were they able to let the phenomena develop further It would seem reasonable that suggested phenomena would not elicit such a response of anxiety unless the experimenter had also suggested an anxious response—but there is no evidence that he did so. For all these reasons, suggestion does not seem to be an adequate explanation of the subjects' experiences.

PROJECTION

In terms of psychoanalytic theory, such perceptions as have been quoted could be regarded as "projections" of internal stimuli. The usual explanation of mystic experiences and of unusual experiences in general, is to regard them as a "projection" and reinterpretation of repressed infantile memories, or in the case of psychotic hallucinations, as a synthetic product re-establishing object relations. In his paper on Schreber, Freud defined projection: "The most striking characteristic of symptom formation is the process which deserves the name of *projection*. An internal perception is suppressed and, instead, its content, after undergoing a certain kind o distortion, enters consciousness in the form of an external perception." In *Beyond the Pleasure Principle* Freud discussed the genesis of this mechanism: ". . . a particular way is adopted of dealing with any internal excitations that produce too great an increase of unpleasure: There is a tendency to treat them as though they were acting not from the inside, but from the outside, so that it may be possible to bring the shield against stimuli into operation as a means of defense against them. This is the origin of projection, which is destined to play such a large part in the causation of pathological processes." The basic phenomenon to which Freud applied the concept of projection consisted of paranoid hallucinations and delusions. In this view, the function of projection is to defend the person against awareness of his own internal psychological contents, and, consequently, it is these contents that are "projected" and perceived as external to the subject. Although later workers have attempted to broaden the concept of projection, nothing further seems to have been hypothesized about how projection takes place, and the broadened definitions gain wider scope at the expense of explanatory potency.

For the purpose of this discussion, "projection" shall refer to Freud's definition emphasizing its function of defense against the awareness of anxiety-provoking internal content. If we apply this concept to the subjects' experiences already quoted, we see that the content of their perception did not consist of affect, motives, or ego-alien ideation but, rather, was composed of sensations referable to such qualities as force, light, and motion. Such sensory qualities do not lend themselves readily to explanations centered on defense against drives (or even the effect of style on stimulus interpretation). Although a "need" may be ascribed to the subjects (e.g., to have unusual experiences), it is not at all clear what the mechanism would be that would give them the experiences they had. Neither do the experiences seem to be reconstructions of lost objects. The classical concept of "projection" does not seem to explain these data.

DREAMING

Were the subjects asleep, and were their experiences actually dreams? When occasionally questioned specifically by the experimenter, A and B felt sure they had not been asleep when the reported phenomena occurred. They referred to the continuity of the vase and the table percept throughout most of the experiences in question. The vivid phenomena seemed to be superimposed on that continuity. On some occasions, the subjects specifically mentioned that they had fallen asleep for a brief time, as they had become "suddenly" aware that their heads had fallen forward and that there had been a break in the continuity of the concentration. Nevertheless, the subjects could have had brief periods of sleep of which they were not aware. The perceptual continuity they experienced would argue against a dream state, as does the fact that their experiences did not have the complex structures normally associated with dreaming.

HYPNAGOGIC STATE

However, there are important similarities to be noted between the subjects' experiences and the hypnagogic state described by Silberer. Silberer defined hypnagogic phenomena as being a regression to autosymbolic thinking, an "easier" way of thinking, occurring when an effort to think took place in a state of drowsiness. Although the subjects stated that they were not asleep during the occurrence of vivid phenomena, they did report episodes of drowsiness in many of the experimental sessions. Thus, one of Silberer's defining conditions for hypnagogic phenomena was present. The other necessary condition, the effort to think, was not present in the specific sense indicated by Silberer's examples, as these subjects were performing a type of perceptual concentration or perceptual thinking, with *abstract* thinking specifically blocked. However, if we accept Silberer's generalization of the second condition (the effort to think) as "an interference with falling asleep," then both conditions would appear satisfied, since the effort to concentrate on the vase would constitute such an interference.

Important differences are present, however. Although it

as clear that the meditative state was one differing from
ormal, awake consciousness,[3] the subject described drowsy
hases as brief episodes interfering with the special state of
ccessful concentration. "Successful" meant being attentively
bsorbed in a perceptual experience with the exception that
e experience usually included as one of its dimensions a re-
ective awareness of the experimental situation, except when
e process reached a high level of intensity. At such times
e subject felt even this connection, or anchor, to be loosen-
g, and experienced anxiety leading to his terminating the
xperience. According to the subjects, it was during the suc-
essful, attentive phase that the vivid phenomena occurred.
lso, the content of the vivid phenomena was much more
morphous than the clear, dreamlike symbols described by
ilberer and seemed to build up gradually rather than make
sudden appearance.

ENSORY TRANSLATION HYPOTHESIS

To account more adequately for the experimental data
ited, I would like to postulate the process of *sensory transla-
ion*. Sensory translation is defined as the perception of psy-
hic action (conflict repression, problem solving, attentive-
ess, etc.) through the relatively unstructured sensations of
ght, color, movement, force, sound, smell, or taste.[4] This
ypothesis is related to Silberer's concept but differs in its
eferents and genesis. In the hypnagogic state and in dream-
g, a *symbolic* translation of psychic activity and ideas oc-
urs, but, although light, force, and movement may play a
art in hypnagogic and dream constructions, the predominant
ercepts are complex visual, verbal, conceptual, and activity

[3] The subject would define this different state of consciousness in
erms of difficulty in verbalizing what had happened, an inability to
aintain a complete and certain memory of it, and the "feeling" of
ifferent "dimensions" to the experience. The definition of the state
EEG terms remains to be done, although relevant data have been
btained by other investigators.

[4] There is an indication in the *New Introductory Lectures* that
reud had an idea tending in the same direction: "It is easy to imag-
e, too, that certain mystical practices may succeed in upsetting the
ormal relations between the different regions of the mind, so that,
or instance, perception may be able to grasp happenings in the
epths of the ego and the id that were otherwise inaccessible to it."

images. "Sensory translation" refers to the experience of nor
verbal, simple, concrete perceptual equivalents of psychic ac
tion. It comes into operation as a consequence of the altere
cognitive mode brought about by the experimental instruc
tions, which focus on perceiving instead of thinking. The a
tered cognitive mode does not appear to be one of sleep o
drowsiness.

This postulate lends itself well not only to the data quote
above, but to the analysis of other, more detailed, reports tha
suggest a possible retranslation back to the stimuli them
selves:

A; 63rd session: ". . . when the vase changes shape . . .
feel this in my body and particularly in my eyes . . . there i
an actual kind of physical sensation as though something i
moving there which re-creates the shape of the vase." Here
this subject may be experiencing the perception of a resyr
thesis taking place following the de-automatization of th
normal percept; that is, the percept of the vase is being recon
structed outside of the normal awareness, and the process o
reconstruction is perceived as a physical sensation.

G; 60th session: ". . . shortly I began to sense motion an
shifting of light and dark as this became stronger and stronger
Now when this happens it's happening not only in my visio
but it's happening or it feels like a physical kind of thing. It'
connected with feelings of attraction, expansion, absorptior
and suddenly my vision pinpointed on a particular place, an
this became the center for a very powerful . . . I was in th
grip of a very powerful sensation, and this became the center.
The perception of motion and shifting light and darknes
may be the perception of the movement of attention amon
various psychic contents. "Attraction," "expansion," "absor
tion," would thus reflect the dynamics of the efforts to focu
attention—successful focusing is then experienced as bein
"in the grip of" a powerful force.

G; 78th session: ". . . that feeling of pulling on the top o
my head, and then this awareness all of a sudden that
wasn't occupying my body, at least not completely, as I usu
ally do." Here the pulling may be the splitting of the norma
synthesis of body self and mental self, leading to a feeling o
being "suspended," or levitation.

G; *93rd session*: ". . . I felt this strong, strong pull in my thoughts. I could feel it as I have never felt anything before—just really making contact, and it was a glorious kind of feeling because it was such a powerful way of thinking, using the mind. It's almost as though something has opened up a whole patch of doors in my mind that haven't been opened before and that all this power had come rushing to and fro, that it was a connecting link between something out of the natural laws of the universe and me, my thoughts. . . ." Perhaps this experience was a relatively direct perception of the release of psychic energy, presumably through a lifting of defensive barriers occurring as a consequence of the experimental program.

REALNESS AND THE REALITY FUNCTION

Not only were these percepts unusual, they were often vividly *real*, seemingly palpable. Both A and B stated on some occasions that they were sure the experimenter must be able to see what they saw, even photograph it. It is necessary to account for the realness of these perceptions. There are ample clinical data demonstrating the great variability in the *realness* of our sensory percepts: 1) In states of depersonalization or derealization, perception is intact but the percepts "feel" unreal or lack the "feeling" of reality. 2) Persons who have had mystic experiences or who have taken LSD report states of consciousness that they feel are "more real" than normal. 3) In the case of some dreams, their "realism" may persist into the waking state. *Thus, realness and sensation are not a unity, but the concurrent operation of two separate functions.* Realness (the quality of reality) and reality testing (the judgment of what is external versus what is imaginary) likewise appear to be two different functions, although they usually operate in synchrony.

Freud discussed reality testing as a learned judgment: "A perception which is made to disappear by an action is recognized as external, as reality; where such an action makes no difference, the perception orginates within the subject's own body—it is not real." "The antithesis between subjective and objective does not exist from the first. It only comes into being from the fact that thinking possesses the capacity to bring before the mind once more something that has once been perceived, by reproducing it as a presentation without the external object having still to be there." Freud explained hallucinations as a consequence of a topographic regression, a reversal of the normal path of excitation so that the perceptual systems are stimulated from within. Federn attempted to deal with the problem of loss of the *feeling of reality* (as opposed to reality testing) seen in estrangement and depersonalization, by postulating that the sense of something being real required an adequate investment of energy (libido) in the ego boundary. Although his concepts are murky, they point toward the notion of a *quantity* of "realness."

REALITY-TRANSFER HYPOTHESIS

The experimental data and clinical examples cited above warrant the hypothesis that there is a specific ego function that bestows the quality of reality on the contents of experience. I would like to hypothesize that this function can be influenced and that the quality of reality can be displaced, intensified, or attenuated—a process of *reality transfer*. In the meditation experiment, the sensory percepts are invested with this quality, resulting in the vivid, intensely real experiences reported. Why does this take place? An initial speculation is that, since in the meditation experience the object world as a perceptual experience is broken down or dedifferentiated, the cognitive organization based on that world is disrupted in a parallel fashion. An ego function capable of appropriately bestowing reality quality must be linked developmentally with the organization of logical, object-based thought. It seems plausible that an alteration in that organization would affect the reality function. In the meditation experiment, the subject is instructed to banish analytical, logical thought and to allow perception to dominate the field. In a formal sense, these instructions constitute a regression to the primitive cognitive state postulated for the infant and young child, a state in which the distinction between thoughts, actions, and objects is blurred as compared to the adult. Such a regression is likely to be enhanced by the passive-dependent relationship with the experimenter. The body immobility, reduction in sensory input, and the rela-

vely stabilized retinal image, are additional factors capable
f producing perceptual and cognitive disorganization. If we
dd all these forces together, we see that the experimental
meditation procedure is potentially a very powerful technique
or undoing the normal cognitive and perceptual modes. Such
n undoing might be expected to result in a mobility of
reality quality," permitting its displacement to internal stim-
li, a displacement congruent with the regressive push of
he specific experimental situation.

E-AUTOMATIZATION

At this point it would be appropriate to discuss the concept
f "de-automatization," as it is relevant to the understanding
f meditation as well as other altered states of consciousness.
Hartmann explicates the concept of automatization as fol-
ows: "In well-established achievements, they (motor apparatuses) function automatically: the integration of the somatic systems involved in the action is automatized, and so
s the integration of the individual mental acts involved in it.
With increasing exercise of the action, its intermediate steps
isappear from consciousness . . . not only motor behavior,
ut perception and thinking, too, show automatization." "It
s obvious that automatization may have economic advantages
n saving attention cathexis in particular and simple cathexis
f consciousness in general. . . . Here, as in most adaptation
processes, we have a purpose of provision for the average ex-
pectable range of tasks." Thus, automatization performs the
unction of eliminating details and intermediate steps of
awareness so that attention is freed for other purposes.
Gill and Brenman developed further the concept of de-
automatization: "De-automatization is an undoing of the
automatizations of apparatuses—both means and goal struc-
ures—directed toward the environment. De-automatization
s, as it were, a shakeup which can be followed by an advance
r a retreat in the level of organization. . . . Some manipula-
ion of the attention directed toward the functioning of an
apparatus is necessary if it is to be de-automatized." Thus,
de-automatization is the undoing of automatization, presum-
bly by *reinvesting actions and percepts with attention*.

The experimental procedure produces a de-automatization

of normal perceptual modes, permitting the operation of sensory translation. At the same time, a de-automatization of the reality function occurs such that the sense of reality normally bestowed on objects is now "transferred" to abstract psychical entities. As stated earlier, the experimental pressure away from abstract thought and toward pure perception fits this explanation.

External Stimuli

PERCEPTUAL EXPANSION HYPOTHESIS

A further possibility remains. Some of the visual phenomena of the meditation experience (reported in the first experiment and present throughout the long-term project) such as loss of the third dimension of the vase, diffusion of its formal properties, and a tendency toward a homogenous color field, appear to be a result of a de-automatization leading to a breakdown of the percepts in the direction of a primitive visual experience. However, the more striking perceptions, of force, movement, and light—as well as other entities to be described below—may possibly be the product of a de-automatization that permits the awareness of new dimensions of the total stimulus array. These experiences are not necessarily in the direction of a less-organized dedifferentiation as such, but of a real sensation that apparently is at variance with everyday perception. Such a concept of de-automatization as a liberating process leads to a third explanatory hypothesis for the meditation phenomena: *perceptual expansion*—the widening of perceptual intake to encompass "new" external stimuli, with a new perceptual route strongly implied. Perceptual expansion is made possible by de-automatization of the selective gating and filtering processes that normally are in constant operation.

There is a developmental concept implicit in such a hypothesis; namely, that our earliest experience is probably one of being in more direct contact with numerous, vivid, primitively organized stimuli. As we mature, a learning process takes place in which stimuli and percepts are organized toward a high level of differentiation based on formal characteristics. This learning process not only takes place at the ex ense of the vividness and variability of sensory stimuli, but possibly involves a loss of special perceptual functions other than those to which we are accustomed. There is evidence to support this concept.

Werner, in a statement based on studies of eidetic imagery in children as well as on broader studies of perceptual development, states that the image ". . . gradually changes in functional character. It becomes essentially subject to the exigencies of abstract thought. Once the image changes in function and becomes an instrument in reflective thought, its structure also changes. It is only through such structural change that the image can serve as an instrument of abstract mental activity. This is why, of necessity, the sensuousness and fullness of detail, color, and vividness of the image must fade." The experimental work of Kohler illustrates this concept. In reviewing his experiments on the effects of wearing distorting lenses for days at a time, Kohler concludes, "We are confronted here with a peculiar relationship between optical and physical facts. We always find that it is the physical dimensions of things which have a tendency to become visually correct. This is due to the fact that physical dimensions are among the most frequent and symmetrically distributed stimuli. Consequently, it is with these stimulus qualities that unique perceptual experiences of straightness, right angularity, and good form tend to become associated. It is always the physically unique stimuli which gradually become the reference standards for our percepts. This is the reason why in the process of adaptation it is always the world with which we are familiar which wins out in the end. It does so in the interest of simplicity and economy." From another field of inquiry, Shapiro has summarized evidence for the primacy of color responses in children, with particular emphasis on Rorschach data. He writes ". . . although the Rorschach data did not indicate that color responsiveness *per se* diminishes with development, they do indicate unmistakably that the relative significance of the color as an essential and overriding aspect of the percept diminishes." Shapiro concluded, ". . . color perception as such is a more immediate and passive experience than form perception, requiring less in the way of perceptual tools for organizing capacity. It is associated with a passive perceptual mode, and it becomes more dominant more compelling in quality, and perhaps antagonistic to form articulation in conditions in which active perceptual organ izing capacity is impaired or only rudimentary." Further sup port for the concept of selective automatization is found in the report by Von Senden of the visual experiences of con genitally blind persons who began using the visual function for the first time following surgery for removal of lens cata racts. His accounts support the idea that, as perceptual learn ing takes place, the vivid qualities of stimuli decrease in pro portion as formal organization is imposed upon them through perceptual learning. The gain in economy and utility through automatization is paid for by a foreclosure of possibilities, a dulling or "jading" of sensory experience that is an all-too common occurrence. The extent of this loss of vividness and detail resulting from automatization can be appreciated when one undergoes an experience of de-automatization through such techniques as meditation, use of LSD-25, sensory isola tion, or spontaneous mystic experience: colors may appear to have gained (temporarily) a new richness and vividness so that the natural world is seen in a "fresh" state. Again, this makes good sense developmentally, for intensity and sensory richness are usually not important stimulus properties for the accurate manipulation of objects.

If, as evidence indicates, our passage from infancy to adult hood is accompanied by an organization of the perceptual and cognitive world that has as its price the selection of some stimuli to the exclusion of others, it is quite possible that a technique could be found to reverse or undo, temporarily, the automatization that has restricted our communication with reality to the active perception of only a small segment of it. Such a process of de-automatization might then be followed by an awareness of aspects of reality that were formerly un available to us.

To return to the data from the meditation experiment, it may be that the simpler perceptions of color, light, energy, force, and movement represent a shift of the *normal* per ceptual processes to aspects of the stimulus array previously screened out—or it may be that these percepts are registered through the operation of *new* perceptual processes. In the

ourse of the experiment, certain reports of A and G were
ery suggestive of this latter possibility. They seemed to be
truggling to convey their perception of unfamiliar reality dimensions, difficult to verbalize exactly, requiring metaphors,
nd seemingly encountered in another realm so that they
poke of "coming back," "elsewhere," "the other place." The
ollowing data are very striking in their implication of a type
f new perception:

G; 14th session: (While looking out the window after the
neditation period) "I am looking differently than I have ever
ooked before. I mean it's almost as though I have a differ-
nt way of seeing. It's like something to do with dimensions.
t's as though I am feeling what I am looking at. It's as
hough I have an extension of myself reaching out and seeing
omething by feeling it. It's as though somebody added some-
hing, another factor to my seeing."

G; 62nd session: ". . . things seem to sharpen and there
s a different nature to the substance of things. It's as though
'm seeing between the molecules . . . the usual mass of
olidity loses its density or mass and becomes separate."

A; 58th session: "The only way I can think of to describe it
s being suspended between something and something, be-
ause the world all but disappears, you know, the usual world,
while some sounds intrude very little, so that I'm in a world
f converging with that, whatever it is, and that's all there is."

G; 64th session: ". . . I've experienced . . . new experi-
nces and I have no vehicle to communicate them to you. I
xpect that this is probably the way a baby feels when he is
ull of something to say about an experience or an awareness
nd he has not learned to use the words yet."

A; 60th session: ". . . it's so completely and totally out-
ide of anything else I've experienced."

G; 66th session: "It was like a parallel world or parallel
ime. . . ."

A; 26th session: ". . . it's the only way I can describe it
. . walking through the looking glass . . . in walking through
he looking glass I would become ethereal and, you know,
ilmy and somehow don't have the same kind of substance
o me that I do otherwise and then when it begins to come

back . . . it was like having walked back out of the cloud somehow and becoming solid as I did so."

G; 74th session: ". . . solid material such as myself and th vase and the table . . . seems to be attributed then with th extra property of flexibility such as in its natural, fluid state It's almost as though we are, myself and the vase and the door a form which has lost its fluidity the way water loses its prop erty of fluidity when it is frozen . . . we're without the abilit to exercise one of the properties that we have when we thinl of ourselves in the conditioned state of solid matter, but i you can remove that impediment . . . of a way of thinkin (and this is what this condition seems to do), this new ele ment gives the ability to recognize this validity that otherwis I'm not aware of."

The postulated new perceptual route is possibly that re ferred to by the subjects when they use the term "feeling." B this they do not mean feeling in the usual sense of touch, no the sense of feeling an emotion, but rather perception tha cannot be located in the usual perceptual routes of sight hearing, and the like. In summary, it may be that the unusua experiences here cited are perceptions of unusual stimulu dimensions, modified in some way by the subject, but neve theless constituting a new perceptual experience made possi ble by the de-automatization of the ordinary perceptual route that normally dominate consciousness.

Some support for this hypothesis is present in the evidenc that there exists in us psychological capacities different fron those we usually employ or with which we are familiar. Vo Neumann has observed: "Just as languages like Greek or San scrit are historical facts and not absolute logical necessities, i is only reasonable to assume that logics and mathematics ar similarly historical, accidental forms of expression. They ma have essential variance, i.e., they may exist in other form than the ones to which we are accustomed. Indeed, the natur of the central nervous system and of the message system that it transmits indicates positively that this is so. W have now accumulated sufficient evidence to see that what ever language the central nervous system is using is character ized by less logical and arithmetical depth than what we ar used to." In his discussion of the brain as computer, he advanced the idea that the human brain programs itself to think logically, with the implication that other superordinate thought functions are inherent in our brain. The creative, preconscious solution of problems is a common experience of another mode of functioning. Specifically in the perceptual sphere, it is relevant to cite observations on synesthesia, especially the association of colors with sounds. This function is found more commonly in children, and tends to disappear as the child grows older. From the point of view of adaptation, it seems plausible that synesthesia is biologically superfluous and therefore would lose out to other perceptual and cognitive processes that provide a more direct biological reward. Evidence for parasensory modes in telepathy experiments is difficult to evaluate, perhaps because such possibilities are discordant with our present scientific cosmology. If there is any validity to the work that has been done in such investigations, it would seem reasonable to conclude that telepathic phenomena represent the operation of perceptual channels ordinarily not utilized or available. The subjective data of the classical mystic experience, of drug states, and of acute psychosis can also be cited in support of the hypothesis of perceptual expansion. In these diverse accounts from varied cultures and epochs, we read the claim that new dimensions are perceived, physical, spiritual, or unclassifiable. These widely disparate authors report certain basic, *similar* perceptions: the unity of existence, timeless properties of the self, and multiple worlds of existence beyond the familiar. The similarity of their perceptions may simply reflect their similar basic psychological structure. Because they are perceiving their own internal psychological structure and modes of activity, their experiences are basically similar despite cultural differences. Logically, however, we must grant the possibility that these unusual experiences contain the percepts of actual characteristics of reality, normally not perceived.

Inside or Outside?

In trying to decide between the two major possibilities for interpreting unusual experiences—the perception of something that is actually internal versus the perception of something that is actually external—and allowing for the presence of both possibilities in one situation, we come quickly to the basic epistemological problem that we have no way of knowing, with certainty whether or not a percept refers to an external source. Why not test the "knowledge" claimed by the subject of an unusual experience and see if it results in greater success in dealing with the world? But which world? Even in the most precise area of physics, we find contradictory worlds—the world of quantum mechanics and the world of special relativity: ". . . any theory which tries to fulfill the requirements of both special relativity and quantum theory will lead to mathematical inconsistencies, to divergencies in the region of very high energies and momenta." If such incongruencies exist there, we can expect even greater difficulty in matching a set of data of the order of mystic revelation with the incredibly complex field of psychological and biological dimensions where a "test" would take place. Unless such a test of new knowledge were in the same dimensional plane as the knowledge itself, the results would not be relevant.

The evidence of scientific experience, thus far, is solidly behind the psychological theories that assume an internal origin of the "knowledge" or stimuli of unusual experiences. However, we cannot exclude the possibility that the classical mystic experience, LSD reactions, certain phases of acute psychosis, and other unusual experiences represent conditions of special receptivity to external stimuli ordinarily excluded or ignored in the normal state.

PART VII

THERAPEUTIC APPLICATIONS

From the very start of the modern rediscovery of psychedelics, these drugs have been involved with mental health. In
the beginning, when they were regarded as psychotomimetics
or hallucinogens, their value was seen in research, in building
models of madness, which would enable the basic etiologies
of schizophrenia and similar disorders to be reconstructed in
the laboratory so that, when their patterns were known, cures
could be devised. Later on, it was felt that if those who had
to deal with the mentally ill took these substances themselves, they would be better able to know what the experiences of their patients were, and by this sensitization become better and more empathic therapists.

When it was observed that small doses of these drugs increased the capacity for visualization, moved thinking to
more-basic and primitive levels, and left the patient more
open to his own feelings and needs, therapists began sup-
plementing their therapies with such small doses, and *psycholytic* therapy began. When it was also observed that some
subjects went into mystical and ecstatic states from which
they returned fundamentally changed, psychotherapists began
administering psychedelics in sufficiently large doses to produce these states, and *psychedelic* therapy began. Although
investigation into therapy with these drugs has now come to
an almost total halt because of government restriction of their
use, the best picture of the current state of the art is given in
the collection of papers edited by Harold Abramson (1967).
More recently, Caldwell (1968) has published an exception-
ally good account of psychedelic and psycholytic therapy and
related it to the historical events around the use of these
compounds as well.

The opposition to the use of psychedelics in therapy seems
to arise primarily from fear of the transforming power and

intensity of the responses these drugs evoke. It has been far easier to view this power with alarm than to try to find ways of controlling it. Especially since the term "ecstasy" has been raised in connection with some of the responses to these compounds, the gloomy tradition that pleasure is offensive to God has been revived. Those experiments that seem to indicate, however vaguely, that something is amiss with a psychedelic are publicized without regard to their validity, and contrary evidence is ignored. Psychedelics are not a panacea, but declaring them anathema will not make them go away, and will even make the situation worse by polarizing their proponents and opponents in opposite positions of irrationality. A balanced approach that would permit proper evaluation and use of these agents has been absent, and a scientific scandal of the first rank has been created.

In this section, a collection of papers on the use of psychedelics in therapy is presented. Except for the program at Spring Grove (Kurland, 1967), no active major research program in psychedelic therapy is currently in existence. In the first paper, Masters and Houston discuss the use of psychedelics in individual therapy. They note that psychedelics create new and unique opportunities to achieve the solution of problems and promote personality integration, and argue for new approaches based on the characteristics of psychedelic experience itself.

Blewett deals with the use of psychedelics in groups. The approaches required for group use differ from those of conventional psychotherapy, but seek fundamentally the same aims. He feels that group experiences with psychedelics fulfill important needs that individual experience cannot provide, and that the two should be blended.

Hoffer deals with the use of psychedelics in the treatment of alcoholism, an area in which psychedelic therapy has been notably successful. He discusses the history of the use of psychedelics in this area and the indications and contraindications for such use.

Kast discusses a study on the use of LSD with dying patients and presents some psychodynamic formulations about the experience of dying. This is an area generally ignored, perhaps because of our feelings about the inevitability of death. It is also an example of a new area for treatment, in which the use of LSD might be of great service.

The paper by Izumi is reminiscent of the era in which therapists took the new psychedelics in order to better understand their patients. In this case, the drug was taken to facilitate the design of a mental hospital that would provide a properly therapeutic environment for patients. The hospitals that have been built as a result of these experiences have been the first major innovations in mental-hospital construction in many years, and herald an era in which buildings will be people-oriented, in contrast to the present, when people are required to be building-adapted.

TOWARD AN INDIVIDUAL PSYCHEDELIC PSYCHOTHERAPY

ROBERT E. L. MASTERS AND
JEAN HOUSTON

Widespread therapeutic use of LSD-25 and similar psychedelic drugs did not begin until the 1950s. By 1965, there had appeared in scientific journals more than two thousand papers describing treatment, of thirty to forty thousand patients, with psychedelics (Buckman, 1967). Since 1965, the literature has continued to grow and now includes book-length works as well as the shorter reports published in journals and anthologies. Yet spokesmen for the American psychiatric establishment continue to tell the public that there is no evidence to demonstrate the value in therapy of psychedelic drugs.

Reports of therapeutic successes have come from hundreds of psychotherapists working in many of the countries and cultures of the world. The psychedelic drugs have been used as "adjuncts" or "facilitating agents" to a variety of existing psychotherapeutic procedures. Some efforts have been made to develop new, psychedelic therapies specifically grounded in the drug-state phenomena and the new models of the psyche that have been suggested by the psychedelic experience.

The diversity of the approaches to therapeutic use of psychedelics makes the evidence supporting their value for therapy all the more impressive. Individuals and groups of therapists of various persuasions have worked with one or more of an ever-expanding family of psychedelic drugs and with a great many drug combinations. Dosages administered have varied enormously—in the case of LSD, anywhere from 10 to 1500 μg or more. The psychedelic treatment has been considered as consisting of from one to well over one hundred drug sessions.

In general, therapists working with small doses—such as 25–50 μg of LSD—do so only to facilitate conventional therapy, most often psychoanalysis. Such doses may heighten suggestibility and facilitate recall, association, and emergence of unconscious materials. This type of treatment might involve weekly sessions that continue for months or even years.

When the very massive dose is administered—LSD: 750–1500 μg—the intent is to achieve the therapeutic result in a single, overwhelming session. The patient's values are changed and personality otherwise altered by means of a transcendental-type experience akin to a religious conversion. This type of treatment has been used mostly with alcoholics.

Other therapists work with a "moderate" dose—LSD: 150–400 μg. Exact dose is individually specified on the basis of the patient's body weight, drug sensitivity (if that can be determined), and personality factors. The dose should be sufficient to allow for a full range of psychedelic response; at the same time, the patient should not be overwhelmed or made confused or unable to communicate effectively. A brief therapy, one or a few sessions in a few weeks or months, is the aim.

Types of conditions repeatedly stated to respond favorably to treatment with psychedelics include chronic alcoholism, criminal psychopathy, sexual deviations and neuroses, depressive states (exclusive of endogenous depression), phobias, anxiety neuroses, compulsive syndromes, and puberty neuroses. In addition, psychedelics have been used with autistic children, to make them more responsive and to improve behavior and attitudes; with terminal cancer patients, to ease both the physical pain and the anguish of dying; and with adult schizophrenics, to condense the psychosis temporarily and to help predict its course of development.

Almost all therapists reporting these successes have stated that the incidence of recovery or significant improvement was substantially greater than with other therapies used by them in the past. The treatment typically required much less time and was accordingly less costly for the patient.

Treatment with psychedelics has most often been described as ineffective in cases of hysterical neurosis and hysteria, stuttering neurosis, infantile personality, and long-term neurotic invalidism. Despite reported successes, compulsive syndromes, criminal psychopathy, and depressive states are also mentioned as contraindicated. The risks frequently have been considered too great for paranoids, severely depressed persons, outpatient psychotics and prepsychotics, and those with a history of suicide attempts or who may be currently suicidal. However, as we have previously suggested (Masters and Houston, 1966), psychedelic therapy may be indicated in cases where suicide seems probable and imminent. By his being enabled to die symbolically and then be reborn, the patient's need to die may be subsequently eliminated.

That psychedelic drugs have value for psychotherapy has usually been most vigorously challenged or denied by therapists who have done no work at all with the drugs. Lack of adequate controls to allow more-objective assessment frequently is mentioned. However, it is very hard to devise fully satisfactory controls where such drastic alterations of consciousness are involved. Some veteran workers with psychedelics believe meaningful controls to be impossible. On the other hand, what one research team regards as adequate double-blind conditions has been achieved by administering a light dose of LSD (50 μg) to the control group, while the experimental group received 450 μg. The small dose produced definite changes in consciousness but did not permit a full-fledged psychedelic reaction (Unger, et al., 1966).

Other charges from opponents of psychedelic therapy have attributed bias and excessive enthusiasm to workers with the drugs. Certainly, some of the early papers were extravagant, as tends to happen with new therapies. But the time has long passed when psychedelics could be hailed as a panacea; and it should be remarked that the bias of the advocates only rarely approaches that of some "distinguished" critics. Some of these critics seem ideologically and emotionally threatened by psychedelic therapy. This has been especially true of psychiatrists heavily committed to psychoanalysis. Psychedelics emerge at a time when analysis is increasingly under strong attack. Much of the opposition to the drugs is thus understandable, but also unjustifiable.

Finally, psychedelic therapy has been assailed as too dangerous. Very definitely, the evidence does not bear this out; and in fact, when the drugs are administered by those therapists and researchers who are most effective, the "dangers" are negligible. This is borne out by studies involving many thousands of patients and experimental drug subjects.[1]

Selection and Preparation of the Patient. Ideally, the patient for psychedelic therapy should be intelligent, well educated, imaginative, strongly motivated to recover, and physically healthy. These are not essential, but they do increase the prospects for a successful treatment. Severe heart and liver conditions, and pregnancy, can rule out psychedelics altogether. In general, the disorder should be one considered responsive to psychedelic therapy. However, exceptions might be made in the case of the patient who, apart from his particular illness, is mature and presents most of those personality and background factors mentioned as conducive to therapeutic psychedelic experience.

Once the patient is selected, he is prepared, over a period of at least several weeks, for the psychedelic session. In a series

[1] For example, Pollard, J., Uhr, L., and Stern, E. (1965): no "persistent ill effects" in experiments with eighty subjects over a five-year period; Masters, R. E. L., and Houston, J. (1966): no psychotic reactions or unfavorable aftereffects in 206 sessions over a combined fifteen years of research; Unger, S., et al. (1966): one adverse reaction in 175 cases treated, and that one "readily reversible"; and Cohen, S. (1960): in one thousand LSD administrations to experimental subjects, less than one in one thousand psychotic reactions lasting over forty-eight hours. In therapy patients, per one thousand administrations, there were 1.2 attempted suicides, 0.4 successful suicide, and 1.8 psychotic reactions. The results compared favorably with incidence of complications following electroshock treatments in common use. As compared to almost any other therapy, LSD seems outstandingly safe when properly used.

of interviews, the therapist establishes rapport and instills a strong belief in the possibility of successful treatment. The patient is advised about what to expect, a thorough case history is taken, and there may be some preliminary psychotherapy. In our own work, the research subject was made to look beyond relief from his symptoms to his whole life situation and his hopes for the future. The therapy should aim not just at symptom relief, but at effecting maturation and actualization of potentials.

Psychedelic Psychotherapy. In our experience, LSD usually provides the more-profound and multivarious psychedelic experience. Other researchers prefer other drugs and drug combinations; and we, too, have effectively utilized psilocybin, mescaline, and peyote. Which psychedelic is most effective has yet to be determined.

Selection of the LSD dose is on the bases indicated earlier. In most cases, we have worked within the range of 200–400 μg. Some persons have reacted intensely to only 100 μg. We conceive of therapy as consisting of from one to five sessions at approximately weekly intervals. The patient should understand that his treatment will not last beyond a few sessions at the most, and possibly only one. Failure to achieve success within five sessions indicates a need for non-drug therapy. After six months to a year, and if the problem remains, another psychedelic session might be scheduled. Often, analytic therapies bring a patient to the threshold of recovery, but then require subsequent psychedelic therapy to push the patient into health.

The LSD treatment is conducted in a comfortable, aesthetically pleasing, spacious room, in no way suggestive of a clinical setting. In this supportive and stimulating setting, the therapist wears ordinary street clothes or something more casual, depending on the needs of the patient. No medical or scientific "uniform" should be worn. The session should be presented less as therapy than as educational and developmental experience. The therapist steps out of his role as "doctor" and becomes more the patient's mentor and guide, who will lead him through the unique world of psychedelic experience and enable him to profit from it.

We always introduce the analogy of Vergil and Dante in

the *Divine Comedy*. As Dante was led by Vergil through all imaginable spheres of reality, so the patient is led through the wonders of the psychedelic world. Just as Vergil was not Dante's psychotherapist, but effected important therapeutic changes in the poet, so the guide may also effect therapeutic changes, but again, in a context pre-defined as much more than simply therapy. *Therapy* is here too limited a concept, and may impose limitations both on the patient's experiences and the benefits he can derive.

LSD alters consciousness in numerous and dramatic ways, and many of these are therapeutically utilizable. Psychological effects of LSD-type drugs include the following (Masters and Houston, 1966):

Changes in visual, auditory, tactile, olfactory, gustatory, and kinesthetic perception; changes in experiencing time and space; changes in the rate and content of thought; body-image changes; hallucinations; vivid images—eidetic images—seen with the eyes closed; greatly heightened awareness of color; abrupt and frequent mood and affect changes; heightened suggestibility; enhanced recall or memory; depersonalization and ego dissolution; dual, multiple, and fragmentized consciousness; seeming awareness of internal organs and processes of the body; upsurge of unconscious materials; enhanced awareness of linguistic nuances; increased sensitivity to non-verbal cues; sense of capacity to communicate much better by non-verbal means, sometimes including the telepathic; feelings of empathy; regression and "primitivization"; heightened capacity for concentration; magnification of character traits and psychodynamic processes; an apparent nakedness of psychodynamic processes that makes evident the interaction of ideation, emotion, and perception with one another and with inferred unconscious processes; concern with philosophical, cosmological, and religious questions; and, in general, apprehension of a world that has slipped the chains of normal categorical ordering, leading to an intensified interest in self and world and also to a range of responses moving from extremes of anxiety to extremes of pleasure. These are not the only effects of the psychedelic drugs, but the listing should suffice to convey some idea of their potency and the range of experiences they afford.

According to the functional model of the drug-state psyche advanced by us previously, there are four major levels of consciousness in the psychedelic experience. Each has its characteristic phenomena, and each can be of value in the therapeutic process. The tendency is for the patient to move through progressively "deeper" and more-complex levels of awareness. These four levels of consciousness we term *Sensory*, *Recollective-Analytic*, *Symbolic*, and *Integral*. The patient ideally proceeds from the first, comparatively shallow, Sensory level, through the Recollective-Analytic and then the Symbolic, to the deepest, Integral level. The terms describe the major phenomena, and the deeper the level reached, the more profound the personality changes that may occur.

The progression only rarely is completed. The patient may never get beyond the Sensory level, although this only happens rarely and in cases of very poor management by the therapist or extremely strong resistance by the patient. Much more often, the deepest level reached will be the second or the third. It also happens that the patient may move back and forth among the first three levels, and there are border areas where experience cannot be precisely identified in terms of the schema. Despite qualifications, the model seems to us more valid and useful than any other.

Psychedelic experience begins on the Sensory level. Probing into personal problems should not begin before the patient has adequately experienced that level. Experiences include altered visual perceptions, with objects changing form, and a heightening of colors; synesthesias (cross-sensing: seeing sounds, hearing colors); changes in the body image; and intensification of all the senses. With eyes closed, vivid eidetic imagery may be seen. Awareness of time is altered as mental processes accelerate, and the patient feels that "hours" of subjective experience occur within a few minutes of objective (clock-measured) time. The patient has been told previously that such changes may occur and that he should accept and delight in them. The instruction is now reinforced, as the therapist emphasizes the beauty and wonder of the patient's experience. Resistance and attempted reimposition of normal categorical orientation results in confusion or anxiety.

The patient has previously been given to understand the distinction between subjective and objective time, and how much more, in the psychedelic state, he can experience within any clock-measured unit. On the Sensory level, he is taught ways to profitably use the time distortion. For example, he may be told to create a short story within two or three minutes of clock time, while being told that he will have more than enough subjective time to do so. Some patients create elaborate vignettes under these conditions. Later, on a deeper level, they can utilize this ability to condense lengthy memory sequences or other materials beyond the usual condensation of psychedelic time distortion.

The extent to which mental processes are accelerated in psychedelic experience remains to be measured, and few researchers have even shown much interest in the phenomenon. However, in mental-experiential terms, it is clear that the ten to twelve hours of objective time of the LSD session may be at least the equivalent of three or four times that period. This could be a major reason for the unusual effectiveness of psychedelic therapy as a "brief" therapy. Just on a subjective time basis, the LSD session may be the equivalent of fifty to one hundred hours or more of other treatment without time distortion.

The patient should be exposed to a rich variety of sensory stimuli on this first level. Objects, when touched, may seem vibrantly alive, and when looked at, may seem to breathe or undergo successive transformations. An orange that is handed the patient may appear to be a golden planet; from a piece of cork may emerge a series of striking "works of art." Joyous music usually is played to help direct him emotionally. Typically, the patient will announce that he is hearing music as if for the first time. All the senses are given an opportunity to respond "psychedelically." What we are aiming for by encouraging these types of experience is perfectly exemplified in the following statement by a young woman:

After I had felt that hours must have gone by and then learned that it was only five minutes! after I had seen flowers open and close their petals and held in my hand a peeled grape that became, before my eyes, a tiny brain! and after I had closed my eyes and seen one beautiful vision right after another! well, then I decided that *anything* must be possible, including the transformations of character and personality I had heard about, and to some extent believed, but which only now I really felt confident could happen.

Thus the Sensory-level experiences have the important function of deconditioning the patient from his old ways of thinking and feeling. He should come to regard the psychedelic drug state as one in which "anything can happen." He should feel that his mind has resources never tapped before and that now have been made constructively available: these can be utilized to resolve conflicts, do away with habitual destructive response patterns, and effect still other beneficial changes.

Eventually, the patient should begin to find everything increasingly meaningful. A stone, a sea shell, or some other object may be contemplated intensely and at length until the patient initiates a philosophical or religious inquiry into the nature of the universe and man's place in it. From this he will go on to examine his particular situation in the world. The emotional tone deepens and intensifies perceptibly. The visual and some other sensory distortions yield to more-normal perceptions. As these and other reactions are noted, and as concern focuses on personal problems, the patient is considered to have reached the Recollective-Analytic level of the psychedelic experience. This deepening of consciousness almost always will occur spontaneously in sessions predefined as therapeutic or developmental. In any case, we emphasize again that the therapist should not force the patient into premature examination of his problem. The patient cannot be allowed to remain indefinitely on the Sensory level, but he must be permitted to have a full experience of it. Otherwise, there is little chance that the deepest, most therapeutic levels of awareness will be reached.

The problem of resistance is most troublesome on the Sensory level. It frequently takes the form of a somatic complaint, perhaps nausea or pain. Less often, but much more dramatically, it may take the form of extremely intense pleasure sensations that the patient will not want to relinquish. Some psychedelic therapists deal with resistance by interpretation or just by identifying it for what it is. The resistance can be handled more effectively and profitably, however, if drug-state phenomena are utilized. For example, a patient complaining of a pain in his shoulder can be asked to transfer the pain to a foot, then an elbow, and finally to his hand. Often this will be done, and then the patient is handed some not-too-sympathetic object and is told to "put the pain in the object." Then the therapist places the object out of sight and begins to talk about something else. The patient has had evidence that therapeutic change can come about in unusual and impressive ways in a psychedelic session. Naturally, such a technique would not be used unless the pain is clearly functional.

Since the patient's heightened suggestibility is such a major factor in psychedelic therapy, it is helpful for the therapist to be familiar with the literature of clinical and experimental hypnosis.[2] Aaronson (1967c) is probably correct in stating that there must be important relationships between the hypnotic and the psychedelic states.[3] However, phenomenological differences are great, and in psychedelic therapy the patient should be a much more active participant than the patient in hypnotherapy.

On the Recollective-Analytic level, a large part of the phenomena are familiar ones in the literatures of psychoanalysis and hypnosis. The unconscious materials are unusually accessible, and the patient may recall or live through traumatic experiences from his early life. The events may be seen (eidetic images), or felt to be occurring, or vividly remembered. The patient, perhaps assisted by the therapist, can immediately review the recollection or age regression with an adult consciousness that interprets the events more appropriately than the child did. Even as the trauma is recalled or relived, a coexisting adult consciousness can draw mature conclusions. Even if abreaction does not occur, interpretation by the mature consciousness may still prove therapeutic.

On the Recollective-Analytic level, the concern is with literal life-historical materials—persons, events, behaviors, values—past and present. Some therapists ignore the patient's remote past and emphasize analysis of recent behavior. The

[2] Cf. Cooper, L., and Erikson, M. (1959): We have profitably utilized modified versions of Erikson's hypnotic techniques on countless occasions.

[3] Aaronson, (1967c) has suggested that the patient, to experience symbolic dramas, must have spontaneously entered a hypnoidal state. However, after, or even during, the dramas, a critical intelligence may be operative, and the patient may describe and even look for meanings in what is occurring. Possibly a consciousness has entered a hypnoidal state, while another, secondary consciousness, remains outside that state and observes.

patient is made to examine in detail irrational, illogical, and self-damaging attitudes and behaviors. He admits the need for change, considers alternatives, and, alone or with the therapist's help, restructures his values. With some frequency, here, unconscious philosophical assumptions become conscious. (A recurrent emerging recognition, in our work, has been the patient's sudden knowledge that he always has considered matter, including his own body, to be evil or inferior. This notion, he feels, was forced upon him early, by his church or his parents. It may have been causative of sexual or other disorders, and usually has impaired sensory perception in one or more spheres.) The value-changes include improving the self-image. Most undogmatic psychedelic therapists probably would agree that (Unger et al., 1966):

In general, pathological functioning in the patient is presumed to have been determined by a reinforcement history which would have predisposed toward root "defects" in the self-system (self-image, self-esteem, self-trust, sense of basic worth), and associated value-attitude distortions and "inadequacies." The major effort of psychedelic therapy is reconstructive, premised on the possibility—via the psychedelic reaction—of rapidly establishing and then consolidating the patient's functioning on a core of positive self-acceptance and regard.

When therapeutic change is effected by essentially persuading the patient to restructure his values, increase his self-esteem, and begin to behave in more-effective ways, the success of the brief treatment owes even more than usual to the patient's suggestibility, prolonged concentration, and intense affect in the psychedelic state. These are factors conducive to learning and behavioral change.

There also occur on this level therapeutic events more characteristic of psychedelic experience, although hypnotherapy can provide some rather similar examples. These cases sound bizarre, but the benefits, however strangely arrived at, are genuine. For instance, one research subject (S) was a woman in her thirties who, two years earlier, had become frigid and begun to experience intense pain at the time of her menstrual period. No organic cause was found. During her session, S's life was reviewed in great detail but without apparent benefit. Later, however, she began to insist that she was aware of a "second self" that in everyday life was constantly rebuking her and calling her an evil and unworthy person. This second self, she said, would speak to her daily in a voice that was heard by her "subconsciously." Now the voice was louder, and she was fully conscious of it. S then entered into a dialogue with the second self. With our encouragement, she refuted point by point the various, actually unfounded, accusations as the voice made them. Finally, S became very jubilant and told us the second self had been vanquished, had admitted being a "malicious liar," and had promised not to trouble her again. S said she now knew that she was a good person who did not have to punish herself by denying herself orgasm and inflicting menstrual pain. In fact, she was subsequently free of the frigidity and pain. Three years later these gains were preserved.

It may be argued that S found it easier to abandon her symptoms than to admit their cause. Other interpretations also might be made. In any case, there was no replacement by another symptom.

In another of these curious cases, a mannish female, who denied homosexual tendencies, had been discussing at some length the combination of facial expressions and gestures and ways of speaking that made her appear masculine despite her strong wish to look feminine. She felt that if she looked into a mirror she would be able to isolate the components of her mannishness and eradicate them, and then go on to develop feminine replacements. When she looked into the mirror, however, she immediately started to weep, became extremely nauseous, and ran into the bathroom. She came back, sat silently for a while, and then appeared more composed. Questioned, she said she had seen the face of her brother when she looked in the mirror.

This woman had brought with her to her session, "for some reason, I just thought it might be important," a five-by-seven-inch photo of her brother. He had quite distinctive features, and it now became evident that her own facial expressions were a mimicking or even, as she suggested, a caricaturing of those features. As she continued discussing his mannerisms and way of walking, she moved around the room, and the mannishness seemed to be falling away. She felt "frightened at something coming up inside me, maybe femininity," but was urged to continue "permitting your own real femininity to emerge." The final "freedom," she said, came when she complied with an instruction to, calmly and without fear or anger, tear up the photograph and slowly drop it, piece by piece, into the wastebasket. The feminization achieved in the session was striking; we thought it best not to explore the relationship to the brother and why she might have chosen to imitate or mock him.

It is always important to follow up the patient for weeks or months after the therapeutic session, until the new behavior patterns become firmly entrenched. Contact with the patient during the first two or three days after the session is especially important. The patient's remaining hypersuggestibility to the therapist makes reinforcement particularly effective. Supportive counseling with praise and encouragement and assignment of behaviors made possible by the therapeutic change may be all that is required. In other cases, a more elaborate postsession psychotherapy will be needed. Without proper follow-up care and the patient's co-operative efforts to preserve his gains, there are frequent partial or total relapses.

"Descent" to the Symbolic level usually depends on the previous occurrence of important insights along with a thorough examination of personal problems, goals, and other values. These allow subsequent symbolization of the psychodynamic and other materials, and participation by the patient in symbolic dramas that can lead to major therapeutic gains. The prolonged concentration on personal problems, with a deepening, intensifying affective climate, also helps effect transition to the more-profound levels of consciousness.

Few of the drug-state phenomena have greater therapeutic potential than the Symbolic-level participation by the patient in mythic and ritualistic dramas that represent to him in terms both universal and particular the essentials of his own situation. Acting out the myth or ritual can produce profound catharsis and "rebirth," and so effect personality changes deeper and more sweeping than those possible on shallower levels of consciousness.

Here, eidetic images become of major importance as an instrument for therapeutic change. The patient closes, or is told to close, his eyes. Spontaneous or suggested first experience on this level is likely to be of historical events and then evolutionary processes. When the historical events are experienced, the patient may observe or feel himself a participant in famous battles, coronations, the building of the pyramids. He may walk along the Piraeus with Socrates, or bear witness while a witch is tried or a saint martyred. The events may be eidetically imaged in intricate and voluminous detail.

Similarly, the patient may observe or feel himself to be a part of evolutionary process. He might "become," or be told to become, "that primordial piece of protoplasm floating in an early ocean." After that, he may experience a reliving of the evolutionary sequence on up through the emergence of man. The descriptions may be extremely rich and go far beyond the patient's capability under non-drug conditions. If tapes are played back later, he will typically deny conscious knowledge of much that he experienced and described at this point. These episodes facilitate later experiencing of more-therapeutic imagery.

The Symbolic-level "world" of myth and ritual, the world of legendary and fairy-tale themes and figures, of archetypes and other timeless symbols and essences, is more profound and meaningful than the historical and evolutionary sequences. Here, where the symbolic dramas unfold, the patient may find facets of his own existence in the persons of Oedipus, Faust, Don Juan, Parsifal, or similar figures; and he plays out his personal drama on these allegorical and analogic terms. Or he finds ways of attaining new levels of health and maturity by participation in rites of passage and other ceremonies and initiations.

Those who have not experienced them find it difficult to understand what is meant by eidetic images. It is somewhat as if a technicolor motion picture were being projected inside one's own head, with the possibility that one may become an actor in the drama. The images are usually seen with the eyes closed, although sometimes they can be projected into a gazing crystal or upon a flat, blank surface. They are typically brilliantly illuminated and vividly colored, exceeding in beauty and richness anything seen in the external world. Not all patients have eidetic images, and some see only abstrac

orms or swirling masses of color. However, especially with
dequate drug dosages, representational imagery, too, has oc-
urred in most persons with whom we have worked.

Eidetic images may be related to dream images, but are
much more vividly experienced by a waking consciousness.
On the deeper psychedelic levels, eidetic images are organ-
zed into highly structured dramas wherein the symbols arise
rom the personal-historic data, and insights become viable
nd plastic to the myth-making process by the patient's evo-
ation and examination of them on the Recollective-Analytic
evel. The meaning of the symbols is clear, or becomes so, and
he dramas unfold without the incoherence and illogic of the
dream. The dramas tend to be purposive and to aim at the
ealing and growth of the person. The patient has no sense
hat he is creating them—it is as if, by applying proper stim-
di, a previously inhibited entelechy has been made free and
unctional, "choosing" the symbolic dramas as a means to
ffect its healing goals.

Ideally, the patient's participation in the symbolic dramas
will be total, including ideation, affect, sensation, and kines-
hesis as integrated dynamic constituents of the drama. The
dramas also can unfold on a verbal-ideational plane without
eidetic imagery, but then there may be lesser response in-
ensity. In the psychedelic theater of symbols, the chief func-
ion of eidetic images seems to be to enhance imaginary
events by drawing into the image-ideation complex the addi-
ional factors of affect, sensation, and kinesthetic involvement, in order to add full richness and transformative power
o the experience.

In one of our cases, a professor of philosophy, deeply religious, brought to his session complaints of a castration
complex (diagnosed by a psychiatrist), inadequate sexual
unctioning, general sensory impairment, an "abstract, intel-
ectualized approach to life," various tensions, a Rorschach
diagnosis of latent homosexuality (which he thought to be in-
correct), and an over-all sense of being "cut off" from full
participation in life. He did not want to deal with the castra-
ion complex directly, but hoped to become better able to
"relate to things and others more completely," establish bet-

ter contact with the sensory realm, "experience life as a cre
tive person," and reorient some of his attitudes and valu
with regard to sex.

His experience of the Sensory phenomena was pleasurabl
On the Recollective-Analytic level, he re-experienced, wi
profound emotion, the death of his grandmother when l
was not quite four years old. There was also a vivid recolle
tion of identifying sexually with a little neighbor girl. I
recalled believing he had killed his grandmother by a "magic
act," the smashing of a doll, and when she was buried he ha
felt that "a part of myself was being buried with her." Th
incident, he said, had left him cut off from "the concre
world" and also had been a "symbolic autocastration." He fel
too, that he still had to liberate himself from identificatic
with the neighbor girl. These, with other regressions, men
ories, and insights, continued for some time, producing em
tional discharge and recurring episodes of nausea. He la
down on a couch to consider his need to achieve a full mar
hood by overcoming the old guilt, the effects of the "aut
castration," and the feminine identification. Symbolic dran
experience began, consisting of a series of vividly imaged ri
uals, which he describes:

I suspended my thoughts for a while, and the material simply bega
to come up. I soon had an image of a group of people dancing. The
seemed to be primitive people, but of white skin. They were dancin
around something raised, a pole or platform, and there was a snal
associated with this ceremony. They were dancing, dancing, trying
bring something to life. I had a sense of labor and duration. At th
point I was lying on the couch and was having periodic spasms
the legs, seeming to come from that point of tension at the base
the penis. These spasms continued through the long series of prim
tive rituals.

This rite he did not understand except that it seemed i
be a preliminary to something more important still to com
Next was a puberty rite:

In the next ritual there were boys present, and they were havir
intercourse with an older woman, with the earth mother. Then I sa
the image of a huge female figure over me and, at that momen
there was a bursting reaction as of liberation, and the figure seeme
to move quickly away. I became very ill and dashed to the bathroo

o vomit. I retched violently. This was the most intense of the vomiting spells and seemed to involve my whole body. I had a sense of spitting up deep anxiety—from the innermost part of my body, from my very toes. There was a realization that I was vomiting up my identification with the Female—an identification which had led to terrible anxiety about being castrated. As long as I identified with the Female, I seemed to be castrated, and unless I got to this level and liberated myself, contact with women in my life would ultimately lead to a sense of castration.

There then followed two additional sequences, one a "warrior initiation rite," and the other an unnamed primitive-Christian ritual that "accomplished the salvation" of the patient and "made [him] whole." In all episodes, participation was on all levels: imagery, emotion, ideation, physical sensation, kinesthesia.

I returned to the couch again, and again saw dancing, this time faster and more violent, like a war dance. I think this was the initiation ceremony for new warriors. . . . Then I saw a group of boys killing an older man. This was the father. Then they began eating him. I felt that I was also there mutiliating this man. I pulled off his penis and testicles and, at that moment, saw vividly his mutilated body and the wound in his groin. I felt a deep release of tension and, I believe, I vomited again.

Then I returned to the couch and saw more dancing. This time the people were dancing around a raised platform, on which people were tied by their arms on supports, perhaps two or three males. Then I had the awareness that I was lying down on my back and that someone was placing hot coals in a circle on the lower part of my abdomen, near my penis. I was afraid. Then I accepted the situation and entered into the ritual. I ritualistically accepted my own castration. At that moment, a man appeared in front of me, in the same position that the large woman had been in the first ritual. I knew that he was the Savior. I could not discern his features. His face seemed to be white, without any features, and I could see only his bust. As soon as he appeared, I threw over his left shoulder a piece of animal skin; it seemed to have hair and to be a piece of goatskin. At this moment I knew I was saved from castration.

Then I noticed that the people were on a field and were tearing the Savior to bits and eating his flesh. Then I felt that I was the Savior and was lying on my back being nailed to a cross. Then the cross was lifted up, and at this moment I was a spectator viewing the Savior from a distance as he was being lifted up on the cross on the top of a hill for all the people. From the time the Savior appeared, I had a deep sense of peace and integration. I felt that I was saved and that I was whole.

Therapy on the Recollective-Analytic level can provide insights essential to growth, remission of symptoms, and even elimination of neuroses; but Symbolic-level work can abruptly and in fundamental ways transform the personality, freeing creative talents and actualizing potentials, as well as accomplishing usual therapeutic goals.

In the case just summarized, the patient afterward felt more masculine, more tranquil; and self-esteem was heightened. He was more energetic, with more-intense sensory experiences. One week after the session, "everything" seemed to be going extremely well. In succeeding weeks, he accepted leadership positions he would not, and felt he could not, have accepted previously. He resolved with his collaborator on a book some long-standing conflicts that had made the project seem hopeless. His philosophical understanding was improved. Five months after the session, the book collaboration was progressing excellently. He was "really discovering what scholarship means." There was "a continual stream of penetrating insights and deepened philosophical understanding." He now had "an integrated view of the world." Personal relationships no longer were "on an abstract level." Instead, he had a "continuous sense of immediacy, a sense of existing in the moment, a total commitment to what is being done at the moment." There was a "continuously heightening relatedness to nature—something qualitatively new, a sense of belonging to nature that was not present before. This relatedness to nature has had an important effect upon my relationship with my wife . . . now there is a shared feeling level to the relationship that never existed before. I have also a deepened sense of what it means to be a father and, along with this, a much better relationship with my children. I think, and apparently my students agree, that my teaching never has been better." A year later he felt that he was continuing to make developmental gains. Objectively, he was achieving more. He reported himself aware "of a positive dimension of sex as a means of relating to the world." "In short," he summarized, "I am happier with myself than I have ever been, and others seem to be happier with me too."

All this was the product of a single LSD session, with occasional supportive follow-up. In the magnitude of the gains, it is exceptional, but it does show what is possible.[4]

Integral-level experiences may follow successful experiencing of the Symbolic level. These are religious and mystical experiences, intensely subjective and private, and once they have begun, the therapist no longer has any part to play. The emotional content is extremely powerful, but serene. The patient feels that he has reached the ultimate depth level of consciousness, there to experience fundamental reality, essence, Ground of Being, or God. The effects are the well-known ones of overwhelming religious conversion, "cosmic consciousness," or "peak experience." As mankind's religious literature abundantly records, the personality can be instantly and profoundly transformed. Subsequent changes in behavior can be extraordinary.

Unfortunately, Integral-level experiences are rare, even with normal subjects. Possibly, with further research, we might be able to bring them about much more frequently. If we could, we would be able to achieve what some men throughout most of human history have pursued with single-minded dedication—and, achieving, have sometimes been able to alter history's course.

Only the religious experiences are therapeutic, effecting a basic change in values from which most of the other benefits seem to flow. Those who have mystical experiences (with "fusion" and loss of self-awareness) on this level are mature, well-developed personalities with little need for change. Their accomplishments already are commensurate with capacities. The mystical experiences are awe-inspiring and beautiful, but tend to confirm the individual's life pattern. Possibly the most fundamental value changes occur in a religious context because, in our society, religion is the source of basic values for most persons. One goes back to this source; and then new, mature, and self-actualizing values replace the immature and distorted ones deriving from childish interpretations of and responses to sectarian dogmas. The profound emotion of this

[4] This case is given in much greater detail in our book *The Varieties of Psychedelic Experience*, along with other detailed Symbolic-and Integral-level cases. The complexity of these deep levels and the experiencing of them can be only suggested here.

level may "imprint" the person with insights and the experience of harmony with a basic and beneficent substratum of reality.

Concluding Remarks. It should be clear that expanded therapeutic and research use of psychedelic chemicals is warranted. Given the present extent of mental illness, it should also be considered urgent. It also is essential that we develop effective, specifically psychedelic, psychotherapies. The psychedelic drug as an "adjunct" to old, and in some cases obsolete, therapies will not provide us with equal benefits.

THE PSYCHEDELICS AND GROUP THERAPY

DUNCAN BLEWETT

The psychedelic drugs offer certain rather profound advantages in the group psychotherapy situation. Examination of these, as well as the disadvantages or hazards related to the group psychedelic process, requires a comparison of group psychedelic experience with that of the more conventional situation. Any group process depends upon the development of the individual subjects within the particular context of the group. Since in group psychedelic sessions this process is so compressed and accelerated, it is advisable first to consider the effect of the drug upon the individual and then to trace the reflections of this in the group process.

Psychedelic and Conventional Group Therapy

In psychedelic and non-psychedelic groups, there is a similar development of basic trust between members, which increases group cohesiveness and permits greater freedom of expression and self-exploration. This leads, in turn, to therapeutic advance through the broadening of self-understanding. In this process, each group member acts both as a mirror and as an alternative pattern of adjustment for each of the other members. Each person finds himself in a gradually growing environment, in which his perspectives may

nlarge, his potential modes of response increase, and his
defensive strictures relax.

The essential difference between psychedelic and conventional group therapy is the speed with which developments
occur. In the psychedelic session, the sequence of events is
remarkably compressed in time. This compression sacrifices
neither quantity of experience nor the totality of emotions
involved. It includes the whole process of therapy, from the
establishment of trust and transference to the final development of self-confidence and self-acceptance in a realistic ap-
praisal of personal defects and personal strengths. It results in
a dramatic acceleration of events and a vastly magnified intensity of emotional response within the psychedelic session.
The strong emotions that must be discharged to loosen crip-
pling cathectic bonds may be released under psychedelics in
a matter of a few hours, and the emotional turmoil may become so overwhelming that the individual "loses control."
Where individual therapy permits the gradual development
of freedom in the individual, in the psychedelic situation
this becomes a surrender of confining, defensive self-inter-
pretations.

Process of Group Psychedelic Treatment

The great advantage of group psychedelic treatment is the
shortening of the therapeutic process. Its disadvantage is the
intensity of the resultant reaction. The therapist must be able
to give his attention to the group for an extended continuous
period of time. It should be recognized that even though the
most intense psychological effects will occur in about three
hours, the latter stages of the experience are also likely to be
of marked importance. After the initial crescendo of alterations, logical and conceptual reasoning begins to reassert itself. The submergence of the individual in his experience
ends, and he becomes, as he usually is, both participant in
and observer of his experiences. He must be able to symbolize
his experience in order to use it. It is not sufficient for an
individual to experience something in order for him to gain
knowledge. Before he can conceptualize his experience, he
must be able to tell himself in one set of symbols or another

what has happened. For instance, to answer the question, How do you feel now? you must be able to step back and observe how you are feeling, and apply some word or conceptual symbol to that feeling, before you "know" what you are feeling.

This objectivity—the capacity to "step back and observe" the experience—begins to reappear about three and one-half or four hours after the ingestion of the drug. It gradually increases, and it permits the individual to explain to himself the nature of his experience and what he has found out about himself. He retains sufficient freedom from his defenses and sufficient acceleration of mental processes to be particularly insightful and efficient in this task of formalizing his insights and storing his findings in memory. Because of the vastness of the experience and the complexity of the self, sessions should be extended to permit this process to go on, and should not be terminated until there is general agreement among the participants to do so.

The intensity of the experience and its overwhelming effect upon the individual also render difficult the mechanics of psychedelic therapy. The question of when to terminate a session is different for patients in a hospital as opposed to outpatients. If possible, group members should be admitted overnight to a hospital where they can sit up and continue the session until they are ready to sleep. Where this is not possible, they should stay together in a large room or suite, accompanied by a "sitter" familiar with the drug experience. If this arrangement is also not possible, a "sitter" should accompany each of the subjects home, and arrangements should be made for a trusted person to spend the night with him. The "sitter" should spend sufficient time with the subject and his attendant to bridge any gaps and be sure that they are comfortable with one another.

Psychedelic States and Personality Dynamics

In order to be able to discuss the problems encountered in different methods of group psychedelic treatment, it is important to understand the psychological processes involved in the experience. Chwelos et al. (1959) has classified these psychological changes as involving (1) prolongation of subjective time, (2) enhancement of perceptual clarity, (3) acceleration of thinking, (4) emotional lability, with increased intensity of emotion, (5) added depth in all mental processes, (6) increased sensitivity and empathic awareness of the feelings of others, (7) a feeling of depersonalization, and (8) psychotic changes including thought disorder and delusional and referential thinking. These changes are not independent, and the relationships between them aid in understanding the underlying process in which they originate.

The ability to judge time is learned, and is one of the major elements in the socialization and maturation of the individual. It involves developing a relationship between a given quantum of objective time and a corresponding quantum of subjective experience. Psychedelic drugs alter this time-metering process by prolonging subjective time and enhancing stimulus input per unit of objective time. The enhanced input involves a corresponding acceleration of ideation and a widening of the scope and meaning of concepts through a flood of novel associations. This overextension of concepts results in their melting and blending in such a way that classification begins to break down. The connection and association of concepts is made nearly instantaneously. Not only is each concept distended in terms of the associations it evokes, but any combination or comparison of concepts produces a vast array of new possibilities, ideas, connotations, and similarities.

Customarily, consciousness acts as a reducing valve on the amount of information permitted into awareness, but the drug disturbs this function, and the subject's thought processes are swamped with an "information overload." Ideation becomes so rapid and extended as to be more aptly described as intuition. What would normally be regarded as overinclusiveness of concepts becomes in the psychedelic experience the basis for remarkably speeded, enriched, and extended modes of ideation. In psychotomimetic reactions, however, the overgeneralization disrupts thought processes and produces intense confusion and bewilderment.

Experience defines value and belief systems in all aspects of the learning process through which concepts are formed. These values and beliefs form the yardstick by which an individual measures the worth and meaning of himself and the events, people, and objects of his environment. They determine the choice of coping mechanisms. Out of them develop what Freud (1936) refers to as the "ethical, aesthetic, and personal pretensions" of personality. These pretensions render unacceptable certain aspects of self, and open a cleavage between the actual and the ideal self. Repression does not rid the self of these unacceptable aspects but merely covers them over, and they remain hidden.

In the psychedelic experience, as the concepts blend and classification breaks down, those concepts that represent the pretensions of the individual also blend, melt, and break down, with other, often opposite, concepts. These particular beliefs and values, which represent classifications of right and wrong, acceptable and unacceptable, lose their pre-emptive power and value. Repressed material breaks through into consciousness as the barriers disappear.

The self-concept and its system of defense mechanisms are intricately interwoven. The breakdown of defenses induces depersonalization. Because defenses limit our ability to see ourselves with clarity and objectivity, the therapeutic potential of the psychedelics resides in the fact that, through depersonalization, they permit a temporary escape from the prison compound of one's own conditioning. The result is a confrontation with the self, with no means of defense against one's own scrutiny or enmity.

At this point the individual must either struggle to reassemble his shattered defenses—an agonizing process very likely to induce the extreme anxiety and confusion of the psychotomimetic response—or he must forgo his customary defenses and surrender them by accepting a revision of his self-concept. This point of surrender is the crux of the experience, for it forms the great divide in the individual's psychological response to the impact of the drug. On the one side lies the process of psychotomimetic response in the form of psychotic depersonalization and its accompanying loss of orientation for time, space, and identity. On the other side psychedelic reactions appear to extend through a series of levels of ego loss into the experience of transcendence, or peak experience.

That which is yielded up in the process of surrender is a value or pretension about the self. As repression breaks down and a particular item begins to find its way into awareness, the individual tries to maintain his defenses. The interpretation that initially forced the repression colors the imagery that arises, and this may take on frightening or revolting characteristics. As long as the pretentious interpretation is clung to, the imagery will be frightening, unacceptable, and distressing. Surrender is the letting go of the interpretation. Because of the psychological proximity of the self-concept and its defenses, this act of surrender calls for undergoing and overcoming the ultimate fear that is locked in each man's heart: If I should come to know myself completely and still hate and revile myself—what then? What if the self is unacceptable, completely unwanted—an entity without purpose or meaning?

The deeper and more anguished my self-hatred, the more I am likely to fear the ultimate revelation of myself to my own scrutiny. Yet it is the person with the greatest self-rejection who feels the most severe distress and is most likely to be undergoing therapy. To the individual in the group, therefore, surrender is likely to be equated with the destruction of the self through its submergence in the terrible power of the images. In this struggle, it is the balance between faith and anxiety that becomes the overwhelming fact of consciousness. In this context, faith refers to the expectation of love and to the acceptance of trust that pain will bring understanding and be bearable. Anxiety is the anticipation of pain and is increased by unwillingness to accept pain and the fear that it may prove unbearable.

When the individual can look into and accept the manifest images of the repressed, he effaces the conditioned interpretation through which alone they are seen as disgusting, meaningless, artificial, or terrifying. The acceptance of the repressed portion of the self is accomplished by the acceptance of the images. Repression has distorted reality by not recognizing those aspects of the self that have been interpreted as unacceptable in the light of the conditioned pretensions. Acceptance of the imagery by being able to project love toward it means that beauty has been found in the repressed area of the self and that compassion is extended toward it. The breach is healed, the severed aspects of the self rejoined, and the individual feels a great release of tension and anxiety and an unaccustomed sense of peace. With defense needs gone, repressed energies are released, heightening the feelings of reality and depth. The individual is psychologically open, where he was defensively closed.

The release of a particular area of repression alters only that area of the conditioned attitudes toward the self. Other, perhaps deeper, areas of repression remain unchanged. Self-surrender is not an event that occurs only once, but must be repeated as additional repressed material is released. Each repetition becomes easier because of the positive reinforcement given by each previous self-surrender. Sometimes, however, the strong emotional impact of the particular repressed material emerging may intensify the difficulties encountered. This is why psychotomimetic reactions may occur even after an individual has experienced a number of psychedelic sessions.

Effects of Enhanced Interpersonal Communication

The openness of the undefended self produces the increased sensitivity and empathic awareness of the feelings of others cited by Chwelos et al., and reported almost universally by subjects who have taken one of the psychedelics in a group session. Indeed, subjects generally cite it as the most outstanding aspect of the experience. Communication, cleared of the distortions of defensive screening, becomes so unusually direct, clear, and proximate that it is a process of empathic bonding. The release of psychic energies formerly trapped in repression and resistance lends to all psychological functions a novel clarity and profundity. This is what is referred to in the vernacular as being "turned on."

It should be noted that the compressed intensity of the psychedelic session will affect the therapist through his own sensitivity and empathy, even more than may be the case with conventional therapy. The therapist may well find himself drawn into a profound self-examination. To overcome fear and to help the patient gain insight is the aim of the therapist. But what guarantee can he provide to the individual who fears and reviles himself, that self-knowledge will lead to self-acceptance and self-compassion? The quality of transference grows from his conviction that to know all is to forgive all, and to find what is, is to locate the grounds for compassion. But does he really believe it? Does he impart it properly? Myriad questions of this sort are likely to come up in his own mind with such insistence that they cannot be brushed aside. The therapist should be prepared to deal with them.

This effect on the therapist is the result of the reduction of the defenses of the group members. Customarily, persons communicating are relating to each other through their defensive screening. Breaking down barriers on the patient end of the communication channel puts pressure on the defenses of the therapist, and they tend to become permeable, often before he realizes what is happening. The empathic bonding between participants in the session is the inevitable consequence of the breaking down of defensive walls. It can develop only to the extent that the participants accept themselves and each other, because in depersonalization the individual feels emotionally naked and vulnerable. It takes place when each individual becomes open with the others and can engage in emotional give-and-take with little or no reservation. The participants are able to feel a union so complete as to verge upon the telepathic. Generally the communication of feeling in this bonded state occurs in the form of rather gross, holistic, undifferentiated feelings of pleasantness or unpleasantness.

When one member of the group becomes anxious, hostile, depressed, or confused, the other members of the group become aware of his discomfort. This is not encountered as an external fantasy impinging upon them, but as an endogenous process. They find themselves casting about seeking an explanation for their discomfort within their own functioning and experience. One of the skills each group member must acquire is the ability to detect the source of disturbing feelings. The therapist will be able to mark this development by a shift in the group from statements like, "I feel anxious, but I don't know why," to statements like, "Somebody is

feeling very anxious." There will then be a further shift t
forms indicating that the members of the group have come t
recognize where the feelings are coming from. The partici
pants will direct questions about what is wrong at particula
group members. This is not simply a matter of projection
for, at this stage, the group will agree as to who is disturbed
the therapist will note signs of disturbance in that person
and if the individual himself is not too withdrawn, he wil
readily admit his discomfort.

The empathic bond is the vehicle upon which the group
process proceeds so rapidly. As defenses fall, the intensifica
tion of each individual's functions lends a critical and acut
poignancy to any element of rejection, for the rejected aspec
of the self is mirrored with tremendous insistence and clarity
Where it is projected, the individual finds the other group
members frightening or revolting. In either case, he will be
come anxious, withdrawn, and probably paranoid, until th
rejection is overcome.

Occasionally a subject will react with anger, hostility, o
grandiosity, rather than withdrawal. Agitation and excite
ment may build to a point where restraint is necessary. T
prevent negative consequences for the group, it is well to as
sure the participants in advance that should they lose con
trol, there is nothing to worry about because the therapis
and other group members will simply hold them until, afte
a few minutes, they will have worked through the disturbin
material. This assurance protects all the group members from
anxiety, and if, as rarely happens, restraint is needed, it make
it easy for them to co-operate with the therapist.

In such a situation, it is unwise to terminate the sessio
with chlorpromazine, because the disturbance and anxiet
are then the most vivid memories of the session, and th
individual is denied the possibility of working through th
problem. The physical contact required in restraint is ofte
helpful in the same way the holding technique is usefu
with disturbed children. A patient mired in a problem ma
be released by administering an additional dose of the drug
Because he will often be unwilling to take more for fear o
adding to his distress, and because most psychedelics ar
rather slow-acting, carbogen or DMT might be considered

These problems are important, because with any technique the hazards become greater as the speed of progress is increased. Such troublesome reactions are rare, however, and occur in less than 2 per cent of the cases treated.

Patterns of Psychedelic Group Therapy

Psychedelic group therapy may be used in three fundamental ways: (1) with participants selected on the basis of clinical considerations alone (Type A), (2) as an adjunct to conventional therapy in groups that have been working together for some time (Type B), and (3) in a program of regular drug sessions in which group membership is not constant (Type C). Other approaches may be possible, but they are probably only variations of these basic approaches.

In a Type A group, the therapist selects from among his patients those whom he deems most apt to benefit from a psychedelic drug experience. The advantage of this approach is that it is designed to minimize treatment time. When successful, it accomplishes in one session what would otherwise require a prolonged course of conventional therapy or several individual psychedelic sessions. Its disadvantages are that participants must adapt not only to the drug, but to the strangeness of the individual group members to one another. This enhances the probability of a psychotomimetic reaction. Additional group sessions may be scheduled, which, however, diminishes the advantage of any time gained.

Intensive preparation of the subject should precede the session, and aftercare should follow. If possible, patients should be kept in a hospital during the night following the session. Participants should be interviewed by the therapist on the following day or soon afterward.

Type A treatment relies on the effect of the overwhelming psychedelic experience. Dosage levels too low to induce the critical experience of surrender leave the individual trapped in his pretensions. Massive doses may release material too fast and too heavily charged with emotion for the subject to find symbols to encode the experience until so late in the session that much is forgotten and repressed again. Very heavy demands are placed on the therapist during the session, and ideally he should have an assistant familiar with psychedelic experience sitting in on the session. Group size should never involve more than three patients unless the therapist has help, and no more than five in any case.

In Type B group psychedelic sessions, drug administration may be scheduled at various times during a conventional group treatment program. While this method does not produce the same marked economy in treatment time as Type A, it speeds the group process greatly and may produce profound insight. The spacing of the sessions can be regulated to shorten plateaus in the group learning experience. It offers the advantages of both group therapy and psychedelic treatment. Some possibility of a psychotomimetic response remains, but the danger is much reduced.

In Type B treatment, dosage levels can be varied to suit the occasion. Group process can be accelerated by the use of doses of LSD as low as 25–50 μg. The group size should be relatively small, with five members optimum. The therapist will probably not need any help during a session, and the introduction of a stranger will inhibit the group.

Type C treatment, like Type A, focuses attention on the psychedelic experience itself. Before the treatment, the individual patient meets for several sessions with a group comprising therapists, "sitters," patients experienced in the use of the drug, patients currently under treatment, and group preparing to undergo psychedelic treatment. This extended group functions as a self-help fellowship, in which understanding of one's own difficulties can be gained, and problems and anxieties aired. Group participation gives the patient assurance that others, whom he knows and with whom he has discussed the experience, have taken the drug and found it useful for problems not unlike his own. Subjects and therapists can select from the extended group a congenial set of participants for maximizing therapeutic possibilities in any particular psychedelic session. Advanced patients can use what they have learned in previous sessions to function as sitters or participants with less-advanced patients, thus enhancing their own personal sense of worth, service, and accomplishment.

Many critics of psychedelics have pointed out that the

seem to produce cults. There is a degree of truth in this observation, since people who have shared in any major experience find it interesting to talk to one another and compare notes. The unusual, complex, and exciting qualities of psychedelic experience create an attraction among users, and the therapist can utilize this treatment potential. As with Alcoholics Anonymous, this group can provide valuable support between sessions. It provides an other-directed outlet for the patient. At the group's inception, it can be given a strong community-service orientation. Although the therapist is a member of the group, its structure is egalitarian.

The larger interest group will increase in size as time passes, but should probably not exceed twenty-five members. As individuals recover, an appreciable number will drop out. More than two large groups with a maximum membership of twenty-five will not be necessary. The larger groups fill some of the functions of a halfway program, permit the training of patients as "sitters," and provide a place to which ex-members can return if they have difficulties. It also makes follow-up studies easier, and provides a pool of stabilized subjects for projects dealing with psychedelics.

In the Type C treatment program, dosage will be variable among members of any group, with experienced subjects requiring lower doses. The number of participants in any session depends upon the goals of the sessions. Group size is an important determinant of experience. When one takes the drug alone, the emphasis is on self-analysis, and it seems almost impossible to communicate with others. Moved into a group, the subject, first by self-surrender, becomes able to give without reservations stemming from areas of self-rejection. Subsequently, he learns to accept when he learns to regard what another person has to offer as being as valid, worth while, and beautiful as his own way of doing things.

Use of Psychedelics by the Therapist in Therapy

Because it is difficult to learn about interpersonal relationships in an individual session, some therapists begin to take the drugs with their patients to maximize the empathic process. This kind of activity limits the number of people

with whom the therapist can be effective to only one or tw
at a session. Repeated use by the therapist of up to thre
or four sessions a week at which he takes drugs is very fati
guing and may leave him exhausted after a few months. I
addition, there is always the possibility of psychological c
physical injury from excessive use, even though the data ar
negative with respect to the likelihood of such injury. In an
case, very small doses (on the order of 30 μg of LSD) ar
sufficient to establish the empathic bond.

The more sophisticated objection that the therapist wh
takes the drug with his patients has rendered his profe
sional judgment at least partially inoperative can be met b
a system that calls for the screening of all treatment dec
sions made during the session by a colleague before they ar
put into effect. Of more profound concern is the fact tha
in the shared experience of altered reality, particularly wit
delusional patients, the therapist may lose his own capacit
to distinguish the delusional from the real and may even rein
force the patient's delusion by accepting the premises upor
which it is based. Therapists should be certain of their hol
upon reality under psychedelics before venturing into treat
ment sessions, particularly with schizophrenic patients.

It should be noted that when a therapist takes LSD, h
enters a state in which he can communicate with schizo
phrenic patients in a direct, close, empathic fashion. Thi
communication opens the door to effective psychologica
treatment for schizophrenia. The schizophrenic is lost in time
and a therapist who will enter the paths of his disordered
thinking, once he can establish trust, can lead the patien
out of the disorder. It is not always sufficient to call out fron
the forest's edge to rescue someone lost. One must some
times go in himself.

There is one other problem involved in this method o
treatment. The therapist may feel that the subject is wastin,
time in largely unproductive hypochondriacal or psychoti
periods. Often, however, these difficulties are steppingstone
to self-acceptance. Because of the therapist's close contac
with the patient, he is better able to help him reach an
maintain a stabilized experience. In so doing, he may in
advertently "help" too much and permit the subject to sta

bilize the experience without working through his difficulties and areas of lack of self-acceptance.

Despite these difficulties, the occasional co-use of the drug by the therapist in appropriate situations can add remarkable power to the therapeutic program in the most difficult cases. When used as a training technique, it sensitizes the therapist and teaches him the characteristics of the psychedelic process as nothing else can.

The Effect of Group Size on Group Process

When drugs are used in a group of two individuals, the results are a high level of intensity and a continuous pressure to relate to the same person. The concentration of the bonding makes it difficult to withdraw even briefly. Any suspicion or hostility is excessively disruptive, and its effect tends to be prolonged. In a group of three, the withdrawal of one individual to engage in self-analysis can occur from time to time, leaving the others to relate to each other. Relationships can be shifted as needed, and temporary negative feelings are much less destructive and more quickly overcome. The group of four leads to a high level of intellectual stimulation and to very excellent discussion, but the level of group empathy is lower than in the group of three. The group of four may break up into two dyads, or three may form a group leaving the fourth member out. The effects of psychedelics on larger groups are unknown and not likely to be known in the near future because of existing government restrictions on needed research.

Some Specific Techniques for Furthering Psychedelic Group Processes

Although there are individual variations in drug reaction and in the nature of the therapy sessions, the first two or three hours after the onset of the physical or perceptual changes that mark the beginning of the experience are apt to be full of stress. Before the sessions begin, it is well to have the participants agree that while the early hours of the session will be free time, devoted to enjoyment and experience, and especially the enjoyment of music, they will make the

effort to communicate and work with each other when th
therapist deems it advisable.

Procedures that foster the examination of one's own dy
namics and those of others are extremely useful. Role-playin
of all kinds is helpful. Assuming the role of an actor wh
plays a number of characters, male and female, young an
old, bitter and harsh, loving and gentle, is difficult but use
ful. Finally, the actor is called upon to role-play himself c
the other members of the group.

Another useful procedure is to have the therapist presen
a subject with a card bearing the name of an emotion (e.g
fear, anger, joy, sorrow, etc.). The subject is then suppose
to feel that emotion so strongly that the others can identif
it. While this appears to be an investigation of commun
cation, it is actually a training in how emotion function
This method also teaches the participants how to recogniz
their own emotions, how to change them and, to some ex
tent, how to control them.

Another technique that has been found to be particularl
useful is for the group to become a junta governing a coun
try. Each of the members in turn takes the role of dictato
or director, the others serving as his cabinet. Each cabine
minister must try to work out a method by which he ca
overthrow and succeed the dictator, but must make certai
that none of his fellow cabinet ministers can achieve th
position. The dictator's role is to assign to each minister th
role or task that best suits him. It must be a position in whic
the person will work hard. The dictator tries to keep powe
by skillfully motivating and manipulating the others. Thi
very simple game brings the person to an understanding o
how others attempt to manipulate him and why they choos
the methods they do for him. Other games are possible t
highlight other aspects of functioning. The therapist ma
choose some, but it is very likely that the patients will in
vent their own games to explore problems useful to them.

Conclusion

In conclusion, there is little doubt that individual an
group psychedelic therapeutic experiences have much to of

fer and that the therapist should aim at giving both kinds of experience to each patient. As there has been much discussion but no research on the order in which these should be undergone, this still remains a matter of clinical judgment.

TREATMENT OF ALCOHOLISM WITH PSYCHEDELIC THERAPY

ABRAM HOFFER

Introduction

Alcoholics Anonymous, the great self-help group-therapy movement, is the only established treatment for alcoholics. Until much more is known about the personal (biochemical and psychological), familial, and social factors that contribute to alcoholism, so it will remain. Most new therapies are merely adjunctive to AA and will continue to be so until it is shown that they have therapeutic value when used alone. In my view, psychedelic therapy is best used as a preparation for AA.

When Bill W. and Dr. Bob founded AA, alcoholism had not been accepted as a disease, either by society at large or by the medical profession. Society considered it a moral problem, but found itself confronted with an interesting dilemma, for only a small proportion of the total drinking society drank excessively. No moral sanctions were required for the majority, who eventually made social drinking an integral part of the culture.

The majority who remained moral drinkers could not understand why a minority became intemperate or alcoholic. Moral sanctions were applied on the premise that excessive drinking arose from defects of character, defects of will, and defects in society. These sanctions included education, persuasion, incarceration, and banishment. Unfortunately, the most stringent measures had little permanent effect, and the proportion of *the drinking society* (a concept developed by

Dr. H. Osmond) remained the same or increased. Medicine also considered alcoholism a non-disease.

The founders of AA introduced the medical model first to alcoholics, later to society, and finally to the medical profession. This concept was very appealing to alcoholics because it gave them a satisfactory explanation for their misfortunes. If they were sick and not evil, then they might expect the same sort of treatment they would receive if they developed pneumonia or diabetes. Bill W. and Dr. Bob also introduced the concept of allergy, which thirty-five years ago was incorporated into medicine as a new group of diseases.[1]

But AA insisted that alcoholism was more than a physical illness. It also carried strong personal responsibility. An alcoholic could not be censured for being an alcoholic, but he could be for doing nothing about it.

Society resisted the idea that alcoholics are sick, since it got no guidance from a reluctant medical profession. Doctors expect diseases to be more or less definable, to have treatment that may be ineffective but must be in common use, and to have a predictable prognosis. When they became convinced that AA did help large numbers of alcoholics remain sober, they gradually accepted alcoholics as patients. Even now, the majority of hospitals are extremely reluctant to admit alcoholics who are drunk, and many doctors dread seeing them in their offices. Eventually AA forced the profession to accept the fact that alcoholism, which has been estimated to afflict 5 per cent of the population, is a disease. This marked the beginning of the final solution to the problem. For, having accepted the disease concept, doctors were challenged by the enormous problems, and, in a matter of a few years, several major therapeutic discoveries were made.

The newer adjunctive therapies developed for alcoholism may be divided into the psychological and the biochemical

[1] Dr. Walter Alvarez recently told me that when he wrote a paper on food allergies at the Mayo Clinic about fifty years ago, he was severely criticized by his colleagues. Only strong support from one of the Mayos, who discovered that he himself had a food allergy, protected Álvarez from even-more-powerful assault. Medicine seems very reluctant to take unto itself new diseases.

Psychotherapy, deconditioning therapy, and psychedelic therapy are examples of purely psychological therapy, while sugar-free diets for relative hypoglycemia, mega vitamin B_3, megascorbic acid, and adrenocortical extracts (or extracts of licorice) are examples of pure chemotherapies.

Psychedelic therapy is the only therapy that has prepared alcoholics to become responsible members of AA, when previously they had been unable to do so.

Psychedelic Therapy

We must distinguish sharply between psychedelic reactions and the means for inducing them. Failure to understand this distinction has led to several futile researches, best exemplified by the study of Smart and Storm (1964), which was widely circulated in an extreme form before publication of the watered-down version.

Psychedelic therapy refers to a form of psychotherapy in which hallucinogenic drugs are used in a particular way to facilitate the final goal, which for alcoholics is sobriety. The drugs may be mescaline, LSD, psilocybin, and many others, as well as combinations. It is therefore trivial to test the effect of LSD or other hallucinogens on alcoholics in such a way that there is no psychedelic reaction. In fact, these trivial experiences have led to trivial data, as reported by Smart et al. (1966), who claimed that a group of ten alcoholics given LSD did not differ in outcome from a group of ten given another psychoactive drug. Close examination of their report shows that no therapy was given, nor was there any encouragement of discussion of problems. The experience was not psychedelic, but was more in the nature of an inquisition, with the subject strapped to the bed, pretreated with dilantin, and ill from 800 μg of LSD. Since no investigator has ever claimed that LSD used in this way does have any therapeutic effect, this experiment suggests that LSD used with no therapeutic intent or skill is not apt to help. One of the subjects given LSD by Smart et al. described his experience in comparison with a psychedelic reaction he received from smaller quantities of LSD in Saskatchewan. The experiences and the outcome were quite different.

Psychedelic therapy aims to create a set and a setting that will allow proper psychotherapy. The psychedelic therapist works with material that the patient experiences and discusses, and helps him resynthesize a new model of life or a new personal philosophy. During the experience, the patient draws upon information flooding in from the altered environment and from his own past, and uses it to eliminate false ideas and false memories. With the aid of the therapist, he evaluates himself more objectively and becomes more acutely aware of his own responsibility for his situation and, even more important, for doing something about it. He also becomes aware of inner strengths or qualities that help him in his long and difficult struggle toward sobriety.

The book *The Use of LSD in Psychotherapy and Alcoholism*, edited by H. A. Abramson (1967), contains the best collection of scientific papers on psychedelic therapy.

Around 1952, Osmond and I had become familiar with psychotomimetic reactions induced by LSD. There was a marked similarity between these reactions and schizophrenia and the toxic psychoses. Delirium tremens is one of the common toxic states. It occurred to us that LSD might be used to produce models of dt's. Many alcoholics ascribed the beginning of their recovery to "hitting bottom," and often "hitting bottom" meant having had a particularly memorable attack of dt's. We thought that LSD could be used this way with no risk to the patient. We treated our first two alcoholics at the Saskatchewan Hospital, Weyburn, Saskatchewan, and one recovered.

Other early pilot studies were encouraging, and we increased the tempo of our research until at one time six of our major psychiatric centers in Saskatchewan were using it. As of now, we must have treated close to one thousand alcoholics.

Within a few years after our first patients were treated, we became aware that a large proportion of our alcoholics did not have psychotomimetic reactions. Their experiences were exciting and pleasant, and yielded insight into their drinking problems. It became evident that a new phenomenon had been recognized in psychiatry. Osmond created the word *psychedelic* to define these experiences, and announced this at a meeting of the New York Academy of Sciences in 1957.

Following this, our researches were aimed at improving the quality and quantity of psychedelic reactions. Within the past ten years, major studies, under the direction of Dr. Ross MacLean, Hollywood Hospital, New Westminster, British Columbia, and under the direction of Dr. S. Unger at Spring Grove State Hospital, Baltimore, Maryland, have added materially to our knowledge of the effect of psychedelic therapy on alcoholism.

I will not review the results of psychedelic therapy in detail. This has been done in the books edited by H. A. Abramson and in *The Hallucinogens* by A. Hoffer and H. Osmond (1967). The one striking conclusion is that every scientist using psychedelic therapy with alcoholics found the same proportion of recoveries. Whether the experiments were considered controlled or not, about 50 per cent were able to remain sober or to drink much less. This seems to be a universal statistic for LSD therapy.

Contraindications

Diseases such as schizophrenia and/or malvaria (Hoffer and Osmond, 1962), are contraindications for the use of psychedelics, because subjects who have them are unlikely to have psychedelic reactions and are much more likely to have prolonged depressions and other psychotic reactions. These can lead to severe anxiety or panic, to suicide, and, very rarely, to other violent acts. Recurrences may occur several months later, but it is difficult to decide whether this is a recurrence of the LSD reaction or a resurgence of schizophrenia.

But even schizophrenics and malvarians will not be harmed by LSD therapy if the treatment is conducted in a hospital and if any resurgence of schizophrenia is treated promptly and vigorously with mega vitamin B_3 (nicotinic acid or nicotinamide) and other chemotherapy. LSD therapy is unlikely to help them, however, and I have not given them LSD unless they have been normal for two years on vitamin B_3 medication. The two main uses for schizophrenics would be in demonstrating to them that the perceptual and other changes they had judged real can be induced by drugs and in helping them remove certain isolated delusions.

How to Select Subjects for Psychedelic Therapy

When the indications for psychedelic therapy are clear, it is important to measure the likelihood of a bad reaction. When this is done, unexpected reactions will be less surprising and more easily controlled. There are two objective tests I have found very helpful. These are the HOD (Hoffer-Osmond Diagnostic) test and the mauve factor test.

a. *The HOD test.* This test consists of 145 cards. Each card, as in the individual form of the Minnesota Multiphasic Personality Inventory, contains a question or a statement on one side. The cards are numbered from 1 to 145 on the other side. The subject is told that this is a symptom check list. He is asked to read each card and then to place it in a box marked TRUE or FALSE, according to how he sees his own situation. After he has sorted the shuffled cards, the TRUE cards are recorded by number.

The questions were designed by Hoffer and Osmond (1961). A thorough study was made of hundreds of schizophrenic patients, of dozens of autobiographies of schizophrenics, and of many psychotomimetic and psychedelic experiences. From this information, questions were created that would test the experiential world, thought, and mood of subjects. Normal subjects would place most cards in the FALSE box, while schizophrenics would tend to place them in the TRUE box. High scores, therefore, indicate psychopathology.[2]

Every subject is given the HOD test, and if his scores are high, he must be re-examined clinically very carefully to rule out early or pseudoneurotic schizophrenic reactions.

The following example illustrates one case in which this precaution was not followed. The subject was helped by his reaction, but had his therapist taken seriously the results of his HOD test, he would have spared a recurrence of mild schizophrenic reactions.

Mr. A. B. (age thirty-five) was admitted to the psychiatric

[2] An HOD manual is available from Modern Press, Saskatoon, Saskatchewan, Canada (1967).

ward for two months in 1963 complaining of bouts of depression, anxiety, stammering, and homosexuality. He had been treated five years before with improvement that had lasted until a few months before this admission. During the interval, he had become a successful educator.

He scored very high on the HOD test, with several scores being in the schizophrenic range. (Depression score was 8, perception score 9, paranoid score 9, and total score 71.) He was given 300 μg of LSD and had a moderate reaction. One week later, he received 500 μg. This time he abreacted a good deal of psychological material. This experience was more bizarre than the first one. He also heard voices speaking to him in a foreign tongue. This is very rare in psychedelic reactions. He was much improved after this for four years. Then (June 1967) he suffered re-experience of certain portions of his LSD reactions. During his 500-μg reaction, a large portion of the experience was not perceptual, but consisted entirely of changes in thought. These now came back to him. He began to block frequently, and for two days became very delusional and paranoid about his family doctor. He was a very intelligent man, so, with great determination, he discussed his paranoid ideas with his doctor. His doctor was very helpful, and in two days the paranoia was gone. He was referred to me. It was fairly certain that he had suffered a transient schizophrenic reaction that could certainly not be ascribed to LSD taken many years before. With reassurance and vitamin B_3, he quickly began to improve, and his HOD scores became normal.

b. *The malvaria test.* Irvine (1961) and Hoffer and Mahon (1961) reported that the majority of schizophrenic patients excreted a substance in their urine that stained a mauve color on a paper chromatogram when sprayed with Ehrlich's reagent. Since then, repeat studies on thousands of cases in our laboratories and fewer cases in other independent laboratories have corroborated these findings. Because the chemical was not identified, we called it the mauve factor. The mauve factor also was found in a minority of non-schizophrenic patients. The frequency with which the mauve factor appeared in various diagnostic categories is shown in Table 1.

TABLE 1

DISTRIBUTION OF MAUVE FACTOR AMONG SEVERAL DIAGNOSTIC GROUPS

Group	Number	Per cent who have factor
Schizophrenia		
acute—first admission	30	90
acute—first and readmissions	300	75
treated, still ill	500	50
treated, well	100	0
All neurotics	300	27
All alcoholics	100	33
All physically ill	400	10
All normals	100	5
All first-order relatives of a schizophrenic or malvarian	200	33

This distribution was obtained from patients tested at the University Hospital, Department of Psychiatry, from 1960 to 1966 by Hoffer and Mahon, from patients tested at Saskatchewan Hospital, Weyburn, under the direction of H. Osmond from 1960 to 1962, and from patients tested at Moose Jaw Union Hospital, Department of Psychiatry, under the direction of Dr. P. O. O'Reilly from 1963 to 1966. The three laboratories used the Hoffer and Mahon (1961) method. Because the mauve factor was present in all groups, Hoffer and Osmond (1962) proposed the diagnostic term malvaria. A malvarian is any human who excretes the mauve factor. Malvarians are all homogeneous with respect to a particular biochemical abnormality. No similar claim can be made for any other psychiatric group, except syphilis, where the criterion is a serological test, or perhaps pellagra psychosis, where the criterion is a chemical test.

Malvarian alcoholics differ from other alcoholics in several other characteristics. (1) Malvarian alcoholics scored much higher on the HOD test (Hoffer and Osmond, 1961). (2) They infrequently responded to LSD with a psychedelic reaction, while non-malvarian alcoholics responded like normal subjects. (3) They had prolonged reactions to LSD more requently. (4) So far, not one of the sixty malvarian alcoholics treated has achieved sobriety because of treatment with LSD. It seems, therefore, pointless to give malvarian alcoholics LSD therapy. Since one third of our alcoholics were malvarian, one can assume a similar proportion will be found at other places. I suggest that psychedelic therapy can be made more specific, and the percentage of recoveries will rise, if the malvarian alcoholics are detected and placed in another treatment category. If there are good reasons for giving malvarians LSD, special precautions must be observed. These are: (1) to treat them with mega vitamin B_3 therapy until they are normal and non-malvarian, (2) to start medication once more the day following the session and to continue for several months. I do not give LSD to any malvarian without following these precautions.

Malvarian alcoholics need not be ignored. The majority will respond very well to mega vitamin B_3 therapy. This is described in a book by Hoffer and Osmond, *New Hope for Alcoholics* (1968).

A recent report by R. Smith (1968) suggests that most alcoholics respond to mega vitamin B_3 therapy. Smith treated over five hundred very ill chronic alcoholics with 4 gm or more per day of nicotinic acid and followed them for six to eighteen months. Smith described this group as the most recalcitrant, or sickest, group in his experience. Most of them had repeatedly failed AA and other alcoholism programs. From this series, about 15 per cent showed no response. About 20 per cent showed an excellent response, meaning that they had achieved a state of normal sobriety and required no medication other than the nicotinic acid. About 40 per cent were classed as good, i.e., they were working, feeling better, but required other medication and slipped now and then. The remaining 25 per cent felt better but did not behave better.

When alcoholic slips did occur, they were of much shorter duration. One alcoholic who invariably had had four-to-six-week bouts for many years drank for only one day when taking nicotinic acid. He reported that contrary to his usual experience, he felt no elation from eight or nine drinks.

Smith's data suggest that one need not wait for the diagnosis of malvaria before using mega vitamin B_3. They also suggest that in Smith's series the malvarian alcoholics are more apt to be found in the group who showed an excellent response, that is in about 20 per cent of the population.

Summary

I have described briefly the Saskatchewan origin of psychedelic therapy. This is a form of psychotherapy wherein particular changes in thought are facilitated by hallucinogenic drugs. Both are essential components. In general, hallucinogenic drugs alone or psychotherapy alone have been ineffectual in helping alcoholics. Many workers have condemned psychedelic therapy when in fact they have merely used drugs and none of the other components of the program.

Every therapy has contraindications. Psychedelic therapy is no exception. They are schizophrenia and malvaria, and high HOD scores. They are contraindications because individuals with these characteristics are unlikely to be helped and because they are more likely to have prolonged undesirable reactions.

When alcoholics have schizophrenia, malvaria, or high HOD scores (uncomplicated by acute intoxication), they will respond well to mega vitamin B_3 therapy.

A CONCEPT OF DEATH

ERIC C. KAST

Any meaningful concept of death can only originate in an intact, living, and functioning central nervous system. This system cannot transgress the limits of its power of conceptualization, and one of these is that it cannot imagine its own termination. Therefore, ideas about death must by necessity be developed in the living state by extrapolation and anticipation of an unknown, frightening, helpless, and ominous state: a state that we all dread and that fills us with terror. Such extrapolations, when they occur in certain contexts, are usually considered mental aberrations, or even mental disease.

If obsessive and compulsive fears about future events overwhelm a patient, we consider him mentally ill. We are continually confronted with uncertainties about the future, and a certain degree of concern about it is considered "normal." But if the concern is excessive or if it handicaps functioning, we consider it worthy of treatment. Because death sometimes casts a strong shadow over most of our lives and at times interferes with the adequate functioning of the human organism, I shall treat this issue, the conceptualization of death, as a mental illness, and divide my discussion into etiology, pathology, physiology, and treatment.

Etiology

As far as we know and as far as we can extrapolate, animals do not have any concepts of death. They exhibit behavior of fear, and when in pain suffer for the moment, but there is no evidence that they experience the disease of conceptualizing death.

Interest in, concern with, and preoccupation about death are apparently strictly human affairs. The specter of its own termination fills the central nervous system with terror and forces it to fill the vacuum created by the possibility of its own ceasing with various delusions and fantasies, not unlike those seen in toxic psychoses and in schizophrenia. These delusions about "death" also inhibit our ability to make commitments and decisions. The ideas of guilt and sin, and the image of retribution, inhibit our ability to deal with life in an appropriate and effective way. These ideas and images have been exploited more or less intentionally in political struggles, and organized religion has exploited them to maintain its hold over the masses. They have also given rise to beautiful and meaningful productions of art and poetry, as has most mental illness.

Like other psychic aberrations, death produces specific defenses. One of these defenses against the ceasing of the central nervous system itself is the construction of a *concept* of death. The word "death" does not really refer to this self-ceasing, but has a future-oriented connotation. It refers to "what happens afterward." This conceptualization can be viewed as a defense against flooding of the central nervous system with a severe alarm reaction, causing great cortical and subcortical excitation. The defense is a structuring of the anticipated self-ceasing.

Anatomy of Death: What Does Death Look Like?

We are walking along a street, and a man walks ahead of us. Suddenly we note that he staggers, and we are filled with ominous dread. Then the terrible catastrophe occurs, awakening a long-forgotten fear: the man falls, limp, like a bag, without stretching out arms to brace the fall. The following moment of silence extends over all, encompassing the heavens. The world stands still in utter horror. Then the tears begin to flow, the wailing starts, and life begins again, in grief. Restitution of the moment of horror has begun.

What is so terrible about the image we all fear to view? First, the man lying down is horizontal, a position we assume only in sleep. His face is blue, the tongue protrudes, and his eyes look glassy, seem to soften before us. His feet stick up in the air; one can see the soles of his shoes and his socks under his pants legs.

All of these signals create the greatest alarm in the viewer. The erect position and the control it implies are carefully cherished and protected. "Up" is associated with light and hope in our minds, "down" with darkness, pain, and punishment. The appearance of helplessness and loss of control we view as a demonstration of our vulnerability, as a reminder that our paths, which seem glorious, may suddenly be cut short. These threatening signals evoke in us intensive anticipatory activity.

Physiology

Anticipation is based on verbal (second signal) (Platonow, 1959) ability to conceptualize and to enact future events in theory. Various ways of dealing with future contingencies are thus tested out with the aim of arriving at the most survival-oriented one.

The next moment is always unknown to us. Signals we have

received in the past and processed in the central nervous system permit us to postulate about the next moment and what it will bring. This obvious fact serves as a vital tool for human survival. It permits us to judge the likelihood of future events and prepare for them accordingly. Struggles and perils of great magnitude have been survived by humans on the basis of the ability to read signals in the present, process and store the information, and anticipate future events. This anticipation evokes different affects, depending on the likelihood of survival and the possibility of avoiding tension. In painful states anticipation deals with the solution of the conflict between narcissistic restoration (re-establishment of ego boundaries by exclusion of the pain-producing part), and castration fears (fear of the loss of the body part containing pain) (Kast, 1966b).

The usual method of solving this conflict is a regressive movement toward primary-process thinking, toward narcissistic restoration and diminishing emphasis on the reality principle. Such regression diminishes dread of loss of a body part. When one is confronted, however, with such formidable and catastrophic possibilities as loss of the whole body, such methods of solution appear inadequate. Restorative attempts are made to avoid the specter of loss of a functioning body, which signifies loss of control. Grief and ritual surrounding the aftermath of dying are examples of such restorative attempts.

However, the invention of the concept of "death" itself must be regarded as one of the most important restorative attempts. When a central nervous system, living and attached to an executive tool, a body, observes a non-functioning central nervous system, it receives highly alarming signals. The horizontality and helplessness observed must be structured, somehow, as the living central nervous system anticipates this ominous and unknown future for itself.

The concept of "death" is such a restorative structuring, the form of which depends on the cultural, social, religious, and personal background of the individual.

The isolation implied in the apparent sensory deprivation of a helplessly horizontal man is especially frightening. The anticipation of that period of isolation demands relief.

Treatment of Death

This relief from the dread of isolation and helplessness can come from a number of sources. Successful anticipation, producing affective peace in the face of most disturbing signals, can be achieved by enlarging the idea of self to include more or less stable continuing structures. These structures may encompass identifications with more-stable, enduring persons, like aggressors, even those responsible for the current dilemma (overseers in concentration camps, for example). A social movement may represent a continuing structure through which the idea of the self may be enlarged, as seen in social revolutionary action (Guevara, 1965). In combat, sometimes even in hopeless combat, victory becomes more important than survival. This happens if the results of combat are viewed not as a solution for the individual's problems, justifying the risk of death, but as a solution for the group or society as a whole. The member of the group becomes a small element of the struggle, and the struggling group becomes a surviving entity.

Elaborate systems have been designed to assure the image of continuing existence. These extension-of-life systems, however, obviate the continuation of the clearly impotent executive tool, the body. They, for the most part, substitute a greater, more potent body. God is viewed as a king in charge of the self after "death," guiding, lauding, or punishing, as the case may be, but in some way substituting for the former gratifying functions of the body, as well as for those dealing with moral and superego control of these functions.

A different way of dealing with this distressing and, at times, paralyzing and terrorizing image of horizontality and impotence is to attenuate all anticipations, including this one. Existentialist views, with their attention to the moment, the here and now, supply a means of drawing attention from the dismal specter of the future to the relatively more pleasant present. However, this emphasis on the moment, and relative neglect of the future, precludes the use of a very important survival tool of the human race—anticipation.

Another way of dealing with the inappropriate anticipation

is through the use of psychedelic drugs. In addition to other factors, to be discussed below, favorably influencing feelings about impending death, it has been shown that LSD does limit the impact of anticipation on human activity. The importance of the moment and the immediate sensory input accompanying it outweigh considerations of the future, no matter how dismal they may be. In order to explore the value of LSD in the treatment of "death," the following study was undertaken.

In dealing therapeutically with a topic of such finality and depth as death, it is difficult to follow the usual format of a scientific presentation. Of necessity one must treat the material from a more holistic and philosophic standpoint. The investigations in this report were designed to make the last months of patients with a terminal illness more meaningful and less distressful.

Before attempting to increase the meaning of the last days of a patient's life, one must first ask basic, fundamental questions:

1. Is any interference at this time justified?
2. If so, what direction should such interference take?
3. How much will it interfere with the religious and philosophic attitudes of the patient?

While observing patients during the final months of life, one can see certain defense mechanisms developing in an attempt either to structure death and subsequent "existence" or to deny all possibility of death and assume an eerie positivism that seems surrealistic in character (Field, 1956). The usual clinical approach to death is by a combination of both, and it seems to take an extraordinary toll of a person's ability to relate to his environment and communicate with his family. He becomes isolated and is deprived, to a large extent, of his ability to experience realistically and deeply these last months or weeks of greatest importance in his life. Therefore, interference seems justified if it enables the patient to see and feel with greater intensity. Of course, such medicinal interference must not tamper with the patient's religious ideas and must have the latitude to permit any philosophic interpretation. This study attempts to explore LSD as a means of increasing the perceptive powers of a dying patient. Lysergic acid diethylamide (LSD) has been reported to enhance the depth of feelings without structuring the individual's interpretation of these increased feelings (Hyde, 1960). Increased communication lessens suffering and isolation, and there is always the possibility that increased perception may enable the patient to penetrate, to some extent, the mysteries of cessation of existence.

To explore the means of making the last months of a patient less distressful is the second purpose of this study. It is difficult for a healthy person to appreciate in its full extent the anguish of the dying. This is rather surprising if one contemplates the tenuousness of healthy existence and the ubiquity of death. It is commonly stated that the terminal patient has "pain." This is a semantic convenience. Pain has been defined as a cortical (psychic) elaboration of the flexion reflex (Kast, 1966a). In this view, pain is a response to a central-nervous-system, probably frontal-lobe, processing of a noxious sensory input. Acute pain is felt by an otherwise intact human as the need to flex away, to remove the rest of the body from the pain-producing part.

The observer sees distress in the dying patient and looks for a related experience in his own life. He thinks of a sensory input from which he, at one time or another, wanted to escape, to flex away; and he imagines that this is what the distressed person wants. The observer tries to relate the agony of the gravely ill patient to some pain-producing sensory experience of his own. This is only an approximation, however. The preterminal patient suffers "pain," to be sure, like metastatic bone pain, but he is also depressed, nauseated, uncomfortable, distended, wet, and afraid. He feels the need for flexion; and he must escape from his whole situation, as discussed above, rather than one part of his body. He wishes for what death can provide; but of course, he is afraid of dying and losing control. In a previous study (Kast, 1964b) we have shown that LSD is capable of reconciling the patient with a mutilated body image and thus reducing the need for flexion. The reconciliation was accompanied by such relief and joy that it was decided to enlarge the scope of the investigation

Further impetus to such an investigation was given by the observation that LSD produces changes in the body image (Liebert, Werner, and Wapner, 1958) and facilitates disregard of unpleasant sensory input in favor of a feeling of beneficent oneness and "universal unity" (Huxley, 1956).

Method

Eighty patients suffering from terminal malignant disease with an estimated life expectancy of weeks or months were selected. Only patients who had been informed of their diagnosis were included. An interview was conducted in which the patient's condition and prognosis were discussed, and he was invited to participate in this investigation. It was emphasized that there was no curative value in LSD.

No psychological tests, personality profiles, or projective tests were used; they are impractical in debilitated patients and in patients under the influence of LSD. The following parameters were observed:

1. The patient's mood was evaluated by global estimate and classed in one of five categories:

    a. deeply depressed
    b. depressed but distractable
    c. appropriate affect
    d. euphoric
    e. hypomanic.

Serial numbers were assigned to the categories with "deeply depressed" designated as one and "hypomanic" as five.

2. The patient's approach to life and death was appraised by interview and classified as approximating one of the following statements:

    a. "I want to die; life has nothing to offer me" (negative attitude toward life).
    b. "I like to live, but it does not mean anything and it does not matter" (indifferent).
    c. "Life is great; the concept of death does not frighten me" (positive attitude toward life).

3. Care was taken to isolate pain from other distress, and pain was graded by the patient as:

   a. none
   b. mild
   c. severe
   d. intolerable.

Serial numbers were again assigned with "none" designated as zero and "intolerable" as three.

4. Sleepiness was observed and classed as:

   a. sleepiness
   b. no difficulty
   c. slight sleeping difficulty
   d. insomnia.

A numerical average was established per time unit, "sleepiness" counting one and "insomnia" counting four.

5. Metaphysical notions of the patients were recorded and classed as:

   a. carefully structured, paranoid, or hallucinatory
   b. vague "oceanic" feelings of mystical unity.

No placebo control was used because of the obvious and immediate differentiation of LSD from placebo by the patient as well as the observer. After the interview we gave 100 μg of LSD hypodermically to insure uniformity of absorption. A trained observer was at the patient's bedside until the termination of the experiment. Upon the appearance of fear, panic, or the desire to rest, the patient was given 100 mg of chlorpromazine intramuscularly, which induced sleep within thirty minutes. The patients were interviewed daily for the subsequent three weeks. In addition to the above observations, the following questions were asked after the experience had worn off (three weeks after administration):

   a. Would you like to repeat the experience?
   b. Was it a pleasant experience?

c. Did you learn or gain insight from the experience?
d. Did it interfere with or offend religious ideas?

Results and Discussions

As expected, the over-all improvement rate of gravely ill patients after 100 μg of LSD administration was considerable during the first eight or ten hours. About half of the patients became upset around six hours after administration, and the experience was terminated with chlorpromazine at that time. Only ten patients were able to tolerate the experience for more than ten hours without having some frightening image that necessitated termination. However, contrary to our previous experience, only 10 per cent, or eight patients, did not wish to repeat the administration, compared to 33 per cent in our previous study, in which the experience was not terminated and the patients were permitted to experience the whole gamut of feelings, even when the frightening images made their appearance. The relatively high percentage of patients whose experience was terminated can be accounted for by the fact that these were debilitated patients who tired easily.

Thus it seems that an avoidance of the tiring and, at times, the frightening images, can add to the patient's willingness to repeat the experience.

Seventy-two patients gained a special type of insight from this experience (Table I). This "insight" was a greater lucidity and tridimensionality with which they viewed events in and around themselves. Through this insight, communication

	WILLING TO RE-PEAT EXPERIENCE	FOUND IT PLEASANT	GAINED INSIGHT THROUGH EXPER-IENCE	EXPERIENCE DID NOT INTERFERE WITH RELIGIOUS FEELING	EXPERIENCE "WENT TOO FAR"
YES	68	58	72	7	12
NO	8	11	4	71	62
UNDE-CIDED	4	11	4	2	6

PATIENTS' REACTION TO THE EXPERIENCE 3 WEEKS AFTER THE ADMINSTRATION OF LSD

TABLE 1

was greatly facilitated, both between observer and patient and among the patients themselves. It also created a sense of cohesion and community among the patients, excluding those who did not "know" the experience. This greatly enhanced the morale and self-respect of the patients involved.

Only seven patients felt that the experience in some way interfered with the privacy of their religious and philosophical ideas. These were the patients who experienced strong hallucinatory or frightening images, and whose experience had to be terminated early. It is interesting to note that the unstructured question "Did it go too far?" was universally understood. The twelve patients responding positively were among those with frightening images, whose experience had to be terminated early.

While the depression returned to a certain extent, a definite lifting of the mood was noted for approximately two weeks (Graphs 1 and 2). The explicit pain was reduced considerably (Graph 3). Of course, one must take into account the fact that at the end of ten hours only a small percentage of the patients were awake. However, for the ensuing ten days a definite pain reduction was also noted.

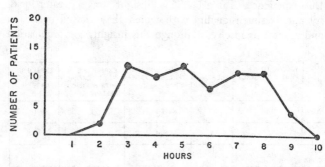

TIME OF CHLORPROMAZINE ADMINISTRATION

(TERMINATION OF LSD EXPERIENCE)

GRAPH 1

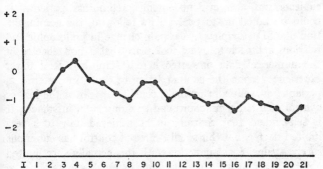

AFFECT

AVERAGE NUMERICAL EVALUATION OF MOOD;
  PLUS 2-HYPOMANIC REACTION
  PLUS 1-EUPHORIA
  ZERO-APPROPRIATE AFFECT
  MINUS 1-SLIGHT DEPRESSION, DISTRACTABLE
  MINUS 2-DEEP DEPRESSION

GRAPH 2

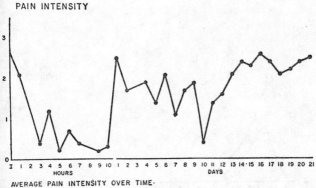

PAIN INTENSITY

AVERAGE PAIN INTENSITY OVER TIME.
0 NONE
1 MILD
2 SEVERE
3 INTOLERABLE

GRAPH 3

The happy, oceanic feeling so often experienced by normal
subjects was also evident among preterminal patients. It
could be noted up to twelve days following the administration of LSD (Graph 4). A certain change in philosophic and
religious approach to dying took place that is not reflected in
the numerical data presented here (Graph 5). Real terror
experienced upon the contemplation of death in preterminal
patients, as well as in normals, consists of fear of the loss of
control of internal functions and environmental influences. It
is self-evident that control can be achieved only to a very
limited degree, but this small degree of control has enormous
survival value. In conjunction with this actually very limited
ability to influence internal and external events, goes a
fantasy-feeling of power to shape one's fate and an adult elaboration of the infantile feeling of omnipotence and omnipresence. The realization of imminent death obviously deals a
heavy blow to that fantasy.

During and after LSD administration, acceptance and surrender to the inevitable loss of control were noted; and this
control is anxiously maintained and fought for in non-drugged
patients. LSD administration apparently eases the blow that

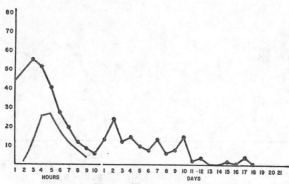

METAPHYSICAL

NUMBER OF PATIENTS EXPERIENCING METAPHYSICAL REACTIONS:
SOLID LINE—OCEANIC FEELING (see text)
BROKEN LINE—HALLUCINATORY, PARANOID REACTION

GRAPH 4

ATTITUDES TOWARD DEATH

AVERAGE NUMERICAL EVALUATION OF ATTITUDES TOWARD LIFE AND DEATH
1. I WANT TO DIE, LIFE HAS NOTHING TO OFFER TO ME.
2. I LIKE TO LIVE, BUT IT DOES NOT MEAN ANYTHING TO ME.
3. LIFE IS GREAT, THE CONCEPT OF DEATH DOES NOT FRIGHTEN ME.

GRAPH 5

SLEEP PATTERNS

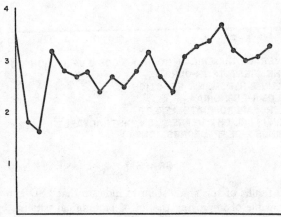

ORDINATE REPRESENTS NUMERICAL AVERAGES INDICATING:
1. SLEEPINESS
2. NO SLEEPING DIFFICULTY
3. SLIGHT SLEEPING DIFFICULTY
4. INSOMNIA

GRAPH 6

impending death deals to the fantasy of infant omnipotence not necessarily by augmenting the infantile process, but by relieving the mental apparatus of the compelling need to maintain the infantile fantasy. Parallel to the general improvement in the patient's feelings, mood, and conflict situation, sleep patterns improved for approximately twelve to fourteen days (Graphs 6 and 7).

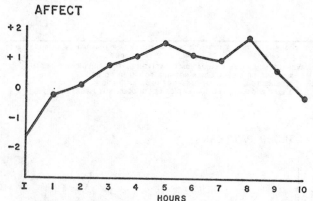

AVERAGE NUMERICAL HOURLY MOOD EVALUATION FOR
THE FIRST TEN HOURS:
PLUS 2-HYPOMANIC REACTION
PLUS 1-EUPHORIA
ZERO-APPROPRIATE AFFECT
MINUS 1-SLIGHT DEPRESSION, DISTRACTABLE
MINUS 2-DEEP DEPRESSION

GRAPH 7

The results of this study seem to indicate that LSD is not only capable of improving the lot of preterminal patients by making them more responsive to their environment and family, but it also enhances their ability to appreciate the subtle and aesthetic nuances of experience. This increased delicate sensitivity is as marked as that usually encountered in normal volunteers subjected to LSD. Here, however, this imagery not only gives aesthetic satisfaction, but creates a new will to live and a zest for experience that, against a background of dismal darkness and preoccupying fear, produces an exciting and promising outlook. Patients who had been listless and depressed were touched to tears by the discovery of a depth of feeling of which they had not thought themselves capable. Although short-lived and transient, this happy state of affairs was a welcome change in their monotonous and isolated lives, and recollection of this experience days later often created similar elation. Of course, these subtleties cannot be appraised in numerical terms. In human terms, however, the short but profound impact of LSD on the dying patient was impressive.

In summary, the drug effect consisted of a lessening of the patients' physical distress and a lifting of their mood and outlook that lasted about ten days.

LSD AND ARCHITECTURAL DESIGN

KIYO IZUMI

LSD was used to help me, as an architect, while designing facilities for the care and treatment of the mentally ill. The object was to understand some of the experiences and problems of the mentally ill, so these problems could be considered in the building design. My personal notes following each LSD experience, recorded discussions, and subsequent reexamination of the events are the source material for this paper. In one sense, the following discussion may be premature, as I have subsequently had no LSD experience in the surroundings that were designed, in order to test the design solutions.

The circumstances and events that led to my series of LSD experiences started in 1954. At this time, Dr. Griffith McKerracher asked me to prepare architectural studies putting into effect the recommendations of a report by Dr. Paul Haun of Pennsylvania on the existing Saskatchewan Hospital at Weyburn, Saskatchewan.[1] The problem was what to do with

[1] Kahan, F. H. (1965), a history of the Yorkton Psychiatric Center and the related social, political, administrative, economic, and psychiatric situations in Saskatchewan.

this existing psychiatric hospital, which had been built in 1921 and had been improved very little during its lifetime. Meanwhile, the Saskatchewan Plan, a regional psychiatric community hospital program, was being developed by the Psychiatric Services Branch of the Provincial Department of Public Health, under the direction of Dr. F. S. Lawson. This plan envisaged a number of small psychiatric centers throughout the province, related to regional general hospitals (Lawson, 1957).

The usual survey of literature was undertaken, and existing hospitals were studied, particularly the few recent ones, but it was apparent that very little information was available. While the psychiatric and related programs were being detailed, we attempted to establish the premises and principles of architectural design that would be applicable to the renovation of the existing hospital and also to the construction of a new hospital. There were many periods of intense discussion with all concerned, particularly with the therapy staff and Dr. Humphry Osmond, Superintendent of the Saskatchewan Hospital at Weyburn. Dr. Osmond prepared notes on the functions of a psychiatric ward, describing the patients' disabilities and setting out general principles for design related to the patients' needs. He contended that buildings exhibit general qualities of either "sociofugality" or "sociopetality," the former preventing or discouraging the formation of stable human relationships and the latter encouraging, fostering, and even enforcing them. Using Dr. Osmond's notes as a basis for design, an architectural counterpart was developed that recognized three levels of human association: the personal association, when a person is by himself; relatively intimate association with a small number of people; and association with a large group. The architectural solution was eventually resolved into a semicircle, with small "retreats" on the periphery, spaces for large group activity in the center, and, in the intermediate area, spaces for small groups. The design concept, which evolved from initial study and research, was called the "sociopetal" concept (Osmond, 1957a; Izumi, 1957; Izumi, 1958).

Despite the progress we had made, many of the significant and more detailed psychiatric considerations and their archi-

ctural counterparts still eluded me. Through a grant from
e Commonwealth Fund in New York, Dr. Humphry Os-
ond, psychiatrist, Dr. Robert Sommer, psychologist, Francis
uxley, social anthropologist, and myself as the architect,
rmed a research team to determine what architectural ele-
ents might have psychiatric significance.

At the same time, Dr. Osmond and Dr. Abram Hoffer,
irector of Psychiatric Research at the University of Sas-
atchewan, had been experimenting with a number of what
e now known as the "psychedelic" drugs, including LSD.
hese drugs were then called "psychotomimetics" or "hallu-
nogens" because of the similarity of some of the perceptual
xperiences they induced to naturally occurring experiences
f the mentally ill. As I was still having difficulty comprehend-
g "secondhand" the perceptions of my psychological, socio-
gical, anthropological, and psychiatric colleagues, who ex-
ained in their own terms the problems of their patients, it
as suggested that I might benefit from an LSD experience.
lthough the psychiatric and architectural programs had de-
eloped to a point where I was able to appreciate the nature
d scope of what the psychiatric services were attempting to
o, I still was unable to grasp the real and significant prob-
ms of a mentally ill individual as related to a building
vironment.

SD Experiences

My first LSD experience was conducted at my home under
e guidance of Francis Huxley and Dr. Duncan Blewett, a
sychologist who had had considerable experience with LSD.
s the intention was just to introduce me to the experience,
o attempt was made to structure the situation to relate to
e problem of designing facilities for the mentally ill. It was
ought that I should "enjoy" the experience. My wife was
so to participate, but she had some difficulty because she
ecame nauseated quite quickly and vomited. As a result, her
SD experience was brief and slightly unpleasant, although
e did experience some of the perceptual phenomena dis-
ssed below.

After an initial reaction of "tightness," not unlike the invol untary muscle contraction one experiences on plunging in cold water, I became aware of how acute my perception wa In fact, it appeared that I was freed completely from a parti deafness of my left ear as well as from my acute astigmatisr Briefly, the perceptual highlights of my first LSD experien were:

1. I was able to read, without my glasses, the titles of books on my library shelves, which were about fifteen fe away.

2. I could hear clearly, through a closed door, the sound of our dogs' toenails tapping the floor, as the pair of chihuahu moved in the service areas of our house, which were som thirty feet away.

3. I experienced in a most intense form vivid color and te ture, not only through the appropriate senses but also throug the interactions of different senses. In fact, I heard color smelled colors, saw sound and texture in a form that seeme almost a direct feeling of tactility with my eyeball or opt nerve. In short, I was experiencing an unusual and extensiv range of perceptual phenomena simultaneously. I had nev had such experiences, although I was aware that they cou occur.

4. I found myself unable to distinguish between space ar time. I had the feeling of being suspended in time, of beir completely "immobile," and yet my increased awareness of "happening" did not appear contradictory, but more rea When I walked across the room, time moved with me. Whe I stopped, time also stopped. When I backed up to my origi nal position, time also seemed to return to its original pos tion, although the time "consumed" was also present. A parently, the sense of time as developed from assimilation of physical time, which is evolved from the arbitrary divisio into units of the daily rotation of the earth, has little rel vance to the kind of perceived time that may occur in drean or, as in this case, be induced by LSD. I do not know ho these kinds of time are related.

During the entire period, I had to lie down intermittent and turn my thoughts "inward" to experience the infini

riety of visual scenes, which were accentuated by the music
at Francis Huxley turned on. When he recited poetry or
lked of his family, I became part of the poetry or the per-
nalities he described.

At one point a friend dropped in and started to eat a piece
chicken that had been placed on the table for me. He
emed to consume the chicken instantly, and yet took an
finitely long time to eat it. It seemed to me that there was
end and no beginning, that he started to eat even be-
re he had picked up the chicken and continued to eat after
put it down.

Some ballet music by Offenbach carried me to heights of
e perception of sound in a total sense that became indis-
nguishable from myself. I was the music. I was one note
d all the notes, floating in a sea of sound. Observers noted
at I flinched involuntarily when there were flaws in the
cord or in the playing of the music itself. This is particu-
ly interesting, in view of the fact that I have very little
ckground in music.

When evening came, we went for a walk. It was a clear,
oonless prairie night with the sky full of stars. I became
ncerned by a person walking toward us along the street. It
emed that he took an extremely long time to come toward
, pass us, and continue on. The sound of his footsteps
emed to go on and on and on, like a broken record, al-
ough he did not appear to change in size as he approached
d then moved farther away.

When I stood still and looked up into the prairie sky, I
rceived that the world was turning. My immediate reaction
as that I was in one of Van Gogh's paintings, which shows
cypress tree and, behind it, the stars and the whole sky,
hich are drawn as if on the end of a pinwheel. Subsequently,
ace taking LSD, I have been able to appreciate qualities
the paintings of Utrillo and El Greco that I had not recog-
ized previously. In the case of El Greco, his attenuation of
e human figure now seems to me to have a lifelike quality
which there is a sense of the passage of time. In Utrillo's
ainting of a street scene with no human beings in it, I now
nse the loneliness and pathos of a person. This differs from

the sense of "emptiness" that such a painting normally con
veys to me.[2]

My next LSD experiences were in situations that the men
tally ill might face in a typical institution. These occurred a
the University Hospital in Saskatoon, under the supervisio
of Dr. Abram Hoffer, and at the Saskatchewan Hospital i
Weyburn, under the supervision of Dr. Humphry Osmond

The first highlight of these experiences was a kind of psy
chic rapport with those who are sympathetic, regardless o
whether this is expressed or unexpressed. I could feel clearl
the hostility of another person, and this hostility seemed t
intrude, making me wary. Subsequently on the wards, amon
people whose faces were unfamiliar, an element of fear wa
added when such an intrusion occurred. Also, if another pe
son was fearful, I could sense his apprehension.

I became acutely aware of different kinds of environmen
These can be expressed simply but not quite accurately b
applying such adjectives as hard, soft, warm, cool, hot, cole
resilient, and so on, to the visual, acoustical, tactile, olfactor
and other qualities. The total effect of the environment was
compound of all these qualities, further confused, enhance
and certainly rendered ineffable by the faulty perception o
time. Past, present, and future seemed interchangeable, ye
retained a continuity. Time as an element was all-encompass
ing, yet specific. For example, a long corridor seemed to tak
longer to traverse when the repetitive elements coincide
with a unit of time. This unit of time is a personal measure
ment resulting from one's own body rhythm, such as one
heartbeat, breathing, or other physiological phenomeno
Time was dependent not only on the visual rhythm of th
physical surroundings, but also on the acoustical rhythm o
the building itself, which was affected by the usual buildin
noises such as the sounds of motors, fans, footsteps, type
writers, cleaning equipment, bells, and also such more con
trollable elements as piped-in music. A "comfortable" roor

[2] Izumi, K. (1961–62), a discussion of certain relationships of a
to the problem of environmental design and, in particular, the re
sponsibilities of the artist when he participates in creating an enviror
ment for other people.

eemed to have a visual and acoustical rhythm appropriate
o its spatial, visual, and tactile qualities.

During the period 1954–58, I had access to all wards in
he Saskatchewan Hospital in Weyburn and had many oppor-
unities to talk with various patients, both in the wards and
n the dining room. Later, while under LSD, I mingled with
patients at the University Hospital in Saskatoon. In addition,
ome former patients have recorded their comments in let-
ers to Dr. Hoffer and Dr. Osmond, and information relevant
o the building environment has been transmitted to me.

I began to comprehend many of the patients' remarks and
oncerns. For example, how a room "leaked" and a patient
aw himself flowing away. He could see his body becoming a
gelatinous and fluid form that flowed and oozed out through
racks and openings other than the doors and windows. Some-
imes his soul or mind seemed to take on a "gaseous" form
hat appeared to be "escaping." To be "startled" by the mo-
notony of one color, such as beige throughout the institution,
nay sound contradictory, but there was such a phenomenon,
which could immobilize a patient. Similarly, the ubiquitous
errazzo floor, suspended ceiling, and similar "uniformity"
added to the patient's confusion in relating himself to time
and space. He could be close to his bed spatially, but because
of the number of beds and their arrangement in a room,
he time required to reach his own bed could seem interminable. In contrast, where a room contained only one bed,
t appeared to be "closer." In general, an increase in the
number of similar elements in a room seemed to increase the
patial and/or time dimension of the room.

It was important to be able to enter a space unobtrusively
and easily, to be able to do this without the feeling of
being on stage or of being observed, and to feel that you were
not intruding on somebody else's psychic space. This later feeling was particularly acute when passing another person
or groups of people in a "hard" corridor. I felt that the corridor should be "soft," "absorbent," and even "resilient," so it
could bulge out where necessary to allow another person to
pass.

The hard, glaring, and highly reflective surfaces of polished
errazzo floors, glazed-tile walls, and white ceiling tiles cre-

ated spaces of unusually intimidating qualities, particular
if other people were also in this space. The acoustical qua
ities of such enclosed space heightened the effect of "tautness
and this quality became indistinguishable from psychic an
physical tensions.

The following quotation is an extract from a letter directe
to me, via Dr. Abram Hoffer, from a former patient who wa
aware of my interest in environmental needs.

The Schizophrenic needs more space around him than other pe
ple do. *Everyone has a space around him which makes him feel fr*
and comfortable. This area varies with individual needs, involvi
privacy more than floor space.
There is the space needed for freedom of movement—according
the person's ability to balance; and another "space" which a perso
needs to be able to relate his thoughts to what he is doing witho
distraction. Environment is not just a "place." It is the feel of t
surroundings which can be changed by personalities exerting infl
ence over it or him.
A Schizophrenic needs extra buffers for his senses to keep hi
comfortable in his surroundings. By buffers I mean the social an
emotional freedoms to co-ordinate the body to the environment in
manner which protects freedom to make decisions without interfe
ence, where personal property is concerned.
Other people cannot understand why the Schizophrenic is so fa
or so slow, so ambitious or so lazy, so happy or so sad, etc. First
all, the disease is not caused by the environment. It is caused by
biochemical lesion and has an inheritance factor. This does not mea
that the environment is not important. It becomes more so.

The above example, which is typical of the kinds of uniqu
experiences that may occur and differ with each individua
indicates how the visual and otherwise-perceived environmer
can be related to how one *is* at any given time. Under LSI
I experienced complete interdependence between mind an
matter in terms of the perceived environment. Apparentl
this projection and injection of your "psyche" into the el
ments around you is also typical of many of the mentally i

Yorkton Psychiatric Centre Design Considerations

Some of the insights I acquired under LSD were ap
plied in designing the Yorkton Psychiatric Centre, which wa
the first regional mental health center constructed under th
Saskatchewan Plan. The initially proposed circular form fc

he building, the "sociopetal" concept, was rejected by the
administration and others concerned as being "too far out."
Certainly it was "unfamiliar" as a building form to the "normal" people involved in building this facility for the mentally
ill. Nor was there an opportunity to test its "comfort" quality
with those who were mentally ill. It is interesting to note
that Dr. T. E. Weckowicz (1957) investigated the perceptions
of some of the patients at the Saskatchewan Hospital in Weyburn. Although his research proceeded independently from
our work on the sociopetal concept, he concluded: "The larger
spaces should be circular, as we are all living in a circular
world (the horizon is round) and our senses are more adapted
to a circular space than to a rectangular one."

The building code and hospital construction standards under which grants were made at that time would not permit
the sociopetal design, but sufficient "reinterpretation" was
given to permit construction of the Yorkton hospital in its
present form. Subsequently, at the request of Mr. Gordon
Hughes, Director of the Hospital Design Division, Department of National Health and Welfare, our firm assisted in
revising the standards for the design and construction of facilities for the care and treatment of the mentally ill (Department of National Health and Welfare, 1965).

The final design for the Yorkton Psychiatric Centre was
for a building complex comprising several small rectangular
buildings. The unusual qualities of these buildings are difficult to describe verbally or to illustrate visually. Essentially,
they provide a unique spatial experience in which all the
building elements are familiar. There are none of the illu-
sionary qualities that architects so often try to achieve, such
as the illusion of a space being larger than it actually is or
an enclosing wall being non-existent.

Certain design premises were established at the outset, since
not only the timidity of the administration, but also my own
LSD experiences suggested a more cautious approach than
would have taken otherwise. By cautious approach I mean
that I did not exercise the prerogatives of an architectural
artist, since my LSD experiences had made me appreciate the
significance of the perceived environment. I felt that the true
"success" of the architectural design depended on the accuracy

of my perception of how other people perceived. There wer
more periods of intense discussion, not only with my co
leagues on the therapy team but also with the patients then
selves. I found myself increasingly able to comprehend th
patients, through their various ways of communicating.
am sure that those who have taken LSD in conjunctio
with the care and treatment of the mentally ill would concu
that their ability to communicate with the patients was er
hanced by their experiences.

The most significant principles and premises of design wer
the following:

1. To provide as much privacy as practicable.
Each patient needs a place to retreat to when he fee
threatened. This place of his own can serve its function eve
if it is quite limited in size.

2. To minimize ambiguity in architectural design and d
tail.
Ambiguity emerges when different functions are indistinguisl
able from each other or when objects appear to be som
thing other than what they actually are. Ambiguous functior
and structural details create uncertainty in the mind of th
observer. Well people usually respond to such uncertaint
with tension, but people whose perception is affected by the
illness can experience real distress when faced with ambiguot
situations.

3. To create an environment without intimidating qua
ities.
Each patient needs encouragement to preserve his own i
dividuality and identity so that he will not be lost in th
mass of other patients. The spatial and functional arrang
ments that are necessary to assist in hospital administratio
should never overwhelm the patient. If the environment co
tributes to a feeling of security, reliance on mechanic
methods of control can be reduced.

4. To create spatial relationships that reduce the frequenc
and intensity of undesirable confrontations.
A mentally ill person should not be faced with an undu

umber of choices in his daily life, particularly in choosing
ompanions from a large number of strangers. Spaces should
e arranged to permit each patient to interact with a small
roup without being confronted by unfamiliar faces.

To meet the need for privacy, each patient was provided
with his own room with all the basic elements that implied
his privacy. As the construction budget did not permit private
oilets and related facilities, we placed these in spaces that
rovided the essential privacy in terms of place and time. Each
athtub and each toilet is in a distinctly separate confined
pace that is controlled by the patient-user.

To avoid environmental ambiguity, we provided logical
isual terminations in the architectural detailing. Junctions of
he walls to floors and to ceilings were clearly defined, with
ach plane surfaced with material appropriate to the total
oncept. Doors, windows, and other openings were designed
with size, proportion, location, and related details that en-
anced the "suchness" of the qualities of each. Windows were
laced on the exterior wall, with returns on both sides and at
he top, so that each window has a certain entity and integ-
ity. This is in sharp contrast to the appearance that would
ave been created if the windows had been continued across
he exterior wall either vertically or horizontally, which hap-
ens when one uses patented wall cladding systems.

Heat, light, and sound sources were designed to avoid creat-
ng confusion, as many of these sources become indistinguish-
ble to a patient who is experiencing perceptual changes and
istortions. For example, air noise emanating from a grill
eside a light source can be confusing and disturbing. For
his reason, the combined fittings that are used quite com-
only in commercial buildings were not used in the psychi-
tric hospital. In selecting illumination type and distribu-
ion, we tried to avoid creating silhouettes of faces and
odies, while still allowing sufficient contrast to give good
nodeling of facial features and other elements in space.
Ve used no clocks or signs that might appear to be floating,
nsecure, or defying gravity.

Doors were placed to allow maximum convenience in fur-
iture arrangement within the room, to provide desirable

visual privacy when opened, and to try to reduce the sense
confinement when closed. Doorways and other entrances
social spaces were designed to minimize the effect of bei
"on stage" as one entered the room or the space. Contr
between rooms visually, texturally, and acoustically was a
minimized, while, at the same time, a certain uniqueness
these qualities appropriate to each separate room or spa
was maintained.

In social rooms, a sufficient variety and number of cha
were always provided, and these were arranged in such a fa:
ion as to avoid the feeling that one was intruding, even wh
all the chairs were occupied. Very few combined seats we
provided, and these were for two persons only. As comm
cially available chairs and other furniture were not suitab
most of the furniture was manufactured in accordance wi
our specifications. Some of the features were extended ar
rests so that the hands could be seen when placed on the:
generally higher backs to give greater support and also a ser
of enclosure, and covering-materials with color and tact
qualities that enhance the feeling of comfort.

The nurses' station was treated visually to try to minimi
the effect of a "police" station, while still permitting ma
mum supervision. The "police" station impression was a har
over from previous hospital design concepts. There was mu
discussion and controversy over the necessity for a nurs
station in the traditional sense. Psychologically, there is
need for a permanent location where the patient knows th
he will be able to get in touch with a staff member. But
was felt that it was undesirable to follow the tradition
pattern of locating a nurses' station in a way that convey
the feeling that it was a "control" center.

A most challenging problem was how to create spatial re
tionships such that, at any given time, the individual patie
would not be confronted with an undesirable proportion
strange faces. To some extent, we were assisted by the a
ministrative decision that there would be no more than thi
patients in each completely separate building unit, but ev
this number can create problems, especially if outpatie
are intermingled with inpatients. In Yorkton, the patie
were distributed in three groups of ten, and the arrangeme

f the primary and secondary social spaces was designed to
ry to minimize any feeling of overconcentration or overcrowd-
g. The "module" used to avoid overconcentration and over-
rowding of people was based on "psychic" boundaries rather
han the prevalent square-feet-per-person ratio, which is typical
f most building and other design standards. There is an in-
reasing awareness of the need to understand the relationship
f psychic boundaries to social behavior and environmental
esign. Dr. Edward T. Hall, in his book *The Hidden Dimen-
ion* (1966), discusses personal space and the varieties of
hysical relationships stemming from cultural, psychological,
nd social differences. Dr. Robert Sommer has written nu-
erous papers in which he discusses the ecology of privacy,
he distance for comfortable conversation, and other matters
hat have a direct bearing on architectural design (Sommer,
960, 1962, 1966a, 1966b).

The above discussion indicates both the complexity of the
esign problem for a psychiatric center and the common-
ense approach to the architectural solution. It is evident
hat, with few exceptions, existing facilities for the care and
reatment of the mentally ill have been designed without at-
ention to significant and relevant details of this kind. This
s understandable, as one of the most difficult tasks is for
he architect, along with his colleagues from other profes-
ions, including psychiatry, psychology, social work, and administration, to appreciate fully the significance of what may
ppear to the well person to be minute and inconsequential.

There is no way of establishing to what extent LSD con-
ributed to the architectural solution, but it is my firm con-
iction that, without my LSD experiences, many of these in-
ights might not have been possible. Certainly they would not
ave been possible within the relatively short period allowed
or design. Perhaps, given the time and the opportunities for
nore-intensive discussion, a similar sort of understanding
night have been achieved. However, I doubt whether any
orm of discussion would have had an impact equivalent to
ny firsthand experiences under LSD.

One of the most difficult problems is for one person to
grasp the experience of another through his description of
t. How do you convey to a child that if he touches a red-

hot element on an electric stove, he will burn himself ar feel pain? Even if he knows pain from another situation, it extremely difficult to appreciate fully the kind of pain th will result from touching a red-hot element. It is a uniqu experience. Even the most imaginative person would find difficult to "experience" it from someone else's description.

How does one fully comprehend the overwhelming sen of fear that a person can feel while standing at the top of staircase, with time distorted and confused with space? Up a point, presumably, you can simulate this by standing at th edge of a precipice with no visible means of support and a tually swaying forward, but taking the precaution of havir somebody pull you back. However, if your appreciation of th time interval that it would take to be pulled back were s distorted that it seemed to take an interminable time, instea of a matter of a second, what would your reaction be?

What does it mean to walk into a quiet room and be co fronted suddenly with the "thunder" of disordered color. What does it mean to fall upward? To feel the arid taste a dry, hot desert sun and sand while in a pool of water? T feel and see yourself "leak"? To be turned inside out so tha you see and feel yourself as in a reverse mold? To a degre through our intellectual powers and imagination, we can sens and appreciate what this might mean. However, a secondhan experience does not have the power to induce the kind concern necessary to discipline the mind to follow minut details of principles of design.

It is too easy for most of us to ignore or to acknowledg superficially the fear, the anguish, and the excruciating ps chological pain of a mentally ill person. We may scoff at as impossible, a figment of the imagination. We may feel tha it is a lie. But to sit beside a patient who is transfixed upo seeing a noise or hearing an intense hotness, as a steam hea ing system suddenly activates itself through hidden pipe and to participate in this "reality," is a convincing experienc that reminds you forcefully of your responsibility as an a chitect when you are designing environments for these peopl

You may not have, under LSD, an identical experience even the whole range of experiences of a mentally ill perso But sometimes, by participating or often by sensing in

econdhand way, you do become more sensitive to the prob-
ems and the reactions of the mentally ill. You begin to un-
lerstand the anguished verbal outburst, the physical cringing,
he tensing of the muscles, the desperation, the anxiety,
ind the fear that is expressed in an infinite variety of forms,
ind you can relate these reactions to various environmental
situations, some of which are within the architectural do-
nain. You can appreciate the hesitancy, like a tidal-wave
torce, that holds a person back from entering a room because
:he placement of the doorway provides almost a theatrical
setting and exaggerates the feeling that he would leave himself exposed from the rear after he entered. You can identify
with the feeling of rejection that a patient may feel as he
enters a room, not because the room is too large or too small
but because it is inconsistent with the psychic dimensions of
the number of people who are already there. This feeling
may be exaggerated further if all the chairs are occupied or
are arranged in some geometric pattern that conflicts with
the psychic spatial boundaries. You become aware of the
feeling of constraint and the overwhelming inability to move
when there is no physical way to escape except through a door
that is almost like a stage exit and has a transom above it
that looks like a guillotine. You begin to realize the significance of even the smallest detail and, most important, to realize that it is not your perception but how other people perceive that is important in making design decisions. As a result
of my LSD experiences, my ability to anticipate, to project, almost to pre-experience some of the difficulties that a
patient might experience through distorted perception, has
been heightened.

The Responsibility of the Architect

As an architect, my LSD experiences have been profoundly humbling and have led me to reassess my role as a
designer. To me, the most significant aspect of an LSD experience, for an architect, is the increased awareness he can
gain of the variety, the depth, and the intensity of experiences evoked by the infinite number of stimuli occurring in
our environment. This heightened awareness can have a dy-

namic effect on his approach to designing the part of the en vironment that may become his responsibility.

There appears to be no doubt that the design concern that have been discussed are important in the specific case of designing facilities for the care and treatment of the men tally ill. The degree to which the architectural environmen supports the medical program at the Yorkton Psychiatri Centre, and at other hospitals that have been designed with perceptual considerations in mind, has not yet been meas ured and may be difficult to measure. However, there is a slow accumulation of information confirming the validity o the argument that the environment does have contributor effects and merits serious concern. Some of this informatio comes from former patients and chronic patients who, in thei lucid moments, have described their environmental needs.

The intense experiences of my own relationship to the vis ually and otherwise perceived environment have raised funda mental questions in my mind. Perhaps it would be more cor rect to say that they have reinforced a previous conviction regarding the art of architecture. There is now no doubt in my mind that the art of architecture as practiced today by contemporary architects as a purely visual aesthetic experi ence is, if not just a shallow exterior decorators' kind o pursuit, at best a selfish and inconsiderate imposition. This is not to say that there is no place for a form of architecture comparable to the other fine arts, but the nature of the ar tistic "responsibility" needs to be commensurate with the occasion. The prevalent practice of permitting an architect to insist on an esoteric approach is not only inconsiderate of the user but may in fact be harmful. In designing facilities for the care and treatment of the mentally ill, for example, the architect should be cognizant of the fact that the most im portant objective in this particular situation is to facilitate the art of alleviating human suffering. Matters of grave con sequence are involved, which makes it vital that design de cisions not be based on intuition, governed by esoteric pref erence, or left to chance.

The ever-increasing problems occurring in our man-made environment indicate the complete inability on the part of both designers and others to realize the significance of other peoples' psychic and perceptual problems and their effects on behavior. There is a growing conviction that ignorance of the relationships between a person's psychic environment and its physical counterpart has contributed to some of the difficulties experienced in our urban centers. I believe, along with others such as Dr. H. Osmond, that there is much to be learned from LSD experiences, even when these experiences are limited to their relevance to mental illness. The relationships between psychic environment and its physical counterpart, as we are beginning to understand them with the mentally ill, are simply an exaggeration of situations in the urban community. Similar forces prevail, and the design criteria are just as valid for so-called normal individuals as for the mentally ill, since, at a critical time, the elements are just as significant. For example, the concept and the subsequent definition of privacy stem from the same basic considerations, whether they are related to the use of a toilet or a yard. The essential principles governing the provision of privacy in the environment are identical for the mentally ill living in a hospital and for so-called normal people living in the suburbs. Architectural aesthetic concepts should recognize the perceptual and psychic needs of a human being, as these are part of an individual's aesthetic experience of his environment. At the present time, our ignorance of these needs is all too evident in many of our designed structures, whether they be housing projects, educational facilities, or even airports.

When an architect is given the opportunity to create an environment affecting many lives, he should also accept the challenge to produce design solutions that enhance the human experience. I am firmly convinced that architecture, as a form of expression, can be considered an art only when it reflects an understanding of the perceptions of the consumers of the designed environment, rather than the perceptions of the architect.

PART VIII

SOCIOLOGY OF PSYCHEDELICS
IN THE CURRENT SCENE

The influence of psychedelics on behavior is paralleled by a concomitant influence on social structures and ways of responding to them. Certain aspects of the hippie life-style (Brown et al., 1967) are merely some of the more visible consequences. Others include the greater tolerance for direct expression of all fundamental needs in the most direct terms, as illustrated on a verbal level in any of the "underground newspapers"; the development of particular styles of dress, and of painting and writing; and the development of such things as communal living arrangements. Most of these changes have occurred among young middle-class people, of the sort expected to be concerned with college and subsequent career, so that their parents are left worried and wondering about what happened. At least two of the books that deal with drugs or psychedelics focus on the college campus situation in line with this kind of concern (Young and Hixson, 1966; Nowlis, 1969).

Any widely used substance is likely to develop culturally specific customs around its use. Alcohol, to cite one example, has given us bars, pubs, cocktail parties, cocktail dresses for women, and night clubs. Psychedelics have also produced many of these changes, as well as churches and all the appurtenances of a new movement promising revolutionary change. The psychedelic experience can alter one's view of the world so drastically that all one's relations to the world come under close scrutiny. One would have to go back to the religious ferment that produced the Quakers and other, similar groups to find a comparable time. Leary's slogan "Turn on, tune in, drop out," however misused, is really an expression of the fundamental changes that occur in the ways of looking at things and the subsequent ways of behaving that flow from these alterations. As a slogan, it becomes an exhortation, but its origin and fundamental sense remain descriptive.

It would be remiss not to note that bad trips are possible and do occur from the use of these substances. Louria (1966, 1967), for instance, has stressed these in his opposition to the use of at least major psychedelics. Even granting that his sample is biased because it is based on hospital admissions, these represent a significant problem. It is probably also the case that conventionally trained physicians treat these cases inadequately and react with a panic culturally appropriate to the older generation, when a calm hand and new methods of treatment might be of more help. The widespread use of psychedelics argues against any high frequency of bad trips, even though they are often taken in very bad situations without adequate safeguards. In an effort to meet some of the problems resulting from the bad trip, the community of psychedelic users has organized in many cities rescue services in which appropriate kinds of help can be given to those who are suffering from a bad trip. Because of the way these services have to operate, there is no way of evaluating their methods. The important need for places in which the drugs can be taken by individuals screened to avoid psychiatric abnormality, under controlled conditions and professional supervision, has not been met by our culture, and this failure only serves to make a bad situation worse and make self-fulfilling the prophecies of disaster.

One of the significant factors in the increasing attention to psychedelics has been the mass media. For the news media, no news and good news are bad news. A paucity of interesting items fails to sell papers and lowers Hooper ratings. There is no question but that the role of the press has been significant in creating interest in psychedelics, fear of psychedelics, and the existence of a psychedelic movement. In his paper, Braden presents a very sensitive analysis of the dilemma and role of the press with regard to the psychedelics. He points out the difference in the kinds of coverage given by newspapers and magazines, and shows how newspaper attitudes may be formed and how they affect subsequent coverage.

Little is known of the life-styles of psychedelic users other than through broad and glib generalizations. Blum and his associates (1964) attempted a study of this, but found it difficult to study any very extensive or representative sample. One way out of the sampling problem is to study various small groups of users and to find out what is common and unique to each. Cheek, Newell, and Sarett present a paper that covers several such groups in extension of Blum's pioneering work.

The paper by Einhorn is as much manifesto as exposition. It discusses the psychedelic scene, and also shows how that scene affects one of the participants in it. It places the effects of psychedelics within the broader context of the technological and communications revolution characteristic of the middle third of this century. It shows how all these developments fulfill McLuhan and Fiore's dictum (1967) "the medium is the massage," even though the effects of psychedelics indicate that the massage may also be the medium.

LSD AND THE PRESS

WILLIAM BRADEN

There is a legend, hallowed in journalism, about a newspaper photographer who was assigned to cover an anniversary of the first sustained nuclear reaction at the University of Chicago. Arriving on campus, the photographer addressed himself to the assembled scientists, including Vannevar Bush, Enrico Fermi, Arthur H. Compton, and Harold C. Urey. "Now, fellows," he said, "I got three pictures in mind. First, you guys putting the atom in the machine. Then splitting the atom. And finally all of you grouped around looking at the pieces."

I had always supposed the story was apocryphal—until just the other day, when I was approached by an excited photographer who works for the same Chicago newspaper I do. "I've got a terrific idea," he said. "You take me out some night to one of those LSD parties. I'll set up my camera and take pictures of the whole thing. All this weird stuff that happens. Who knows? We might come back with a picture of God."

I like to think he was putting me on. Taken together, however, the two anecdotes provide a reasonably accurate idea of the befuddled manner in which the press has often groped to understand anything radically new and complex—including nuclear energy, space flight, and now psychedelic drugs.

We are able now to cover the atom and space beats with a high degree of competence and sophistication, due in large part to the development of specialist reporters. At my own newspaper, for example, we do not have simply a science writer: we have one reporter who is assigned exclusively to the physical sciences and a second reporter assigned to the biological sciences. A third reporter is a nationally respected authority on evolution and DNA.

It seems fair to say, however, that the nation's newspapers as a whole are still befuddled about LSD. And there are several reasons for this state of affairs.

Consider first the plight of a typical city editor. Assuming he wants to provide responsible coverage of LSD phenomena, who might he assign to the job?

The medical writer? Perhaps. But that would certainly limit the scope of the investigation, and the writer would probably tend to reflect the attitudes and concerns of the medical establishment.

The religion editor? Well, he or she is pretty busy as it is putting together the Saturday church page and trying to deal with the day-to-day hard news generated by the ecumenical movement and squabbles over birth control and priestly celibacy. The overworked religion editor seldom has the time, space, or inclination to dabble in metaphysics.

The police reporter at detective headquarters? Unfortunately, he is often enough the final choice. But obviously not a very good one.

What about that new cub reporter with the degree in sociology? He could explore the subject from the standpoint of its social impact and social origins. Not a bad idea maybe. But again, too limited.

The travel editor? He's never taken that kind of trip.

The difficulty with the psychedelics, of course, is that they cut across so many areas—law and psychology, physiology and philosophy, Eastern and Western religions. As a result, the city editor may decide to fall back on the talents of that Jack-of-all-knowledge, the general-assignment reporter.

In the old days, any reporter worth his paycheck was supposed to be capable of handling any story on any subject. The theory was that he would ask himself the same questions that the uninformed layman would ask, and that he would supply the answers in terms that could be understood by a Kansas City milkman or a little old lady in Dubuque. For years, reporters all over America were writing stories with these two mythological readers in mind. And the theory in fact was not such a bad one, until we got quite deep into the twentieth century. I still remember, however, the night the first Sputnik flashed across our innocent Western skies. There was turmoil in the city room as the general-assignment reporters placed frantic telephone calls to sleepy astronomers and physicists. We didn't even know what questions to ask. After only a few days of struggling with apogees and perigees, it became all too evident that we needed our own rocket expert, and in time a top investigative reporter was groomed to take over the field. I don't know if the little old lady in Dubuque can understand every word he writes, but she can rest assured at least that her information is accurate.

The late Professor Jacob Scher used to tell his journalism students: "Do all you can to simplify. But keep in mind there are some things that are just damned hard to understand. They're difficult. And if you simplify beyond a certain point, you won't be telling the truth about them." Obviously the issues raised by the psychedelics are incredibly complex and damned hard to understand. A general-assignment Da Vinci would have trouble enough explaining all of them, if he understood them himself, and here again it is clear that complexity demands at least a degree of specialization and a fundamental background in a number of areas.

Newspapers in recent years have produced their experts on outer space, as well as education, labor, politics, urban planning, and human relations, to the point where major city rooms have come to resemble miniuniversities. As yet, however, they have not developed any comparable authorities on inner space, if such a thing is possible, and it must be admitted in consequence that newspapers in general have done a bum job in telling the many-faceted story of LSD.

Some patterns are revealed by a visit to a newspaper morgue, where the files contain hundreds of clippings about LSD. The clippings were scissored from newspapers across the country, and there are very few of them that date prior to 1963. The few early ones are optimistic, and they tend to treat LSD as a possible new wonder drug:

> DRUG HELPS
> MENTALLY ILL   (1960)
> RECALL PAST
>
> HOW "NIGHTMARE" DRUG   (1961)
> AIDS ADDICTION FIGHT

As early as 1951, readers of the Chicago *Daily News* were informed that a psychiatrist had told "how a white powder given in so tiny an amount it could not be seen by the naked eye transformed normal people into strange, psychotic-like individuals in thirty minutes [and] hinted at the exciting possibility that mental illness could be caused by a toxic substance produced in the bodies of people who have broken down under stress." "A New Shock Drug Unlocks Troubled Minds," readers of the *This Week* newspaper supplement were told in 1959. "It has rescued many drug addicts, alcoholics, and neurotics from their private hells—and holds promise for curing tomorrow's mental ills." It has "excited psychiatric workers all over the world."

By 1963, however, the pattern had shifted, and the volume of stories since then has appeared to multiply almost in geometric progression. It is not a coincidence, moreover, that 1963 was the year Dr. Timothy Leary took his departure from Harvard University. That was the year the press really discovered LSD, having first discovered Dr. Leary, and until recently there has been little success in divorcing the one subject from the other. As far as the drug is concerned, the change in emphasis can be detected from a sampling of 1963 headlines:

A WARNING ON LSD:
IT CARRIES WILD KICK
DRUG BRINGS HALLUCINATIONS;
USE IS GETTING OUT OF HAND

MEDICS WARN THRILL DRUG
CAN WARP MINDS AND KILL

Of psychedelic drugs in general, readers of the Washington *Post* learned in 1963: "They have been blamed for at least one suicide, and for causing a respectable married secretary to appear nude in public." Since that year, newspaper readers on the whole have learned very little else of consequence about the drugs; the coverage by and large has been of the cops-and-robbers variety, concentrating on police raids, drug-control bills, suicides, and fatal plunges.

As indicated, this sort of treatment can be attributed in part to a lack of reportorial expertise. Before taking a closer look at newspaper handling of the subject, however, another important factor should be pointed out.

It might be argued that the current emphasis on the negative aspects of LSD is at least partially inherent in the very nature of that curious stuff we call "news."

There is a common complaint that every newspaperman must have heard at least a thousand times in his lifetime. It goes something like this: "Why do you always print bad news? Why is the front page always full of war and crime, murders and disasters? Why don't you print some of the *nice* things that happen? Why don't you write stories about all the good people who lead decent lives?"

"Because you wouldn't buy our paper any more" is an obvious and an honest answer. "You'd run right out and buy some other paper." And why? Because a newspaper is supposed to print the news, and news is based on conflict. Dog bites man: that's news. More to the point, news deals with *exceptions*. Its stock in trade is the exceptional event that runs counter to ordinary experience, and that is why man bites log is *really* news. In the same sense, war, crime, and disasters are all exceptions to the normal rule, and therefore they are news. If a man rises in the morning and does not murder his wife, that is not news. If people live in harmony and do good works, that also is not news. I believe a satirist once wrote a Walter Lord type of book titled *The Day Nothing Happened,* offering an hour-by-hour chronicle of events in some hypothetical American city. One by one, with murderous suspense, these ordinary events built up to a shattering climax in which the sun went down and everybody went peacefully to bed. I can't imagine the book sold very well, but there is probably a lesson in it for those people who complain about news content.

Many complain that the "good teen-ager" has had a bad press, that his image has been ruined by a few bad teen-agers. The fact is that the good teen-ager is not news, because he is not exceptional. By the same coin, a good trip on LSD is not news either. But a bad trip: that's news. And a bad trip that ends in suicide or a psychotic break: that's really news.

Newspapers since World War II have been giving more and more space to interpretation of news events—to what is known in the business as "think pieces." But their primary function, as it has always been, is still to tell the news—to record the daily glut of occurrences; and since news by definition is almost certain to be bad, it is perhaps unfair to fault the newspapers too much for doing what they are supposed to do.

Having said this, however, I must add that the run-of-mill coverage of LSD has more often than not been superficial at best and violently distorted at worst. Since 1963, the newspapers have had almost nothing to say about the potential benefits of psychedelics in psychotherapy and related fields, including the treatment of alcoholism. As evidence of the breakdown in communications, reflecting also the breakdown in legitimate research in this country, witness this pathetic little column-closer, which was filed in 1967 by an Associated Press reporter in Germany:

> HAMBURG (AP)—The hallucinatory
> drug LSD is being used by Czech au-

thorities as a possible cure for alcoholism, according to Radio Free Europe
monitors.

End of story, in the paper where I read it. Americans can
no doubt be thankful at least that they still have Radio Free
Europe to keep them posted.

Two news stories in particular were probably of major importance in turning the tide of public opinion decisively
against LSD. They broke within a week of each other, in April
of 1966. One involved a five-year-old Brooklyn girl who suffered convulsions after swallowing an LSD sugar cube that
had been left in a refrigerator by her uncle. The other concerned a former medical-school student, Stephen H. Kessler,
who was charged with the stabbing death of his mother-in-
law, also in Brooklyn. "Man," he told police, "I've been flying
for three days on LSD. Did I rape somebody? Did I kill my
wife?"[1]

Kessler vanished into Bellevue Hospital for mental tests,
and that was the last news I have seen about him. But the
case since then has been cited repeatedly in newspaper columns to support the assertion that LSD "can lead to murder." *Post hoc, ergo propter hoc,* of course. If indeed it was a
case of *post hoc.*

Later in the year, in a story on the League for Spiritual
Discovery, writer Thomas Buckley noted rather wistfully in
the New York *Times,* ". . . the increasing use of LSD poses
social, medical, and religious questions that do not seem to be
receiving the attention they deserve." Soon after that, however, the drug was to receive considerable attention in the
very influential pages of the *Times:*

LSD SPREAD IN U.S. ALARMS DOCTORS AND POLICE
AUTHORITIES SEE EDUCATION AS
KEY HOPE IN CURBING PERIL
OF THE HALLUCINATORY DRUG

[1] It was at this point that Sandoz Pharmaceuticals withdrew its
new-drug application, citing unfavorable publicity, and thus cut off
most legitimate LSD research in this country.

Under the three-column headline, in a lengthy story that attracted widespread attention, Gladwin Hill wrote on February 23, 1967, that LSD had become "the nation's newest scourge." Setting out to prove it, he reported some horrifying examples—including the case of a teen-age driver whose car had crashed into a house and killed a child; in a trancelike state, trying to climb the walls of his cell, the youth shouted: "I'm a graham cracker. Oops, my arm just crumbled off." There was no reference to any possible beneficial uses of LSD. As for the drug's supposed consciousness-expanding qualities, the article quoted an expert on the subject, California's Attorney General Thomas Lynch, who said that LSD represents "a flight from reality." Lynch did not say what reality is; but then Hill apparently neglected to ask him.

Reporters who wonder if LSD has any mystical or insight-producing properties can always find out by asking a cop, a doctor, or a legislator.[2] Illinois State Senator Robert Cherry, for example, has been quoted as stating, "This drug puts these people in the world of nothing." Dr. J. Thomas Ungerleider has said flatly, "There is no basis in fact for their claims." John Merlo, an Illinois state representative, has observed that the mystical claims for LSD are "pure bunk," which he may have picked up from Commissioner James L. Goddard of the Food and Drug Administration, who told a House Government Operations subcommittee in Washington that mind-

---

[2] I came across an interesting question to ask people who scoff at psychedelic mysticism. I had written a newspaper article on the subject, and next day I received a telephone call from a prominent psychiatrist who established his authority immediately by informing me that he had recently been quoted on LSD by *Time* magazine. "I just thought I would tell you," he said, "that users of LSD do not have a mystical experience." I resisted the temptation to ask how it had been up there on Mount Sinai; instead, it occurred to me to ask him:

"Doctor, do you believe that anybody ever has a mystical experience?"

"What do you mean by that?" he asked.

"I mean like Paul on the road to Damascus and all that. All of these saints we read about. Did *they* have mystical experiences?"

"Well . . . I'm sure they thought they did."

"But did they really?"

"No."

stretching claims for LSD are "pure bunk." (Presumably it takes a subcommittee to study a subculture.)

If there are no experts available, the reporter can always decide for himself. Thus, one reporter gave the subject a fair shake recently. He watched an LSD party and even went so far as to listen to a Jefferson Airplane record, all of which led him to conclude concerning "the mystique" of LSD, "Tomorrow will come, and that other world—the straight world, the world of reality—will take over." Or as another reporter saw it, the hippies take LSD "to elude a world they don't like, and to create an artificial one in which they feel more comfortable." Nobody has yet suggested that hippies may take LSD to elude reporters.

The newspapers indeed are full of news about psychedelics:

CLUBS BLAST LSD, SEX MAGS[3]

MYSTERY OF NUDE COED'S FATAL PLUNGE

NAKED IN A ROSE BUSH

HER SON'S TRAGIC TRIP

STRIP-TEASING HIPPIE GOES WILD
IN LAKESPUR ON LSD

"NIGHTMARE" DRUG PERIL GROWS

HOME DRUG LAB
RAIDED IN BRONX

BOBBY BAKER KIN IN TREE NUDE

BANANA SMOKING
UNDER U.S. STUDY

Some terrible things are reported. A team of investigators in California, for example, came across a former disk jockey

[3] California Federation of Women's Clubs.

who said he had lost his job after taking LSD, and what's more, he didn't care. A medical man found: ". . . LSD users are suddenly overcome with religion." As far back as 1960, *This Week* had recovered from its original optimism, and Dr. Franz E. Winkler was warning readers of the supplement that he had detected certain "ominous symptoms" in some LSD users. "LSD," the doctor noted, "breaks the fetters of our disenchanted existence and releases the mind to a flight into a fairyland sparkling with colors and sounds and sensations of unearthly beauty. Under its influence, all confinements and separations fade, and the world becomes a place in which individuals need no longer be lonely but become members of an all-encompassing whole. Under such influences, people receive creative inspirations, become inclined to accept the reality of a spiritual world, and at times, even sense the existence of a supreme being." And this is all wrong and immoral, of course. Because it's too easy. In fact, it's a sin.

Parents, do you know the danger signs? You do if you read a 1967 syndicated series by Ann Honig, which ran among other places in *Chicago's American*:

"Parents who suspect their offspring are turned on via LSD should be suspicious if the youngsters suddenly espouse a oneness with God and the universe, if they are suddenly superknowledgeable about life and love, if they hear and see things no one else does, if their pupils are dilated."

Of course there are real LSD tragedies, and nobody should minimize them. Certainly the press cannot be accused of minimizing them.

BAD LSD TRIPS INCREASE, the headline over an Associated Press story reported in May of 1967. And so they probably had. But this raises an interesting possibility I remember discussing one time with Jean Houston, and I believe we agreed that the press might be partly responsible for creating a sort of self-fulfilling prophecy. One dimly recalls a halcyon time, in the beginning, when nobody spoke much about bad trips, and the psychedelic experience was almost always very nice and rewarding. Perhaps that was never the case, or it could be that fewer bad trips in the past were merely a result of a smaller drug population and/or far less publicity. But the other possibility remains.

Just suppose. Here all of a sudden is this Greek chorus of doctors and psychiatrists warning young people to avoid LSD: it might drive them crazy. And the warnings are dutifully passed on by the press. This doesn't stop the young people from taking LSD, of course; but it could possibly create a subliminal anxiety that results in either a bad trip or in a panic reaction at some later date. Since LSD subjects are so highly suggestible, as is well known, it could be that they oblige the doctors and the press by doing exactly what they were told they would do. They flip out.

In my own case, I was having dinner one night with a bearded psychiatrist of formidable appearance. This was some months after I had participated in a legal psychedelic experiment at a psychiatric hospital, for a newspaper story, and while the trip had not been a pleasant one, I had not given it any thought for some time, and I had not been worried about it in any way. Between courses, the psychiatrist declared: "The real tragedy of LSD has only now come to light. People think they might have a bad trip for a few hours, and that's all they have to worry about. But we now know the frightening truth that *nobody comes back unharmed*. In *every* case there is some degree of brain damage." Oh? And where had the good doctor heard that? Well, he said, he had heard it just the other day at a medical-school symposium. And whom had he heard it from? He had heard it from this doctor sitting right next to him at the symposium, he forgot his name. And where had *he* heard it? He had heard it on a recent visit to the West Coast, where the research had been done. Where on the West Coast? My dinner companion didn't know. Who had done the research, and how was it done? He didn't know that either. He called for the dessert menu.

Driving home, like the man in the joke, I kept telling myself: "Now is not the time to panic. Now is not the time to panic." And then, finally: "Now. *Now* is the time to panic!" Without dwelling on the details, I will say only that I spent a very bad week, and I can certainly understand now those stories about rational Westerners who mentally disintegrate under the suggestive curse of an African witch doctor. In my own mind at least, the experience lends credence to the hypothesis that the press and the medical profession between them may have contributed to a similar situation by continually emphasizing the dangers and negative aspects of the psychedelic experience.

One might ask why the press has been so willing to go along with the doctors in this connection, to the point of distorting the over-all truth about LSD. There is in fact a fundamental dilemma involved here, and it is one that editors run into rather frequently. In short, should a newspaper tell the truth, or whole truth, when the public safety might be better served by silence or half-truths?

An obvious example is the development of a riot situation in a community. Should the local newspapers call attention to the situation and thereby possibly aggravate it by directing other malcontents to the scene? In most cases, newspapers withhold such stories during the early stages of mob action, and especially so if the disorder is still on a relatively small scale.

It would be hard to argue with that decision. But I recall a less-obvious version of the same basic problem. A rare solar eclipse was soon to occur, and our newspaper was flooded with urgent messages from individuals and organizations dedicated to the prevention of blindness. We were urged to tell our readers there was no safe way to look directly at the eclipse. It so happens that a safe eclipse viewer can be made with exposed photographic negatives, but the anti-blindness lobby said the procedure was too complicated, and many people undoubtedly would botch the job. Well, what should we do? Should we, in effect, fib and play it safe? Those who wanted us to do so were interested only in preventing blindness—not an unworthy motive, certainly—but the eclipse, on the other hand, was a phenomenon of considerable interest. Did we have the right to deny people the experience of seeing it and studying it? In the end, we decided to tell the truth. We published carefully worded instructions telling how to construct a safe viewer.[4]

The parallel to psychedelic drugs is obvious. Medical men quite properly are interested in the prevention of suicide and psychosis, and there are strong pressures on a newspaper edi-

---

[4] To my knowledge, nobody went blind.

tor to conform. Besides, there is no foolproof method to guarantee a safe view of the psychedelic world, and editors, in addition, are often cowed by the medical profession. If a doctor says LSD is a deadly peril, how is an editor to argue with him? The result sometimes is a certain timidity on the part of the press in any situation involving a medical judgment. It is understandable, then, if many editors decide to play it safe and treat LSD simply as something that flew out of Pandora's box.

Still, there is no obligation to overdo it.

There was widespread rejoicing when the first study was published in 1967 indicating that use of LSD might result in abnormal chromosome breakage. That would certainly solve the problem very neatly, obviating the necessity to deal with all those sticky questions the psychedelics had raised, and the press in some cases did its best to improve upon the findings. The syndicated series by Ann Honig began with the observation, "LSD may cause cancer in drug users—and deformity and death in their children." But the series itself was relatively restrained in comparison to the headlines and advertising that accompanied it in *Chicago's American*. There was an interesting escalation from story to headline to promotional copy. For example the headline:

LSD: FOR THE KICK THAT CAN KILL

Then the printed advertising blurbs:

LSD: THE "FLY NOW,
DIE LATER" DRUG

"Altho many acid-users have committed suicide or murder while high on LSD, an even grimmer indictment has been placed against it. A well-known genetics expert has found that 'harmless' LSD damages human chromosomes . . . and eventually causes cancer! Find out the frightening facts. Read 'LSD: The Tragic Fad' starting Sunday in *Chicago's American*."

"Why does a young person suddenly want to jump out of a window? Or shoot a number of people? Or eat the bark from a tree? Learn what the use of the drug LSD can do to a person. . . ."

And finally the spot radio announcements, prefaced with the remark that acid-heads think LSD is harmless:

"Well, they're wrong—*dead wrong*. People who take LSD eventually get cancer."

In the series, writer Honig sought to analyze why so many young people turn to LSD. The conclusion: "LSD offers a new mystique, a new entree to the in-group, a new rebellion against their elders, a new thrill. Also it's cheap, easy to make." And so much for that. The writer went on to comment upon the experience of a San Mateo high school superintendent who raised $21,000 to finance an "anti-LSD film" and then asked the students "whom they would trust as the narrator." He was "shocked" by their answer.

"Nobody," said the students.

Small wonder, one might add.

This isn't to say that all newspapers in all cases have taken a limited and wholly negative view of psychedelics. There have been thoughtful pieces, here and there, now and then. My own newspaper, for example, devoted a four-page section to the religious implications of LSD experience, and it also offered vigorous editorial opposition to proposed legislation making LSD possession a crime in Illinois. Occasionally one comes across an isolated headline:

> LSD CHEERS UP
> DYING PATIENT,
> DOCTOR FINDS
> DRUG BRINGS A NEW
> ZEST FOR LIFE

There has, however, been very little of substance printed. Seldom is any attempt made to explain the nature of the LSD experience, except in terms of the acting-out behavior it sometimes produces. Even in the New York *Times*, one may be told simply that LSD ". . . produces hallucinations or alters thought processes in various ways." At best, a reader may find that the experience enhances sensory perception—pretty colors are seen—and sometimes he is told that the experience breaks down the ego and produces a "mystical" state of mind. But what constitutes a mystical state of mind is left to the imagination. Now and then a perceptive reporter notices that LSD cultists talk a lot about Hinduism and Buddhism. They are interested in something called Zen, and they like to read *The Tibetan Book of the Dead*. But the implications of all this are not pursued; no effort is made to explore or explain the Eastern ideas that hold such fascination for the drug takers. The newspapers report that young drug users are in revolt; they do not say precisely what values are challenged by that revolt, and they do not say what alternatives exactly are offered by the drug movement. This is partly the fault of the cultists themselves—"mumblers about Reality," a *Life* reporter called them—and it is also due in part to the ineffable character of the psychedelic experience. But it is the fault, too, of the press. It is easy to see why the attractions of LSD seem so inexplicable to those puzzled adults who get all their information from the newspapers. There is one LSD question that is rarely asked in the press, and when it is asked it isn't answered in any depth. In the case of psychedelics, many reporters seem to remember only Who? What? Where? and When? They forget the most important question of all, which is Why?

One split-off of this has been the emergence of the underground press to represent the non-straight viewpoint—the San Francisco *Oracle*, the Berkeley *Barb*, the *Seed* in Chicago, and the *East Village Other* in New York, to name but a few. These improbable newspapers even have their own Underground Press Syndicate (UPS) to service them with news and features. Colorful sheets, sometimes highly original in their content and design, they are of course just as much out of balance on the one side as the regular press is on the other. But if nothing else, they indicate that newspaper readers abhor a vacuum just as much as nature does, and reporters who are still concerned about the fifth W might find a few clues in the pages of the underground journals. (I did like the classified ad I saw in one of them: "You're welcome. St. Jude.")

Recently, a modification in press attitudes seems to have occurred, with the development of a distinct drug subculture focused in such areas as San Francisco's Haight-Ashbury, New

York's Greenwich Village, and Chicago's Old Town. The newspapers in these cities have been fascinated by the psychedelic hippies, and at times the fascination has verged on obsession. In New York, the *Times* has devoted many columns of newsprint to their doings, and in San Francisco, the *Chronicle* sent a bearded reporter out to spend a month prowling the acid dens. (You guessed it: "I Was a Hippie.") Even the seventy-eight-year-old historian Arnold Toynbee showed up mingling with the flower children of Haight-Ashbury, where he wrote a series of dispatches for the London *Observer*.

In general, the tone of most stories has been sympathetic. United Press International produced a long feature that compared the hippies favorably with their beatnik predecessors, and a similar piece by the Associated Press seemed to agree with the assessment of a San Francisco florist it quoted: "These kids are good kids. They don't steal and they don't fight. But they should wash their feet more often."

Toynbee thought the hippies were just splendid, seeing in them certain similarities to St. Francis. I think seriously that the flowers had a lot to do with taming the savage press—it's hard to bad-mouth a little girl who hands you a posy—but even more important perhaps is the fact that the concentration of amiable hippies has taken the publicity spotlight off Dr. Leary, on whom it had been shining almost exclusively. He's a very nice fellow. But no single individual can dominate a situation without rubbing many people the wrong way, and he is perhaps a trifle old for his role. The kids as a whole come off better.

In any case, the press at times has seemed on the verge of suggesting that the hippies might just possibly have something to say. They have nudged at least a few observers to inquire into their motivations—"Why do they act like that?" —and the newspapers have actually reported a few efforts to answer that question. Toynbee said that the hippies are rebelling against American conformism, which he blamed partly on the Puritans and partly on Henry Ford (a nation of car drivers has become habituated to regimentation by traffic cops, who tell them where and how they may drive). One columnist concluded that hippies ". . . suffer from something the more fashionable sociologists call 'anomie.'" And of course somebody, in this case a psychiatrist, had to drag Marshall McLuhan out of the wings: "We must understand that we are dealing with the first generation raised on TV, and everything is instant. It is a generation that expects instant gratification."

Not very good, so far. But better than nothing.

So much for the newspapers. Summing up, we have suggested that the essentially negative attitude toward LSD in this area may be attributed to three primary factors: (1) no experts, (2) the nature of news, (3) eclipse syndrome. And we have proposed that newspapers may be partly responsible for the bad trips and panic behavior they fill their pages with.

Turning briefly to radio and television, there is little to say, since these media have virtually ignored the drug movement. The one important exception has been the "talk shows," both on radio and television. Some of the talk programs run up to three hours or longer, often with audience participation by telephone, and they have produced many excellent debates and discussions by experts representing every conceivable point of view on psychedelics. In other areas of programing, however, one would never guess that such a thing as LSD existed. I have never seen or heard any reference to it in a dramatic presentation, and that is understandable perhaps when you consider the fire television comes under when it shows a young person smoking even a Lucky Strike. In fact, the only substantial network show I recall on LSD was the CBS documentary, narrated by Charles Kuralt, on the psychotherapeutic sessions at the Spring Grove (Maryland) State Hospital. That was very good. But, also, that was in May of 1966. And, to my knowledge, there has been nothing since.

It is painful to admit that the major magazines have probably done a better job than newspapers in reporting on LSD, and that *Time* and *Life* between them have possibly done the best job of all. Between 1963 and 1967, *Life* carried at least ten pieces on LSD, including an important cover story on March 25, 1966. (Another cover story, on psychedelic art, appeared on September 9, 1966.) *Time* discovered LSD in 1954 and has since published at least eighteen pieces on the drug. Other major stories have appeared in such magazines as *Newsweek, Look, Playboy, Reader's Digest, The Saturday Evening Post, The Nation, New Republic, The Atlantic,* and *Harper's.* In fact I recall the first time I learned about LSD—in a 1963 article by Noah Gordon in *The Reporter* magazine.

With some exceptions, the magazines have plumbed the subject to a far greater depth than most newspapers have. They, too, have given heavy play to the dangers involved—as the *Reader's Digest* saw it, "LSD will remain about as safe and useful as a do-it-yourself brain surgery kit for amateurs" —but they also have been willing to examine psychedelics from other viewpoints, and in general they have treated the drugs with a balanced perspective. To my knowledge, incidentally, *Look* senior editor Jack Shepherd did the one thing journalistic reporters on LSD almost never do: he took the drug himself (and had a detestable trip).

A curious and significant by-product of the fuss over LSD came in 1967 in the form of a widespread effort, especially in the magazines, to give a better image to marijuana, the psychedelic near beer. The proliferation of articles provoked a suspicious complaint from a hippie friend of mine who prefers his fruit forbidden: "Man, are you aware there's a *conspiracy* in the magazines to make pot legal?" And indeed I could appreciate his growing paranoia on the subject; in July alone, *Life, Newsweek,* and *Look* carried stories sharply questioning the wisdom of marijuana penalties, and *Newsweek* devoted a cover story to the issue.

Life has described marijuana as "a mild euphoric drug," adding: "Pot is not physically addicting, nor need it lead to crime, immorality, or stronger drugs."

Newsweek: "Indeed, the prohibitive laws against marijuana in America today, like those against alcohol in the 1920s, have not significantly diminished its use and, in fact, may have increased it."

Look: "The severity of the Federal marijuana law far exceeds the danger of the drug. The law needs an overhaul, with smoking marijauna reduced from a felony to a misdemeanor, as with LSD."

The Nation: "It is difficult to fashion a serious case against smoking marijuana, except that a user will find himself in serious trouble with the police."

New Republic: "The worst thing about marijuana is the laws against it, which should be repealed."

While the magazines outshine the newspapers in reporting on LSD, their coverage is good only by comparison, and nobody could truly grasp all the varied implications of the psychedelics just by flipping through the slicks. In the last analysis, however, anybody in America today who is really interested in the subject can learn what is accurately known about it, which isn't much, by reading both the magazines and the newspapers (underground and above), by listening to the radio and television discussions, by dipping into the large number of books such as this one. And that, perhaps, is all one can ask. As for those who are not really interested, they will resist the best efforts of the media to inform them. As somebody has said, you can't reason people out of an opinion they did not arrive at by reason to begin with.

THE ILLICIT LSD GROUP—
SOME PRELIMINARY OBSERVATIONS

FRANCES E. CHEEK, STEPHENS NEWELL, AND MARY SARETT

There is reason to believe that the illicit use of LSD-25 is widespread and increasing, particularly in the young, well educated, and middle class, though to date only two studies have provided objective information about the situation. Blum and his associates (1964) interviewed twelve members of one illicit LSD group, while Ludwig and Levine (1965) examined the use of psychedelic drugs by narcotics addicts at Lexington. Both these studies focused in large part upon psychological aspects of the problem, such as characteristics of the users, perceived consequences, and so forth. However, illicit LSD use is also of great interest to sociologists, both in terms of the nature and significance of the deviant groups in which the drug is usually taken, and in terms of the social processes involved in the development and course of the career of the illicit user. This paper presents some preliminary observations of illicit LSD groups.

Our investigations to date suggest that while solitary LSD use unquestionably occurs, it is not the prevailing pattern. This may derive in part from the need for supervision because of the unpredictable effects of the drug upon behavior, and in part from problems of access. We have found that LSD tends to be taken in groups of at least two persons, and sometimes as many as twelve or fifteen. The group is likely to consist of a core membership of users, supplemented by hangers-on who may decide to take the drug or not.

Our interest in the nature and significance of these groups associated with the illicit use of psychedelics was sparked by observations we made in the course of clinical investigations of the therapeutic efficacy of LSD with alcoholics (Cheek et al., 1966). We found that when we administered LSD to our patients in group settings, remarkably strong attachments developed between the investigators and the patients, and among the patients themselves, more intense than those arising without LSD and persisting long after the patients had left the hospital. We wondered whether these attachments might not be important in the marked attitudinal and behavioral changes that occurred in the course of therapy.

Sociologists have long recognized and commented upon the significance of such close and intimate relationships in the development and alteration of personality. Cooley (1937) calls small, face-to-face, intimate associations "primary groups" and sees them as the "springs of life." Parsons (1954) comments that it is hard for anyone to change his own behavior or that of others without strong positive emotional attachments.

We were interested to see whether attachments like those we saw in our clinical settings arose in the illicit groups, and how these might be related to changes in attitudes and behavior. We also wished to examine the formation and development of illicit LSD groups, the characteristics of their members, their social structures and modes of functioning, their goals, and their relation with other such groups and with society at large.

We were aware that such investigations of illicit use would

present many difficulties. In the first place, as Blum has pointed out in *The Utopiates* (1964), studies of the use of LSD present special problems of reliability, in that reality distortions may characterize the perceptions not only of the users but also of the investigators. To counteract this, Blum suggested that such studies include informed as well as dispassionate observers. For this reason, the present research team included members who had not taken the drug at all, members who had taken the drug only once in a clinical setting, and members who had taken the drug many times in a variety of settings.

A second problem was that we would have no way of knowing the degree of representativeness of the groups we studied, though we could attempt to sample a variety of the types of groups (oriented toward sex, magic, mysticism, etc.) that our informal explorations suggested.

Thirdly, we did not know whether the LSD users would be willing to be studied, in view of the illegal nature of their activities. Fortunately, we had a very good entree to the situation. A few years before, a member of our research team had been contacted by one of the psychedelic churches. This was followed up with the thought of future studies of illicit use. One contact led to another, and a very good relationship had been established with the psychedelic underground.

The preliminary observations reported here derive from a pilot study conducted in order to test the feasibility of such research and to begin to develop appropriate techniques and instruments. Three groups of illicit users in a northeastern seaboard city were studied. The largest group, which was examined in greatest detail, included seven or ten core members and about twenty-five peripherals. Most of the members were young, well-educated, middle-class homosexuals. The two smaller groups each consisted of a core of three and a periphery of five or six persons, mostly heterosexuals.

Method of Procedure

In the study of the large, homosexual group, several methods were used: (1) informal observations of drug and non-drug activities of the group over a period of one year; (2)

tape-recorded interviews with the three group leaders, in which standardized interview schedules were used to examine the characteristics both of the group and of the individual users; (3) self-administered questionnaires filled in by twelve members of the group. The two smaller, heterosexual groups were studied by means of interviews with the leaders.

The "Inventory of Group Characteristics" was used to collect group data. This was based on Hemphill and Westie's list of group characteristics (1950) and covered such matters as history of development of the group, modes of introduction of new members, types of activities of the group, hedonic tone, intimacy, goals of the group, and so forth.

For the tape-recorded interviews, from which were obtained individual data, "The Inventory of Psychedelic Experience" was developed. This covered such matters as background data (age, sex, etc.), use of drugs (non-psychedelic), and use of psychedelic drugs. Under use of psychedelic drugs were included questions regarding the amount of experience of the person with the various psychedelics, usual dosages taken, frequency of use, settings in which the drug was taken, purposes of LSD use, perceived consequences, attitudes regarding control of LSD, proselytism, and so forth.

Results

A. The Homosexual Group

1. Pattern of Growth

The homosexual group had come into being about one and a half years before the study. It grew out of a large, loosely organized group, all in the age range nineteen to thirty, consisting mostly of female homosexuals who had known one another over a period of years. One of this group began to take LSD in connection with an association with the people around Dr. Timothy Leary at Castalia, and she was very eager to introduce her friends to it. The others were curious, had seen articles about LSD, and heard it was a consciousness-expanding drug. Though somewhat apprehensive, three of them decided to take it with her.

From this nucleus of four, the group of illicit users began to grow. For the first few months, new members derived largely from the original group and from other long-term friends who were curious about the drug. About five or six people were introduced to the drug at this time. However, not all the original group wished to join the LSD group. When asked how those who did not join differed from those who did, our informants replied that these were likely to be people who lived at home and who tended not to be independent in their thinking.

After the first few months, the group suddenly began to grow rapidly as a result of contacts with psychedelic organizations like the Neo-American Church. "Everything began to change. We started to meet new people, we started to want to meet new people. Prior to that we had been solely in contact with homosexuals." Several of the newcomers, mostly experienced users, began to take LSD with the group on an occasional basis. Additionally, old friends who were curious about the drug, or new acquaintances who could be checked out readily, continued to be a source of new members.

The structure of the group now began to change. In addition to the core members who saw one another frequently, a peripheral group emerged who attended the parties irregularly. Some of these took LSD with the group, and nearly all smoked marijuana. At the time of the study, the group consisted of about seven core and twenty-five peripheral members.

2. The Members

Seventeen of the group were female, fifteen were male. The age range was nineteen through forty-five, with a median of twenty-four years, six months. Twenty-one were single, eleven were married. Sixteen had attended college for four or more years, six had had some college, eight had graduated from high school, while the education of the remaining two was unknown. Twelve of the group were professionals (social workers, university professors, school teachers, and so forth), six were artists, dancers, or musicians, seven were students, five were in white-collar occupations, one was a housewife, and one was unemployed.

Seven had participated in the group during most of the one and one half years of its existence, twenty for only about one year, five for less than a year. Seven had very frequent contact with the group, at least once per week with constant telephoning, ten were involved only once or twice a month, and fifteen made occasional appearances.

One had not taken LSD at all, four only once, ten twice, nine from ten to twenty-nine times, six from thirty to ninety-nine times, two more than one hundred times.

3. Homogeneity of Attitudes and Life Styles

The core members of the group were all Jewish and homosexuals, though some of the peripheral members were neither. The group as a whole consisted mostly of young-adult, professional, middle or upper-middle class persons.

One of our informants described the group as ". . . not overrebellious non-conformists. We are pretty strongly individualists." She felt that they were all characterized by a lack of dogmatism in their beliefs, while their political orientation tended to be both liberal and passive. Our informants showed some ambivalence with regard to the desirability of similarity of attitudes and life-style in the group. On the one hand, all seemed to feel that they enjoyed the sharing of their interests, but there were complaints that the situation was too confining. One person felt that the inclusion of more heterosexuals in the group would help to broaden their orientation.

4. Stratification of the Group

The three core members whom we interviewed might be regarded as a coalition of leadership, for they initiated, planned, and organized the activities of the group. Also, they had had more experience with the drug than the others, and status in the group was said to be partly a function of "level of development" in relation to the drug. This was variously defined as "lack of paranoia," "loving more," "insight into our own being," "seeing that choices exist and being able to make them," and so forth.

5. Introduction of New Members

In view of the need for secrecy, because of the illicit nature of the activity around which the group was organized, the introduction of new members presented special problems. While the original major source of new recruits was old and trusted friends, later, when the contacts of the group suddenly expanded, new acquaintances were sometimes intro-

duced. In general, the recommendation of a friend was suffi
cient to check out new members.

One of our informants described how the group locate
new members, as follows:

Usually one or another of us meets somebody who strikes us a
being a particularly beautiful type of person and . . . it's like a who
kind of sharing thing, like wow! you're beautiful, I want to share yc
with my friends and I want to share my friends with you. (Beautif
was defined as "unpretentious," "on our level intellectually," "ho
est," "doesn't try to put on a big act.")

On the other hand,

We would not invite people that are strictly conformists, an
would not invite people who are narrow-minded. We would not i
vite people who have a very middle-class fear of drugs and, quot
addicts, and we would not invite people whom we haven't anythir
in common with.

Potential members were invariably introduced to the grou
at a social occasion and brought into a drug session only late
after an informal consensus of the members. It was not re
garded as necessary to ask permission, though notice was us
ally given beforehand when a visitor was to be introduced
If the visitor was congenial to the others, one of the co
members would slip around his neck a diffraction-jew
necklace of a type originally purchased at Castalia. Then
would be left up to him whether he wanted to continue t
come or not.

If a new member wished to take the drug, he would sa
something like, "Oh, I'd like to take a trip," and the grou
would reply, "Okay" or "Well, no." Before taking the dru
he would be asked to read Leary's *The Psychedelic Experienc*
allowed to observe a drug session, and carefully coached wit
regard to what might happen.

In the beginning, the group felt the whole world shou
be turned on; later they became "very, very, very careful.
On the whole, members were negative to signs of depressio
in the would-be drug taker, to "extreme reactions," and t
those who were "weak personally." One member felt, how
ever, that even "prepsychotics, psychotics, and schizophrenics
might benefit from LSD.

Thus, whereas in its early stages the group actively tried to interest others in becoming involved and taking LSD with them, this pattern had altered by the time we began our study. Our informants felt that a few might still proselytize, but in general, new members were not sought out. "They come because they met us, and they stay if they like us." Some people were said to remain with the group even though they were afraid to take the drug.

6. Types of Activities of Group

This was an informally organized group. No formal records of activities were kept, though some kept notes of the times they had taken LSD and the dosages. Also, there were no regularly scheduled meetings. The group, or part of it, would get together about once a week, but close friends might meet more often and spend much time on the telephone. Drug sessions occurred about once a month; the other meetings were social.

Sessions were usually held at the apartment of one of the three core members whom we interviewed. When the group first formed, ritual played an important part in the taking of LSD. Elaborate ceremony was planned around its ingestion, one such move being to dissolve the sugar cubes in a "common vessel" of tea to be passed among the members. A cornucopia for "natural" foods, and objects such as shells and driftwood, was often placed in the middle of the room; candles and incense were lit, poetry or psychedelic literature read, and Indian music played.

At the time of our study, some ritual was still employed in initiating new members on their first "trip," but the group had become impatient with lengthy preparations. As the capsule had largely replaced the sugar cube, the partaker of LSD now typically tended to pop it in his mouth, and "sit around and squirm and smoke a lot" waiting for the drug to take effect.

Drug sessions could be divided into two categories: (1) work sessions with LSD, and (2) play sessions with LSD.

The purpose of a work, or "housecleaning," session was to enable the individuals to get rid of their psychological "hangups." Such a session, occurring about once a month, was preceded by a week or more of meditation on problems. The sessions were kept small (two to four persons), only one pe[r]son taking a large dose of LSD (250–500 μg), the others tak[k]ing 80–150 μg. This was done so that only one person woul[d] go deeply into himself, the others acting as "guides," wh[o] might function as "mirrors" or a "bridge" between the tw[o] worlds.

Props were almost always used, but "at these sessions yo[u] try to keep the artifacts down, you know, and the music pa[r]ticularly soft and pleasant, and you try not to disturb any[y]body else."

At the beginning, marijuana might be smoked to allay ten[n]sion, and after three or four hours, smoked again to prolon[g] the "high," boost the experience, or break up "repetitiv[e] game patterns."

There was very little verbal communication in this type o[f] session, but psychic communication was felt to be very stron[g] so strong in fact that in one instance a member who wa[s] "going through hell" in one room caused the guide, wh[o] was in another room, to lose her identity altogether. Distress[s]ing as this was to both, the guide let it continue, feeling tha[t] the other had to "work (her problem) through or it woul[d] always be there."

Sessions usually began in the evening, and might last a[ll] night. Afterward, all present would have a meal together a[t] the apartment or a favored restaurant. Then a kind of grou[p] therapy session would take place in which the experience[s] were "interpreted" rather than "analyzed." Sometimes, how[w]ever, the person who had taken LSD therapeutically would no[t] want to discuss it until several days later.

Play sessions were described as looser in structure. Thes[e] were sometimes planned and sometimes arose spontaneousl[y] They might take place anywhere and might include peopl[e] not on LSD. Play sessions quite deliberately had no "ob[b]jective." They were primarily for fun, emphasizing the sen[n]sual. Usually, all would go outside and "just look at th[e] world." Members might take a trip to the country, walk i[n] a park, visit a museum, go to a concert, play, or movie. A[ll] these activities were characterized by a strong feeling of "to[o]getherness." There was a preoccupation with externals, an[d] in contrast to work sessions, emphasis on interaction—co[m] ersation, laughter, "ego play." When inside, the group often played with toys such as kaleidoscopes or plastic bubbles. Like the work sessions, play sessions would invariably end with a common meal.

The members whom we interviewed felt that the original distinction between "work" and "play" sessions was now beginning to disappear. One felt that the two should be combined into a single drug session because ". . . it can be very annoying to be in a session where you're really into yourself and nothing else." Another said,

Usually we find that we accomplish more in terms of psychological development and working through problems at a play session than we will on a work session. This is something that we've only recently discovered. . . . You know, you go after something and chances are you're going to miss it.

We asked about "bad trips." Our informants stated that all members have had moments of fright under LSD, but that only one case of real panic had occurred, and drug-induced psychosis had never erupted in this group. Warmth and reassurance on the part of the guide was thought to be the best way to handle "bad trips" should they occur.

Non-LSD sessions took place at least once a week. These were usually parties held at the home of one of the core members, at which the guests, who might include non-drug friends of the members, would converse, eat, dance, or play with a homemade stroboscope. Alcohol, usually beer or wine, was drunk sparingly by some. Marijuana was always available. DMT also had been tried, but none of these was ever mixed with large amounts of alcohol. The group also enjoyed going to nice restaurants, movies, or plays, without drugs.

All the members of the research team commented on the air of innocent gaiety that seemed to pervade the group. All their activities tended to be at once more childlike and more restrained than those at the alcohol parties typical of this age group. For instance, at Easter, the group regularly had an Easter-egg-coloring party.

If they wanted to smoke pot, they smoked pot . . . and if somebody wanted to paint an egg, they painted an egg, and finally we all got together and decided we were going to scramble all the eggs and eat them, so that we did all together.

7. Hedonic Tone, Intimacy, Potency

The atmosphere of the group was described by all a pleasant and gay, with no fighting and little griping or com plaining. One member described the group as "like a family There's a special kind of love that everyone has for everyon else." The word "love" was frequently mentioned—"there' lots of love and affection around," and affection was expresse physically: "We kiss, we kiss a lot—we're a real kissing group.

On the other hand, physical sex was said not to be a par of their drug experience, while drug-involved mass sex wa apparently rare and hardly ever discussed. An orgy involvin one boy and three girls did once occur spontaneously, how ever, and was said by one (who had not been on LSD a the time) to have been "a beautiful thing . . . very interes ing." Nevertheless, sex-oriented or sado-masochistic group that exist primarily for this purpose were disapproved of.

Our informants all felt that the members of the grou had developed a very intimate knowledge of one anothe However, they stressed the fact that this intimacy was no sought, but just came up in relation to the drug experienc "You can't take LSD with somebody and not know wha they're like inside."

The members we interviewed all felt that this group ha more significance for them than others they had belonge to. Their best friends were in the group, both because the tended to introduce people they were specially fond of to th group—"I love you so I want to share you with my grou and my group with you"—and because relationships tende to become very close in the group. But all stressed the fac that they had outside friends and interests.

8. Group Goals and Shaping of Behavior

At its first drug experience, the goal of the group was mys tical experience, as a result of the Castalia influence of th girl who introduced the others to LSD. This soon shifte to an interest in personality development and growth. " think everybody's goal is to attain a high degree of produc tivity and peace of mind, freedom to make choices in a situa tion." Apart from this general common goal, the individua members had a variety of interests they wanted to explor under the drug. One, a scientist, wanted to examine the cr teria for genius, another to experiment with ESP and telepathy. However, ". . . we have a lot of ideas about what we'd like to do, but we haven't really gotten down to doing anything yet."

One of our informants attributed the interest of the group in personal development to its special character.

I think this group has a particular kind of makeup in its general homosexual background, and I really feel that you have people who are more apt to be interested in changes than you might have in an ordinary, heterosexual group.

The members felt that changes in their homosexual orientation had occurred, and this was described as follows:

The human personality is like a diamond and has many facets, and I think what's happened to me or to Letty* and Matilda by talking to them is that you discover that your homosexuality is just a facet of your behavior and that it's allowed to be a facet that's dominating, and there's no reason for that.

Another member described changes she had seen in the following ways:

Well, first myself. I went back to school and I got a better job. I took a position of authority which I'd never had before, and Matilda went back to school, even though she's teaching. We've definitely increased our activities, very social things and it used to be anti-social things. We used to go out to bars, but now we've been having a lot of home gatherings or we've been going out to some kind of activity, either music or art kind of functions.

9. Attitudes Toward the Law

The group is composed of people who are law-abiding aside from their involvement with LSD and marijuana. There have been one or two who have taken narcotics in the past, an occasional charge of petty larceny, one arrest in connection with picketing, one of prostitution; and most, as mentioned before, are practicing homosexuals. All except the last of these are not generally characteristic of the group.

Their attitude toward the illegality of their drug activity is pretty well summed up by one member, who compares the present legal situation to prohibition. They think these laws both ineffective and unwise, serving only to drive people un-

* Names are fictitious

derground, perhaps into the hands of the Mafia, or to
". . . encourage kids out for kicks or to break the law on prin
ciple."

The group, in fact, tends to ". . . find it amusing tha
something like this should be illegal." Another says, "We'r
breaking a law we don't believe in." And still another: "I'v
taken illegal drugs before and I felt guilty, but I never hav
(a guilty feeling) about LSD; I honestly believe in the drug.

10. Attitudes Toward Society at Large

Our informants reported that most of the members fee
less conflict between their own styles, values, and attitudes
and those of society, than they did prior to taking LSD. Aske
about a tendency to withdraw from the concerns of society a
a result of taking the drug, one member replied: "On th
contrary . . . the only thing it's done is make us more dis
criminating in our choice of friends." She adds that they hav
less compulsion to do things they really don't want to do
and have a clearer perspective on this. Regarding society's goal
and norms, she says she isn't sure what these are any more
but that she is much surer of her own. "And I would sa
(these) are productive and beneficial both to ourselves an
for society in general."

LSD plays a large part in the value system. "Everyon
should experience this thing . . . no doubt it would chang
the whole world."

B. The Two Heterosexual Groups

The two heterosexual groups developed in a similar way
from a nucleus of close friends to a small core plus periphera
members. However, neither of these groups grew large, as th
homosexual group had done.

One group consisted of two men in their mid-twenties, bot
members of the artistic, literary world. Each had had previou
LSD experience. They took the drug together for a perio
of about one year, at which time a homosexual threat ende
the relationship. During this time, eight or nine visitor
participated in drug sessions with the two core members
but most only came once; two others came more than once
but not more than three or four times. By and large, thes

visitors were also involved in the arts, and most had taken the drug before joining the group.

Our informant thought that this group had not grown larger because they were not people "prone to group activities." When taking LSD they did not want to be infringed on by someone else's personality:

Generally I find that most people have a tendency to bring me down, bring the level of experience down, so I don't feel it is desirable for myself to take it in large groups unless I know that we have a strong rapport.

As in the homosexual group, active proselytizing was not a policy.

Most of the time it went this way: Like we were always discussing it with many people, everyone was talking about it, I guess, and we said, "We're going to get some LSD, do you want to get some?" and they'd say, "Yeah, here's my five dollars." And we'd all throw our money in and we'd all get the LSD on the same day. Now some of the people, we'd say, "Okay, we're going to get it today. We're going to take it like Saturday. Do you want to take it Saturday?" and some of them would say, "No, I can't," and they'd take their cube and go home. The others would stay, and it was like a consumers' co-op.

While this sounds rather casual, only those who were "intellectually curious or fairly open and ready to accept" were invited, and not "anybody that looked in any way deranged or was mad or looked violent." Nevertheless, a need for care in introducing new members was not stressed.

Drug sessions almost always took place at the home of the informant, about once every three months, occasionally more often. The drug was usually taken around six on a Saturday morning (when the two had got home from work), orally, without ceremony. The usual dosage was 250 μg, or so they assumed, although our informant had once taken 1500 μg. Various props were used, including Indian classical music, candles, the informant's paintings. The two would then settle down, either talking or silent, almost always with music.

Intimate personal matters were not discussed under the drug or after. There was exploration of self in postdrug sessions, but on a sort of mystical Jungian level. Therapy was not the object of the enterprise for this group. The goal was, in the words of our informant, "The clear light. Total mystic state. God." However, in addition to this mystical interest, one of the purposes of the sessions was to explore telepathic communication and "extrasensory vibratory experiences." One of the men was very interested in black magic and demons, and our informant told us that once, when both were under LSD, "I saw him one day sit there in a chair and change physically into some sort of hissing, spitting, demonlike, catlike, strange thing."

At the close of the experience they usually went out to eat, often macrobiotic food, and ate heartily; if they ate in, it was usually fruits and nuts.

The day after, they were generally tired and would sleep late, after which our informant would usually paint.

The main reason I took LSD was to get ideas for painting, and I always painted afterwards. I felt that it greatly enriched my creative sense.

While the two were taking the drug together, their already close friendship increased—enhanced, our informant felt, by the drug, but ending, as we have indicated earlier, with a homosexual threat. Our informant told us:

When he and I took it the last time, Penny (our informant's girl friend) was in the room and I was very much digging her. I was watching Penny change from a Vermeer into a dwarf, you know, run across the floor, and I was having a great time with that, and Paul apparently felt rejected in a certain sense, and I felt his rejection, though I tried to overcome it, and then he had a homosexual thing going in his own mind which he didn't tell me anything about till later, but I suppose I sensed it . . . as far as mutual sharing the experience, it didn't come off.

The second heterosexual group consisted of two men and the girl friend of one. Our informant and his girl had already taken LSD together when they met the second man, and they introduced him to LSD. During the next six months, till the group broke up when the second man had to leave the city, the three took the drug together. From time to time one or two others took the drug with them, usually people who had not previously taken it. Our informant attributed the lack of growth of the group to the fact that the three core members had developed a sort of private feeling that tended to exclude others.

The members of this group, and the visitors, all were in their twenties, "working people," with some college background but by no means professional. They tended to hold similar religious and political views, and the short life of the group was attributed to this similarity:

The reason, I think, these groups have only lasted a certain amount of time is that the people were very similar, and they exhausted their common experience in a fairly short time.

The major requirement for visitors to the group seemed to be an emotional bond, "people of whom we were fond enough to want to share the experience with," and these people would probably have "a certain openness, not a lot of grasping, a person who wasn't likely to be very demanding of any other person in the group." On the other hand, people would not be brought in ". . . if it seemed likely that there was going to be some personal problem [that] might arise in an LSD session so all their attention would be diverted." The group did not actively try to bring new people in; however, ". . . the group had a sort of rapport and freedom about them that would naturally make other people curious and maybe envious."

The drug was taken every Sunday. As the two men worked at night and got home at two or three in the morning, they would turn on then or get a few hours' sleep first and then turn on. Sessions were usually held in the same place—the apartment of the second man. Concertos by Vivaldi, Indian music, and madrigals were played. No books or poetry were read during the session, though they would always make reference to Leary's *Manual*. Incense and candles were used, and psychedelic jewels served as a centering device.

Our informant and the other man ordinarily took either 250 or 500 µg of LSD; the girl never exceeded a 250-µg dose. On two or three occasions, our informant took 1000 µg.

While the location of the sessions, the times, and the props were always planned, there was no plan made for their content.

Only in the sense that sometimes we'd say that another time
should go to the Botanical Gardens, and there was never any form
area of exploration to concentrate on.

A typical session was described as follows:

We would take it, just casually, not in a ritualistic way, and th
while we were waiting for it to take effect, we usually would separa
out and try to achieve a state of quiet in ourselves. We'd intera
very little. However, while there was very little interaction on a
tional level, there would be a great deal of communication on a su
rational level. We would become well aware of the presence and t
state of mind of the other persons in the group. . . . Then t
group would gradually begin to drift together, and then we wou
sort of discuss what was happening, and we would explore this a
and that area, and after about four or five or six hours we'd do som
thing if we were going to do it, such as going to the Botanical G
dens or bicycling or to a museum.

Though sometimes they went out, all on the dru
". . . usually Sunday in this city is a very harsh experienc
and we'd end up getting back in the house as soon as possibl
because of the harshness and ugliness of what was going o
there." On one occasion, at the zoo, a bad situation arose f
the other man. "There were masses of people, it was on
Sunday, and it frightened him, so that we felt we should g
him out of the zoo as quickly as possible, and once we got
the Botanical Gardens nobody was there, and it was ve
beautiful and we had a nice time."

On a few occasions the one man and his girl would go o
together for sexual experience during the session. This w
described as producing "sexual intensification" and "total em
tional involvement," though our informant reported that h
own sex experience under the drug ranged from impotence
ecstasy. The first was more frequent when he began to a
tempt sex under the drug.

Sessions typically lasted about fourteen hours and the
would eat ritually at the end, about half the time going ov
to eat at one particular place. If at home, they would hav
fresh fruits, bread, wine, and cheese.

The atmosphere of the group was very warm. "It became
very emotional and satisfying unit, a very loving unit." Ou
informant described the goal of the group as follows: "Tryin

to achieve a natural unity with the cosmos and with our-selves."

Discussion

The purpose of this pilot study was to examine the feasibility of studying illicit LSD groups and to begin to develop adequate techniques and instruments for this purpose. We have hesitated about presenting observations so preliminary and little representative. Indeed, our inclusion of information regarding the two smaller, heterosexual groups was an attempt to set in some perspective the material we presented in greater detail on the homosexual group. On the other hand, we decided that such presentation would be useful because of the paucity of objective information in this area. In this spirit, we would like to comment upon what we have observed.

In the first place, all the illicit LSD groups showed different patterns of growth and development, apparently in conformity with the personalities of their core members. The homosexual group grew rapidly and has existed for several years. The two heterosexual groups remained small and went out of existence after a few months, when the core membership was seriously disrupted. In both heterosexual groups, the members we interviewed felt that their groups did not grow larger because they were not "prone to group activities." On the other hand, the homosexual group included in its founding members several very active, energetic, extroverted types.

Each group tended to include persons similarly young, middle class, and fairly well educated, and in each the members were described as being alike in terms of social, political, and religious attitudes and opinions. This similarity was deemed desirable by the users because of the intimate nature of the contact that took place under the drug. On the other hand, it was also felt that some variety in the orientation of the members was desirable in order not to exhaust the common experience of the group. Indeed, the decline of one of the heterosexual groups was attributed in part to lack of variety in the membership.

None of the groups tended to function as active proselytiz-

ers, though the homosexual group reported that they ha
initially acted in this way. Various reasons, apart from th
legal situation, were given for not introducing people casuall
to the drug. This ranged from a sense of responsibility fc
what would happen to the initiates, to a simple disinclinatio
to share so intimate an experience with just anybody. In a
groups, caution was expressed about giving the drug to sever
neurotics or potential psychotics.

All three groups were informally organized, with a sma
core of active members and a larger periphery who partic
pated less frequently. The informality of the three group
was shown by their lack of formal records and regularl
scheduled meetings. It is of interest that while various prop
such as incense, music, and flowers were routinely associate
with drug use in all three groups, in none did a very rigi
form of ritual develop. On the contrary, in the homosexua
group, even the work session/play session differentiation, wit
which they had begun, disappeared in time.

We noted many similarities, such as a common meal afte
the experience, in the three groups. Indeed, we felt tha
none of the groups tended to develop a specific style or "cul
ture" of its own, but that all borrowed heavily from the gen
eral "psychedelic" culture, with little subsequent modifica
tion. We felt it possible that some of the ways in which the
became similar—e.g., food preferences (like most psychedeli
people, the members of all three groups favored fruits, nuts
vegetables, and cheese)—might be related to the effects of th
drug experience itself. Others, like the language patterns (al
used words like "acid," "beautiful," "wow"), probably de
rived in part from interaction with other psychedelic user
and also from exposure to the psychedelic "culture" in the
psychedelic journals and the popular press.

While the groups did not show great eagerness to "turn on"
non-psychedelics, all of them seemed very eager to get i
touch with other psychedelics. In part, these contacts were
made in order to ensure sources of supply. Group member
also greatly enjoyed and profited from sharing informatior
regarding the various drugs available and special methods o
producing interesting effects. In addition, they could gossip
about the psychedelic community and the efforts of the po

lice. These interactions served to develop and disseminate the psychedelic culture.

It is also true that the popular press, with its many articles on the psychedelic group, helped to spread among the groups themselves a knowledge of rituals, language, and habits of the others, so they were able to develop a common style and a sense of identity. It seemed to us that while all the psychedelics differed greatly from the rest of society, they tended to be more like one another in appearance and attitudes than other sections of society did.

We did find variability in the groups with regard to their goals in using the drug, although, probably as a result of Leary's influence, mystical experience was seen, or had at one point been seen, as a goal in all cases. Both heterosexual groups could be described as seeking "the clear light," though one group additionally leaned in the direction of personality growth and the other toward magic and "vibratory experiences." After a very brief flirtation with mysticism, the homosexual group had settled down to self-therapy.

In all the groups, we were told of increased intimacy and closeness related to the drug experience. However, this was associated with different effects in each. One of the heterosexual groups broke up when one of the men became jealous of the other's relation with his girl. In the other heterosexual group, the three core members developed "a sense of unity which tended to exclude others." On the other hand, the homosexual group, which had a more extroverted style, developed considerable freely expressed warmth and intimacy, which was readily shared with outsiders. Also, only in the homosexual group was self-therapy seen as a major purpose, and indeed only in this group did the members report marked personality benefits. Our preliminary observations suggested to us that these benefits were related to the warmth and intimacy of this group.

For instance, a young man who had recently begun to associate with the group told us he had taken LSD about eight times over a two-year period in other contexts. Then, in a state of "fear and desperation," he went off to Florida, where he stayed for about five months. Toward the end of this time, when he was beginning to feel ready to return North in order to begin a new life, he happened to meet one of the core members of the homosexual group, who was visiting Florida. Suddenly ". . . everything changed." He came North, got a job he very much likes, and when interviewed, was happily enjoying the warmth and friendship of the group. He felt that the LSD he had taken in another context had opened him up and prepared him for changes, but only in the warmth of the homosexual group did he begin to realize his potential. It seemed to us that the support of this group, plus its basically conventional orientation, helped its members to develop and maintain conventional lives.

In another case, one of the core members lost his job as a result of being taken to a psychiatric hospital in an LSD panic attack. Becker has pointed out that such a crisis can often be the first step in a frankly deviant career (Becker, 1963). However, this young man simply got himself another job, in which such an item on his record would not cause him trouble. It is also of considerable interest that this panic attack occurred away from the group, when he took LSD with some friends he was introducing to the drug.

It appeared that the illicit homosexual group manifested an LSD therapy situation very like our own hospital program with alcoholics. The illicit setting had the advantage of long-term, intimate follow-up of those who took the drug, but the disadvantages of lack of medical supervision and lack of trained psychotherapeutic guidance. As one of our informants said, "We're not psychiatrists and we're not saviors, and all we can do is love somebody."

We were intrigued by the fact that, as in our therapeutic studies, LSD seemed to have opened up the possibility of life changes, though, in the illicit setting, we may or may not approve the nature of these changes. We had observed an increased interest in heterosexuality, but also in homosexuality. However, the drug seemed to function mainly as a catalyst; a warm and supportive group appeared to facilitate the maintenance of changes. We plan to pursue these matters further in the future.

QUITO, ECUADOR

A controversy is raging because a foot powder named Puluapies was elected mayor of a town of 4100.

A foot-deodorant firm decided during recent municipal election campaigns to use the slogan: "Vote for any candidate, but if you want well-being and hygiene, vote for Puluapies."

On election eve, it followed up its advertising with nationwide distribution of a leaflet the same size and color as the official ballot reading, "For Mayor: Honorable Puluapies."

When the votes were counted, the coastal town of Picoaza elected Puluapies by a clear majority, and dozens of other voters in outlying municipalities had marked their ballots for it.

Front page, San Francisco *Chronicle*,
July 18, 1967

FROM DATA COLLECTION TO PATTERN REC-OGNITION: THE SOCIOLOGY OF THE NOW

IRA EINHORN

"The times they are a-changin'"
Bob Dylan

Preface

The rate of present cultural change, though fast becoming visible, far exceeds the ability and tools of the experts who are attempting to measure it; it is not a measurable quantity. What is happening cannot be easily delimited by the man with perspective who stands without. Only those who are involved have a faint chance of being able to describe the ongoing as it goes on. We can't depend on the past, for that which is now has never been before.

I have been involved with psychedelic substances for ten years, having experimented extensively with LSD since 1959. I have watched the few become many, the casualties mount, the mistakes multiply; yet I feel that those on the moving edge of culture will eventually use these new tools in a way that will utterly transform the nature of human consciousness. The cultural revolution that swept Europe at the beginning of the nineteenth century was created by a small number of people; the present revolution, in terms of actual change, has also been led by a small number—that minuscule percentage of people whom Huxley felt had any influence on the human scene. Yet the stage has changed: what was accomplished in fifty years during the course of the nineteenth century can occur today in six months; this refers to constructive as well as destructive change. To understand the world of the present, we must discard a past that has become increasingly difficult to manage—but awake we must, for the nightmare must not be allowed to go on any longer.

1.

> "There are no more political solutions,
> only technological ones. The rest is
> propaganda."
> Ellul—*The Technological Society*

The social matrix within which any emergent tool inheres will determine the nature of its use. Much more important, however, in terms of long-range prediction, is the means by which the information about the tool is transferred. The mechanical process that breaks down a total situation into discrete units allows for a slow dissemination of partial products along a linear chain, unlike an electrical network, which provides for instantaneous transmission of information within a mosaic structure whose extent is limitless.

In Western society during the past five hundred years, the nature of the transfer of information could be understood by statistical models, based on a linear mode that deals with discrete units; this is no longer an adequate mode of structuring in the age of electricity. The emergence of patterns and the consequent ability to perform the task of pattern recognition must now take precedence over the slow collection of data.

We live in the age of color TV—a constantly shifting mosaic pattern of iconic forms, wherein the emphasis is on surface texture and the interrelation of the forms. The inside of an upper-middle-class department store will give you an idea of what I'm referring to: nothing touches anything in a stylized atmosphere of form and color that slowly lulls the mind to sleep.

Within this matrix, we have recently witnessed the arrival of the chemical age. This age was ushered in by the widespread acceptance of the use of a synthetic substance such as LSD, the taking of which should be looked upon as being of an entirely different order from the use of peyote, marijuana, or any of the other naturally occurring psychedelics. The ingestion of LSD is symbolic of a Gestalt switch requiring a process of understanding that goes far beyond the simple matter of figuring the percentage of the population involved in the activity. A basic paradigm involving behavioral decisions has been altered; the nature of this alteration is the important thing to understand, since the rate of transfer of this pattern, in an electronic age, is instantaneous.

2.

"We have no art; we do everything as
well as we can."
Balinese saying

These substances have become popular at an unusual point in human history: they occur during a period of transition from the mechanical to the electronic age. In fact, for many people they provide the first real introduction to the distinct difference between the "straight" world of mechanical technology and the fragmented world of the mosaic pattern—a world in which constant crossing of the interface between any two sectors becomes a common occurrence. The shock of this encounter between the two cultures—the major interface that must be crossed—created by the emergence of electronic technology, is quickly fashioning a new stage upon which the human drama is being enacted. The content of this new electronic environment is the entire old, mechanical environment; this has been made increasingly obvious by pop art, happenings, and the new environmentalist sculpture.

3.

> "It is not time for reflection, but for
> evocation. The responsibility of the in-
> tellectual is the same as that of the
> street organizer, the draft resister, the
> digger: to talk *to* people, not *about*
> them."
>   Andrew Kopkind—*New York
>   Review of Books*

The age of Aristotelian cathartic art is over—that art that
allowed for the release of dammed-up emotions, returning
the individual to his old environment and his old self, free
of that which had been disturbing him. (Going to church to
get happy.) We are no longer contained within the realm of
the proscenium stage, with its single point of view. We have
proceeded from point of view, which allows one to exercise
his sight or hearing without the need to act; to happening,
which creates a situation of total sensory involvement for a
limited time within a limited space; to total environment—
something that "happens" all the time without any limitations
as to time or space (the continuous theater of the street).

We can see the same progression in the psychoanalytic
world as it moved from individual therapy to group therapy
to marathon (twenty-four-to-thirty-six-hour sessions) to a situation similar to that of Synanon, wherein the encounter goes
on continuously, twenty-four hours a day, until the individual
is converted—Wagner's idea of the *Gesamtkunst* functioning
within a totally controlled environment (Bayreuth) that allows for the experience of conversion. We live in the age of
the true believer.

The stage of catharsis (classical tragedy) developed into
the Wagnerian idea of conversion, wherein the energy is released, then redirected within the structure of the situation.

Brecht's concept of the epic theater is a further stage of
this development—a concept that has influenced Artaud,
Warhol, and any number of psychedelic entertainers. They,
however, differ from Wagner in operating on principles of in-

formation overload and alienation (Brecht's *Verfremdungsaffect*). These principles disturb the individual without allowing for release to occur within the situation, thus forcing him to discharge his energy outside the artistic experience. Art then becomes a type of conversion that forces action upon those who are involved in it, after the artistic experience has ended. These situations become ever more necessary as we move closer to the total technological control that Huxley (*Brave New World*) and Orwell (1984) wrote about. Art becomes the microcosmic means by which we are able to understand and perhaps exercise remedial control over the constantly changing macrocosm.

LSD and the other psychedelics are symbolic of the need for means with which to adapt to this change. They are tools that will become standard means for effecting the transition to the new environment, dispensed with as soon as the user has adapted to the all-at-once quality of the new situation, returned to as soon as the ability to live in this new, turned-on world fades. A way by which the possibility of constantly living in the now could be reactivated.

The psychedelics are new forms of energy, whose use will depend upon the situation in which they occur—hence the careful planning of the research worker interested in investigating a few linear parameters; a deep contrast to the teenager who downs 500 μg of LSD and goes out to a rock concert. One has expectations of particular results; the other wishes to experience new structures. One activity is based on a linear model—the expansion and improvement of an old form, the energy being directed to maintaining the old game; the other activity opens up the individual to manifold experiences which will allow him to create a new game. In this brief illustration lies the crux of the battle between the generations.

4.

"Violent eruption, vulcanism; the patient becomes violent, as he wakes up. The madness of the millennia breaks out: Dionysius is violence."
Norman O. Brown—*Love's Body*

The extremes of both the old and the new environments can't visualize a future or live in the present, and their being-in-the-world is characterized by modes of resonance that move in response to similar vibrations; they are respectively the apocalyptic and the totalitarian mentalities. Neither can envision a future or live in the present; they both want out.

The apocalyptic mentality lives with unbelievable intensity in the continuous present, burning himself out in order to produce a break-through into eternity; he wants his revolution and he wants it now. His desire is for a communion with the entire world, an undifferentiated sense of merging that allows for no distinctions; out of this mode arises the psychopath. His ideal is an anarchic chaos that would be hell on earth. Norman O. Brown's *Love's Body* describes this mode, and figures like Dylan Thomas, Charlie Parker, and Richard Fariña embody it.

The totalitarian mentality refuses to let go at all—like Wagner's dragon Fafner, he sits and possesses. He is continually engaged in protecting what he considers to be his—building walls to close off that threatening outside world, grasping, grabbing, tightening his hold on things. His response exists in terms of one dimension: threat → fear → desire for control; he is the paranoid building the perfect wall. His ideal is a collectivity of individual monads that never touch: Jacques Ellul describes the technology that is producing this extreme in *The Technological Society*, and Herbert Marcuse offers us a look at his psychology in *One Dimensional Man*.

These antipodes reflect the extremes of a battle between linear and mosaic structures, both of which will be totally destructive of all that we hold to be human. In the center, attempting to hold these incongruities together, is the schizophrenic, an adequate reflection of the fragmented world in which he is forced to live: linear parents and teachers, mosaic media.

He exists in the midst of a constant tug of war between two forms that have not been able to find an equilibrium. As the tension mounts, in terms of contradictory information, the individual is led in two directions: psychopathic acting out in order to release some of the excess energy (police violence, Vietnam), and catatonic withdrawal in orler to reduce the amount of stimuli coming into the system (the dropout, hippies doing their thing in Haight-Ashbury).

5.

> "Gaston Bouthoul, a leading sociologist of the phenomenon of war, concludes that war breaks out in a social group when there is a 'plethora of young men surpassing the indispensable tasks of the economy.' When for one reason or another these men are not employed, they become ready for war. It is the multiplication of men who are excluded from working that provokes war. We ought to at least bear this in mind when we boast of the continual decrease in human participation in technological operation."
>
> Ellul—*The Technological Society*

Dropping out, into criminality, insanity, or deviant social action from the point of view of the linear world, is increasingly becoming the province of the middle class. It is indicative of one major fact: the characterological model that has controlled Western thought since the Renaissance is rapidly losing its efficacy. The struggle for individual distinction through differentiation and separation is no longer able to structure individual energies in a socially useful manner. The nineteenth and early twentieth centuries explored individuality[1] and all its ramifications, ending in a morass of alienation that we are just beginning to understand.[2]

My generation is tired of defining man in terms of his differences; it wishes to look at another in terms of common factors: that which we can share, that which will bring us

[1] Morse Peckham's *Beyond the Tragic Vision* is a detailed historical study of this problem, concentrating on the nineteenth century.

[2] Kenneth Keniston's *The Uncommitted* is a brilliant study of this problem as it applies to my generation—those born since 1940.

together, rather than that which isolates. The mind divides;
the body unites; hence the neocortex and its environmental
correlates are being tempered by the wisdom of similar bodies. We're learning to touch again in order to escape the hypnotism of overcerebralization. The danger in overemphasizing this can be seen in crowds:[3] touch without responsibility and the ability of a psychopath such as Hitler to utilize their energy.

Social bonds must be sundered through deviation before new community can arise. The energy of many individuals must be directed against the old before there is the realization of a common enemy (the enemy of my enemy is my friend). The step toward a new communion is not far away from this awareness.

It is difficult to communicate how rapidly this is happening to those who are not included within the network of the change. Electricity is here, and those of us who are plugged into it are vibrating with an intensity that our elders can't see or hear.

The development of the Beatles and the entire popular music field in the past few years is reminiscent of the 1909–14 era, when an entire artistic generation rose to heights that have not since been equaled; yet there is a great difference, for Stein, Joyce, Picasso, Matisse, and Schönberg were speaking to an extremely small audience: the pop people are directing their statements to the entire world. The increasingly critical attitude of this new elite[4] with respect to the older

[3] See Elias Canetti, *Crowds and Power*, for a deeper understanding of this most complex of modern problems.

[4] The following news story, illustrating this point, appeared during the end of July in the San Francisco *Chronicle*:

> Beatle George Harrison yesterday hit back at a member of Britain's ruling Labour Government for criticizing fellow Beatle Paul McCartney for taking drugs.
> In Parliament Friday, Minister of the State at the Home Office Alice Bacon said she was horrified to read that McCartney said he discovered God through the hallucinatory drug LSD.
> Yesterday, Harrison flew into London with

generation, and their ability to dramatize their feelings, are rapidly changing the consciousness of an entire generation.

6.

> "We want our revolution, and we want it now."
> Popular song

America has managed to avoid an actual revolution even though there has been much talk about it since the power shifted from a European elite to an American elite back in '76. The image of that shift galvanized popular movement after popular movement, in other places, as the American revolutionary spirit slowly calcified and then died. After 1918 the spiritual center of the revolution shifted toward Russia: she has gone through the same changes as the United States. The battle between Stalin and Trotsky was essentially over the point of a nationalistic or an internationalistic revolution; as the recent split with China demonstrates, the nationalistic Stalin won. China is now the center of those downtrodden internationalist hopes, and Mao's recent appeals to his own people lead one to believe that they are still alive.

> his wife, actress Pattie Boyd, from Athens, where they have been vacationing with McCartney and a third member of the Beatles, John Lennon.
> Harrison said: "As far as I am concerned, these people are ignorant. I have worked out my life, and it is up to them to work out their own."

This same tone can be seen in the full-page ad that the Beatles and a number of other prominent British citizens took out in the London *Times* concerning the laws on marijuana.

7.

> "I ain't gonna work on Maggie's farm
> no more."
>   Bob Dylan

Bob Dylan was the symbolic center of the first phase of this alienation. He was able to externalize the disgust of an entire generation for values that have become extremely hypo critical. We no longer wish to eat the menu. His changes have almost singlehandedly created the entire context of contempo rary popular music, although the recent shift to the more positive vibrations of the Beatles and the San Francisco sound indicates an audience that is no longer satisfied with expres sions of constant sadness and disgust. These positive vibra tions have been greatly enhanced by the use of the variou psychedelics.

The utter destruction of the Haight-Ashbury, which has now become that terminal sewer that seems to lurk at the end of every American social experiment, as a result of its enormous media coverage and consequent commercialization somewhat dampens this optimism, although there is ever indication that the original spirit has been rapidly trans planted throughout this country and Europe.

California is quickly becoming overpopulated and over extended financially—the paradise has a serpent lurking in the garden.

But this shift to the more-positive aspects of experience is a significant one; for we are slowly learning to be peaceful, a necessity in this tense, overcrowded world. The undercurrent of these feelings is a strong revival of the religious instinct with the great emphasis being placed upon the Eastern re ligions and their sure sense of the necessity of maintaining an adequate ecological balance with the natural world. This factor is in strong contradistinction to our Western urge to destroy the natural world.

This is concomitant with a psychological shift from Freud ian (masculine, father) to Jungian (feminine, mother) psy chology among psychedelic people. The mother is returning.

to prominence, and the father is rapidly disappearing from the American home:

Throughout their responses, the conclusion was inescapable that the wives cared far more about what their husbands *did* than about what they *were*, as persons. About one third of the women not only put their own role as mothers first, but indicated that the husband was essentially outside the basic family unit of herself and her children.[5]

The psychedelics are quickly becoming standard tools in the process of self-education that more and more of our youth are undergoing. They are similar to the autotelic toys that Dr. Sheridan Speeth[6] has developed, in that they can be used with a minimum amount of instruction, thereby freeing the student from the restricting bonds of an educational system that is becoming increasingly obsolete. The age of constraint has come to an end, making it mandatory to shift from negative to positive reinforcement in the education of any individual. This should not frighten us, for it does not mean that the id has taken over; it refers to the loosening of the bonds of the superego and a consequent dependence on the self for values and decisions. God is dead, and so is the father. The obsolescence of the educational system has been greatly exacerbated by the generational war, which is making it more difficult for the young to identify with anyone who is markedly older than they. This has almost entirely destroyed the vertical transmission of value (Dad and Mom are enemies, so I deny them and everything about them), placing an overwhelming load on the peer group, which is now the major

[5] Marya Mannes, New York *Times*, November 15, 1965.

[6] "If the stereotyping of responses and the suppression of novelty in the use of material are to be avoided, information should be taught with only so large a level of motivation as needed to maintain relevant activity. Both monkeys and men are motivated by curiosity, and show continued activity as long as they have an effect on the surroundings. This is called playing or research in different contexts. It has been shown that by making an irrelevant reward contingent on performing some action which had previously been performed 'for fun' one destroys its intrinsic ability to motivate. This suggests that the 'educational' toy is preferable to the irrelevant social rewards of the schoolroom as a support for the early learning process. There are deleterious effects produced by doing the right thing for the wrong reason." Quoted in the *East Village Other*, July 1–15, 1967, from *Toys That Teach*, Dr. Sheridan Speeth.

educating force in the country, and ruining the sense of trust that is an absolute necessity for the adequate functioning of any society.

This shift is indicative of a major social crisis, for it indicates an unconscious desire to escape from history (our present nightmare)—sensible in an age that bombards an individual with a wide range of choice just as he is supposedly beginning to solidify his sense of identity.

This is leading a great number of the psychedelic generation to adopt modes of existence that reduce the range of choice. They are forming tribes and re-establishing rites of passage that enable them to create a stable identity within a context that is manageable. The mythic mode of addressing the world is upon us again.

The parent is enemy, and the progressive change in attitude toward these individuals during the past forty years is quite instructive in gauging where individual energy is directed. When the Freudian ethos was just emerging in this country, the analyst had to work many hours in order to convince the individual that he possessed a deeply repressed hatred for his parents. Ten years later, this tension had become a part of the conscious process, being experienced as a neurotic symptom. Now it has become a structural part of the personality, expressing itself as a character defect.

There are two further stages of this process: one, violence directed against the parents, the father in particular, which is slowly freeing an entire generation from the past, has emerged in rock song, short story, and action; the other, envisioned in Philip Rieff's *The Triumph of the Therapeutic* in terms of the entire society, is one of total detachment. As soon as he is able, the child will go on his own way with hardly a glance backward. This trend indicates a flow of energy from the family to structures (groups, extended families, communities) that will utilize the energy in a fashion that is more satisfactory to the individuals involved.

8.

> "Violence has no place in America!
> Anybody who preaches violence should
> be shot like a dog."
>> Ira Blue on KGO Radio, San Fran-
>> cisco

The danger of this newly generated violence—a problem faced by the society in its entirety, as psychoanalysis is telling us (people are increasingly troubled with problems of aggression rather than the standard problem of sexuality—a question of release rather than one of symbolic transformation), has been dramatically presented to us in the July 1967 *Esquire*. There, the very presentation of the problem indirectly serves as an advertisement for the thing it supposedly is condemning. This is a result of the extreme amount of free-floating anxiety that is presently afflicting our culture. This anxiety is able to localize itself around a vast range of behavioral paradigms; anything that is advertised proclaims, "Be like me," and will be copied. This is another way of saying that there is no negative advertising.

The attempt to handle the drug problem in the schools is an excellent example of the failure to understand this fact. The constant publicity that marijuana and LSD have received, although a vast amount of it has been extremely pejorative, is the single most important reason for its widespread use. In an atmosphere of generational disaffiliation, the quickest pathway to an adolescent action is an adult "No."

The previous generation (a generation is now from three to ten years) was plagued with sexuality and its attendant problems. This generation has accepted the sexual revolution and is confronted with a much more difficult problem—violence, and its counterpart, religion.

"My own belief is that . . . these new mind changers (the psychedelic drugs) will tend in the long run to deepen the spiritual life . . . , and this revival of religion will be at the same time a revolution . . . religion will be transformed into an activity con-

cerned mainly with experience and intuition—an everyday mysticism underlying and giving significance to everyday rationality, everyday tasks and duties, everyday human relationships."
Aldous Huxley

The religious revival, which Timothy Leary is attempting to symbolize in rather outmoded ways, is a distinct product, along with violence, of information overload—something I mentioned a little earlier. Sex has become so available, along with other physical stimulants, that a point of satiation has been reached in a number of people (boredom is a phenomenological way of describing this psychological mode of being). This can produce two characteristic patterns: acting-out, with the tendency toward crowds and mass behavior, as a result of the modern context; and withdrawal into a low-stimulus environment, leading the individual in the direction of religious experience.

This return to religion in the face of our highly technological society will eventually produce the greatest shock, for the tepid beliefs of our conforming parents are about to be replaced by fanatic adherence to ways of being that closely resemble the messages of Christ in the Gospel of St. John, the Buddha, Lao Tzu, and other great men whose words are mouthed and then quickly neglected as soon as the words are asked to become action in a situational context. What will the country do with a hundred thousand teen-age Buddhas?

These impulses have certainly been accelerated by the advent of psychedelics, but those who are familiar with the course of cultural history in the past hundred years will not be surprised at either the attitudes or their offshoots in art and other forms of behavior. What was happening to a small group of Europeans from 1860 to 1920 is now occurring in America on a vast scale.

A percentage of our mental institutions must be changed into *ashrams*,[7] allowing the individual who has been disturbed by his psychedelic experience to complete his trip in a

[7] Meditation rooms should be set up in all our big-city hospitals, using, where possible, the techniques that Joe Kamiya has developed in the conditioning of EEG patterns at Langley Porter Neuropsychiatric Institute in San Francisco.

supportive atmosphere,[8] thus creating positive instead of negative identities on a model proposed by Erik Erikson for the handling of juvenile delinquents. This would allow the society to use its available sources of energy instead of subverting them, thus protecting itself against this segment of the population through the use of non-violent means—an obvious necessity, for direct physical contact within the confines of this country must result in damage far beyond our ability to sustain or afford: Newark and Detroit are adequate demonstrations of this fact.

10.

> "The time has come," Tate said, "for
> honesty to overshadow everything else."
> Negro worker in response to riots

A new kind of honesty is slowly appearing, a tribal kind that will eventually do away with the unconscious—Eskimos talking about last night's dream, hippies discussing their last acid trip—everything up front. This is also a product of our electronic technology, which is providing us all with external examples of what we thought to be buried deep within: the unconscious is now out there instead of in here. An example on a highly public level was the dissenting opinion written by Justice Douglas in a homosexual case, wherein he refused to vote for the deportation of a man on the basis of an action that was regularly engaged in by men who were high up in both the legislative and executive branches of the government.

These factors, somewhat influenced by psychedelics, in combination with the general turmoil loose in the country, have created a situation that is explosive.

People who are classically trained or possess any sense of history are willing to accept a large amount of treachery and dishonesty—unlike those without historical models; to the latter, it looks and feels bad; they will be compelled to hurl their bodies into the breach. They know only the moment, and

[8] R. D. Laing extends this concept to all so-called mental illness in his *The Politics of Experience*.

wish to feel good. If they don't, they will act to bring about this sense of well-being. *Now* is their cry. The free speech movement at Berkeley and the statements of Mario Savio are an obvious example.

The analogical method of thought is alien to those who do not possess historical training, for they have no basis for comparison; instead they use a situational logic that might seem crude to their more-educated betters, though their responses certainly speak of a more honest confrontation with things as they are. They do not wish to have their wounds dipped in the healing pages of time, for they do not wish to make history; they want to live *now!*

This situational thinking is deeply mirrored in the recent development of hip slang, which is reminiscent of Old Norse in both its extreme brevity and its situational nature (words take on meaning in respect to the total context in which they inhere): "freak" is an example of a word being used by the hippies in a way that is absolutely opposite to the way it is used by the normal culture.

11.

> "We know everything except how to
> make democracy work and what to do
> with ourselves. We know everything ex-
> cept what is most important for us to
> know."
> Robert Hutchins

The erosion of middle-class values is quite obvious to anyone who has been involved in the psychedelic scene, for the desire for psychedelics is running high among many whose entire life is "straight." They have little to sustain them, for they live on within the skeleton of a structure that has become much too confining, projecting the outward manner of a life that no longer lives within—empty as the latest TV show, valueless as last night's plastic dinner. They hope to use LSD and other psychedelics to refashion a world that is quickly collapsing. The downfall of the work-oriented Protestant ethic adds to an already difficult situation for the predominantly middle-class people who are involved in this shift from postponed to immediate gratification—not the future, *now*. Both the upper and the lower classes escape this problem, for they are used to obtaining immediate gratification, the upper class using it as a means of demonstrating their continual mastery of the environment, having been trained since childhood in means of doing this (the constant round of dancing, boating, golfing lessons); the lower class taking its pleasure when it is available (our crowded Friday night bars), for who knows what tomorrow will bring?

The shift of a middle-class individual to the ethic of immediate gratification produces an immense burst of energy (the release of all that energy stored away for future use), but after a while a monumental boredom sets in, since the techniques of constantly generating experiences that produce immediate gratification are just not available to this class of people.

The middle-class pot scene is a perfect example of this kind of behavior. As pot filters into a middle-class scene, parties shift from being occasions at which pot is smoked to the reason for which parties are held. Pot is no longer used as a means for improving communication, but as a means by which communication is impeded. The group is together, and nothing happens. Here we face one of the major problems of our time, that of leisure. A partial solution has been provided by the emergence of new craft and artistic movements (the desire to do something, no matter what, well). This is the situation that originally activated the entire Haight-Ashbury area. It is one way in which the hippie movement is very much in the vanguard of contemporary culture, for as automation increases, we are all going to be faced with the problem of occupying ourselves. Those, like the hippies, who are learning today to be the artists of their own beings, have a decided head start on the rest of the culture.

12.

"Today we can be relevant only if we
are Utopian."
Shane Mage

The United States is the most powerful nation the world
has ever known; what it does today, the world will do tomorrow. Our culture (used in the anthropological sense) is being
imported by every other nation in the world at an ever-
increasing rate; the models we provide will determine the
fate of tomorrow's world.

In this respect the psychedelic vanguard is attempting to
provide both a model for others and an answer to an important question: how are we to treat those who will not be able
or allowed to work in our rapidly automating society? The
obvious answer is a guaranteed annual income[9] that would
pay a living wage to everyone for doing what he chooses. This
would allow many people to spend a great deal of time re-
constructing their environment,[10] so that our cities can eventually become places that are desirable for human habitation.
Gunnar Myrdal, in his *Challenge to Affluence*, implies just
this.

13.

"Small communities vibrating in the
woods, they are the important thing."
Quentin Fiore

Some aspects of the psychedelic community are struggling
to provide an alternative in art, economics, and community

[9] See *Free Men and Free Markets*, by Robert Theobald, and *The
Guaranteed Income*, edited by Theobald, both Doubleday Anchor
books, for an extended discussion of this most important concept.
[10] This idea will shortly go into effect in riot-torn areas of Jack-
sonville, Fla., where Negroes will be paid to reconstruct their own
destroyed and dilapidated areas.

organization that will allow for a more positive presence to enter the arena of American life.

Such groups as USCO, the Diggers, and Drop City were the beginning of a trend that might provide positive alternatives to those who have learned the importance of small groups, ecology, and ritual. They are still too recent to provide anything else but hope, yet their spirit is a rare brightness in the midst of a rather bleak picture.

What follows is a partial description of the present, with a few suggestions, no salvation; for the days of our sentimental lusting after finality must come to an end. There is no end; it all goes on, within you, without you, with you, without you.

Epilogue

"As cultures die they are stricken with the mute implacable rage of that humanity strangled within them. So long as it grows, a civilization depends on the elaboration of meaning, its health is maintained by an awareness of its state; as it dies, a civilization opens itself to the fury of those betrayed by its meaning, precisely because that meaning was not sufficiently true to offer a life adequately large. The aesthetic shifts from creation of meaning to the destruction of it."

Norman Mailer

"As for me, I answer that we are all in a state of frightful hypertension."

Antonin Artaud

"A ritual approach is a historical approach. Ritual is, simply, a re-enactment of the past. The great revolutions in human society are changes in the form of symbolic representation; reorganizations of the theatre, of the stage for human action."

Norman O. Brown

History is a nightmare from which we have awakened.

"The methods now being used to merchandise the political candidate, as though he were a *deodorant*, positively guarantee the electorate against ever hearing the truth about anything." (my italics)

Aldous Huxley, 1958

PART IX
CONCLUSION

PSYCHEDELICS AND THE FUTURE

HUMPHRY OSMOND AND BERNARD S. AARONSON

Those older men and women exercising structural and moral authority (Paterson, 1966), often called collectively the Establishment, have been alarmed by psychedelics for rather less than five years. Their attitude might be described in the terms Aneurin Bevan used for an old man approaching a young bride: ". . . fascinated, sluggish, and apprehensive." The impetuous young, however, always at the heart of any anti-establishment movement, rush in with all the rash ardor of Romeo and Juliet. Medical men, though less worried about morals or legality, are properly concerned with the health of the young lovers, and have been debating, not without acrimony, whether the entrancing psychedelic bride is a delicious and sexy houri or a poxy doxy.

This fascination of older folk with psychedelics and the climate attached to them becomes evident in the propaganda devoted to them by many government agencies, professional associations, and other interested people. While this has been aimed ostensibly at discouraging the young from taking or continuing to take these substances, the means employed seem unlikely to achieve such an end. The cause of pornography has frequently been well served by those whose strident warnings abjured others from seeking what, until then, they had hardly noticed. Public men have, quite unwittingly, by their ignorance, evasion, and downright lies, egged on their children and grandchildren to explore these experiences. It appears sometimes as if they were trying to discredit themselves in the eyes of the young. It may not be their intention, but it seems to be their achievement.

Our connection with this intergenerational controversy began about sixteen years ago, when one of us, after a troubled night, was standing at a table stirring a glass of water in which silvery white crystals were dissolving with an oily slick. Would it be enough or too much? He was uneasy: he would be disappointed if nothing happened, but what if the mescaline worked too well? Suppose he poured half of the full glass into an adjacent flower vase? He did not relish the possibility, however remote, of finding a small, but discreditable niche in literary history as the man who drove Aldous Huxley mad. His fears proved groundless. Although the bitter chemical did not work as quickly as he had expected, in due course it etched away the patina of conceptual thinking.

Much has happened since that smogless May morning in Hollywood. Neither Aldous Huxley nor he would have predicted that *The Doors of Perception* (1954) was going to have such an immense impact on an ever-increasing number of people. Those substances, then known as hallucinogens or psychotomimetics, and which he later called psychedelics (Osmond, 1957b), have, for good or evil, become far more widely known and no longer the concern merely of the specialist and scholar. They are part of our vocabulary, a source of both vexation and inspiration.

Less than ten years after the senior author's spring visit to Hollywood, Pandora's box was unexpectedly opened. Since then, members of the Establishment have been sitting on the lid of the empty box, unaware that this posture is both undignified and futile. It is the fate of establishments to be taken by surprise in spite of ample and repeated warnings. Once they have become aware that something is amiss, they often act precipitately, with little forethought or caution, and transform a minor inconvenience or even possible benefits into catastrophe. There was plenty of warning that psychedelics were apt to be of interest to people and also to become more available so that this long-standing human taste could be indulged more easily. It required no gift of prophecy to recognize this, for history shows that man has been an inveterate experimenter with chemicals, usually derived from plants, that make him happier or livelier, or alter his perceptions and awareness. In his sumptuous and magnificent book *Soma: Divine Mushroom of Immortality* (1969), for example, R. Gordon Wasson, the mycologist-scholar, has shown convincingly that the *Rig Veda*, one of the oldest and greatest of man's religious works, devoted about one tenth of its collection of over one thousand psalms to celebrating the plant god Soma. Wasson, with wonderful persistence, caution,

nd intuition, makes a good case for soma being the mush-
oom *Amanita muscaria*, or fly agaric, the classic toadstool of
he birch forests of the world. Psychedelics are a very ancient
nd influential human interest.

What has the Establishment been doing about them? If
ne had listened only to its members from a recent president
n down, one might have been convinced that psychedelics
ad no future at all because of the development of ever-
rowing and increasingly specialized law-enforcement agen-
ies to remove the nuisance permanently. In the past year or
wo, the tone has changed somewhat, along with other over-
ptimistic estimates. On the other hand, if one listened only
o supporters of the psychedelic movement, one might be led
o suppose that an age was borning in which from earliest
hildhood, and possibly the prenatal state, we would all be
xposed to the delights and virtues of wholly beneficial sub-
tances. The facts do not support either of these extreme posi-
ions, but extreme positions rarely depend on facts. Long be-
ore the official Establishment had asked itself what sort of
roblem it might be facing, legislation was being prepared,
ills hurriedly passed, statements of an alarming kind made,
nd vigorous legal and police action taken. This was not admirable, but it was no more admirable of the psychedelic
movement to imply that there were scarcely any dangers at-
endant on these remarkable substances and that we should
ll hasten along the road to the "joyous cosmology," taking
nything anyone offered, and trusting it would be enough,
nd not too much.

The Establishment's posture is not difficult to understand,
or it is that of all establishments everywhere when faced
vith innovation. It consists in saying, "No, you don't. Father
(or Grandfather) knows best. Be good and do as you are told,
or if you don't, it will be the worse for you." Before planning
nd passing legislation or developing new policing proce-
lures, it might seem prudent to assess the effectiveness of
uch actions, and consider whether police activities might
ot have unintended consequences as bad as or worse than the
vils to be remedied. This is especially true in the United
States, where prohibition, with all its admirable intentions,
nerely provided a golden opportunity for gangsters to become

multimillionaires and spread the habit the legislation was in
tended to curb. The most likely outcome of prohibition i
the early twenties was that, since many people did not fee
that drinking alcohol was immoral, even though it might hav
become illegal, the law would be widely subverted. Criminal
would then have an opportunity to provide these disaffecte
citizens with their needs. The police would be liable to b
corrupted, the law itself brought into disrepute, and becaus
most people would come to feel that prohibition itself is
farce, they would tend to consider that the law is a racket
too. This is a high price to pay for an unattainable socia
benefit.

Other legislation aimed at preventing people from takin
substances, such as psychedelics, that they want to take shoul
surely be examined in this context. As we have noted, this i
an interest that men have pursued for millennia with grea
persistence and in a variety of ways, ranging from self-inflicte
tortures and austerities to taking dangerous substance:
Drugs are only one of many possible ways of achievin
these experiences, and are by no means the most objec
tionable from a medical viewpoint. From earliest times, psy
chedelics have been regarded as strange and sacred and hav
been part of many great religious ceremonies. They are cer
tainly as enduring and interesting for mankind as alcoho
although, since the rise of modern agriculture, alcohol ha
been probably easier to obtain. On the other hand, cannabi
has been used for many centuries. It may not be a simpl
matter to head off people's interest in psychedelics; it has no
been easy to head off interest in alcohol. Had it been possibl
to prevent people from making alcoholic drinks, prohibitio:
would have been feasible. As it was, everyone could make hi
own fermented drink in the bathtub, and before long, th
well-meant laws to curb drinking had become meaningles
and socially harmful.

In 1966, the government did not seem to have considere
these early experiences much, and appeared to believe tha
by preventing Sandoz from manufacturing and distributin
LSD to research workers, the problem would soon be resolved
Indeed, one of us was told by an aide of the late Senato
Robert F. Kennedy that the ex-Attorney General of th

United States was surprised to learn "that preventing Sandoz from selling LSD (which, of course, they were not doing, but giving it away only to accredited researchers) would not solve the problem." Even though Senator Kennedy was a young, active, and unusually well-informed man, he was ignorant of this, although he quickly acquired the necessary information. The elderly men who govern most countries apparently failed to ask or have impressed upon them the questions facing those who wish to control the use of psychedelics.

During World War II, British and American intelligence services briefed their generals by first giving an opinion as to what was most likely to happen, followed by a statement of what they considered the best possible outcome in the circumstances, and finally, the worst possible construction. The general officer, knowing the conclusion of his intelligence service, could then make his own decision, basing it on optimism, pessimism, or a middle way, as he saw fit. Suppose it had been our task to advise statesmen on the future of psychedelic substances, what would we have told them, assuming that we knew that they were already more or less limited to a policy of control? From this point of view, the best possible thing that could happen would be for people to lose interest in psychedelics once and for all, and for the sources of supply to dry up forever. The worst that could happen for the Establishment would be for supplies of psychedelics to become greater and easier to make in a climate of sustained or increasing interest, thus producing a situation resembling prohibition at its worst.

How would these two extreme estimates relate to the most likely outcome? It would be surprising if an interest so long sustained ever disappears completely. Indeed, our age is one in which interest in these matters seems more likely to increase. Today, at least in North America and Europe, there are larger numbers of highly mobile young people, many of them fairly well-to-do, than ever before in history. Most have been reared with less severity than previous generations and have largely escaped the terrible blows that death, illness, starvation, and poverty frequently inflict on the young. They are sufficiently uncowed by the world to be highly critical of how it is run, and have the energy, time, and opportunity to express dissatisfaction and explore new ways of improvin matters. Their education has taught them how to use l braries and other modern information-retrieval systems. Mar of them became interested in psychedelics in the early si ties, and while this preoccupation may fluctuate, it seems ur likely that it will disappear completely. The interest of th Indians in drugs survived the full force of the Spanish I: quisition, and it is unlikely that even the severest legislato intend to emulate that mighty institution in policing the children and grandchildren.

In addition, with regard to the control of the substanc themselves, more have been discovered and rediscovered du ing the past decade and a half than in any similar period i history. It seems likely that more will be found during th next ten years. Some of these will be discovered in plants an others synthesized. Every discovery makes it easier to sugge not only new places in which to look for active substance but also new ways of making them. We predict that withi the next twenty-five years, and perhaps sooner, simple pro esses will be discovered by which reasonably safe psychede ics can be made in any kitchen or basement with materia available in stores, pharmacies, and fields or gardens. Son believe the best way to avoid these dangers would be to sto all research on psychedelics. In our opinion, this would be ol jectionable, since these substances have great interest for ps chology and psychiatry and since there is, as we have show here, growing evidence of their therapeutic usefulness. would also not succeed in stopping the clandestine exper ments in the synthesis or use of these substances, for fo bidden fruits not only taste sweeter, but develop an esoter interest. Presumably this "occult" science, because it wou be "illegal," would not be published in official scientific jou nals. A sort of underground science would develop, which : least would be deplorable, and might be very dangerous.

In our imaginary briefings, the statesmen would be tol that the most likely outcome during the next decade woul be that the interest in these substances would be maintaine though it is likely to fluctuate from year to year. Although number of new psychedelics will be discovered, there is n convincing evidence that the era of "bathtub" psychedeli as yet arrived, allowing them to be made in ease and safety at home. Should this occur, the resulting situation will resemble that of prohibition.

Statesmen must surely ask themselves whether it is wise to invent new crimes or inflate misdemeanors into matters of great importance. The roster of criminal law is large; by adding new laws that are difficult to enforce, respect for the law may be decreased. Certain kinds of new laws may be expensive luxuries that societies in the course of change simply cannot afford. We believe that the interest in psychedelics will be maintained in the foreseeable future. If police and similar agencies devote much of their energy to controlling the substances, the overt interest may become less conspicuous. Prosecuting people does not necessarily change their opinions, but may invest forbidden activity with glamour and make those undertaking it discreet. It is said that crime has been increasing greatly in recent years, and one wonders whether this is a propitious time to add a whole new series of crimes to the burden of an already overladen police and magistracy.

Already there are laws of such severity on the statute books that judges, juries, and police often shy away from using them, although, from time to time, unlucky people receive very harsh punishment, which seems unfair both to them and to their contemporaries. It seems unlikely that occasional severities will do much to change the general picture. However, in politics as elsewhere, men have rarely shown a sense of history or adequate foresight, and the same legislators who promise a tough line against psychedelics talk blithely about reducing the voting age to eighteen. If these statements are sincere, and they plan to continue their opposition to psychedelics when they have reduced the voting age, one wonders whether we are not becoming tired of politics.

In our opinion, the Establishment has behaved as establishments usually do, bolstered with the authority they possess by virtue of their social and political position. They have not been any less admirable than members of the psychedelic movement who claim that as a result of their experiences they have a deeper knowledge of the human heart and a greater understanding of the meaning of things. By their claims, their actions must be judged by a higher standard than the actions of the Establishment, which does not make such claims. one asks whether mind-expanding experiences have increase the ability of members of the psychedelic movement to u derstand the views and fears of their elders more compassio ately than they feel they themselves have been judged, w believe the verdict must be "not proven." Aldous Huxley on urged a leading figure in the psychedelic movement to remer ber that it is "important to do good stealthily." His exceller advice has not always been heeded. If indeed insights hav been acquired as a result of psychedelic experience, the should be used for the general good rather than for person ends.

In this controversy, medical men have tended to be range on the side of the Establishment. This is understandab enough, for they are frequently closely associated with it, an often among its members. Unfortunately, they sometimes u their enormous medical authority to justify prejudices deri ing not from medical knowledge, but from the social an moral climate in which they happen to live. This has occurre repeatedly throughout history, and the same error has bee made by some of the most distinguished medical men.

An excellent example of this is provided by the case Henry Maudsley, one of the most enlightened psychiatris of his day, and for whom a leading mental hospital in Londo is presently named. In his fine paper "Masturbational Insa ity," E. H. Hare (1962) notes that Maudsley wrote, "In th life of the chronic masturbator, nothing could be so reaso ably desired as the end of it, and the sooner he sinks to h degraded rest the better for himself, and the better for th world, which is well rid of him." Hare comments on thi ". . . the besetting sin of the psychiatrist [is] a tendency t confuse the rules of mental health with morality." Maudsley views were part of the conventional wisdom of his age. Eve as late as 1892, the Dictionary of Psychological Medicine d scribed the effects of masturbation as "moral and mental shij wreck, the whole nature is deteriorated. . . . mental facultie become blunted. . . . The miserable wretch would comm suicide if he dared, but rarely has the courage . . . and sink into melancholic dementia." Writing in 1911 on the trea ment and prevention of this grievous condition, Ivan Bloc stated, "In the treatment of masturbation, the methods of the older physicians who appeared before the child armed with great knives and scissors and threatened a painful operation or even to cut off the genital organs may often be used and often effect a radical cure." Psychoanalysts, too, were involved in this nonsense. Ernest Jones, the biographer of Freud, for instance, wrote in 1918 that neurasthenia derived from excessive onanism and seminal emission (Comfort, 1967).

Masturbation was of no interest to medicine until about 1720, following the publication in 1710 of a book called *Onania, or the Heinous Sin of Self-Abuse,* to tout a patent medicine. Indeed, in 1644, masturbation was recommended as a remedy against "the dangerous allurements of women." After the publication of *Onania,* the negative view taken up by medical men and educators became the source of some of the most harmful iatrogenic miseries, exceeded only by the great nineteenth-century pandemic of bleeding. Right up to the 1930s, in both England and the United States, extraordinary garments, a combination of straitjacket and chastity belt, were sold by makers of surgical and medical instruments to curb "the deadly vice of onanism."

What relevance has this to psychedelics? Medicine, in its views, is in tune with the morality of the age in which it is practiced, and indeed, has been more or less identified with morality for millennia. Medical men have to choose a middle course to avoid overidentification with the establishments of their day. Medical men who went along with the Nazi race theories are one dismal example of how current social values can destroy medical ethics. In the case of masturbation, physical and psychological injury was inflicted on at least six generations of children and adults. Panic and terror spread among parents who were urged to be ever alert to spot young masturbators. Children became morbidly preoccupied with this attractive but deadly vice which excited the grownups to such frenzy.

Perhaps we are about to indulge in yet another of these medicomoral autos-da-fé. The sequence of events is easy to spot. First, a few medical men associate themselves with a particular moral viewpoint that they consider has some medical importance. They soon find evidence, sometimes dubious, to confirm their convictions. Using this evidence, they begin to suggest solving the moral problem by medical means. In the psychedelic context, users have been infringing on the contention of the medical establishment that any pharmacological substances used on human beings lie within its bailiwick. The psychological changes resulting from drug use are those older folk frown upon and sometimes find repugnant and frightening, in contrast with such acceptable social tranquilizers as alcohol or barbiturates. There is also the possibility that those who use psychedelics might be injuring themselves or their offspring. The recent impassioned discussions of the possible effects of LSD on chromosomes is paralleled by similar discussions over masturbation. It was stated with the utmost confidence that not only would the secret vice result in the collapse and insanity of those who practiced it, but should they be unfortunate enough to survive to adulthood, their children would suffer for their sins. There was no evidence for this, but it did not prevent men of the highest integrity from stating that it was undoubtedly so.

There are real dangers associated with the psychedelic substances known today. These dangers are of many kinds and call for concern from medicine and its allied sciences. However, before discussing these dangers and how they might be alleviated, it may be well to remind those who urge medical men to make public pronouncements to frighten and dismay the young that, given the morality of medicine, its place in society, and the age of the experienced medical man, the doctor is rarely the best person for the task. He is liable to exaggerate such dangers as exist and is apt to aid and abet extreme measures, in keeping with the morality of the day, that may not alleviate the sufferings of the victims of the immoral condition and may even make it worse.

Psychedelics are liable to arouse moral indignation, because emotions are always likely to be deeply stimulated when someone else is indulging in new pleasures that may alter social values, especially when the users are young and rash and often brash as well. Medicine has a duty not to make this confusion and uncertainty any worse. Physicians are not police. Their duty is to inform the public as truthfully as they can, without excessive bias, resounding moral statements, or validation of punitive actions carried out as treatment. Medicine must avoid becoming a precipitate partisan in complex moral and social issues such as those posed by the modern advent of psychedelics.

After such perplexities, it is tempting to leave the solution to the reader's ingenuity. Yet authors customarily give their opinion and venture at least a few steps beyond the threshold of their ivory tower. The uses and dangers attending these substances must be discussed accurately and dispassionately. Men like Dr. Stanley Yolles, Director of the National Institute of Mental Health, do not seem convinced that "drug abuse," which includes the unauthorized use of a variety of psychedelics, will be eliminated in the foreseeable future.[1] If this is indeed so, strenuous efforts must be made to reduce those dangers attendant on clandestine use. We require a variety of social strategies rather than freezing in a catatonic posture and boasting that this immobility is firm resolution. The very brief banning of LSD-25 research in 1966 was a classic example of precipitate, unintelligent action springing from high government levels. Since then, some research has been restored to a limited degree, but expansion has not been greatly encouraged, nor is an atmosphere of panic and politicking conducive to clear thinking, planning, and diligent, long-continued inquiry. Legitimate, rather than amateur and bootleg, research is necessary; yet one of the most gifted and distinguished researchers in the country was not able to obtain permission to do this sort of work. Others, too, have been discouraged by the sluggishness of the various bureaucracies that must be consulted.

The muddled and ambiguous situation regarding the effect of LSD-25 on chromosomes[2] might call for restriction of re-

[1] Yolles, Stanley F. Speech quoted in *Hospital Tribune*, Monday, June 16, 1969.

[2] Today (July 1969) reports of chromosome changes are bewildering to those not experts in this field. The various conflicting statements suggest that the science of studying chromosomes requires an art as great as that needed to interpret Rorschach inkblots. In that famous and often valuable test, the non-expert must rely on his own estimate of the reliability of the particular person who administered and reported on the test. Great difficulties arise when men of good repute publish findings that seem, at least to the naïve, to be dia-

search with this particular drug to those people for whom such changes, if they do indeed occur, would be of comparatively little importance. Other psychedelics, which have never been implicated in this way, could be used more widely. Subjects for LSD might include some of the several million afflicted by severe and chronic alcoholism, patients suffering from intractable pain in fatal illnesses (Kast, 1964a), and older people still curious for new experience to enlarge their understanding of themselves, others, and existence. While not everyone might choose to die with his mind stimulated by LSD, as did Aldous Huxley (Huxley, L. A., 1968), rather than dulled by morphine, such matters call for careful consideration, for each of us owes God a death. It is folly to restrict and hamper research in all directions because it may be dangerous in some. If damage to chromosomes should be proved, and this has not yet been done, some substances may be less harmful than others, and it may be possible to discover protective measures. As a number of medicines in regular use are also suspect, and since some virus diseases and certain radiations produce similar changes, inquiries here would serve a wider purpose. Indeed, because of the possibility of chromosome-damaging substances in various medicines and foods, it would be prudent to inquire at once into such protective substances. For instance, it has been shown (in animals) that the teratogenic effect of thalidomide (Frank et al., 1963) can be prevented by greatly increasing the intake of niacin (vitamin B_3). It is not known if this protective effect extends to humans, but if it does, the thalidomide tragedy, in which so many babies were deformed, might have been simply and cheaply avoided.

---

metrically opposed and irreconcilable. There is a danger that, because of reports in the press based on earlier studies that suggested unequivocal damage to chromosomes, some people who were frightened away by this information will now decide that there is no danger whatever. It may even be thought that this was another trick like that deplorable episode in Pennsylvania, where it was reported with considerable circumstantial detail that a number of young men had gazed at the sun under the influence of LSD-25 and were permanently blinded, suffering grave retinal damage. This proved to be false. Thus are credibility crevasses created.

Many years ago, Carl Jung[3] told one of us that by the middle years of life, childhood experience had usually done its worst and became of lessened importance as a source of intrapsychic distress. Queen Elizabeth I put it to her godson, Sir John Harrington, who invented the water closet, "When thou dost feel creeping time at the gate, these fooleries will please thee less." She also reflected, "The days of man's life are plumed with the feathers of death." As the years pass by, many men and women become more concerned with the purpose and meaning of life, rather than with the drive to succeed in it. This is an important area of inquiry for psychedelic research.

Just as important, and at present receiving just as little attention, is our need to explore ways to help people prepare themselves for the rapid, all-pervasive, social and technological changes characteristic of our times. In terms of science and technology, as compared with previous ages, many of us have lived through the equivalent of centuries of change. This torrent of change is itself anxiety provoking, for there are no structures to handle the kinds of change that change the structures themselves. Few moralists seem to have noticed yet that the progress of medicine has made it harder for us to reflect upon death and so savor life to the full. To come to terms with both life and death, each must be measured with the cold eye of the reflective mind; change must be faced.

Until about half a century ago, everyone everywhere was raised in the ever-present shadow of death. The autobiographies, biographies, and histories of forty years ago show that those plumed feathers were never far away. Life and death were inseparables, the subject of gossip and conversation. Many people were preparing themselves for their own deaths all their lives, for, unhampered by insurance statistics, they saw death as ever present. Death seems to have become taboo today and has taken that place of secrecy from which sex has just been freed. This exchange of prisoners seems hardly worth while. It is usually possible to abstain from sex, should one want to; death allows no abstentions. As a Ghanaian truck driver put it, "Death takes no bribes."

[3] Jung, C. Personal communication to H. Osmond. November 1955.

A generation has grown up in whose life death is an u familiar and unnatural event, almost an affront. Their expe ence does not countenance illness for which nothing can I done. But death has only been postponed, not defeated, ar has dominion over people who have scarcely dared speak h name in polite company. Our forebears linked holy living ar holy dying, and considered the two an art. In a society such ours, which has become almost idolatrous about living inde nitely, it is becoming bad taste to discuss death. Our po: tion is not unlike that in Victorian love stories, in which t authors managed to write about love and passion with fe open references to sex, although its absence made its pr ence all the clearer.

Those concerned with the religious aspects of psychedeli should make special efforts in this direction. Many membe of the Establishment are in their middle and later years, ar there is little doubt that they recognize that they "owe God death," in spite of the efforts of their physicians and surgeon Research into these matters should be pursued with arde for while the risks are small, the rewards are likely to I great. This still leaves the question of whether these su stances have ill effects on the young and whether such ill e fects can be much reduced, easily corrected, or complete avoided. Since controlling the manufacture, distribution, ar use of psychedelics is still uncertain, although their contai ment seems to be possible, at least for the moment, even th might break down during the next few years, as we note earlier.

If Victor Gioscia (1969) is correct, and there is an LS subculture, the dangers, particularly to those under thirty, i quire very careful consideration. Leaving out chromoson damage, perhaps the most dramatic misfortune is the d velopment of a schizophreniform illness. There is no doul that this can happen, though it is not clear how often it doe Certain myths current among some young drug takers increa the danger. One of the most unfortunate is that the appr priate remedy for a bad trip is another one, frequently with larger dose than that which produced the first one. This n tion is on a par with the alcoholic slogan of having a hair, even the tail, of "the dog that bit you." The sensible respon to a bad trip is not to have another, but to seek competent advice and guidance without delay. Some people, who are clearly developing schizophrenia and have disturbances of perception (Hoffer and Osmond, 1966a) combined with usually depressed mood changes, with anxiety and sometimes thinking difficulties, take psychedelics because they have heard, or hope, that they will help. The most probable outcome is a severe and prolonged bad trip, or sometimes the precipitation of a more-severe and acute illness. If these dangers were more widely known and understood, many young people would avoid trying to treat themselves by these desperate means and avoid much unhappiness and distress.

A number of simple and effective ways of exploring and measuring perceptual anomalies, including the HOD (Hoffer and Osmond, 1961; Kelm, Hoffer, and Osmond, 1967) and EWI (El-Meligi, 1968a, 1968b; El-Meligi and Osmond, in press) tests already exist. By means of these and similar instruments, and by improving public knowledge about schizophrenia, it should be possible to diagnose and treat it far earlier and more successfully than usually happens today. Delaying treatment or aggravating the condition with mixtures of impure and often unknown chemicals in inept attempts at self-treatment only makes things worse. However, by no means all, or even most, who sample the bewildering array of often dubious substances said to be psychedelic become gravely ill or likely to be so. Official propaganda paints a uniformly gloomy picture, which paradoxically increases rashness by its exaggeration. This same kind of overstatement was used to discourage masturbation, sex, drinking, dancing, smoking, using make-up, primping, and other disapproved activities. The results have been unimpressive. However, even if it were shown that there were few physiological objections to young people taking pure and reliable psychedelics except for those with a tendency to schizophrenia, it does not follow that all controls should be removed.

Each one of us must learn his own culture before he can either align himself with its values or object to them in a manner likely to produce constructive change. In most cultures, the attainment of this is symbolized by the accordance of certain rights, such as the right to marry, hold prop-

erty, vote, go to war, receive the death penalty, and oth
positive and negative awards withheld from children an
those not sufficiently acculturated. In some cultures, cer
monies take place to mark entry into adult status, and ritu
markings may also be applied in order to indicate the statu
of the new adult. Psychedelics taken before the stabilizatio
of knowledge about cultural norms, because of their capaci
to alter perceptual constancy, might result in a reduced capa
ity or wish to internalize the already fluctuating and fra
menting values of our industrial society. The Establishmen
by its hasty and apparently not fully enforceable ban on thes
substances, seems to have worsened matters by making the
symbolic of intergenerational differences.

Since the mistake has already been made, what can t
done? Societies that have sought and used psychedelic e:
perience, however achieved, have nearly always had some kin
of initiation ceremony, often of a religious kind, aimed
focusing expanded experience in a way that will enhance th
participant's identification with and appreciation of his ow
society. In the United States at present, only indigenous I
dians are permitted a religion employing psychedelics, an
they have achieved this only by much stubborn courage. Sure
bona fide religious groups interested in these matters who a
prepared to conduct themselves in a manner in keeping wit
safety and public decency, should be encouraged and su
ported. They are likely to serve a valuable social function i
the future. Even the cynical who are not wholly myopic ca
understand that banned and persecuted religions frequent
spread more quickly and become more attractive in times
change. Persecution, even with the good intention of preser
ing health, is liable to have unintended consequences. In h
morality *Island*, Aldous Huxley (1962) discussed these ma
ters and illustrated them with the learning, perceptivenes
wit, and delicacy in which he had few rivals.

Mankind's interest in the psychedelic experience is unlikel
to lessen with increase in leisure. This gives us a greater o
portunity to be concerned not only with survival, but wit
the quality of those human relationships that are the stuff
life. Wasson (1969) shows in his great book that this is one
mankind's oldest interests. In the years that lie ahead, ne

rugs, although there will probably be many more of them, will not, we think, be the focus of greatest interest. Already various forms of hypnosis, learning-theory applications, and electronics that evoke and reproduce these experiences are being explored. Those young people who are alert to them and interested will learn how to use them, and some may be doing so even now. If this happens, the Establishment will have to decide whether it disapproves of the chemicals producing the experience or the experience itself. Very few of those dealing with these matters legally, scientifically, or politically seem to have concerned themselves with this critical issue. Medically, the non-drug methods eliminate many of the current objections to the psychedelic experience as a hazard to health. The social problems, however, especially those of acculturation, would not necessarily be greatly changed.

If such capacities, however induced, become widespread, their impact is likely to resemble some massive mutation. Perhaps this is necessary if we are to adapt to that new world that we are building with such a strange mishmash of cunning, inspiration, apprehension, and folly. The sociological, psychological, political, and other consequences of psychedelic experience, however induced, occurring in the majority or even a substantial minority of a postindustrial population, is likely to affect most of us far more than a few space jaunts or carefully selected heroes and heroines. The record is merciless: practical men of sound sense are nearly always wrong about the future, though never lacking in certainty. While the winds of change strum to gale force around us, they perform their ostrich acts and proclaim that they have everything under control. But the gale does not blow itself out because of their rhetoric, and to survive, we need to set a course that carries us into the future. Some years ago one of us wrote Osmond, 1957a):

. . these agents have a part to play in our survival as a species, for that survival depends as much on our opinion of our fellows and ourselves as on any other single thing. The psychedelics help us to explore and fathom our own nature.

We can perceive ourselves as the stampings of an automatic socioeconomic process, as highly plastic and conditionable animals, as congeries of instinctive strivings ending in loss of sexual drive a death, as cybernetic gadgets, or even as semantic conundrums. All these concepts have their supporters and they all have some deg of truth in them. We may also be something more, "a part of t main," a striving sliver of a creative process, a manifestation Brahma in Atman, an aspect of an infinite God immanent and tra scendent within and without us. These very different valuings of t self and of other people's selves have all been held sincerely by m and women. I expect that even what seem the most extreme notio are held by some contributors to these pages. Can one doubt that t views of the world derived from such differing concepts are likely differ greatly, and that the courses of action determined by tho views will differ . . . ?

. . . I believe that the psychedelics provide a chance, perhaps or a slender one, for homo faber, the cunning, ruthless, foolhard pleasure-greedy toolmaker, to merge into that other creature who presence we have so rashly presumed, homo sapiens, the wise, t understanding, the compassionate, in whose fourfold vision art, po tics, science, and religion are one. Surely we must seize th chance. . . .

And so it stands today. We predict, to use the Iron Duke phrase to Creevey, that it will be "a nice-run thing: th nicest-run thing you ever saw. . . ."

PART X

SPECIAL SECTIONS

CONTRIBUTORS

JOHN W. AIKEN founded the Church of the Awakening in 1963 and retired from general medical practice in New Mexico in 1964. Since then, he has lectured to various metaphysical and religious groups throughout the United States.

DUNCAN BLEWETT is Professor of Psychology at the University of Saskatchewan.

WILLIAM BRADEN is a reporter with the Chicago *Sun-Times* and author of *The Private Sea: LSD and the Search for God.*

FRANCES CHEEK is Chief of the Section of Experimental Sociology at the Bureau of Research in Neurology and Psychiatry in Princeton, New Jersey.

JONATHAN CLARK is Associate Professor of Education at Boston University, and Director of the Boston University Psycho-Educational Clinic. He is a consultant to the Massachusetts Department of Correction.

WALTER HOUSTON CLARK, now retired, was Professor of Psychology of Religion at the Andover Newton Theological School in Newton Center, Massachusetts.

ARTHUR DEIKMAN is Associate Professor of Psychiatry at the University of Colorado Medical Center, Denver, Colorado.

IRA EINHORN, formerly a college teacher, is currently a writer concerned with problems of the youth revolution.

JAMES FADIMAN is President of the Transpersonal Institute and is a psychological consultant to management in San Francisco, California.

WILLIS HARMAN is Director of the Educational Policy

Research Center at the Stanford Research Institute, and Professor of Engineering-Economic Systems, Stanford University, Palo Alto, California.

ABRAM HOFFER, formerly Professor of Psychiatry, University of Saskatchewan, and Director of Psychiatric Research, Department of Public Health, Saskatchewan, is now engaged in private practice in Saskatoon, Saskatchewan.

JEAN HOUSTON is a director of the Foundation for Mind Research in New York City and is a co-author of *The Varieties of Psychedelic Experience* and *Psychedelic Art*.

KIYO IZUMI is Professor of Social Sciences and Chairman of the Human Information and Ecology Programme at the University of Saskatchewan.

ERIC KAST is Assistant Professor of Medicine and Psychiatry at the Chicago Medical School and Director of the Pain Clinic, Mount Sinai Hospital, Chicago, Illinois.

WERNER P. KOELLA is Chief of Biological Research, Roberts pharm, Inc., Basel, Switzerland, and Professor Affiliate at Boston University and Clark University.

STANLEY KRIPPNER is Director of the William C. Menninger Dream Laboratory, Maimonides Medical Center, Brooklyn, New York.

JEFFREY LINZER is a dormitory counselor at Rutgers University, New Brunswick, New Jersey.

ROBERT E. L. MASTERS is a director of the Foundation for Mind Research in New York City and a co-author of *The Varieties of Psychedelic Experience* and *Psychedelic Art*.

RALPH METZNER, former editor of the *Psychedelic Review*, is with the Counseling and Testing Center, Stanford University, Palo Alto, California.

TOD MIKURIYA is Director of Research at the Everett A. Gladman Memorial Hospital, Oakland, California, and consulting psychiatrist to the Alameda County Health Department Drug Abuse Program.

ROBERT MOGAR is Professor of Psychology at San Francisco State College, San Francisco, California.

STEPHENS NEWELL is a Research Associate in the Section

of Experimental Sociology, Bureau of Research in Neurology and Psychiatry, Princeton, New Jersey.

WALTER PAHNKE is Director of Clinical Sciences at the Maryland Psychiatric Research Center, and Assistant Professor of Clinical Psychiatry at the Johns Hopkins University School of Medicine, Baltimore, Maryland.

PAUL RADIN, now deceased, was at one time affiliated with the Bureau of American Ethnology and wrote many articles and books on North American Indians, including *An Autobiography of a Winnebago Indian*.

JERRY RICHARDSON is an insurance underwriter in San Francisco, California.

MARY SARETT is a Research Associate in the Department of Experimental Sociology, Bureau of Research in Neurology and Psychiatry, Princeton, New Jersey.

E. ROBERT SINNETT is Director of the Mental Health Section, Student Health Center, and Professor of Psychology, Kansas State University, Manhattan, Kansas.

PETER STAFFORD is a writer on psychedelics in New York City and co-author of *LSD: The Problem-Solving Drug*.

ALAN WATTS is a philosopher and President of the Society for Comparative Philosophy in Sausalito, California.

BIBLIOGRAPHY

Aaronson, B. S. *Some Quantitative Properties of Verbal Behavior in Psychotherapy.* Unpublished doctoral dissertation, University of Minnesota, 1955.

Aaronson, B. S. *Hypnosis, Depth Perception, and Schizophrenia.* Presented at Eastern Psychological Association meetings, Philadelphia, Pa., 1964a.

Aaronson, B. S. "Hypnotic Induction of Colored Environments," *Perceptual and Motor Skills* 18, 30, 1964b.

Aaronson, B. S. *Hypnosis, Being, and the Conceptual Categories of Time.* Presented at New Jersey Psychological Association meetings, Princeton, N.J., 1965.

Aaronson, B. S. "Behavior and the Place Names of Time," *American Journal of Clinical Hypnosis* 9, 1–17, 1966a.

Aaronson, B. S. *Hypnosis, Time Rate Perception, and Psychopathology.* Presented at Eastern Psychological Association meetings, New York, N.Y., 1966b.

Aaronson, B. S. "Distance, Depth, and Schizophrenia," *American Journal of Clinical Hypnosis* 9, 203–7, 1967a.

Aaronson, B. S. "Hypnosis, Responsibility, and the Boundaries of Self," *American Journal of Clinical Hypnosis* 9, 229–45, 1967b.

Aaronson, B. S. "LSD: Experimental Findings," *International Journal of Parapsychology* 9, 86–90, 1967c.

Aaronson, B. S. "Mystic and Schizophreniform Perception as a Function of Depth Perception," *Journal of the Scientific Study of Religion* 6, 246–52, 1967d.

Aaronson, B. S. "Hypnosis, Time Rate Perception, and Personality," *Journal of Schizophrenia* 2, 11–41, 1968a.

Aaronson, B. S. "Hypnotic Alterations of Space and Time," *International Journal of Parapsychology* 10, 5–36, 1968b.

Aaronson, B. S. "Lilliput and Brobdignag—Self and World," *American Journal of Clinical Hypnosis* 10, 160–66, 1968c.

Aaronson, B. S. "Psychosynthesis as System and Therapy," *American Journal of Clinical Hypnosis* 10, 231–35, 1968d.

Aaronson, B. S. "Hypnosis, Depth Perception, and the Psychedelic Experience." In Tart, C. T. (ed.) *Altered States of Consciousness.* New York: Wiley, 1969a, pp. 263–70.

Aaronson, B. S. "The Subject as Programmer," *American Journal of Clinical Hypnosis* 11, 245–52, 1969b.

Aaronson, B. S., and Mundschenk, P. *Some Spatial Stereotypes of Time.* Presented at Eastern Psychological Association meetings, Washington, D.C., 1968.

Aberle, D. F. *The Peyote Religion Among the Navaho.* Chicago: Aldine, 1966.

Abramson, H. A. (ed.) *The Use of LSD in Psychotherapy.* New York: Josiah Macy, Jr., Foundation, 1960.

Abramson, H. A. (ed.) *The Use of LSD in Psychotherapy and Alcoholism.* Indianapolis: Bobbs-Merrill, 1967.

Ackerknect, E. H. "Medical Practices." In Steward, J. H. (ed.) *Handbook of South American Indians.* Washington: United States Government Printing Office, 1948.

Adams, J. K. "Psychosis: 'Experimental' and Real," *Psychedelic Review* 2, 121–44, 1963.

Alpert, R., and Cohen, S. *LSD.* New York: New American Library, 1966.

Amarel, M., and Cheek, F. E. "Some Effects of LSD-25 on Verbal Communication," *Journal of Abnormal Psychology* 70, 453–56, 1965.

Arieti, S. *Interpretation of Schizophrenia.* New York: Bruner, 1955.

Author unknown. "Yage, the Psychedelic Vine," *Explorations Magazine* 9, 17–18, 1966.

Ayer, A. J. *Language, Truth and Logic,* 2d ed. New York: Dover, 1946.

Babbitt, Irving. *The Dhammapada.* Oxford University Press, 1936. (Paper ed.) New York: New Directions, 1965.

Bagchi, B. K., and Wenger, M. A. "Electrophysiological Correlates of Some Yoga Exercises," *International Congress of Neurological Sciences, First Session* 3, 141–46, 1957.

Barron, F. "Motivational Patterns in LSD Usage." In DeBold, R. C., and Leaf, R. C. (eds.) *LSD, Man & Society.* Middletown: Wesleyan University Press, 1967.

Bateson, G. (ed.) *Perceval's Narrative: A Patient's Account of His Psychosis.* Stanford: Stanford University Press, 1961.

Beard, R. *Everyman's Search.* New York: Arthur James, 1950.

Beck, S. J. "Errors in Perception and Fantasy in Schizophrenia." In Kasanin, J. S. (ed.) *Language and Thought in Schizophrenia.* New York: Norton, 1964.

Becker, H. *Outsiders; Studies in the Sociology of Deviance.* Glencoe: The Free Press, 1963.

Beers, C. W. *A Mind that Found Itself.* New York: Longmans, 1908.

Benabud, A. "Psycho-pathological Aspects of the Cannabis Situation in Morocco; Statistical Data for 1956," *Bulletin of Narcotics* 9, 1–16.

Bender, L. "D-lysergic Acid in the Treatment of the Biological Feature of Childhood Schizophrenia," *Diseases of the Nervous System, Monograph Supplement* 27, 43–46, 1966.

Bender, L., Goldschmidt, L., and Sankar, D. V. "Treatment of Autistic Schizophrenic Children with LSD-25 and UML-491," *Recent Advances in Biological Psychiatry* 4, 170–77, 1962.

Bergen, J. R., Koella, W. P., Freeman, H., and Hoagland, H. "A Human Plasma Factor Inducing Behavioral and Electrophysiological Changes in Animals: II. Changes Induced in Animals," *Annals of the New York Academy of Sciences* 96, 469–76, 1962.

Bleibtreu, J. *The Parable of the Beast.* New York: Macmillan, 1968.

Bleuler, M. "Conceptions of Schizophrenia Within the Last Fifty Years and Today," *International Journal of Psychiatry* 1, 505–15, 1965.

Blewett, D. B. "Psychedelic Drugs in Parapsychological Research," *International Journal of Parapsychology* 5, 1963.

Blewett, D. B., and Chwelos, N. *Handbook for the Therapeutic Use of D-lysergic Acid Diethylamide 25.* Government of Saskatchewan Department of Public Health, mimeo, 1959.

Bloch, Iwan. *Sexual Life of Our Time in its Relations to Modern Civilization.* Tr. from 6th German edition by M. Eden Paul. Mosby, 1911.

Blofeld, J. "Consciousness, Energy, Bliss." In Metzner, R. (ed.) *The Ecstatic Adventure.* New York: Macmillan, 1968, pp. 124–33.

Blough, D. S. "Effect of Lysergic Acid Diethylamide on Absolute Visual Threshold of the Pigeon," *Science* 126, 304–5, 1957.

Blum, R., et al. *Utopiates: The Use and Users of LSD-25.* New York: Atherton, 1964.

Boisen, A. *The Exploration of the Inner World.* New York: Harper, 1952.

Bowers, M. B., and Freedman, D. X. " 'Psychedelic' Experiences in Acute Psychoses," *Archives of General Psychiatry* 15, 240–48, 1966.

Braden, W. *The Private Sea: LSD and the Search for God.* Chicago: Quadrangle, 1967.

Bradley, P. B., Deniker, P., and Radovco-Thomas, C. *Neuropsychopharmacology.* New York: Elsevier, 1959.

Bradley, P. B., and Elkes, J. "The Effect of Amphetamine and D-Lysergic Acid Diethylamide (LSD-25) on the Electrical Activity of the Brain of the Conscious Cat," *Journal of Physiology* 120, 13P–14P, 1953.

Brown, J. D. (ed.), and *Time* correspondents. *The Hippies.* New York: Time-Life Books, 1967.

Brown, N. O. *Love's Body.* New York: Random House, 1966.

Buck, R. W. "Mushroom Toxins—A Brief Review of the Literature," *New England Journal of Medicine* 265, 681–86, 1961.

Bucke, R. M. *Cosmic Consciousness.* New York: Dutton, 1923.

Buckman, J. "Theoretical Aspects of LSD Therapy." In Abramson, H. (ed.) *The Use of LSD in Psychotherapy and Alcoholism.* Indianapolis: Bobbs-Merrill, 1967, pp. 83–97.

Buss, A. H. *Psychopathology.* New York: Wiley, 1966.

Caldwell, W. V. *LSD Psychotherapy: An Exploration of Psychedelic and Psycholytic Therapy.* New York: Grove, 1968.

Canetti, E. *Crowds and Power.* New York: Viking, 1962.

Carrel, A. *Voyage to Lourdes.* New York: Harper, 1950.

Carstairs, G. M. "Daru and Bhang: Cultural Factors in the Choice of Intoxicant," *Quarterly Journal of Studies on Alcohol* 15, 228, 1954.

Cassirer, E. *Philosophy of Symbolic Form.* New Haven: Yale University Press, 1955.

Castaneda, C. *The Teachings of Don Juan: A Yaqui Way of Knowledge.* Berkeley: University of California Press, 1968.

Chase, P. H. "A Note on Projection," *Psychological Bulletin* 57, 287–90, 1960.

Chayet, N. L. "Social and Legal Aspects of LSD Usage." In DeBold, R. C., and Leaf, R. C. (eds.) *LSD, Man & Society.* Middletown: Wesleyan University Press, 1967.

Cheek, F. E. "Exploratory Study of Drugs and Social Interaction," *Archives of General Psychiatry* 9, 566–74, 1963.

Cheek, F. E., and Amarel, M. "Studies in the Sources of Variation in Cloze Scores: II. The Verbal Passages," *Journal of Abnormal Psychology* 73, 424–30, 1968.

Cheek, F. E., Osmond, H., Sarett, M., and Albahary, R. S. "Observations Regarding the Use of LSD-25 in the Treatment of Alcoholism," *Journal of Psychopharmacology* 1, 56–74, 1966.

Church of England. "A Prayer for the King's Majesty, Order for Morning Prayer," *Book of Common Prayer.* New York: Oxford University Press, 1904.

Chwelos, N., Blewett, D. B., Smith, C. M., and Hoffer, A. "Use of D-lysergic Acid Diethylamide in the Treatment of Alcoholism," *Quarterly Journal of Studies in Alcoholism* 20, 577–90, 1959.

Clark, W. H. *The Psychology of Religion.* New York: Macmillan, 1958.

Cohen, S. "Lysergic Acid Diethylamide: Side Effects and Complications," *Journal of Nervous and Mental Disease* 130, 30–40, 1960.

Cohen, S. *The Beyond Within: The LSD Story.* New York: Atheneum, 1964.

Cohen, S., and Eisner, B. "Use of Lysergic Acid Diethylamide in a Psychotherapeutic Setting," *Archives of Neurology and Psychiatry* 81, 615–19, 1959.

Cole, J. O., and Katz, M. M. "The Psychotomimetic Drugs: An Overview." In Solomon, D. (ed.) *LSD: The Consciousness-Expanding Drug.* New York: Putnam, 1964.

Comfort, A. *The Anxiety Makers.* London: Nelson, 1967.

Cooley, C. *Social Organization.* New York: Scribner, 1937.

Cooper, J. H. "Stimulants and Narcotics." In Steward, Julian H. (ed.) *Handbook of South American Indians.* Washington: United States Government Printing Office, 1948.

Cooper, L. F., and Erikson, M. H. *Time Distortion in Hypnosis,* 2d ed. Baltimore: Williams & Wilkins, 1959.

Crocket, R., Sandison, R., and Walk, A. *Hallucinogenic Drugs and Their Therapeutic Use.* Springfield: Thomas, 1963.

Custance, J. *Wisdom, Madness and Folly*. New York: Pellegrini & Cudahy, 1952.

Dahlberg, C. C., Feldstein, S., and Jaffe, J. Abstract of grant proposal entitled "Effects of LSD-25 on Psychotherapeutic Communication." New York: William Alanson White Institute of Psychiatry, Psychoanalysis and Psychology, 1968.

DeBold, R. C., and Leaf, R. C. (eds.) *LSD, Man & Society*. Middletown: Wesleyan University Press, 1967.

Deikman, A. J. "Experimental Meditation," *Journal of Nervous and Mental Disease* 137, 329–43, 1963.

DeRopp, R. S. *Drugs and the Mind*, 1st Evergreen ed. New York: Grove, 1960 (copyright 1957).

Ditman, K. "Review and Evaluation of Current Drug Therapies in Alcoholism," *International Journal of Psychiatry*, pp. 248–58, 1967.

Dostoevsky, F. "Notes from the Underground." In *White Nights and Other Tales*. New York: Macmillan, 1944.

Ebin, D. (ed.) *The Drug Experience*. New York: Grove, 1961.

Efron, D. H., Holmstedt, B., and Kline, N. S. (eds.) *Ethnopharmacologic Search for Psychoactive Drugs*. Public Health Service Publication No. 1645. Washington, D.C.: U. S. Department of Health, Education, and Welfare, 1967.

Eliade, M. *Shamanism: Archaic Techniques of Ecstasy*. New York: Pantheon, 1964.

Ellul, J. *The Technological Society*. New York: Knopf, 1964.

El-Meligi, A. M. *The Experiential World Inventory: A Non-Projective Aid for the Rorschach*. Presented at the Seventh International Congress of Rorschach and Other Projective Techniques, London, 1968a.

El-Meligi, A. M. *Some Psychological Correlates of Changes Produced by Hallucinogens in Man: A Comparison with Schizophrenia*. Presented at Annual Meetings of the American College of Neuropsychopharmacology, San Juan, P.R., 1968b.

El-Meligi, A. M., and Osmond, H. *Manual for the Experiential World Inventory: A Non-Projective Aid for the Rorschach*. Saskatoon, Saskatchewan: Prairie Press, in press.

Erikson, M. H. "The Induction of Color Blindness by a Technique of Hypnotic Suggestion," *Journal of General Psychology* 20, 61–89, 1939.

Erikson, M. H. "A Special Inquiry with Aldous Huxley into the Nature and Character of Various States of Consciousness," *American Journal of Clinical Hypnosis* 8, 14–33, 1965.

Evarts, E. V. "Some Effects of Bufotenine and Lysergic Acid Diethylamide on the Monkey," *Archives of Neurology and Psychiatry* 75, 49–53, 1956.

Evarts, E. V. "A Review of the Neurophysiological Effects of Lysergic Acid Diethylamide (LSD) and Other Psychotomimetic Agents," *Annals of the New York Academy of Sciences* 66, 479–95, 1957.

Evarts, E. V., Landau, W., Freygang, W., Jr., and Marshall, W. H. "Some Effects of Lysergic Acid Diethylamide and Bufotenine on Electrical Activity in the Cat's Visual System," *The American Journal of Physiology* 182, 594–98, 1955.

Fadiman, J. *Behavior Change Following Psychedelic (LSD) Therapy.* Ph.D. dissertation, Stanford University, 1965.

Fadiman, J., Harman, W. W., McKim, R. H., Mogar, R. E., and Stolaroff, M. J. *Psychedelic Agents in Creative Problem Solving.* San Francisco: Institute for Psychedelic Research of San Francisco State College, 1965.

Farnsworth, D. "Hallucinogenic Agents," editorial, *Journal of the American Medical Association* 185, 878–80, 1963.

Federn, P. *Ego Psychology and the Psychoses.* New York: Basic Books, 1955, pp. 241–60.

Feuchtwanger, L. *Power.* New York: Simon and Schuster, 1928.

Field, H. *The Meaning of Death.* New York: McGraw-Hill, 1956.

Finkelstein, N. "Honghi, Meester?" *Psychedelic Review* 10, 1967.

Flattery, D. S., and Pierce, J. M. *Peyote.* Berkeley: Berkeley Press, 1965.

Fogel, S., and Hoffer, A. "Perceptual Changes Induced by Hypnotic Suggestion for the Post-hypnotic State: 1. General Account of the Effect on Personality," *Journal of Clinical and Experimental Psychopathology* 23, 24–35, 1962a.

Fogel, S., and Hoffer, A. "The Use of Hypnosis to Interrupt and to Reproduce an LSD-25 Experience," *Journal of Clinical and Experimental Psychopathology* 23, 11–16, 1962b.

Ford, A., and Bro, M. *Nothing So Strange.* New York: Harper, 1958.

Foucault, M. *Madness and Civilization.* New York: Pantheon, 1966.

Fowles, J. *The Magus.* Boston: Little, Brown, 1965.

Frank, O., Baker, H., Ziffer, H., Aaronson, S., Hutner, S. H., and Leevy, C. M. "Metabolic Deficiencies in Protozoa Induced by Thalidomide," *Science* 139, 110–11, 1963.

Freud, S. *The Standard Edition of the Complete Psychological Works of Sigmund Freud.* London: Hogarth, 1955, p. 18.

Freud, S. *The Standard Edition of the Complete Psychological Works of Sigmund Freud.* London: Hogarth, 1957, p. 14.

Freud, S. *The Standard Edition of the Complete Psychological Works of Sigmund Freud.* London: Hogarth, 1958, pp. 5, 12.

Freud, S. *The Standard Edition of the Complete Psychological Works of Sigmund Freud.* London: Hogarth, 1961, p. 19.

Freud, S. *The Standard Edition of the Complete Psychological Works of Sigmund Freud.* London: Hogarth, 1963, p. 22.

Freud, S. *Inhibition, Symptoms and Anxiety.* London: Hogarth Press, 1967.

Gendlin, E. T. "Research in Psychotherapy with Schizophrenic Patients and the Nature of that 'Illness,'" *American Journal of Psychotherapy* 20, 4–16, 1966.

Giarman, N. J. "The Pharmacology of LSD." In DeBold, R. C., and

Leaf, R. C. (eds.) *LSD, Man & Society*. Middletown: Wesleyan University Press, 1967.

Gill, M., and Brenman, M. *Hypnosis and Related States*. New York: International Universities Press, 1959.

Ginsberg, A., and Burroughs, W. *The Yage Letters*. San Francisco: City Lights Books, 1963.

Gioscia, V. "LSD Subcultures: Acidoxy *versus* Orthodoxy," *American Journal of Orthopsychiatry* 39, 428–36, 1969.

Goldstein, L., Murphree, H. B., Sugerman, A. A., Pfeiffer, C. C., and Jenny, E. H. "Quantitative Electroencephalographic Analysis of Naturally Occurring (Schizophrenic) and Drug-induced Psychotic States in Human Males," *Clinical Pharmacology and Therapeutics* 4, 10–21, 1963.

Grinker, R. "Lysergic Acid Diethylamide," editorial, *Archives of General Psychiatry* 8, 425, 1963.

Guevara, C. "The Socialist Man," *Journal of Progressive Labor Party* 5, 84–106, 1965.

Hall, E. T. *The Hidden Dimension*. New York: Doubleday, 1966.

Hammer, M., and Zubin, J. *Culture and Psychopathology*. Unpublished manuscript. Columbia University, 1966.

Hare, E. H. "Masturbational Insanity: The History of an Idea," *Journal of Mental Science* 108, 1–25, 1962.

Harman, W. W., McKim, R. H., Mogar, R. E., Fadiman, J., and Stolaroff, M. J. "Psychedelic Agents in Creative Problem-Solving: A Pilot Study," *Psychedelic Reports* 19, 211–27, 1966.

Hartmann, E. "The Sleep-Dream Cycle and Brain Serotonin," *Psychonomic Science* 8, 295–96, 1967.

Hartmann, H. *Ego Psychology and the Problem of Adaptation*. New York: International Universities Press, 1958, pp. 88–91.

Hastings, A. *Language and Memory*. Personal communication, April 18, 1967.

Havens, L. L. "The Placement and Movement of Hallucinations in Space: Phenomenology and Theory," *International Journal of Psychoanalysis* 43, 426–35, 1962.

Heimann, P. *Notes on the Theory of the Life and Death Instincts: Developments in Psychoanalysis*. London: Hogarth, 1952, pp. 321–42.

Heisenberg, W. *Physics and Philosophy*. New York: Harper, 1958, p. 162.

Hemphill, J. K., and Westie, C. N. "The Measurement of Group Dimensions," *Journal of Psychology* 29, 225–41, 1950.

Hennell, T. *The Witnesses*. London: Davies, 1938.

Henri, R. *The Art Spirit*. Philadelphia: Lippincott, 1923.

Hensala, J., et al. "LSD and Psychiatric Inpatients," *Archives of General Psychiatry* 16, 554–59, 1967.

Hesse, H. *Steppenwolf*. New York: Ungar, 1929.

Higgens, J., and Peterson, J. C. "Concept of Process-Reactive Schizophrenia: A Critique," *Psychological Bulletin* 66, 201–6, 1966.

Hill, H. E., Haertzen, C. A., and Belleville, R. E. *The ARC Inventory.* Lexington: Addiction Research Center, 1961.

Hobson, J. A. "The Effect of LSD on the Sleep Cycle of the Cat," *Electroencephalography and Clinical Neurophysiology* 17, 52–56, 1964.

Hoffer, A. "Studies with Niacin and LSD." In Cholden, L., *Lysergic Acid Diethylamide and Mescaline in Experimental Psychiatry.* New York: Grune & Statton, 1956.

Hoffer, A. "LSD: A Review of Its Present Status," *Clinical Pharmacology and Therapeutics* 6, 183–255, 1965.

Hoffer, A. "Comment on the Laing Paper," *Psychedelic Review* 7, 127–28, 1966.

Hoffer, A., and Mahon, M. "The Presence of Unidentified Substances in the Urine of Psychiatric Patients," *Journal of Neuropsychiatry* 2, 331–62, 1961.

Hoffer, A., and Osmond, H. *The Chemical Basis of Clinical Psychiatry.* Springfield: Thomas, 1960.

Hoffer, A., and Osmond, H. "A Card Sorting Test Helpful in Making Psychiatric Diagnosis," *Journal of Neuropsychiatry* 2, 306–30, 1961.

Hoffer, A., and Osmond, H. "Malvaria: A New Psychiatric Disease," *Acta Psychiatria Scandinavica* 39, 335–66, 1962.

Hoffer, A., and Osmond, H. "Some Psychological Consequences of Perceptual Disorder and Schizophrenia," *International Journal of Neuropsychiatry* 2, 1–19, 1966a.

Hoffer, A., and Osmond, H. "What is Schizophrenia?" *Psychedelic Review* 7, 86–116, 1966b.

Hoffer, A., and Osmond, H. *The Hallucinogens.* New York: Academic Press, 1967.

Hoffer, A., and Osmond, H. *New Hope for Alcoholics.* New York: University Books, 1968.

Horowitz, M. J. "The Imagery of Visual Hallucinations," *Journal of Nervous and Mental Disease* 138, 515–23, 1964.

Houston, J. "A Different Kind of Mysticism," *Jubilee*, June 1967.

Huxley, A. *Brave New World.* New York: Harper, 1932.

Huxley, A. *The Perennial Philosophy.* New York: Harper, 1945.

Huxley, A. *The Doors of Perception.* New York: Harper, 1954.

Huxley, A. *Heaven and Hell.* London: Chatto & Windus, 1956.

Huxley, A. *Brave New World Revisited.* New York: Harper, 1958.

Huxley, A. *Collected Essays of Aldous Huxley.* New York: Harper, 1959.

Huxley, A. *Island.* London: Chatto & Windus, 1962.

Huxley, A., Mayr, E., Osmond, H., and Hoffer, A. "Schizophrenia as a Genetic Morphism," *Nature* 204, 220–21, 1964.

Huxley, L. A. *This Timeless Moment.* New York: Farrar, Strauss, 1968.

Hyde, R. W. "Psychological and Social Determinants of Drug Action." In Sarwer-Foner, G. J. (ed.) *The Dynamics of Psychiatric Drug Therapy.* Springfield: Thomas, 1960.

Inge, W. R. *Christian Mysticism*. New York: Meridian Books, 1956.

Irvine, D. "Apparently Non-Indolic Ehrlich-positive Substances Related to Mental Illness," *Journal of Neuropsychiatry* 2, 292–305, 1961.

Izumi, K. "An Analysis for the Design of Hospital Quarters for the Neuropsychiatric Patient," *Mental Hospitals* 8, 30–32, 1957.

Izumi, K. "Some Elements of Hospital Design," part three, *Journal of the Royal Architectural Institute* 35, 99–100, 1958.

Izumi, K. "Some Considerations on the Art of Architecture," *The Structurist*, 1961–62, pp. 46–51.

James, W. *The Varieties of Religious Experience*. New York: Longmans, 1935.

Jarvik, M. E. "The Behavioral Effects of Psychotogens." In DeBold, R. C., and Leaf, R. C. (eds.) *LSD, Man & Society*. Middletown: Wesleyan University Press, 1967, pp. 207–16.

Jarvik, M. E., Abramson, H. A., Hirsch, H. W., and Ewald, A. T. "Lysergic Acid Diethylamide (LSD-25)," *Journal of Psychology* 39, 465–73, 1955.

Jensen, S. "Treatment of Chronic Alcoholism with Lysergic Acid Diethylamide," *Canadian Psychiatric Association Journal* 8, 182–88, 1963.

Johnson, R. C. *Watcher on the Hills*. New York: Harper, 1959.

Jones, A. (ed.) *Jerusalem Bible*. New York: Doubleday, 1966.

Kahan, F. H. *Brains and Bricks*. Regina, Saskatchewan: Canadian Mental Health Division, 1965.

Kaplan, B. (ed.) *The Inner World of Mental Illness*. New York: Harper, 1964.

Karsten, R. *The Head-hunters of Western Amazonas*. Helsingfors: Sinska Zetenskaps-Societeten, 1935.

Kasamatsu, A., and Hirai, T. "Science of Zazen," *Psychologia* 6, 86–91, 1963.

Kast, E. C. "Pain and LSD-25: A Theory of Attenuation of Anticipation." In Solomon, D. (ed.) *LSD: The Consciousness-Expanding Drug*. New York: Putnam's, 1964a.

Kast, E. C. "A Study of Lysergic Acid Diethylamide as an Analgesic Agent," *Anesthesia and Analgesia* 43, 285–91, 1964b.

Kast, E. C. "An Understanding and Measurement of Human Pathologic Pain and the Analgesic Activity of Methrotrimeprazine," *Journal of Drugs* 16, 142–48, 1966a.

Kast, E. C. "An Understanding of Pain," *Medical Times* 94, 1501–13, 1966b.

Katz, M. M., Waskow, I. E., and Olsson, J. "Characterizing the Psychological State Produced by LSD," *Journal of Abnormal Psychology* 73, 1–14, 1968.

Kelm, H., Hoffer, A., and Osmond, H. *Hoffer-Osmond Diagnostic Test Manual*. Saskatoon, Saskatchewan: Modern Press, 1967.

Keniston, K. *The Uncommitted*. New York: Harcourt, 1965.

Kierkegaard, S. In Le Fevre, P. D. (ed.) *The Prayers of Kierkegaard*:

With a New Interpretation of His Life and Thought. Chicago: University of Chicago Press, 1956.

Klüver, H. "Neurobiology of Normal and Abnormal Perception." In Zubin, J. (ed.) *Psychopathology of Perception.* New York: Grune & Stratton, 1965.

Klüver, H. *Mescal and Mechanisms of Hallucinations.* Chicago: University of Chicago Press, 1966.

Knauth, L. "Historia de los Indios de la Nueva España," in *Estudios de Cultura Nahuatl,* Vol. III, 1962.

Knauth, L. "The *Teonanacatl* in Pre-conquest Accounts and Today." Unpublished research report, 1960, p. 1.

Koella, W. P., and Wells, C. H. "Influence of LSD-25 on Optically Evoked Potentials in the Nonanesthetized Rabbit," *The American Journal of Physiology* 196, 1181–84, 1959.

Koestler, A. *The Invisible Writing.* Boston: Beacon Press, 1955.

Kohler, I., transl. by H. Fiss. "The Formation and Transformation of the Perceptual," *Psychological Issues,* 1–173, 1963.

Korzybski, A. *Science and Sanity: An Introduction to Non-Aristotelian Systems and General Semantics.* Lancaster: Science Press, 1933.

Krech, D., Rosenzweig, M. R., and Bennett, E. L. "Effects of Environmental Complexity and Training on Brain Chemistry," *Journal of Comparative and Physiological Psychology* 53, 509–19, 1960.

Krippner, S. "Consciousness-Expansion and the Extensional World," *Etc.* 22, 463–74, 1965.

Krippner, S. "The Psychedelic Artist." In Masters, R. E. L., and Houston, J. (eds.) *Psychedelic Art.* New York: Grove, 1968, pp. 163–82.

Kroger, W. S. *Clinical and Experimental Hypnosis in Medicine, Dentistry and Psychology.* Philadelphia: Lippincott, 1963.

Kurland, A. A. "The Therapeutic Potential of LSD in Medicine." In DeBold, R. C., and Leaf, R. C. (eds.) *LSD, Man & Society.* Middletown: Wesleyan University Press, 1967.

Kurland, A. A., Unger, S., and Shaffer, J. "The Psychedelic Procedure in the Treatment of the Alcoholic Patient: A Research Program at the Spring Grove State Hospital." In Abramson, H. A. (ed.) *The Use of LSD in Psychotherapy and Alcoholism.* Indianapolis: Bobbs-Merrill, 1957, pp. 496–503.

Kurland, A. A., Unger, S., Shaffer, J., Savage, C., Wolf, S., Leihy, R., and McCabe, O. L. *Psychedelic Therapy (Utilizing LSD) in the Treatment of the Alcoholic Patient: A Preliminary Report.* Presented at the American Psychiatric Association meetings, Atlantic City, N.J., May 1966.

Laing, R. D. *The Politics of Experience.* New York: Pantheon, 1967.

Landis, C. *Varieties of Psychopathological Experience.* New York: Holt, Rinehart & Winston, 1964.

Langdon-Davies, J. *On the Nature of Man.* New York: Mentor, 1961.

Laurie, P. *Drugs: Medical, Psychological and Social Facts.* Middlesex, England: Penguin, 1967.

Lawes, T. G. G. "Schizophrenia, 'Sernyl' and Sensory Deprivation," *British Journal of Psychiatry* 109, 243–50, 1963.

Lawshe, C. H., and Harris, D. H. *Purdue Creativity Test.* West Lafayette: Purdue Research Foundation, 1960.

Lawson, F. S. "The Saskatchewan Plan," *Mental Hospitals* 8, 28–31, 1957.

Leary, T. R. "Introduction." In Solomon, D. (ed.) *LSD: The Consciousness-Expanding Drug.* New York: Putnam, 1964a.

Leary, T. R. "The Religious Experience: Its Production and Interpretation," *Psychedelic Review* 3, 1964b.

Leary, T. R. "Languages: Energy and Systems Sent and Received," *Etc.* 22, 431–60, 1965.

Leary, T. R. "The Experiential Typewriter," *Psychedelic Review* 5, 70–85, 1966a.

Leary, T. R. *Psychedelic Prayers.* Kerhonkson, N.Y.: Poets' Press, 1966b.

Leary, T. R. *High Priest.* New York: World, 1968a.

Leary, T. R. *The Politics of Ecstasy.* New York: Putnam's, 1968b.

Leary, T. R., and Clark, W. H. "Religious Implications of Consciousness-Expanding Drugs," *Religious Education* 58, 251–56, 1963.

Leary, T. R., Metzner, R., and Alpert, R. *The Psychedelic Experience.* New Hyde Park, N.Y.: University Books, 1964.

Leary, T. R., Litwin, G. H., and Metzner, R. "Reactions to Psilocybin Administered in a Supportive Environment," *Journal of Nervous and Mental Disease* 137, 561–73, 1963.

Lennard, H., Jarvik, M. E., and Abramson, H. A. "Lysergic Acid Diethylamide (LSD-25): XII. A Preliminary Statement of Its Effects upon Interpersonal Communication," *Journal of Psychology* 41, 185–98, 1956.

Levine, J., and Ludwig, A. "The Hypnodelic Treatment Technique." In Abramson, H. A. (ed.) *The Use of LSD in Psychotherapy and Alcoholism.* New York: Bobbs-Merrill, 1967.

Lewin, B. D. *The Psychoanalysis of Elation.* New York: Norton, 1950, pp. 144–50.

Lewis, M. M. *How Children Learn to Speak.* New York: Basic Books, 1959.

Liebert, R. S., Werner, H., and Wapner, S. "Studies on the Effect of Lysergic Acid Diethylamide," *A.M.A. Archives of Neurology and Psychiatry* 79, 580–84, 1958.

Ling, T. M., and Buckman, J. *Lysergic Acid (LSD-25) and Ritalin in the Treatment of Neurosis.* London: Lambande, 1963.

Louria, D. B. *Nightmare Drugs.* New York: Pocket Books, 1966.

Louria, D. B. "The Abuse of LSD." In DeBold, R. C., and Leaf,

R. C. (eds.) *LSD, Man & Society*. Middletown: Wesleyan University Press, 1967.

Lowie, R. H. "Tropical Forest Tribes." In Steward, J. H. (ed.) *Handbook of South American Indians*. Washington: United States Government Printing Office, 1948.

Ludwig, A. M. "Altered States of Consciousness," *Archives of General Psychiatry* 15, 225–34, 1966.

Ludwig, A. M., and Levine, J. "Patterns of Hallucinogenic Drug Abuse," *Journal of the American Medical Association* 191, 104–8, 1965.

Mach, E. *The Analysis of Sensations and the Relationship of the Physical to the Psychical*. Williams-Waterloo translation. Chicago: Open Court, 1914.

Malamud, J., Zigo, J., White, R., and Krippner, S. *An Analysis of Dream Content, Part I: Rules for Determining Units of Meaning in Dream Protocols*. Brooklyn: Dream Laboratory, Maimonides Medical Center, 1967.

Manzini, B., and Saraval, A. "The Experimental LSD Psychosis and and Its Relationship to Schizophrenia," *Rivista Sperimentale di Freniatria e Medicina Legale delle Alienazioni Mentali* (Reggio-Emilia) 84, 589, 1960. (Abstracted in Sandoz Annotated Bibliography, p. 307.)

Marcuse, H. *One Dimensional Man*. Boston: Beacon, 1964.

Marsh, R. P. "Meaning and the Mind-Drugs," *Etc.* 22, 408–30, 1965.

Maslow, A. H. *Religions, Values, and Peak Experiences*. Columbus: Ohio State University Press, 1964.

Mason, R. E. *Internal Perception and Bodily Functioning*. New York: International Universities Press, 1961.

Masters, R. E. L., and Houston, J. *The Varieties of Psychedelic Experience*. New York: Holt, Rinehart & Winston, 1966.

Masters, R. E. L., and Houston, J. *Psychedelic Art*. New York: Grove, 1968.

McGhie, A., and Chapman, J. "Disorders of Attention and Perception in Early Schizophrenia," *British Journal of Medical Psychology* 34, 103–16, 1961.

McLuhan, M. *Understanding Media: The Extensions of Man*. New York: McGraw-Hill, 1964.

McLuhan, M., and Fiore, Q. *The Medium is the Massage*. New York: Ballantine, 1967.

Merleau-Ponty, M. *The Structure of Behavior*. Boston: Beacon, 1963.

Metraux, A. "Initiation into Shamanistic Career." In Steward, J. H. (ed.) *Handbook of South American Indians*. Washington: United States Government Printing Office, 1948.

Metzner, R. (ed.) *The Ecstatic Adventure*. New York: Macmillan, 1968.

Metzner, R. "Subjective Effects of Anticholinergic Hallucinogens," *Psychedelic Review* 10, 1967.

Metzner, R., and Leary, T. R. "On Programming Psychedelic Experiences," *Psychedelic Review* 9, 5–19, 1966.

Michaux, H. "Light Through Darkness." In Andrews, G., and Vinkenoog, S. (eds.) *The Book of Grass*. London: Peter Owen, 1967.

Miller, D. R. *Survey of Object Visualization*. Monterey: California Test Bureau, 1955.

Mitchell, S. W. "Remarks on the Effects of *Anhalonium Lewinii* (the Mescal Button)," *British Medical Journal* 2, 1625–29, 1896.

Mogar, R. E. "Current Status and Future Trends in Psychedelic (LSD) Research," *Journal of Humanistic Psychology* 4, 147–66, 1965a.

Mogar, R. E. "The Psychedelic Drugs and Human Potentialities." In Otto, H. (ed.) *Explorations in Human Potentialities*. Springfield: Thomas, 1965b.

Mogar, R. E. "Search and Research with the Psychedelics," *Etc.* 22, 393–407, 1965c.

Mogar, R. E. "Psychedelic Drugs and Human Potentialities." In H. A. Otto (ed.) *Explorations in Human Potentialities*. Springfield: Thomas, 1966.

Mogar, R. E. "Psychedelic (LSD) Research: Critical Review of Methods and Results. In J. F. T. Bugental (ed.) *Challenges of Humanistic Psychology*. New York: McGraw-Hill, 1967.

Mogar, R. E., and Aldrich, R. W. "The Use of Psychedelic Agents with Autistic Schizophrenic Children," *Psychedelic Review* 10, 1967.

Mogar, R. E., and Savage, C. "Personality Change Associated with Psychedelic (LSD) Therapy: A Preliminary Report," *Psychotherapy: Theory, Research, Practice* 1, 154–62, 1964.

Murphy, G., and Cohen, S. "The Search for Person-World Isomorphism," *Main Currents in Modern Thought* 22, 31–34, 1965.

Murstein, B. I., and Pryer, R. S. "The Concept of Projection: A Review," *Psychological Bulletin* 56, 353–74, 1959.

Muzio, J. N., Roffwarg, H. P., and Kaufman, E. "Alterations in the Nocturnal Sleep Cycle Resulting from LSD," *Electroencephalography and Clinical Neurophysiology* 21, 313–24, 1966.

Myrdal, G. *Challenge to Affluence*. New York: Pantheon Books, 1963.

Netz, B., and Engstam, P. O. *Lysergic Acid Diethylamide (LSD-25) and Suggestibility. Part II: Effects of a Threshold Dosage of LSD-25 on Hypnotic Susceptibility.* MPI B-rapport nr 17, dec 1968. Stockholm: Militärpsykologiska Institutet, 1968.

Netz, B., Morten, S., and Sundwall, A. *"Lysergic Acid Diethylamide (LSD-25) and Intellectual Functions, Hypnotic Susceptibility, and Sympatho-adreno-medullary Activity. A Pilot Study.* MPI B-rapport nr 19, dec 1968. Stockholm: Militärpsykologiska Institutet, 1968.

Newland, C. A. *My Self and I*. New York: Coward-McCann, 1962.

Nowlis, H. H. *Drugs on the College Campus*. Garden City, N.Y.: Doubleday-Anchor, 1969.

Ogdon, J. H. *The Kingdom of the Lost*. London: Victor Gollancz, 1947.

Ong, W. J. *In the Human Grain: Further Explorations of Contemporary Culture*. New York: Macmillan, 1967.

Orwell, G. *1984*. New York: Harcourt, 1949.

Osmond, H. "On Being Mad," *Saskatchewan Psychiatric Services Journal* 1, 63–70, 1952.

Osmond, H. "Function as the Basis of Psychiatric Ward Design," *Mental Hospitals* 8, 23–29, 1957a.

Osmond, H. "A Review of the Clinical Effects of Psychotomimetic Agents," *Annals of the New York Academy of Science* 66, 418–34, 1957b.

Osmond, H. "Peyote Night," *Tomorrow* 9 (2), 105–25, 1961.

Osmond, H. "Comments on 'Meaning and the Mind Drugs,'" *Etc.* 22, 425–30, 1965.

Osmond, H., and Hoffer, A. "A Comprehensive Theory of Schizophrenia," *International Journal of Neuropsychiatry* 2, 302–9, 1966.

Oster, G. *The Science of Moire Patterns*. Barrington, N.J.: Edmund Scientific Co., 1964.

Otto, R. *The Idea of the Holy*. New York: Oxford University Press, 1958.

Pahnke, W. N. "Drugs and Mysticism," *The International Journal of Parapsychology* 8, 1966.

Pahnke, W. N. "LSD and Religious Experience." In DeBold, R. C., and Leaf, R. C. (eds.) *LSD, Man & Society*. Middletown: Wesleyan University Press, 1967.

Palmer, R. D. "Visual Acuity and Excitement," *Psychosomatic Medicine* 28, 364–74, 1966.

Parsons, T., and Bales, R. F. *Family Socialization and Interaction Process*. Glencoe: The Free Press, 1954, p. 304.

Passouant, P., Passouant-Fontaine, T., and Cadilhac, J. "Action du LSD-25 sur le Comportement, et les Rythmes Corticaux et Rhinencéphaliques du Chat Chronique," *Comptes Rendus de Séances de la Société de Biologie et de ses Filiales* 150, 2237–41, 1956.

Paterson, T. T. *Management Theory*. London: Business Publications, 1966.

Paul, M. "Two Cases of Altered Consciousness with Amnesia Apparently Telepathically Induced," *Psychedelic Review* 8, 4–8, 1966.

Peckham, M. *Beyond the Tragic Vision*. New York: Braziller, 1962.

Phillips, B. *The Search Will Make You Free*. Pendle Hill, Pa.: Friends Conference on Religion and Psychology, 1964.

Platonow, K. *The World as Physiologic Factor*. Moscow: Foreign Languages Publishing House, 1959.

Pollard, J. C., Uhr, L., and Stern, E. *Drugs and Phantasy. The Ef-

fects of LSD, Psilocybin, and Sernyl on College Students.
Boston: Little, Brown, 1965.

Prabhavananda, Swami, and Manchester, F. (eds. and trans.) *The Upanishads: Breath of the Eternal.* (Mentor ed.) New York: New American Library, 1957.

Prince, R., and Savage, C. "Mystical States and the Concept of Regression," *Psychedelic Review* 8, 59–75, 1966.

Psychedelic Review editors. "The Subjective After-Effects of Psychedelic Experiences: A Summary of Four Recent Questionnaire Studies." In Weil, G. R., Metzner, R., and Leary, T. R. *Psychedelic Reader,* New Hyde Park, N.Y.: University Books, 1965.

Puharich, A. *The Sacred Mushroom and the Question of Its Role in Human Culture.* Unpublished research memorandum, 1962.

Purpura, D. P. "Electrophysiological Analysis of Psychotogenic Drug Action. *Archives of Neurology and Psychiatry* 75, 122–31, 1965.

Purpura, D. P. "Neurophysiological Actions of LSD." In DeBold, R. C., and Leaf, R. C. (eds.) *LSD, Man & Society.* Middletown: Wesleyan University Press, 1967, pp. 159–85.

Radhakrishnan, S. *The Hindu View of Life.* New York: Macmillan, 1951.

Radin, P. *The Autobiography of a Winnebago Indian.* New York: Dover, 1920.

Remmen, E., Cohen, S., Ditman, K., and Frantz, J. *Psychotherapy.* Los Angeles: Western Medical Publications, 1962.

Rickers-Ovsiankina, M. R. (ed.) *Rorschach Psychology.* New York: Wiley, 1960.

Rieff, P. *The Triumph of the Therapeutic.* New York: Harper, 1965.

Rinaldi, F., and Himwich, H. E. "The Cerebral Electrographic Changes Induced by LSD and Mescaline Are Corrected by Frenquel," *Journal of Nervous and Mental Disease* 122, 424–32, 1955.

Rinkel, M. "Experimentally Induced Psychoses in Man." In Abramson, H. A. (ed.) *Transactions of the Second Conference on Neuropharmacology.* New York: Josiah Macy, Jr., Foundation, 1956.

Rinkel, M., DeShon, H. J., Hyde, R. W., and Soloman, H. C. "Experimental Schizophrenia-like Symptoms," *American Journal of Psychiatry* 108, 572–78, 1952.

Roseman, B. *LSD: The Age of Mind.* Hollywood: Wilshire, 1966.

Roubicek, J. "Similarities and Differences Between Schizophrenia and Experimental Psychosis," *Review of Czechoslovak Medicine* (Praha) 4, 125, 1958. (Abstracted in Sandoz Annotated Bibliography, p. 174.)

Sandison, R. "Comparison of Drug-Induced and Endogenous Psychoses in Man. In P. Bradley (ed.) *Neuro-Psychopharmacology.* Amsterdam: Elsevier, 1959.

Savage, C. "An Outline of Psychedelic Therapy," *International Journal of Neuropsychiatry*, 241–54, 1967.

Savage, C., Fadiman, J., Mogar, R. E., and Allan, M. "The Effects of Psychedelic Therapy on Values, Personality, and Behavior," *International Journal of Neuropsychiatry* 2, 241–54, 1966.

Savage, C., Stolaroff, M., and Harman, W. "The Psychedelic Experience—A New Concept in Psychotherapy," *Journal of Neuropsychiatry* 5, 4–5, 1963.

Schachtel, E. G. "Projection and Its Relation to Character Attitudes and Creativity in the Kinesthetic Responses," *Psychiatry* 13, 69–100, 1950.

Schacter, Z. M. "The Conscious Ascent of the Soul." In Metzner, R. (ed.) *The Ecstatic Adventure*. New York: Macmillan, 1968, pp. 96–123.

Schultes, R. E. "Botanical Sources of the New World Narcotics," *Psychedelic Review*, 145–46, 1963.

Schultes, R. E. "Botanical Sources of the New World Narcotics." In Weil, G., Metzner, R., and Leary, T. (eds.) *The Psychedelic Reader*. New Hyde Park, N.Y.: University Books, 1965.

Schultes, R. E. "Hallucinogens of Plant Origin," *Science* 163, 245–54, 1969.

Schwarz, B. E., Wakim, K. G., Bickford, R. G., and Lichtenheld, F. R. "Behavior and Electroencephalographic Effects of Hallucinogenic Drugs," *Archives of Neurology and Psychiatry* 75, 83–90, 1956.

Searles, H. F. "Schizophrenia and the Inevitability of Death," *Psychiatric Quarterly* 35, 414–32, 1961.

Selver, C., and Brooks, C. V. W. "Report on Work in Sensory Awareness and Total Functioning." In Otto, H. A. (ed.) *Explorations in Human Potentialities*. Springfield: Thomas, 1966.

Shapiro, D. "A Perceptual Understanding of Color Response." In Rickers-Ovsiankina, M. R. (ed.) *Rorschach Psychology*. New York: Wiley, 1960, pp. 154–201.

Sherman, H. *Wonder Healers of the Philippines*. Los Angeles: Devorss and Co., 1967.

Silberer, H. "Report on a Method of Eliciting and Observing Certain Symbolic Hallucination-Phenomena." In Rapaport, D. (ed. and transl.) *Organization and Pathology of Thought*. New York: Columbia University Press, 1951.

Silverthorn, L. J., Jr. "An Experimental Investigation of Some of the Psychological Changes Associated with the Effects of Mescaline Sulfate." Unpublished doctoral dissertation, University of Kansas, 1957.

Sjoberg, Jr., B. M., and Hollister, L. E. "The Effects of Psychotomimetic Drugs on Primary Suggestibility," *Psychopharmacologia* (Berlin) 8, 251–62, 1965.

Slotkin, J. S. *The Peyote Religion*. Glencoe: The Free Press, 1956.

Smart, R. G., and Storm, T. "The Efficacy of LSD in the Treatment of Alcoholism," *Quarterly Journal on the Study of Alcohol* 25, 333–38, 1964.

Smart, R. G., Storm T., Baker, E. F. W., and Solursh, L. "A Controlled Study of Lysergide in the Treatment of Alcoholism," *Quarterly Journal on the Study of Alcohol* 27, 469–82, 1966.

Smith, P. B. "A Sunday with Mescaline," *Bulletin of the Menninger Clinic* 23, 20–27, 1959.

Smith, R. *Schizophrenics Anonymous Conference*, Fordham University, 1968.

Sommer, R. "Personal Space," *Canadian Architect*, February 1960, 76–80.

Sommer, R. "The Distance for Comfortable Conversation," *Sociometry* 25, 111–16, 1962.

Sommer, R. "The Ecology of Privacy," *Library Quarterly* 36, 234–48, 1966a.

Sommer, R. "Man's Proximate Environment," *The Journal of Social Issues* 4, 59–70, 1966b.

Sommer, R. "Small Group Ecology," *Psychological Bulletin* 67, 145–52, 1967.

Spiegal, H. "Imprinting, Hypnotizability and Learning as Factors in the Psychotherapeutic Process," *American Journal of Clinical Hypnosis* 7, 221–25, 1965.

Stace, W. T. *Mysticism and Philosophy*. Philadelphia: Lippincott, 1960.

Stafford, P. G., and Golightly, B. H. *LSD: The Problem-Solving Psychedelic*. New York: Award Books, 1967.

Stern, H. "Some Observations on the Resistance to the Use of LSD-25 in Psychotherapy," *Psychedelic Review* 8, 1966.

Stern, P. J. *The Abnormal Person and His World*. Princeton: Van Nostrand, 1964.

Swain, F. "The Mystical Mushroom," *Tomorrow*, Autumn 1962. Also in *Psychedelic Review* 2, 219–29, 1963.

Szasz, T. S. *The Myth of Mental Illness*. New York: Harper, 1961.

Takagi, H., Yamamoto, S., Takaori, S., and Ogui, K. "The Effect of LSD and Reserpine on the Central Nervous System of the Cat," *Japanese Journal of Pharmacology* 7, 119–34, 1958.

Tart, C. T. "A Second Psychophysiological Study of Out-of-the-body Experiences in a Gifted Subject," *International Journal of Parapsychology* 9, 251–58, 1967.

Tart, C. T. (ed.) *Altered States of Consciousness*. New York: Wiley, 1969.

Tauber, E. S., and Green, M. R. *Prelogical Experience*. New York: Basic Books, 1959.

Taylor, N. *Narcotics: Nature's Dangerous Gifts*. New York: Dell, 1963.

Teilhard de Chardin, P. *The Phenomenon of Man*. New York: Harper, 1959.

Tennyson, H. T. *Alfred Lord Tennyson, A Memoir by His Son*. New York: Reprint House International, 1899.

Terrill, J. "LSD, Transcendence and the New Beginning," *Journal of Nervous and Mental Disease* 135, 425–29, 1962.

Theobald, R. *Free Men and Free Markets*. New York: Doubleday-Anchor, 1963.

Theobald, R. (ed.) *The Guaranteed Income*. New York: Doubleday, 1966.

Trouton, D., and Eysenck, H. J. "The Effects of Drugs on Behavior." In Eysenck, H. J. (ed.) *Handbook of Abnormal Psychology*. New York: Basic Books, 1961.

Turner, W. J. "Schizophrenia and Oneirophrenia," *Transactions of the New York Academy of Sciences* 26, 361–68, 1964.

Turner, W. J., Almudevar, M., and Merlis, S. "Chemotherapeutic Trials in Psychosis," *American Journal of Psychiatry* 116, 261–62, 1959.

Unger, S. "The Current Status of Psychotherapeutically Oriented LSD Research in the U.S." Unpublished paper presented at the New York State Psychological Association Annual Convention, Grossinger, N.Y., 1965.

Unger, S., Kurland, A., Shaffer, I., Savage, C., Wolf, S., Leihy, R., McCabe, O., and Shock, H. *Psychedelic Therapy*, Third Conference on Research in Psychotherapy, Chicago, Ill., 1966.

Usdin, E., and Efron, D. H. *Psychotropic Drugs and Selected Compounds*. Public Health Service Publication No. 1589. Washington: U. S. Department of Health, Education, and Welfare, 1967.

Verrill, A. E. "A Recent Case of Mushroom Intoxication," *Science* 40, 408, 1914.

Vinar, O. "Analogies Between Schizophrenic Diseases and LSD Psychoses," *Psychiatric Quarterly* 10, 162, 1958. (Abstracted in Sandoz Annotated Bibliography, p. 178.)

Vogt, M., Gunn, C. G., Jr., and Sawyer, C. H. "Electroencephalographic Effects of Intraventricular 5-HT and LSD in the Cat," *Neurology* 7, 559–66, 1957.

Von Felsinger, J. H., Lasagna, L., and Beecher, H. K. "The Response of Normal Men to Lysergic Acid Derivatives (di- and monoethylamides), Correlation of Personality and Drug Reactions," *Journal of Clinical and Experimental Psychopathology* 17, 414–28, 1956.

Von Neumann, J. *The Computer and the Brain*. New Haven: Yale University Press, 1958.

Von Senden, M. *Space and Sight*. Glencoe: The Free Press, 1960.

Wagner, N., and Stegemann, K. "Imagination and Impulse Control in Children." Unpublished manuscript, State of Washington Grant 171, 1964.

Walters, M. B. "Pholiota Spectabilis, a Hallucinogenic Fungus," *Mycologia*, September/October 1965.

Walton, R. P. *Marihuana: America's New Drug Problem*. Philadelphia: Lippincott, 1938, pp. 47–48.

Wasson, R. G. "Lightning Bolt and Mushrooms, An Essay in

Early Cultural Exploration." In *Roman Jakobson: Essays on the Occasion of his Sixtieth Birthday*. The Hague: Mouton & Co., 1956.

Wasson, R. G. Transcript of discussion held in Montreal, November 23, 1961.

Wasson, R. G. "The Hallucinogenic Mushrooms of Mexico and Psilocybin: A Bibliography," *Botanical Museum Leaflets*, Harvard University 20, 1962.

Wasson, R. G. "The Hallucinogenic Fungi of Mexico. *Psychedelic Review* 1, 27–42, 1963.

Wasson, R. G. "Notes on the Present Status of Ololiuhqui and the Other Hallucinogens of Mexico," *Psychedelic Review* 3, 1964.

Wasson, R. G. *Soma: Divine Mushroom of Immortality*. New York: Harcourt, 1969.

Wasson, R. G., and Wasson, V. P. *Mushrooms, Russia and History*. New York: Pantheon Books, 1957.

Watts, A. *The Joyous Cosmology: Adventures in the Chemistry of Consciousness*. New York: Pantheon, 1962.

Watts, A. *The Book: on the Taboo Against Knowing Who You Are*. New York: Collier, 1967. (First published in 1966.)

Watts, A. "Psychedelics and Religious Experience," *California Law Review* 56 (1), 74–85, 1968.

Wavell, S. "Introduction." In Wavell, S., Epton, N., and Butt, A. *Trances*. New York: Dutton, 1967.

Weitzenhoffer, A. M. *General Techniques of Hypnotism*. New York: Grune & Stratton, 1957.

Welker, W. I. "An Analysis of Exploratory and Play Behavior in Animals." In Fiske, D. W., and Maddi, S. R. (eds.) *Function of Varied Experience*. Homewood, Ill. Dorsey Press, 1961, pp. 175–226.

Werner, H. *Comparative Psychology of Mental Development*. New York: International Universities Press, 1957.

Wienpahl, P. *The Matter of Zen: A Brief Account of Zazen*. New York: New York University Press, 1964.

Witkin, H. A. "Individual Differences in Ease of Perception of Embedded Figures," *Journal of Personality* 19, 1–15, 1950.

Witkin, H. A., Dyk, R. B., Faterson, H. F., Goodenough, D. R., and Karp, S. A. *Psychological Differentiation*. New York: Wiley, 1962.

Witt, P. N. "D-Lysergäure-Diethylamid (LSD-25) im Spinnentest," *Experientia* 7, 310–11, 1951.

Wolfe, T. *The Electric Kool-Aid Acid Test*. New York: Farrar, Strauss, 1968.

Worrall, A., and Worrall, O. *The Gift of Healing*. New York: Harper, 1965.

Wyburn, G. M., Pickford, N. W., and Hirst, R. J. *Human Sense and Perception*. Toronto: University of Toronto Press, 1964, pp. 242–335.

oung, W. R., and Hixson, J. R. *LSD on Campus*. New York: Dell, 1966.

aehner, R. C. *Mysticism: Sacred and Profane*. Oxford: Oxford University Press, 1957.

immer, H. *Philosophies of India*. (Bollingen Series, vol. 26) Princeton: Princeton University Press, 1951, pp. 355–463.

insser, W. K. "The Love Hippies," *Look*, April 18, 1967.

ubin, J., and Katz, M. "Psychopharmacology and Personality." In Worschel, P., and Byrne, D. (eds.) *Personality Change*. New York: Wiley, 1964, pp. 367–95.

INDEX